T0366926

MENANDER

III

LCL 460

MENANDER

VOLUME III

EDITED AND TRANSLATED BY

W. GEOFFREY ARNOTT

HARVARD UNIVERSITY PRESS
CAMBRIDGE, MASSACHUSETTS
LONDON, ENGLAND
2000

Library of Congress Control Number 80-154351
CIP data available from the Library of Congress

ISBN 978-0-674-99584-0

Composed in ZephGreek and ZephText by
Technologies 'N Typography, Merrimac, Massachusetts.
Printed on acid-free paper and bound by
The Maple-Vail Book Manufacturing Group

CONTENTS

To Rosemary, Alison, Hilary, Hatau and Deema

PREFACE

This volume completes the new Loeb Classical Library edition of Menander. It again follows the principles adopted in volume one, with the adjustment mentioned in the preface to the second volume. Volume three begins with the preserved portions of those plays (from *Samia* to *Phasma*, in Greek alphabetical order) whose titles are known or can with some some confidence be identified. Next comes a carefully selected group of papyri whose attribution to Menander ranges from certainty (in the case of *Fabula Incerta* 1) to disputable plausibility; the reasons why those that appear have been selected are given in the separate introductions to each member of this elite, while the reasons why some familiar papyri (such as *P.Louvre* 7172 = *P.Didot* 1) have been excluded are set out in the general introduction to this collection of papyri and papyrus fragments. This section concludes with those papyrus fragments of prose summaries of Menander's plays that have not been printed elsewhere in this edition, and with one probable and two certain book fragments that have been added to the Menander store by a papyrus first published in 1966.

Each text and critical apparatus in this volume is based, as before, mainly on close study of good photographs of the relevant papyri, whenever possible. Unpublished photographs of several papyri have been supplied to me; due acknowledgement is made below. I have, however, had the good fortune to see and examine *P.Bodmer* 4 in Cologny and *P.Sorbonne* 72, 2272 and 2273 in Paris, and I should like to express my gratitude here to the Fondation Bodmer and Professor A. Blanchard. Many institutions and scholars have helped me in various ways with advice, useful information and photocopies of publications that were otherwise unavailable to me. If any name has been omitted in the following list, I trust he or she will accept my apology. My thanks are owed and gratefully given to Dr Annamaria D'Angelo, Professors C. Austin, A. Blanchard, Dr R. W. and Mrs Elaine Brock, Drs D.L. Cairns, R. A. Coles, Professor Christina Dedoussi, Dr. Chr. Förstel, Professors I. Gallo, Chr. Habicht, E. W. Handley, Mr J. G. Howie, Professors A. Hurst, J.-M. Jacques, R. Kassel, L. Koenen, P. von Möllendorff, Dr R. Nünlist, Professor P. J. Parsons, Drs R. Pintaudi, A. P. Romanov, Professor G. Reger, Mr L. Scott, Professor W. Stockert, the Accademia di Torino, the Bibliothèque Nationale in Paris, the British Academy, the Fondation Bodmer in Cologny, the Fondation Hardt in Vandoeuvres, the National Library of Russia in St Petersburg and the Reial Acadèmia de Barcelona. Above all I should like to express my gratitude to Professors P. Goold, J. Henderson, and F. J. Williams, whose courteous assistance with editing and proof-reading has been invaluable, and to my wife, whose patient tolerance of my devotion to a dramatist of the distant past has been as rewarding as her loving support.

Leeds   W. Geoffrey Arnott
February 1999

SUPPLEMENT TO THE
BIBLIOGRAPHIES IN
VOLUMES ONE AND TWO

Catalogue Raisonné of Menander Papyri

P. Mertens in *Serta Leodiensia Secunda* (University of Liège 1992) 330–56 is complete up to its date of publication, and includes doubtful as well as certain attributions.

Editions: Single Plays

Aspis. M. Rossi (Milan 1994). J.-M. Jacques (Paris 1998).
Dis Exapaton. E. W. Handley in *The Oxyrhynchus Papyri* 64 (1997) 14–42.
Dyskolos. M. Bissinger (Bamberg 1979).
Epitrepontes. A. Martina (Rome 1997).
Kolax. J. Barsby, in his edition of Terence's *Eunuchus* (Cambridge 1999), appendix II.2 pp. 305–11.
Samia. G. Jäger (Bamberg 1979). M. Lamagna (Naples 1998).

Bibliographies

A. G. Katsouris, *Menander Bibliography* (Thessalonike 1995).

Word Index

G. Pompella, *Lexicon Menandreum* (Hildesheim, Zürich, New York 1996).

SAMIA OR KEDEIA

(THE WOMAN FROM SAMOS
OR THE MARRIAGE CONTRACT)

INTRODUCTION

Manuscripts

B = *P.Bodmer* 25, the first of three plays (*Dyskolos* and *Aspis* follow) in a papyrus codex of the third (or possibly early fourth) century A.D. It contains lines 1–119a, 120–43a, 144–245, 254–406, 411–54, 458–605, 612–737. First edition: R. Kasser and C. Austin, *Papyrus Bodmer XXV. Ménandre, La Samienne* (Cologny-Geneva 1969),[1] with photographs of *P.Bodmer* 25 and also (photographed in its original position: see below) *P.Barcelona* 45.

B = also *P.Barcelona* 45, a small scrap of one page torn from the same codex as *P.Bodmer* 25, containing lines 399–410 and 446–57.[2] First editions: R. Roca-Puig, *Butlletí de*

---

[1] Some time before this authorised publication, P. Photiades made a transcript of parts of this papyrus (vv. 1–166, 174–203, 254–86 and 411–28), and this was circulated among scholars working on Menander at the time. See especially J.-M. Jacques, *Bulletin de l'Association G. Budé* 4.2–3 (1968) 213–39, his edition of *Samia* (Paris 1971) pp. vii and lxxxiii, and O. Reverdin's preface to A. Hurst's French translation of the play (*Bastions de Genève* 1975), pp. 3–4.

[2] The codex was at some stage torn, so that one part of lines 399–406 and 446–54 is in the Bodmer codex, another part in the Barcelona sheet.

la Reial Acadèmia de Bones Lletres de Barcelona 32 (1967–68) 5–13 (in Catalan) = (with some modifications) *Estudios Clásicos* 12 (1968) 375–83 (in Castilian Spanish), both with photographs.

C = *P.Cairensis* 43227, part of a papyrus codex from Aphroditopolis written in the fifth century A.D. The codex originally contained six or more plays by Menander; *Samia* was placed after (but not directly after) *Perikeiromene*. Extant in C are lines 216–416 and 547–686. First edition: G. Lefebvre, *Fragments d'un manuscrit de Ménandre* (Cairo 1907); the same editor's *Papyrus de Ménandre* (Cairo 1911), with a revised text, contains photographs; new and clearer photographs have been published in *The Cairo Codex of Menander (P.Cair. J.43227)* (Institute of Classical Studies, London 1978), plates XXXVII–XLVI.

O.17 = *P.Oxyrhynchus* 2943, a small fragment of papyrus written in the late second or early third century A.D. It contains the ends of lines 119b–d and 120–25, and the beginnings of 134–42, 143a–m (on these numberings, see below). Definitive edition: E. G. Turner, *The Oxyrhynchus Papyri*, 41 (London 1972) 1–4 with a photograph (plate I); this followed a permitted earlier publication by Turner in *CR* 21 (1971) 352–53.

O.16 = *P.Oxyrhynchus* 2831, a small fragment of papyrus perhaps written in the late first or early second century A.D. It was identified by E. Lobel as containing the ends of lines 385–90. Definitive edition: E. G. Turner, *The Oxyrhynchus Papyri*, 38 (London 1971) 29 with a photograph (plate I); this followed a permitted earlier publication by Turner in *Aegyptus* 47 (printed as 1967, but appearing 1970) 187–90, also with photograph.

Berl. = *P.Berlin* 8450, a scrap of papyrus from the Fayyûm written in the late first or early second century A.D. and containing the middle parts of 21 iambic trimeters which have been assigned to the *Samia* by its first editors: W. Luppe and W. Müller, *Archiv für Papyrusforschung* 3 (1983) 5–7 with a photograph (plate 1). It appears as fr. adesp. 1131 in Kassel–Austin, *PCG* VIII (Berlin 1995) p. 459. Although its attribution to the *Samia* is uncertain, it is printed here after the end of B's text as fragment 1.

Fragment 2, printed after fr. 1, is a quotation made allegedly from this play by an ancient grammarian (see introduction to Volume I, pp. xxiv f.).

Pictorial Evidence

A mosaic of (probably) the late fourth century A.D. from the 'House of Menander' at Mytilene in Lesbos. The mosaic is inscribed ΣAMIAΣ ME(POΣ) Γ (*Samia*, Act III), and portrays the moment when Demeas expels Chrysis and the baby from his house before the apparently puzzled gaze of the cook (cf. lines 369ff. of the play). Demeas (his name is written to his left, ΔHMEAΣ) wears a long cloak decorated with double-axe motifs; his left hand holds a stick and his right arm is raised aggressively in the direction of Chrysis (XPΥΣIΣ inscribed above her head), who stands on his right. She is richly attired in a tunic and gown of many colours, nestles the baby in her left arm and looks slightly to her left. On Demeas' left stands the cook

4

SAMIA

(ΜΑΓΕΙΡΟΣ inscribed on his left), portrayed with a remarkably dark face[3] and four dreadlocks on each side dropping over his shoulders. Demeas' age is emphasised by white hair and beard and wrinkles on his face. The cook's position is as far forward as that of Demeas and Chrysis, not in the background (as required by line 368 of the text), and Chrysis is not accompanied by her old female servant (cf. line 373). Standard edition of the mosaic: S. Charitonidis, L. Kahil, R. Ginouvès, *Les Mosaïques de la Maison du Ménandre à Mytilène* (*Antike Kunst*, Beiheft 6, Berne 1970), 38–41 and colour plate 4; a colour plate, chopped off at the bottom, appears also as the frontispiece of the Kasser–Austin edition of the play. Cf. also T. B. L. Webster, *Monuments Illustrating New Comedy* (3rd edition, revised and enlarged by J. R. Green and A. Seeberg, London 1995), I.93 (XZ 31) and II.469 (6DM 2.2); and L. Berczelly, *BICS* 35 (1988) 119–27.

The attribution of the Cairo papyrus fragments to Menander's *Samia*, which G. Lefebvre originally suggested (1907 edition, p. 141) because of two mentions of 'the Samian woman' in them (vv. 265, 353f.; cf. now also vv. 21, 35–36), has been proved correct by the Mytilene mosaic (see above) and the colophon in the Bodmer codex. Stobaeus, however, quotes two short passages from the play (*Ecl.* 4.29.10 = vv. 140–42, 1.6.9 = vv. 163–64) under another title, Κηδεία (*The Marriage Contract*),[4] which

---

[3] On black cooks in ancient Greek comedy see p. 423 of this volume.

[4] The correct spelling is given by only one manuscript (P) at 1.6.9, but corrupted in others to an inappropriate Ἀκηδεία (*Indif-*

5

was perhaps given later to the play (? for a subsequent production) as an appropriate alternative name. No other ancient comedy deals so exhaustively with the impediments blocking a wedding that all the parties to it originally support, and indeed A. W. Gomme wrote long before the Bodmer codex was discovered 'Had it been an eighteenth-century play, it might have been called *Chrysis*, or *The Wedding Postponed*' (*CQ* 30, 1936, 72).

The Cairo papyrus contains 341 lines of the play, 5 of them badly mutilated. The Bodmer codex duplicates 330 of these and adds a further 396, of which over 90 are seriously imperfect. The text of acts III, IV and V of the play is now virtually complete; all the major lacunae come in acts I and II. However, a careful comparison of the most mutilated pages (1–8) of the Bodmer codex, whose tops and bottoms have been torn or chopped off, with those later ones (9–18) which are almost completely preserved, reveals that the scribe kept the relationship between the number of lines on a page and the space between individual lines on that page remarkably constant, and this makes it possible to predict within narrow limits the original number of lines written on the badly mutilated pages, giving a probable total of 412 or 413 lines for pp. 1–8 and 896 or 897 lines for the whole play.[5]

In this edition, however, with considerable hesitation I follow the editions of Kasser–Austin, Austin and Sand-

ference: F at 1.6.9) or Κνηδία (MA at 4.29.10: gibberish, earlier wrongly emended to Κνιδία, *The Woman of Knidos*).

[5] For the detailed calculations see my paper in *ZPE* 128 (1999) 45–48.

bach, together with virtually all modern scholarship, in numbering the lines preserved in B and C consecutively. In consequence I do not (as J.-M. Jacques more wisely does in his Budé edition of the play, Paris 1971) adjust that numeration in order to take account of the gaps mainly in the first eight pages of the Bodmer codex. I add in brackets to my Greek text both Jacques' numbering (hereafter J) and the earlier one used for the Cairo papyrus remains by Körte in his third Teubner edition (Leipzig 1938: hereafter K). The tiny fragments of new lines preserved in *P.Oxyrhynchus* 2943 (see above) between lines 119 and 120, 143 and 144 are here for convenience numbered 119b–d and 143b–m, with 119 and 143 renumbered 119a and 143a.

Neither of the two major papyri preserves a hypothesis, didascalic notice or cast-list. *Samia*'s production date is not recorded, although several (a) structural or theatrical elements and (b) real or alleged references to contemporary personalities and events may be identified as pointers to a more or less precise time of composition.

(a) The structural and theatrical elements include a preponderance of monologues so far unparalleled in Menander (probably over 40% of the play),[6] the use of trochaic tetrameters for the whole of act IV (421–615), and the transformation of ostensibly serious situations into exuberant farce (especially 519–615 with its sudden, high-speed exits and entrances). Before the Bodmer codex was discovered, such elements were generally interpreted as

[6] Cf. J. Blundell, *Menander and the Monologue* (*Hypomnemata* 59, Göttingen 1980) 35–45.

evidence of youthful high spirits or even immaturity in a play produced at the beginning of Menander's career, but views of this kind are based partly on a fallacious equation of youth and slapstick, partly on an earlier ignorance of Menander's widespread employment of trochaic tetrameters at least throughout the first half of his career. In any case it is not the choice of a particular metre or theatrical mode that deserves to be significant in matters of either dating or evaluation, but rather the quality of the writing in that mode or metre and the appropriateness to its particular situation. Thus in *Samia* the long monologue by Demeas that opens act III (205–82) is a masterpiece of imaginative narrative and emotion graphically expressed, revealing also more about the speaker than he consciously intends. Again, the farcical toings and froings of 519–615 contribute positively to a fast-moving and engrossing act composed by a writer in total control of his medium. Expertise, however, can be shown very early in a dramatist's career, as Aristophanes revealed with *Acharnians*, and in our more limited percentage of Menander's surviving but largely undated plays and fragments it would accordingly be wiser to refrain from using the structural and theatrical elements discussed above as pointers to *Samia*'s date.

(b) Six types of reference to contemporary personalities or events are either offered by or can be teased out of what survives of *Samia*. These are first listed and discussed individually; when the information that they offer is combined, a precise date for the play can be suggested:

(1) Chrysis, Menander's title figure, was a native of Samos who was working in Athens as a *hetaira* (21, 25, cf. 392–97) when the elderly Athenian Demeas fell for

her and installed her in his house as his partner. Was Menander here influenced by recent history? In 319 B.C. the Athenian cleruchs went back to Samos after a three-year absence and expelled the native Samians who had returned there under protection from Alexander the Great's successors. However, nothing in what is now preserved of *Samia* actually reveals why or when Chrysis came to Athens, or how long she had been in Athens when she met Demeas as a refugee after the events of 319, or how long she had been living with him. Yet see below.

(2) At 101–104 Demeas' chauvinistic praise of Athens is a stock topic in Athenian drama,[7] but it includes in v. 102 an implication that all is not well with the city. There were many periods of unrest in Athens during Menander's career, with violent changes of government and constitution in Athens, unpopular rule, civil war, external attack, siege and famine,[8] and so it is difficult to link v. 102 with any particular disaster. Yet see below.

(3) At 504 Nikeratos refers to one Diomnestus in terms that would represent him as an unsatisfactory son-in-law, most probably with reference to a recent Athenian scandal about which nothing is now known.[9]

[7] See e.g. K. Gaiser, *Gymnasium* 75 (1968) 193–219, and P. Walcot, *Greek Drama in Its Theatrical and Social Context* (Cardiff 1976) 94–103.

[8] Cf. W. S. Ferguson, *Hellenistic Athens* (London 1911) 111–43.

[9] Early in the fifth century B.C. a Diomnestus of Eretria is said to have come into possession of a treasure, and his family then to have lost it through no moral fault (so Heraclides of Ponticus fr. 58 Wehrli, in Athenaeus 12.536f–537b; see C. Dedoussi, *Entretiens*

9

(4) At 570 Demeas is confronted by an infuriated Nikeratos and he exclaims μονομαχήσω τήμερον, 'Today I'll have to fight a duel!' One-to-one gladiatorial contests may have become a topic of conversation in the city after Cassander μονομαχίας ἀγῶνα ἔθηκεν (instituted a gladiatorial contest) at royal funeral games in Macedonia during 316/5 B.C. (Dyillus, *FGrH* 73 F 1, cited by Athenaeus 4.155a), and it is suggested below that Demeas' remark here could have been inspired by news of that event. However, duels (along with the use of μονομαχῶ and its congeners) were a feature of Greek history, myth and literature from Homer onwards (e.g. *Iliad* 3.264–372 Menelaus and Paris, 23.801–25 Ajax and Diomedes at funeral games, Hdt. 7.104, 9.26, Eur. *Phoen.* 1220, 1300, 1325 Eteocles and Polynices, cf. A. *Septem* 798), and so it could equally well be argued that μονομαχήσω at *Sam.* 570 was merely a comic echo of that tradition, lacking any contemporary historical link.

(5) In 603–604 and 606–608 Demeas mentions Chaerephon and an aged Androcles as ever-present on the Athenian scene. Chaerephon[10] was an Athenian parasite notorious for his habit of gatecrashing dinners, and he became a constant butt of comedians in the city from the time that Menander began writing (e.g. Men. fr. 265 K-A

Hardt 16 (1970) 167–68), but the person named by Nikeratos in Menander was apparently a proverbial example of vicious behaviour, not misfortune. See also note on v. 504.

[10] See especially my commentary on Alexis fr. 213.1 Kassel–Austin (Cambridge 1996) p. 610, for a full discussion with bibliography.

from *Orge*, his first play[11]) until about 310 (Apollodorus of
Carystus fr. 29 K-A, *PCG* II.499, referring to Ophellas of
Cyrene's wedding feast some time before the bridegroom's
death in 309 B.C.). Androcles on the other hand has not
been certainly identified; the name was common in Athens, and there is no evidence to support the view that
Menander's Androcles was also the titular hero of a lost
(and undatable) comedy by Sophilus.

(6) Finally in act V a disgruntled Moschion thinks of
travelling to Bactria or Caria as a mercenary soldier (628–
29: see notes there). In both areas during Menander's career military activity by Greek mercenaries was virtually
continuous.[12] Accordingly Moschion's words cannot be
firmly tied to any one particular date. Yet see below.

The reference to Chaerephon (b.5) apparently dates
Samia to the first ten to fifteen years of Menander's career,
and this makes it more plausible that the reference to duelling (b.4) was inspired by Cassander's new entertainment
and came in a play produced in or around 314 B.C. Such a
date would produce a plausible timetable for a Chrysis
who, after being expelled as a young woman from Samos in
319 (b.1), came in an impoverished state to Athens and
worked there for a year or so as a *hetaira*, then met
Demeas and lived with him long enough to become pregnant and bear the child that presumably died at birth but

[11] Its date is disputed; different sources give 323/2, 321/0 and
(possibly) 325/4 B.C.: see volume I of my Loeb Menander (1979)
xiv–xv, and St. Schröder, *ZPE* 113 (1996) 36–38.

[12] See notes on *Samia* 628 and 629, and the introduction to
Menander's *Sikyonioi* below.

enabled her successfully to suckle Moschion's baby.[13] In 314 B.C. Athens would just have learnt about the despatch of 13,000 mercenaries by Ptolemy son of Lagus to Cyprus and Caria (Diod. Sic. 19.62), and this could have added a topical flavour to Moschion's reference to mercenary service in the latter place (b.6). In 314 too another remark by Moschion—his claim to have shone as *choregos* with his payments for choruses (v.13)—could have touched a nostalgic chord in the audience, for it appears that in the previous year the *choregia* had been abolished and replaced by state funding under legislation proposed by Demetrius of Phalerum, then the despotic ruler of Athens.[14] Finally, Menander is said to have been a personal friend of Demetrius (see the Loeb Menander, I, 1979, xvii–xviii), but the latter's regime seems to have been unpopular with the majority of Athenians,[15] and so Demeas' vague reference to the city's troubles in *Sam.* 102 (b.2) could well have been a studied attempt by Menander to kowtow to his audience's feelings without annoying the friend.

[13] See now especially F. H. Sandbach, *LCM* 11 (1986) 158–60 and S. R. West, *ZPE* 88 (1991) 11–16.

[14] See A. Pickard-Cambridge, *The Dramatic Festivals of Athens* (2nd edition, revised by J. Gould and D. M. Lewis, Oxford 1968) 91–93. The dating of this reform is disputed (line 116 of the *Marmor Parium, FGrH* 239 B.13 = *IG* 12(5).444 gives 317/6 B.C.), but W. S. Ferguson's arguments for 316/5 in *Klio* 11 (1911) 265–76 are convincing; cf. E. Bayer, *Demetrios Phalereus der Athener* (Stuttgart & Berlin 1942) 48–51, S. Dow and A. H. Travis, *Hesperia* 12 (1943) 144–65.

[15] See Ferguson, *Hellenistic Athens*, 61–62.

SAMIA

Dramatis Personae, in order of speaking,
so far as is known:

Moschion, adopted son of Demeas and guilty of
   Plangon's rape
Chrysis, originally from Samos, but now living with
   Demeas as his partner
Parmenon, slave of Demeas
Demeas, a wealthy old man
Nikeratos, a comparatively poor old man, father of
   Plangon
A cook, unnamed

Mute characters: the slaves returning from abroad with
Demeas and Nikeratos and carrying their luggage and
possibly other goods (see the comments between vv. 95
and 96, 105 and 106); the cook's one or more assistants;
Chrysis' old female servant; Plangon; one or more male
witnesses to Moschion's betrothal; Nikeratos' wife; a
young boy or girl bringing water for Moschion's nuptial
bath; a female piper; a slave bringing a strap and pursuing
Parmenon; a slave bringing a torch and garlands; and—if
they can be called mutes—Moschion's and Plangon's baby
and the sheep led on by Nikeratos. There is also a chorus,
perhaps of tipsy revellers, to perform the entr'actes.[16]

---

[16] While this volume was in press, Dr. N. Gonis was kind
enough to send me the text of a tiny scrap of parchment (*P.An-
tinoopolis inv.* 4) from *Samia* which he is publishing in the forth-
coming Festschrift for Professor J. Bingen. Written in the sixth or
seventh century A.D., it contains fragments of the line ends of
vv. 312–15 and the openings of vv. 341–50. There is no divergence
from the text printed here in the Loeb; at v. 347 *P.Ant.* has νος.

ΣΑΜΙΑ

(*SCENE: A street somewhere in Athens, with two houses visible; one belongs to Demeas, the other to Nikeratos. There is a small altar or emblem of Apollo just outside Demeas' front door.*)

(The opening lines of the play, probably about 7 in number, are torn off the top of the first page of the Bodmer codex.)

ΜΟΣΧΙΩΝ

. . . . .

1 (10J)
             ]...ε.[.]υπερ[
        ]ονετι λυπῆσαί με δεῖ;
     ὀδ]υνηρόν ἐστιν· ἡμάρτηκα γάρ.

In the apparatus to this play ed.pr. = the Kasser–Austin edition of the Bodmer codex, apogr. = the transcript of the codex made before that edition (see above, Intro., note 1). New conjectures and supplements of mine are discussed in *ZPE* 121 (1998) 35–44 and 122 (1998) 7–20. 1–119a, 120–42a, 143–215 are preserved in B (ends of 119b–d, 120–28, beginnings of 134–41, 142a–n in O).

14

SAMIA

(The play begins with the entry of Moschion, presumably from the house of Demeas, his adoptive father. He delivers the prologue, whose first 9–11 lines are lost. What precisely they contained is uncertain, but they must have included a mention of Moschion's adoption by Demeas, since Moschion refers to Demeas in v.6 just with an otherwise unexplained third-person pronoun (he; cf. vv. 17, 21–22, 24), and goes on immediately to describe Moschion's earliest years as just after that (v. 7). One possibility is that the prologue opened (like Misoumenos) with general expressions of misery, which the speaker explained vaguely as due to his fear of telling his adoptive father, now due back from a journey abroad, about misconduct that would displease Demeas.)

MOSCHION

. . . . .

] over [1
] why (?) must I cause distress?
] is painful. I've done wrong, you see.

---

2 Either γέγ]ονε· τί (suppl. Austin) or]ον ἔτι.
3 Suppl. ed.pr.

]ο τοῦτ᾽ ἐσόμενον λογίζομαι.

5 φανερὸν] δὲ τοῦτ᾽ ἂν εὐλόγως ὑμῖν ποεῖν
(15J) θέλοιμι,] τὸν ἐκείνου διεξελθὼν τρόπον.
ὡς μὲ]ν ἐτρύφησα τῷ τότ᾽ εὐθέως χρόνῳ,
ὢν παι]δίον, μεμνημένος σαφῶς ἑῶ·
εὐεργέ]τει γὰρ ταὐτά μ᾽ οὐ φρονοῦντά πω.

10 εἶτ᾽ ἐν]εγράφην οὐδὲν διαφέρων οὐδενός,
(20J) τὸ λεγό]μενον δὴ τοῦτο, τῶν πολλῶν τις ὤν·
ὃς γέγον]α μέντοι, νὴ Δί᾽, ἀθλιώτερος·
παχεῖς] γάρ ἐσμεν. τῷ χορηγεῖν διέφερον
καὶ τῇ] φιλοτιμίᾳ· κύνας γὰρ ἔτρεφέ μοι,

4 αὐτ]ὸ τοῦτο ⟨γ᾽⟩ ἐσόμενον suppl. and conj. Sandbach (τουτο B), τοῦτ᾽ εἰς μέσον Austin, Jacques.
5 Suppl. Barigazzi.   6 Suppl. Arnott.
7 Suppl. Oguse.   8 ὢν suppl. Jacques, Oguse, παι]δίον apogr., ed.pr.: B has]διων corr. to]διον.
9 Suppl. Jacques, Oguse.   μεου B.   10 Suppl. several.
11 Suppl. Jacques, Lloyd-Jones.   δὴ Austin, Jacques: δε B.
12 ὃς suppl. Arnott, γέγον]α Austin and Sandbach.
13 Suppl. Arnott.
14 Suppl. ed.pr. (τῇ also apogr.).   φιλοτημιαι with correcting ι above the η B.

---

1 Moschion is directly addressing the audience; cf. D. Bain, *Actors and Audience* (Oxford 1977) 185–89.

2 Sc. Demeas.

3 Sc. just after Moschion's adoption by Demeas.

4 On reaching his 18th birthday a free Athenian boy had to appear before the members of his deme, who registered him as a fellow member (and thus a full citizen) only after a thorough

I reckon it will be (?) [
But sensibly [I'd like] to make this [clear]   5
To you[1] by spelling out the kind of man he[2] is.
I well remember [how], just after that,[3]
[In child]hood I was spoiled—but let that pass.
This [served] me [well], before I learned to think.
[Next], I was registered[4]—an average chap,   10
[That's how the] phrase goes, just like any other.
And I've [become] in fact more wretched—all
Because we're [loaded[5]]! I shone with my payments
For choruses [and] public service.[6] He kept hounds

check of his age and parentage. See A. R. W. Harrison, *The Law of Athens,* 2 (Oxford 1971) 205–207, P. J. Rhodes' commentary on [Arist.] *Ath. Pol.* 42 (Oxford 1981), and D. Whitehead, *The Demes of Attica* (Princeton 1986) 32–33, 258–60, 292–301.

[5] The supplement παχεῖς was a contemporary colloquialism for 'rich'. Having been adopted into a wealthy Athenian family, Moschion was miserable because he realised that his own misconduct with Plangon would prevent Demeas from arranging for Moschion a marriage into an equally wealthy family, which was the social norm for his class.

[6] Up to 315 B.C. very wealthy citizens were required to meet the expenses of costuming and training choruses at Athenian festivals: see A. Pickard-Cambridge, *Dramatic Festivals of Athens*[2] (Oxford 1968) 86–93, and J. K. Davies, *Wealth and the Power of Wealth in Classical Athens* (Salem, NH 1981) 9–37. On public services (which often involved considerable expenditure on behalf of the state) see D. Whitehead, *Classica et Mediaevalia* 34 (1983) 55–74 and *The Demes of Attica* (Princeton 1986) 241–52, P. Veyne, *Bread and Circuses* (translated by B. Pearce, London 1990) 83–200, and P. Gauthier, *Les cités grecques et leurs bienfaiteurs* (Paris 1985) 112–20.

15 ἵππο]υς· ἐφυλάρχησα λαμπρῶς· τῶν φίλων
(25J) τοῖς] δεομένοις τὰ μέτρι' ἐπαρκεῖν ἐδυνάμην.
δι' ἐκεῖνον ἦν ἄνθρωπος. ἀστείαν δ' ὅμως
τούτων χάριν τιν' ἀπεδίδουν· ἦν κόσμιος.
μετὰ τοῦτο συνέβη—καὶ γὰρ ἅμα τὰ πράγματα
20 ἡμῶν δίειμι πάντ'· ἄγω γάρ πως σχολήν—
(30J) Σαμίας ἑταίρας εἰς ἐ<πι>θυμίαν τινὸς
ἐλθεῖν ἐκεῖνον, πρᾶγμ' ἴσως ἀνθρώπινον.
ἔκρυπτε τοῦτ', ᾐσχύνετ'· ᾐσθόμην ἐγὼ
ἄκοντος αὐτοῦ, διελογιζόμην θ' ὅτι,
25 ἂν μὴ γένηται τῆς ἑταίρας ἐγκρατής,
(35J) ὑ[π'] ἀντεραστῶν μειρακίων ἐνοχλήσεται·
τοῦτο <δὲ> ποῆσαι δι' ἔμ' ἴσως αἰσχύνεται·
λέγ]ω λαβεῖν ταύτην· τὸ μεν..[.]..π.[
29 ...].οσε.[.].[

15 Suppl. Sandbach.   16 Suppl. ed.pr.   ξεπαρκειν B
with ξ crossed out.   εδυναιμην B with ι crossed out.
18 απεδουν B with omitted δί written above εδ.
19 τουσυνέβη B with omitted το written above νσ.
καιταργ B with γ crossed out: corr. Austin.   πραμματα B
with first μ crossed out and γ written above it.
21 εισεθυμιαν B: corr. apogr.   τινὸς Jacques: τινα B.
22 εκθιπον B with θ and π crossed out and ε and ν written
above.   ισωσδε B: corr. Austin.   23 τουτομ' B: corr.
Austin.   26 Supp. apogr., ed.pr.   27 τουτοποησαι B: corr.
Arnott, Sandbach.   28 Suppl. Jacques.

---

7 Literally, 'I served as φύλαρχος (the commander of the cav-
alry supplied by the tribe).' At the time of *Samia* this officer's role

18

For me, and [horses]. I starred as a colonel of   15
Hussars![7] I could give modest help to needy
Friends. He made me grow up. I paid my debt
For that, though, nobly: I behaved myself.
And then it happened—I'll put all the facts
Together in one tale, I've got the time.   20
He fell in love with a call-girl from Samos,
Something that's normal, possibly. He kept
It secret, being embarrassed. I found out,
Against his wishes, and I judged that if
He didn't take her under his protection,   25
He'd then be plagued by younger rivals, [but]
He shied at doing it, perhaps because of me.
[I] told (?)] him he should take her [28

*(The next verse preserves only the tops of a few letters, and
then there is a lacuna of some 23 or 24 lines. When the text
resumes, Moschion is still delivering the prologue. In the
gap he must have told how Demeas installed the Samian
girl in his house, and then gone on to mention their next-
door neighbour and his daughter, since the latter is re-
ferred to just as* the girl *in vv. 35-36 without further expla-
nation. Lines 31-34 yield some puzzling phrases: a* male
seeing him bear *31,* everywhere I applied *or* gave *or* added
32, a plural *you* and to our neighbour *33,* smashing the seal
with force *34. One possibility is that Demeas had noticed
how well Nikeratos bore his poverty and had taken him as
a companion abroad with him on a trading venture, and*

was probably more ceremonial than military, and his wealth could
ensure an impressive turnout. See the Gomme–Sandbach com-
mentary, *ad loc.*

(Between vv. 29 and 30 there is a lacuna in B of about 23 or
24 lines. At v. 30 Moschion's prologue speech still con-
tinues.)

30   ].[....].[..].[

(65J)   ].φέροντ᾿ ἰδὼν

            ]ουτος· προσετίθην πανταχοῦ

            ].ησθε πρὸς τὸν γείτονα

            ]α συνθλάσας τὸ σημεῖον σφόδρα

35   φ]ιλανθρώπως δὲ πρὸς τὴν τοῦ πατρὸς

(70J) Σαμί]αν διέκειθ᾿ ἡ τῆς κόρης μήτηρ, τά τε

πλεῖ]στ᾿ ἦν παρ᾿ αὐταῖς ἥδε, καὶ πάλιν ποτὲ

αὗτ]αι παρ᾿ ἡμῖν. ἐξ ἀγροῦ δὴ καταδραμών,

ὡς ἔτυ]χ[έ] γ᾿, εἰς Ἀδώνι᾿ αὐτὰς κατέλαβον

40 συν]ηγ[μ]ένας ἐνθάδε πρὸς ἡμᾶς μετά τινων

(75J) ἄλλω]ν γυναικῶν. τῆς δ᾿ ἑορτῆς παιδιὰν

πολλὴ]ν ἐχούσης, οἷον εἰκός, συμπαρὼν

ἐγι]νόμην, οἴμοι, θεατής· ἀγρυπνίαν

ὁ θ]όρυβος αὐτῶν ἐνεπόει γάρ μοί τινα·

45 ἐπὶ] τὸ τέγος κήπους γὰρ ἀνέφερόν τινας,

(80J) ὠρχο]ῦντ᾿, ἐπαννύχιζον ἐσκεδασμέναι.

32 Corr. Austin: προσετίθειν B.   34]ανθλασας with ν
crossed out and συν written above it.

35 Suppl. apogr., ed.pr.   36 Suppl. Austin.

37 Suppl. ed.pr.   38 Suppl. Jacques.

39 Suppl. Sandbach.   αδώνει᾿ B: corr. apogr., Austin.

40 Suppl. apogr.   41 Suppl. apogr., ed.pr.

42 Suppl. Kassel, Sandbach.   οιχουσης corrected to εχ- B.

43 Suppl. ed.pr. (ἐγιγ]ν- apogr.).   οἴμε B: corr. several.

that during their absence Moschion had helped Nikeratos'
family, perhaps with money, by breaking a seal that se-
cured some of Demeas' property. Continuous sense returns
at v. 35.)

>] the girl's mother[8] got on well   35
> With father's [Samian] lady friend; she[9] spent
> [A lot of time] with them, and [they] in turn
> With us. Well, [as it happened (?)], I had rushed
> Back from the farm, and found them [gathered] in
> Our house here for the Adonis revels,[10] with   40
> Some [other] women. Naturally the rites
> Proved [lots of] fun, and being there with them—
> Oh dear!—I turned spectator, for [the] noise
> They made kept me awake. They carried plants
> Up [to] the roof, they [danced], they had an all   45
> Night party—spread all through the house! I['m scared]

---

[8] Nikeratos' wife, Plangon's mother.   [9] Chrysis.

[10] The festival of Adonis was celebrated by women in Athens during the summer. Adonis, Aphrodite's lover, was killed as a young man by a boar, and his worshippers believed that after his death he spent six months each year with Aphrodite and six months in Hades. For the festival women sowed seeds which quickly germinated and as quickly withered in their pots, which they carried up onto the rooftops. This early growth and early decay seemed to symbolise the life of Adonis. See W. Atallah, *Adonis dans la littérature et l'art grecs* (Paris 1966), M. Detienne, *The Gardens of Adonis* (translated by J. Lloyd, Hassocks, Sussex 1977) and N. Weill, *BCH* 90 (1966) 664–98 and 94 (1970) 591–93.

44, 45 Suppl. apogr., ed.pr.   45 ἐνέφερον B: corr. Austin.
46 Suppl. M. L. West.

MENANDER

ὀκν]ῶ λέγειν τὰ λοίπ'· ἴσως δ' αἰσχύνομαι
ὅτ'] οὐδὲν ὄφελος· ἀλλ' ὅμως αἰσχύνομαι.
ἐκύ]ησεν ἡ παῖς. τοῦτο γὰρ φράσας λέγω
50 καὶ] τὴν πρὸ τούτου πρᾶξιν. οὐκ ἠρνησάμην
(85J) τὴν] αἰτίαν σχών, ἀλλὰ πρότερος ἐνέτυχον
τῇ] μητρὶ τῆς κόρης· ὑπεσχόμην γαμεῖν
καὶ ν]ῦν, ἐπὰν ἔλθῃ ποθ' ὁ πατήρ· ὤμοσα.
τὸ π]αιδίον γενόμενον εἴληφ', οὐ πάλαι·
55 ἀπὸ] ταὐτομάτου δὲ συμβέβηκε καὶ μάλα
(90J) εὔκαιρο]ν· ἡ Χρυσίς—καλοῦμεν τοῦτο γὰρ
57   ].[.]......ν εὖ πάλαι

(Between vv. 57 and 58 there is a lacuna in B of some 26 or
27 lines).

47 Suppl. apogr., ed.pr.   λοιπα B with grave accent above
π.   48 Suppl. Post, Lowe.   οφελοσεστ'ομως B with αλλ'
written above ομ: corr. Arnott, Austin.   49, 50, 51, 52 Suppl.
apogr., ed.pr.   49]σεν B with η written above σ.
51 εχων B with ε crossed out and σ written above it.
ενετυχων B with ω crossed out and ο written above it.
52 υποσχομην B: corr. apogr., Austin.   53 καὶ suppl.
Handley, ν]ῦν ed.pr.   54, 55 Suppl. apogr., ed.pr.
56 Suppl. Sandbach (εἰς καιρόν Barigazzi, Blume).
57 εὖ Arnott, Austin: ου B with ε written above ο.

---

11 Demeas, his father, and Nikeratos, the girl's father, were still
abroad in the area around the Black Sea; Moschion was thus com-
pelled to make his confession to the girl's mother and postpone
the wedding until the return of Demeas and the girl's father. See
A. R. W. Harrison, *The Law of Athens: the Family and Property*

22

To say what happened next—ashamed perhaps
[When] there's no need, but still I am ashamed.
The girl got [pregnant]. Saying that I tell
What happened earlier, [too]. I didn't deny   50
I was to blame, but first I went to see
Her mother, I agreed to marry now,
[I mean] when father's back,[11] I swore an oath.
[The] baby came quite recently, and I've
Accepted it.[12] There's been a lucky break,   55
Quite [opportune], for Chrysis—that's her name[13]
                              ] well, a while ago   57

(After v. 57 there is a lacuna of some 26 or 27 lines. In them Moschion probably ended his prologue by saying that he had sent Parmenon to the harbour to see whether there was any news about his father's return from abroad, and that he would go off in the same direction with the hope of meeting Parmenon. After Moschion's exit, Chrysis enters probably from Demeas' house and delivers a short monologue, whose ending is preserved.)

(Oxford 1968) 17–21, D. M. MacDowell, *The Law in Classical Athens* (London 1978) 86–89.

  [12] Literally, 'I've taken it': sc. into Demeas' house, where Chrysis (as well as Plangon) could feed it.

  [13] After giving the Samian girl's name, Moschion presumably went on to explain the 'lucky break' by saying that Chrysis had herself given birth to a baby (by Demeas) at about the same time as Plangon, but it had been stillborn, died shortly after birth, or been exposed. That delivery had enabled Chrysis to breastfeed Plangon's baby (cf. vv. 77–79, 265–66). See F. H. Sandbach, *LCM* 11 (1986) 158–60 and S. R. West, *ZPE* 88 (1991) 11–16.

23

MENANDER

ΧΡΥΣΙΣ

(in mid-speech)

58   ]..[...].[
σπουδῇ πρὸς ἡμᾶς ἐ[νθα]δ[
60 ἐγὼ δ' ἀναμείνασ' ὅ τι λέγουσ' ἀ[κούσομαι.

ΜΟΣΧΙΩΝ

(121J) ἑόρακας αὐτὸς τὸν πατέρα σύ, Παρμέν[ων;

ΠΑΡΜΕΝΩΝ

οὔκουν ἀκούεις; φημί.

ΜΟΣΧΙΩΝ
            καὶ τὸν γείτονα;

ΠΑΡΜΕΝΩΝ

πάρεισιν.

ΜΟΣΧΙΩΝ
     εὖ γ' ἐπόησαν.

ΠΑΡΜΕΝΩΝ
            ἀλλ' ὅπως ἔσει
ἀνδρεῖος, εὐθύς τ' ἐμβαλεῖς περὶ τοῦ γάμου
65 λόγον.

59 B's σπουδη deciphered and corrected by Turner.
ἐ[νθά]δ' or ἐ[νθα]δ[ί suppl. Jacques.
60 αναμίνασ' B with omitted ε written above ί.
ἀ[κούσομαι suppl. Barigazzi, Sandbach.
61 Suppl. apogr., ed.pr.
63 εποεσαν corrected to -οησ- B.
64 ανδρῖος B with omitted ε written above ῖ.   ἐμβαλεῖς
several: αμβαλεῖς B.

24

SAMIA

CHRYSIS

(catching sight of Moschion and Parmenon rushing back)
[I can see (?)]   58
[Them] rapidly [approaching] us here [now (?)].
I'll wait and [hear] what they have got to say.   60

*(Moschion and Parmenon enter in mid-conversation. They
do not notice Chrysis, who may have retired into the back-
ground, at first.)*

MOSCHION

Have you yourself seen father, Parmenon?

PARMENON

What? Can't you hear? I have!

MOSCHION
Our neighbour,[14] too?

PARMENON

They're here!

MOSCHION
That's splendid!

PARMENON
Well then, you must be

A man, and broach the subject of your marriage
At once!

---

[14] Nikeratos, who accompanied Demeas on his journey
abroad.

25

MENANDER

ΜΟΣΧΙΩΝ

τίνα τρόπον; δειλὸς ἤδη γίνομαι,

(126J) ὡς πλησίον τὸ πρᾶγμα γέγονε.

ΠΑΡΜΕΝΩΝ

πῶς λέγεις;

ΜΟΣΧΙΩΝ

αἰσχύνομαι τὸν πατέρα.

ΠΑΡΜΕΝΩΝ

τὴν δὲ παρθένον
ἣν ἠδίκηκας τήν τε ταύτης μητέρα
πῶς οὐ τρέμεις, ἀνδρόγυνε;

ΧΡΥΣΙΣ

τί βοᾷς, δύσμορε;

ΠΑΡΜΕΝΩΝ

70   καὶ Χρυσὶς ἦν ἐνταῦθ'. ἐρωτᾷς δή με σὺ
(131J) τί βοῶ· γελοῖον· βούλομ' εἶναι τοὺς γάμους
ἤδη, πεπαῦσθαι τουτονὶ πρὸς ταῖς θύραις
κλάοντα ταύταις, μηδ' ἐκεῖν' ἀμνημονεῖν
ὧν ὤμοσεν—θύειν, στεφανοῦσθαι, σησαμῆν

65 Corr. apogr., ed.pr.: γιγνομαι B with ε written above the
first ι and the second γ crossed out.

69 πῶς οὐ Arnott: ὅπως B.

70 χρυσισενταυθα B with ην written above σεν and dicolon
after εντανθα.

72 πεπαυσθαιτε B: corr. several.

74–75 Punctuation by Kamerbeek, Lowe: παρελθὼν·αυτος
B.

26

MOSCHION

How can I? Now the time for action has   65
Come close, I've lost my nerve.

PARMENON

                How do you mean?

MOSCHION

I dare not face my father.

PARMENON

(angrily raising his voice)
                How's it you
Don't fear the girl you've injured and her mother,
You sissy?

CHRYSIS

(intervening to address Parmenon)
           Why shout so loud, you scoundrel?

PARMENON

So Chrysis too is here! You ask me why   70
I'm shouting—that's a joke. I want the wedding
To take place now, and *him*[15] to stop his wailing by
That door, and to remember what he swore
Himself when he went in[16]—to sacrifice, put on

[15] Said doubtless with a gesture in Moschion's direction.
[16] Sc. into Nikeratos' house, when he swore his oath to marry
Plangon (vv. 52–53).

75 κόπτειν—παρελθὼν αὐτός. οὐχ ἱκανὰς ἔχειν
(136J) προφάσεις δοκῶ σοι;

ΜΟΣΧΙΩΝ
πάντα ποιήσω· τί δεῖ
λέγειν;

ΠΑΡΜΕΝΩΝ
ἐγὼ μὲν οἴομαι.

ΜΟΣΧΙΩΝ
τὸ παιδίον
οὕτως ἐῶμεν ὡς ἔχει ταύτην τρέφειν,
αὐτήν τε φάσκειν τετοκέναι;

ΧΡΥΣΙΣ
τί δὴ γὰρ οὔ;

ΜΟΣΧΙΩΝ
80 ὁ πατὴρ χαλεπανεῖ.

76 ποησω B: corr. apogr., Austin.
77 οιμαι B: corr. Austin.   τοδεπαιδιονεχειν B: δε deleted
by Jacques (but Menander could perhaps have written τὸ παιδίον
/ δ᾽ οὕτως: Arnott), εχειν by Austin.
79 φασκει B: corr. apogr., Austin.
80 χαλαπαινεῖ B (with three dots above first ι, ? indicating
error).

17 Parmenon picks out three parts of the wedding ceremony.
On his wedding day the bridegroom conducted a sacrifice

SAMIA

His garland, cut the cake up![17] Don't you think   75
I've ample cause?[18]

                    MOSCHION
              I'll do all that—why must
You preach?

                    PARMENON
          I think you will.

                    MOSCHION
                      The baby, though—
Do we just let *her*[19] feed him, as she's doing,
And claim to be the mother?

                    CHRYSIS
                      Yes—why not?

                    MOSCHION
Father will go mad!

($\pi\rho o\gamma\acute{a}\mu\iota a$ or $\pi\rho o\tau\acute{\epsilon}\lambda\epsilon\iota a$) before the other festivities began (see
also vv. 123, 158, 190, 713, and cf. 211, 222). He wore a garland for
both this and the evening procession when he took his bride from
her house to his (cf. vv. 158, 190, 676). The reference to the cake is
ambiguous. Wedding cakes in ancient Athens were made from
roasted sesame seeds and honey, and here we cannot be sure
whether Moschion means he will chop the seeds before delivering
portions to his friends in advance of the marriage, or whether he
means he will cut the cake and distribute portions to guests in his
house on his wedding day (cf. vv. 125, 190). See especially R. Gar-
land, *The Greek Way of Life* (London 1990) 217–25, and J. H.
Oakley and R. H. Sinos, *The Wedding in Ancient Athens* (Madi-
son, Wisc. and London 1993) 11–37.
    [18] Sc. for shouting (cf. vv. 70–71).
    [19] Pointing to Chrysis.

MENANDER

ΧΡΥΣΙΣ

⟨τί δέ;⟩ πεπαύσεται πάλιν.

(141J) ἐρᾷ γάρ, ὦ βέλτιστε, κἀκεῖνος κακῶς,
οὐχ ἧττον ἢ σύ. τοῦτο δ᾽ εἰς διαλλαγὰς
ἄγει τάχιστα καὶ τὸν ὀργιλώτατον.
πρότερον δ᾽ ἔγωγε πάντ᾽ ἂν ὑπομεῖναι δοκῶ

85 ἢ τοῦτο τίτθην ἐν συνοικίᾳ τινὶ
(146J) ε........[   ].˙.[

(Between vv. 86 and 87 there is a lacuna in B of some 21 or
22 lines).

ΜΟΣΧΙΩΝ

87   ].[
βο]ύλομαι
λά]βοις

90   γ]ὰρ ἀθλιώτερον
(173J)]πάντων· οὐκ ἀπάγξομαι ταχύ;
ῥ]ήτωρ μόνος γὰρ φιλόφρονος
]ότερός εἰμ᾽ ἔν γε τοῖς νυνὶ λόγοις.
τί δ᾽ οὐκ ἀ]πελθὼν εἰς ἐρημίαν τινὰ

95 γυμν]άζομ᾽; οὐ γὰρ μέτριος ἀγών ἐστί μοι.

80 τί δέ; added by M. L. West.   83 τεν corrected to τον
B.   84 υμπομειναι B with first μ deleted.   85 τιθην B:
corr. Lloyd-Jones.   88 Suppl. ed.pr.   89 Suppl. Austin (or
συλλα]βοις, etc.).   90 Suppl. Austin, Barigazzi.
92 Suppl. apogr., ed.pr.   94 τί δ᾽ οὐκ suppl. Kassel,
Oguse, ἀ]πελθὼν ed.pr.   95 Suppl. several.

30

SAMIA

CHRYSIS

        [So what?] He'll calm down   80
Again. You see, my boy, he too's as badly
In love as you are! That persuades the most
Hot-tempered man to make an early peace!
I think, though, I'd put up with anything
Before a nursemaid in some tenement   85
[Was hired to feed (?)] this [baby (?)] . . .   86

*(After Chrysis' remark about Plangon's baby in vv. 84–86
there is a lacuna in the papyrus of some 21 or 22 lines, in
which the conversation between Chrysis, Moschion and
Parmenon must have ended with Chrysis and Parmenon
going off into Demeas' house and leaving Moschion alone
on stage to express in a monologue his worries about what
he should say in explanation to Demeas. Some of this
monologue is preserved on a new page of the papyrus, but
its opening is lost and the next five lines are too mutilated
for coherent supplementation (88 yields only I wish, 89
you[d] take (?), 90 more forlorn, you see (presumably a
reference to himself), 91 of all—shouldn't I throttle myself,
92 speaker alone . . . of friendly), although they all suit a
context where Moschion feels himself pinioned by helpless
despair.)*

MOSCHION

(in mid speech)
I'm rather [doubtful (?)] over what I must now say!   93
[Why don't] I go off to some lonely spot
And [practise], for my fight's not trivial!   95

(Moschion now goes off into the country (probably audi-

31

ΔΗΜΕΑΣ

(178J) ἆ]ρ᾽ οὖν μεταβολῆς αἰσθάνεσθ᾽ ἤδη τόπου,
ὅσον διαφέρει ταῦτα τῶν ἐκεῖ κακῶν;
Πόντος· παχεῖς γέροντες, ἰχθῦς ἄφθονοι,
ἀηδία τις πραγμάτων. Βυζάντιον·
100 ἀψίνθιον, πικρὰ πάντ᾽. Ἄπολλον. ταῦτα δὲ
(183J) καθαρὰ πενήτων ἀγάθ᾽· Ἀθῆναι φίλταται,
πῶς ἂν [γ]ένοιθ᾽ ὑμῖν ὅσων ἔστ᾽ ἄξιαι,
ἵν᾽ ὦμεν ἡμεῖς πάντα μακαριώτατοι
οἱ τὴν πόλιν φιλοῦντες. εἴσω παράγετε
105 ὑμεῖς. ἀπόπληχθ᾽, ἔστηκας ἐμβλέπων ἐμοί;

96–105 are all assigned to one speaker by B (Sandbach gives
96–97 and 102(Ἀθῆναι)–105 to Demeas, and the rest to
Nikeratos).
96 ἆ]ρ᾽ suppl. Arnott.
98 Corr. Arnott: ἰχθνες B.
102 Suppl. apogr., ed.pr.

---

20 The Greek word Πόντος, naming one of the two places
visited by the speaker and Nikeratos on their business trip, is an
ambiguous term, denoting elsewhere both the Black Sea in gen-
eral and more specifically a stretch of land to its south, covering
roughly the northeastern section of modern Turkey. The refer-
ence in vv. 108–11 to fog blotting out the sun, however, makes it
likely that Menander had in mind here the west and northern
shores of the Black Sea, whose enduring fogs were as well known
in antiquity as was its abundance of fish. See especially C. M.
Danoff, *RE Suppl.* 9 (1962) s.v. *Pontos Euxeinos*, 938–49, 955–85
and H.-D. Blume, *Menanders Samia* (Darmstadt 1974) 33–51.

ence left) in order to rehearse the explanation of his past
misconduct that he should give to Demeas. Onto the empty
stage, from the direction of the harbour (probably audi-
ence right), now enter Demeas and Nikeratos in mid-con-
versation. They are accompanied by several slaves heavily
laden with Demeas' baggage, and by one other carrying
Nikeratos' much skimpier luggage.)

DEMEAS

Don't you all notice now a change of scene,
How much this differs from the horrors there?
The Black Sea[20]—fat[21] old men, no end of fish,
Disgusting business. Then Byzantium[22]:
Absinthe and all things bitter. God! But here—   100
Pure blessings for the poor. Oh dearest Athens,
If only you could get all you deserve[23]—
So we who love the city might then be
Completely happy. In you go! Have you
Been paralysed, to stand and gawp at me?   105

[21] The Greek word here is ambiguous: elsewhere it can also
mean 'rich' or 'stupid,' but the natives living to the west and north
of the Black Sea are described as 'fat and fleshy' in the Hippocratic
Airs, Water and Places, ch. 19.

[22] Byzantium (later Constantinople, now Istanbul) lies on the
Thracian side of the Bosporus; it—as well as the Pontus—was
known for its wormwood or absinthe (*Artemisia absinthium*), a
plant which was reputed to add its own bitter taste to everything
growing in the area.

[23] This chauvinistic praise of Athens seems nevertheless to
imply that all was not well with the city; see introduction.

ΝΙΚΗΡΑΤΟΣ

(188J) ἐκ[ε]ῖν᾽ ἐθαύμαζον μάλιστα, Δημέα,
τῶν περὶ ἐκεῖνον τὸν τόπον. τὸν ἥλιον
οὐκ ἦν ἰδεῖν ἐνίοτε παμπόλλου χρόνου·
ἀὴρ παχύς τις, ὡς ἔοικ᾽, ἐπεσκότει.

ΔΗΜΕΑΣ

110   οὔκ, ἀλλὰ σεμνὸν οὐδὲν ἐθεᾶτ᾽ αὐτόθι,
(193J) ὥστ᾽ αὐτὰ τἀναγκαῖ᾽ ἐπέλαμπε τοῖς ἐκεῖ.

ΝΙΚΗΡΑΤΟΣ

νὴ τὸν Διόνυσον, εὖ λέγεις.

ΔΗΜΕΑΣ

καὶ ταῦτα μὲν
ἑτέροις μέλειν ἐῶμεν· ὑπὲρ ὧν δ᾽ ἐλέγομεν
τί δοκεῖ ποεῖν σοι;

ΝΙΚΗΡΑΤΟΣ

τὰ περὶ τὸν γάμον λέγεις
115   τῷ μειρακίῳ σου;

ΔΗΜΕΑΣ

πάνυ γε.

106 Suppl. apogr., ed.pr.   ]ινοθαύμαζον B with the omit-
ted ε written above οθ.
107 εκείνων corrected to -νον B.
108 παμπολου B with the omitted λ written above λο.
109 εο:ικ᾽ B in error.
111 τοεκει with the omitted ις written above οε.
115 Corr. several: μειρακειω B.

(Demeas directs In you go *at his slaves, who speedily carry his baggage into his house. The one who dawdles and gawps was perhaps Nikeratos' slave, reluctant to obey an order from someone not his master but eventually exiting into Nikeratos' house, but he could just as well have been a refractory slave of Demeas'. Nikeratos then turns to Demeas.)*

NIKERATOS

One feature of that region, Demeas,
Particularly puzzled me. Sometimes
You couldn't see the sun for hours on end.
A dense fog, so it seems, blotted it out!

DEMEAS

No—it saw nothing there of note, so it   110
Shone on the people there the least it could!

NIKERATOS

That's really well said!

DEMEAS

                Let's leave that for others
To worry over. But about our talk
Just now—what do you want to do?

NIKERATOS

                        You mean about
This wedding for your son?

DEMEAS

              Yes.

ΝΙΚΗΡΑΤΟΣ

ταῦτ᾽ ἀεὶ λέγω.

(198J) ἀγαθῇ τύχῃ πράττωμεν, ἡμέραν τινὰ
θέμενοι.

ΔΗΜΕΑΣ

δέδοκται ταῦτ᾽;

ΝΙΚΗΡΑΤΟΣ

ἐμοὶ γοῦν.

ΔΗΜΕΑΣ

ἀλλὰ μὴν

κἀμοὶ προτέρῳ σου.

ΝΙΚΗΡΑΤΟΣ

παρακάλει μ᾽ ὅταν ἐξίῃς.

ΔΗΜΕΑΣ

119a   ].γαστυ[

(Between vv. 119a and 119b there is a lacuna in B contain-
ing between 12 and 16 lines of spoken text, as well as the
sign ΧΟΡΟΥ to indicate the break between Acts I and II.
The ends of the last three lines in this gap, however, are
preserved in O.)

115–17 ταῦτ᾽—θέμενοι given to Nikeratos by Kassel, Blume:
no dicolon before ταυτ᾽ and no paragraphus under 115 in B.

117 ἐμοὶ γοῦν assigned to Nikeratos by Fraenkel: no dicolon
before εμοι in B.   γουμ B: corr. Austin.

NIKERATOS

                My reply's   115
Always the same—let's go ahead, good luck to us,
And fix the day!

DEMEAS
You think so?

NIKERATOS
              Yes, I do.

DEMEAS
                   I too
Planned this, before you!

NIKERATOS
(probably as he goes off into his own house)
              Call me when you leave.   118

DEMEAS
    ] town (?)[119a

(After v. 119a there is a gap of perhaps 8–12 lines in the papyri, during which Demeas would have delivered a short monologue, perhaps indicating at first an intention to visit town (cf. v. 119a), but then changing his mind and exiting into his own house when he saw some tipsy revellers approaching along one of the side entrances. These were the chorus, entering for the performance of their first entr'acte.)[24]

[24] Cf. *Asp.* 245–49, *Dysk.* 230–32, *Epitr.* 169–71, *Pk.* 261–66, and my commentary (Cambridge 1996) on Alexis fr. 112 K-A, pp. 300–301.

MENANDER

(ΜΕΡΟΣ Β΄)

ΔΗΜΕΑΣ

119b   ].

119c   ].α.

119d   ἔρχε]ται·

(either ΔΗΜΕΑΣ or ΜΟΣΧΙΩΝ)

120   ]ντ᾽ εἰ καὶ δι.[....]

ΜΟΣΧΙΩΝ

                              οὐδὲ] ἕν

(217J) ἐ]γὼ μελετήσας ὧν τό[τ᾽ ἐνόουν, ἔρ]χομαι.
        ὡς ἐγενόμην γὰρ ἐκπ[οδὼν αὐτὸς μ]όνος,
        ἔθυον· ἐπὶ τὸ δεῖπνον [ἐκάλουν τοὺς φίλ]ους·
        ἐπὶ λούτρ᾽ ἔπεμπον τὰς γ[υναῖκα]ς· περιπατῶν
125   τὴν σησαμῆν διένεμον· ἦ[δον· ἐνί]οτε
(222J) ὑμέναιον ἐτερέτιζον· ἦν ἀβέλτ[ε]ρο[ς.

        119b–125 Line-ends preserved in O (O.17) often supplement
a defective B. 119b–d assigned to Demeas, 120 (from οὐδὲ] ἕν)
onwards to Moschion, by Arnott: O apparently misplaces
μο(σχιων) as its indication of a new speaker to the right margin of
122.   119d ? ἔρχε]ται or προσέρχε]ται Arnott.
        120]..ντοει apparently B.   [οὐδὲ] suppl. Sisti.
        121 ἐ]γὼ suppl. apogr., Austin, τό[τ᾽ ἐνόουν Barigazzi (τό[τ᾽
also Austin), ἔρ[χομαι Turner.
        122 ἐκπ[οδὼν suppl. Sisti, [αὐτὸς] Dedoussi, μ]όνος Austin.
        123 εποι with ο deleted B.   Supplements by Austin,
Barigazzi.   124 Suppl. Merkelbach.
        125 διενιμον B: corr. Austin.   ἦ[δον suppl. Austin, ἐνί]οτε
Sandbach.

38

SAMIA

(ACT II)

*(The second act must have opened with Demeas returning
to the stage. He probably expressed his anger at seeing
Chrysis with the baby in his house, and possibly ended
with a reference to the entry of Moschion by the side en-
trance leading from the countryside; three tattered line-
ends (119b–d) precede the resumption of a more compre-
hensible text, and the three letters preserved from the close
of v. 119d could be part of the verb in a clause such as* my
son *or* Moschion is coming *or* approaches. *The first part of
v. 120 (with only* even *if clearly decipherable) could have
been spoken by either Demeas or Moschion. At the end of
120 Moschion is speaking, having entered apparently with
his thoughts so dominated by what he had done at his
'lonely spot' (v. 94) that he does not notice his father's pres-
ence until v. 127.)*

MOSCHION

Here I [am]—   120
I did[n't] run through anything [I'd planned]
Before! When I was on my own, away
[From here], I sacrificed, [invited my friends] to
The dinner, sent the [women] off to bathe,
Traipsed round distributing the cake. [I sang,]   125
[Some]times I hummed my wedding song. I played

---

125 ($\mathring{\eta}[\delta o\nu$)–126 ($\dot{\epsilon}\tau\epsilon\rho\dot{\epsilon}\tau\iota\zeta o\nu$) so punctuated by Arnott: B has
raised stop after υμεναιον.

126 $\epsilon\tau\epsilon\rho\epsilon\theta\iota\zeta o\nu$ B: corr. apogr., Austin. $\dot{\alpha}\beta\dot{\epsilon}\lambda\tau[\epsilon]\rho o[\varsigma$
suppl. ed.pr.

39

MENANDER

ὡς δ' οὖν ἐνεπλήσθην—ἀλλ᾽, Ἄπολλον, οὑτοσὶ
ὁ π]ατήρ. ἀκήκο᾽ ἆρα; χαῖρέ μοι, πάτερ.

ΔΗΜΕΑΣ
ν]ὴ καὶ σύ γ᾽, ὦ παῖ.

ΜΟΣΧΙΩΝ
τί σκυθρωπάζεις;

ΔΗΜΕΑΣ
τί γάρ;

130 γ]αμετὴν ἑταίραν, ὡς ἔοικ᾽, ἐλάνθανον
(227J) ἔχ]ων.

ΜΟΣΧΙΩΝ
γαμετήν; πῶς; ἀγνοῶ τὸν ⟨σὸν⟩ λόγον.

ΔΗΜΕΑΣ
λάθ]ριό[ς τι]ς ὑ⟨ός⟩, ὡς ἔοικε, γέγονέ μοι,

127 Dicolon in B after ενεπλησθην, indicating that the
speaker now addresses Demeas.
128 Suppl. apogr., ed.pr.   ἀκήκο᾽ ἆρα punctuated as a
question by Austin, Barigazzi.   χαιρεα B: corr. Austin.
Dicolon after πατερ omitted by B.
129 Suppl. ed.pr.   130 Suppl. apogr., ed.pr.
131 ἔχ]ων suppl. apogr., ed.pr.   ⟨σὸν⟩ added by Arnott.
132 Suppl. and corr. Austin:]σνωσεοικ᾽ε B.

---

1 Moschion went off at v. 95 in order to prepare some defence
of his past misconduct that he could use before his father. Instead
of doing that, however, he sank into a reverie about events in his
projected wedding—the preliminary sacrifice (cf. vv. 75 and note,
190, 713; cf. 217, 222), his invitation of friends to the wedding

The fool![1] But when I'd had enough—

(Moschion suddenly now sees his father.)

O god,

Here's father! Has he heard me?—Father, greetings!

DEMEAS
(still angry over what he saw in his house)
Yes, son, to you too!

MOSCHION
Why the black looks?

DEMEAS

Why indeed!

My partner's[2] now [become] my wife, it seems, without   130
My knowing!

MOSCHION
Wife? How? I don't follow what you say.

DEMEAS
[A secret son]'s been born to me, it seems!

---

breakfast, the despatch of the womenfolk to the prenuptial bath in water from a sacred spring (cf. 713 and contrast 167), the distribution of portions of the wedding cake (cf. vv. 74–75 and note, 190), and the wedding song sung normally in the evening procession to the bridegroom's house. See especially Maas in *RE* (1914) s.v. *Hymenaios* 130–34, R. Garland, *The Greek Way of Life* (London 1990) 217–25, and J. H. Oakley and R. H. Sinos, *The Wedding in Ancient Athens* (Madison, Wisc. and London 1993) 11–37.

[2] Literally *'hetaira'* or 'courtesan.' Demeas believes that Chrysis, formerly a *hetaira*, is now behaving like a wife by bearing and nursing a child.

MENANDER

ὅν γ'] ἐς [κόρ]ακας ἄπεισιν ἐκ τῆς οἰκίας
ἤ]δη λαβ[ο]ῦσα.

ΜΟΣΧΙΩΝ

μηδαμῶς.

ΔΗΜΕΑΣ

πῶς μηδαμῶς;

135 ἀλλ' ἦ μ[ε θ]ρέψειν ἔνδον υἱὸν προσδοκᾷς
(232J) νόθον; [μιαρὸ]ν κοὐ τοῦ τρόπου τοὐμοῦ λέγεις.

ΜΟΣΧΙΩΝ

τίς δ' [ἐ]στὶν ἡμῶν γνήσιος, πρὸς τῶν θεῶν,
ἢ τίς νόθος, γενόμενος ἄνθρωπος;

ΔΗΜΕΑΣ

σὺ μὲν
παίζεις.

ΜΟΣΧΙΩΝ

μὰ τὸν Διόνυσον, ⟨ἀλλ'⟩ ἐσπούδακα.

140 οὐθὲν γένος γένους γὰρ οἶμαι διαφέρειν,
(237J) ἀλλ' εἰ δικαίως ἐξετάσαι τις, γνήσιος
142 ὁ χρηστός ἐστιν, ὁ δὲ πονηρὸς καὶ νόθος

140–42 fr. 248 Körte–Thierfelder (Stobaeus, *Eclogae* 4.29.10
citing Μενάνδρου κηνδία (*sic* mss. MA, corrected to Κηδείᾳ by
Austin). See introduction to *Samia* at n. 4).

133 ὅν γ' suppl. Austin (ὅν also Turner), [κόρ]ακας ed.pr.
134–42, 143a–43m Line beginnings preserved in O (143b–m
covering a gap in B).   134 Suppl. Turner.   135 ἀλλ' ἦ
Austin: αλλωμ[O.   μ[ε suppl. Turner, θ]ρέψειν ed.pr.

SAMIA

She'll[3] take [him] now and leave my house—to hell
With her!

MOSCHION

No!

DEMEAS

No? Do you expect me to
Bring up a bastard son in there?[4] That 'no'   135
Of yours is [vile], it goes against the grain!

MOSCHION

In heaven's name, which man of us is born
Legitimate, and which a bastard?

DEMEAS

You
Are joking!

MOSCHION

No, I'm not! I'm serious—
I think there's no distinction when one's born,   140
But if you test them fairly, good men are
Legitimate, bad men are bastards and   142

---

3 Chrysis.
4 Inside his house.

---

136 [μιαρὸ]ν suppl. Arnott.   κοὐ τοῦ Kassel: γ'ουτου B.
137 Suppl. Turner, Austin.
139 ⟨ἀλλ'⟩ added by Arnott, Sandbach.
140]σγενους B: γένους γένος mss. SMA of Stobaeus.
141 εξετασαιτις·γνησιος B: ἐξετάσεις καὶ γνησίως SMA of
Stob.

43

143a καὶ δοῦλος .[   ].[..]s
143b λεγωνεαν[

ΔΗΜΕΑΣ (?)

143c ἀλλ' ἀργύριον [
143d εστα.το.ει.[
143e εἶναι πολ...[

ΜΟΣΧΙΩΝ (?)

143f σὺ ταῦτα συ..[
143g τοῦτον λαβ.[

ΔΗΜΕΑΣ (?)

143h ἄδηλον εἶπ[ας
143i πᾶσαν ἀπο[

ΜΟΣΧΙΩΝ (?)

143j πολὺ μ[ᾶλλον
143k τοιοῦτον[
143l κατα[
143m .[

(After vv. 143b–m, which are line beginnings preserved
only in O, there is a lacuna of some 16 lines before
B resumes with an indecipherable trace in v. 144.
A transcribable, though mutilated, text commences at
v. 145.)

143b λέγων ἐὰν/ἐᾶν or λέγω νέαν O, with paragraphus under
this line.   143d αυτ or αιτ, ολε or ομε O.
Under 143e, 143g, 143i paragraphi in O.
143h, 143j Suppl. Turner.

Slaves [143a

(This page of the Bodmer papyrus is torn or cut off at v. 143a, but another papyrus preserves the openings of the next 12 lines (143b–143m), in which Moschion and Demeas apparently continue their argument about Chrysis and the baby. Too little of each line survives for a coherent interpretation of the drift of that argument. The speech of Moschion beginning at 139 probably continued to 143b, which yields saying "if . . . ," or telling . . . to let, or I say . . . young [lady(?)]. Demeas appears to respond with 143c–e (143c but money, 143d it will be . . . , 143e to be). Moschion may speak 143f–g (143f you . . . these [things (?), 143g take this [opportunity (?)]). Demeas perhaps retorts with 143h–i (143h [you've (?)] spoken a riddle, 143i all). Moschion finally may deliver 143j–m (143j much [rather (?), 144k such). After v. 143m there is a lacuna of about 16 lines before the Bodmer papyrus resumes. Demeas and Moschion are still in conversation, but their subject has changed from the future of Chrysis and the baby—presumably in the lacuna Demeas withdrew his threat to expel them from his house—and they are now talking about the future of Moschion and Plangon. Although vv. 145–50 are badly mutilated, it seems clear that Demeas has just suggested that Moschion should marry Nikeratos' daughter, and been surprised by Moschion's eager agreement. Moschion so far has made no mention of his misconduct.)

ΔΗΜΕΑΣ

145   ] ἐσπούδακας;

ΜΟΣΧΙΩΝ

(273J)   ]ν γαμεῖν· ἐρῶ
    ]ν μὴ τοὺς γάμους

ΔΗΜΕΑΣ
    ].ως, παῖ.

ΜΟΣΧΙΩΝ
        βούλομαι
    ] δοκεῖν.

ΔΗΜΕΑΣ
      καλῶς ποεῖς.

ΜΟΣΧΙΩΝ
150   ]..

ΔΗΜΕΑΣ
  ἂν διδῶσ᾽ οὗτοι, γαμεῖς.

ΜΟΣΧΙΩΝ
(278J) πῶς ἄν, π]υθόμενος μηδὲ ἓν τοῦ πράγματος,
ἐσπο]υδακότα μ᾽ αἴσθοιο συλλάβοις τέ μοι;

ΔΗΜΕΑΣ
ἐσπουδακότα; μηδὲν πυθόμενος; καταν[οῶ
τὸ πρᾶγμα, Μοσχίων, ὃ λέγεις. ἤδη τρέχω

146 Punctuation by Arnott, Austin.
150]..B, perhaps followed by a dicolon.
151 πῶς ἄν suppl. Kassel, π]υθόμενος ed.pr.

46

DEMEAS
] are you serious?   145

MOSCHION
   ] to marry—I'm in love!
] the wedding

DEMEAS
] , son.

MOSCHION
         I desire
[To be—not just (?)] seem [—decent]!

DEMEAS
                  You do well.

MOSCHION (?)
[   ]

DEMEAS
If they[5] agree, you'll marry her?   150

MOSCHION
If you'd heard nothing of the matter, [how]
Could you know I was serious, and chip in?

DEMEAS
Serious? Heard nothing? Moschion, [I] understand
The plight that you describe. Now I'll run off

---

[5] Nikeratos, his wife and Plangon.

152, 153 Suppl. apogr., ed.pr.
152 τέ μοι apogr., Austin: γεμοι B.

47

155 πρὸς τουτονί, καὶ τοὺς γάμους αὐτῷ φράσω
(283J) ποεῖν. τὰ παρ᾽ ἡμῶν γὰρ <παρ>έσται.

MOΣXIΩN

ταῦ[τά γ᾽ εὖ

λέγεις. περιρρανάμενος ἤδη παρα[γαγών,
σπείσας τε καὶ λιβανωτὸν ἐπιθείς, [τὴν κόρην
μέτειμι.

ΔΗΜΕΑΣ

μήπω δὴ βάδιζ᾽, ἄχ[ρι ἂν μάθω
160 εἰ ταῦτα συγχωρήσεθ᾽ ἡμῖ[ν οὑτοσί.

MOΣXIΩN

(288J) οὐκ ἀντερεῖ σοι. παρενοχλε[ῖν δ᾽ ὑμῖν, πάτερ,
ἐμὲ συμπαρόντ᾽ ἐστ᾽ ἀπρε[πές, ἀλλ᾽ ἀπέρχομαι.

ΔΗΜΕΑΣ

ταὐτόματόν ἐστιν, ὡς ἔοικέ, που θεός,

156 γαρεσται B: corr. Austin. ταῦ[τά γ᾽ εὖ suppl.
Jacques (ταυ]τ already ed.pr.). ταῦ[τά γ᾽—159 μέτειμι as-
signed to Moschion by Arnott: B has paragraphi under 156, 158, a
dicolon crossed out after ποειν (156) and changed to a full stop af-
ter λεγεις. 157 περιρανμενος with the omitted α written
above νμ B: corr. apogr., Austin. παρα[γαγών suppl. Oguse
(cf. also H.-D. Blume, Menanders Samia, Darmstadt 1974, 65
n.15). 158 σπείσας apogr.: επεισας B. τὴν κόρην suppl.
Jacques. See also fragment 2 below. 159 Suppl. M. L.
West (ἄχρι ἂν also Oguse). 160 συγχωρήσεθ᾽ Austin:
συγχωρησεσθ᾽ B. ἡμῖ[ν suppl. ed.pr., οὑτοσί Austin.

161 παρενοχλε[ῖν suppl. apogr., ed.pr., [δ᾽ ὑμῖν, πατερ,]
Austin. 162 συνπαρόντ᾽ B: corr. Austin. ἀπρε[πές
suppl. apogr., ed.pr., ἀλλ᾽ ἀπέρχομαι M. L. West.

And see him,[6] ask him to arrange the wedding.   155
On our side, we'll be ready!

MOSCHION
                [Excellent]—
Now I'll [go] in and wash, pour a libation,
Put incense on the altar, and I'll fetch
[The bride!][7]

DEMEAS
                Don't go yet—not until [I find]
Out whether he agrees with us on this!   155 160

MOSCHION
He won't oppose you! It's not right, though, [father],
For me to stay here [in your way—I'm off].

(*Moschion goes off, probably by the side-entrance leading
into the city centre. Demeas, now alone on stage, reflects on
what has happened.*)

DEMEAS
It seems that Chance somehow's a kind of god—

---

6 Nikeratos. The Greek word implies that Demeas points to
Nikeratos' house.

7 In vv. 157–59 Moschion picks out different parts of the wed-
ding ceremony. 'Wash' here is a substitute for the prenuptial bath,
taken normally by bridegrooms as well as brides. The pouring of
libations and burning of incense were essential parts of ritual in
sacrifices at weddings and other occasions. The highlight of Athe-
nian weddings, however, was the bridegroom's journey to the
bride's house and return with her in the evening to his own house.
See especially notes on 74–75 and on vv. 123–25 and 190, and cf.
211, 432–33, 609–610 and 673–74.

MENANDER

σῴζει τε πολλὰ τῶν ἀοράτων πραγμάτων.
165 ἐγὼ γὰρ οὐκ εἰδὼς ἔχον[τα τουτονὶ
(293J) ἐρωτικῶς, ταυ[τ

(After 166 there is a lacuna of 27 or 28 lines. When B re-
sumes, Demeas is coming to the end of the monologue
which he began at v. 163.)

167 (?).....]ε[..] ἐκεῖνον βού[λομαι
(325J) ἔξω καλεῖν. δεῦ]ρ' εἰς τὸ πρόσθεν, δ[ε]ῦρό μοι,
Νικήρατ', ἔξελθ'].

163–64 fr. 249 K-T (Stobaeus, *Eclogae* 1.6.9 citing
Μενάνδρου Κηδείᾳ (so correctly ms. P: Ακηδείᾳ F). See intro-
duction to *Samia* n. 4).

165 Suppl. Lloyd-Jones, Oguse.
166 Suppl. ed.pr.
167 βού[λομαι suppl. Austin.
168 ἔξω καλεῖν δεῦ]ρ' suppl. Arnott (ἐκκαλε]ῖ[ν already Aus-
tin, but before ἐκεῖνον in 167).   δ[ε]ῦρό μοι Handley:
δ[.].ρομαι B, with ο or οι (as correction?) or ηρ (as marginal
identification of speaker: [νικ]ηρ' ?) written above the α.

It watches over many things concealed
From view! I didn't know that [my son here]   165
Was smitten—this [*   *   *   *   *]   166

*(After 166 there is a gap of some 27 or 28 lines, entirely oc-
cupied in all probability by the monologue of Demeas that
began at 163. We have no means of knowing what the miss-
ing verses contained. When the text resumes at 167 Demeas
is still speaking, and now apparently bent on meeting
Nikeratos and asking him to fix the date of Moschion's and
Plangon's wedding for that very same day. Severe mutila-
tion in the papyrus up to v. 193, however, has removed the
first half of each line and consequently made it difficult to
know (i) where Demeas' monologue ends, (ii) whether
Nikeratos was called out of his house by Demeas or entered
spontaneously, and (iii) where the speech divisions pre-
cisely come in the ensuing conversation between the two
old men. The supplements suggested here between vv. 167
and 171 are very uncertain.)*

DEMEAS

(still speaking)
[*   *   *   *   *   I] wish [to summon] him   167
[Outside].

*(Demeas goes to Nikeratos' door and shouts to Nikeratos
inside.)*

                [Nikeratos,] I want you [here]—
[Out] here, in front!

(Nikeratos enters from his house.)

ΝΙΚΗΡΑΤΟΣ

ἐπὶ τί;

ΔΗΜΕΑΣ

χαῖρε πολλὰ σύ.

ΝΙΚΗΡΑΤΟΣ

170   καὶ σύ γε. τί ἐστι]ν;

ΔΗΜΕΑΣ

μνημονεύεις, εἰπέ μοι,

(328J)   ὡς οὐ τὸ πρῶτο]ν ἐθέμεθ' ἡμέραν;

ΝΙΚΗΡΑΤΟΣ

ἐγώ;

ΔΗΜΕΑΣ

]λυτ[α]ι τὴν τήμερον
ι]σθ' ἀκριβῶς.

ΝΙΚΗΡΑΤΟΣ

ποῦ; πότε;

ΔΗΜΕΑΣ

γ]ίνεσθαι ταχὺ
175   τήμ]ερον.

ΝΙΚΗΡΑΤΟΣ

τρόπῳ τίνι;

169–87 Speakers identified mainly by Austin (but 170 up to
ἐστι]ν;, and 186 before [ἀ]λλὰ, Arnott).
169 Suppl. Barigazzi (so also Handley, Sandbach as supple-
ment in 168).   170 Suppl. Barigazzi (but with τί δ' in 170: τί
Arnott, and εστι]ν B in error for ἐστι?).

SAMIA

NIKERATOS
What for?

DEMEAS
Hello to you!

NIKERATOS
[You too! What's up?]

DEMEAS
Tell me, do you remember,　　　　170
We did[n't] fix a date [before]?

NIKERATOS
I didn't?

DEMEAS
[　　　　　] this very day!
[　　　　　] know precisely.

NIKERATOS
Where and when?

DEMEAS
[　　want the wedding (?)] to be soon—
[　　　　　　in fact,] today!

NIKERATOS
How can this be?　　175

---

171 Suppl. Arnott (ὡς οὐχὶ πρότερο]ν already Sandbach).
Dicolon after ἡμέραν uncertain in B.

172]λυτ[α]ι τὴν Austin:]λυτ[.]την B with ι or [.]ι written
above τ[.]τ.

173 Either ἴ]σθ᾽ (ed.pr.) or οἶ]σθ᾽ (Austin).

174 Suppl. ed.pr.

175 Suppl. Jacques, Barigazzi.

53

ΔΗΜΕΑΣ

(333J) [   ]

ΝΙΚΗΡΑΤΟΣ

ἀλλ' ἔστ' ἀδύνατον.

ΔΗΜΕΑΣ

ἐ]μοί· σοὶ δ' οὐδὲ ἓν
            ]γειν.

ΝΙΚΗΡΑΤΟΣ

        ὦ Ἡράκλεις.

ΔΗΜΕΑΣ

        ]ς· οὕτω σοι φράσαι
180   ].ν· ἀλλὰ ⟨δεῖ⟩ τοδὶ λέγειν
(338J)   ]ν.

ΝΙΚΗΡΑΤΟΣ

        πρὶν εἰπεῖν τοῖς φίλοις
        ] δοκεῖν.

ΔΗΜΕΑΣ

            Νικήρατε,
ἐμ]οὶ χαρίσῃ.

ΝΙΚΗΡΑΤΟΣ

                πῶς γνώσομαι;

ΔΗΜΕΑΣ (?)

[   ]

177 Suppl. apparently Paduano.
179 ουτο B with 2nd o crossed out and ω written above it.

SAMIA

DEMEAS

[   ]

NIKERATOS

          But that's impossible!

DEMEAS

[leave everything (?)] to me! For you, there's no
[Reason to worry (?)   ]

NIKERATOS

          Good heavens!

DEMEAS

[   ] to tell you so
[   ] but [I must] say this—   180
[   ]

NIKERATOS

         Before I tell my friends?

[   ] to seem [   ]

DEMEAS

         Nikeratos,
[Do this, and (?)] you'll oblige [me].

NIKERATOS

          How shall I decide?

DEMEAS (?)

[   ]

---

180 ⟨δεῖ⟩ added by Austin.

183 ἐμ]οὶ Austin, χαρίσῃ Kamerbeek:]χαρισ:ην· B with misplaced dicolon and]οι written above χα.   γνωσωμαι B with correcting o written above the ω.

ΝΙΚΗΡΑΤΟΣ (?)

[   ]. τυχόντος μοι φίλον.

ΔΗΜΕΑΣ (?)

185 [   ]

ΝΙΚΗΡΑΤΟΣ
τοῦτ᾽ ἐσπούδακας;

ΔΗΜΕΑΣ

(343J) [   ]

ΝΙΚΗΡΑΤΟΣ
[ἀ]λλὰ συγχωροῦντά σοι
ἐ]στὶν φιλονικεῖν.

ΔΗΜΕΑΣ
νοῦν [ἔχ]εις.

]ν συνοίσει σοι.

ΝΙΚΗΡΑΤΟΣ
λέγεις

[   ]ς.

186, 187 Suppl. ed.pr.
187]τιν B with σ written above the τ.   φιλονεικεῖν B: corr.
Austin.

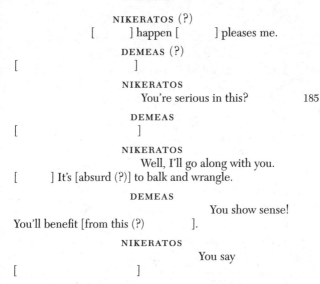

SAMIA

NIKERATOS (?)

[   ] happen [   ] pleases me.

DEMEAS (?)

[   ]

NIKERATOS

You're serious in this?   185

DEMEAS

[   ]

NIKERATOS

Well, I'll go along with you.

[   ] It's [absurd (?)] to balk and wrangle.

DEMEAS

You show sense!

You'll benefit [from this (?)   ].

NIKERATOS

You say

[   ]

(*Here Demeas' conversation with Nikeratos has reached its conclusion, and, despite the sad mutilation of the papyrus hereabouts, it is clear that Demeas has browbeaten Nikeratos—against the latter's protests and better judgment—into accepting the suggestion that Moschion and Plangon should marry that very day. At line 198 Demeas expects Nikeratos to exit into the latter's house in order to attempt the task of persuading his wife to accept the agreement that the two men have made. However, Nikeratos stays on stage, probably dithering in the background; his wife, though she never appears on stage, is always presented as a force to be reckoned with. Demeas meanwhile*

57

ΔΗΜΕΑΣ

Παρμένων, παῖ, Παρμέν[ων,

190 στε]φάνους, ἱερεῖον, σήσαμα.
(348J) [σπυρίδα λαβὼν σὺ (?)] πάντα τἀξ ἀγορᾶς ἁπλῶς
[πριάμενος ἧ]κε.

ΠΑΡΜΕΝΩΝ

πάντ'; ἐμοὶ ⟨δή⟩, Δημέα,

[ἄν τις (?) παρ]αλίπῃ—

ΔΗΜΕΑΣ

καὶ ταχέως· ἤδη λέγω.

ἄγε καὶ μ]άγειρον.

ΠΑΡΜΕΝΩΝ

καὶ μάγειρον; πριάμενος

195 [ἃ δεῖ; (?)]

ΔΗΜΕΑΣ

[π]ριάμενος.

189 Suppl. ed.pr.

190 Suppl. apogr., ed.pr.   ἱερεῖονα· B: corr. Austin.

191 Suppl. Blume (*exempli gratia*).

192 πριάμενος ἧ[κε suppl. Austin.   ⟨δή⟩ suppl. Arnott, Barigazzi.

193 Suppl. tentatively Austin.   Punctuation after ταχέως by Sandbach.   ηδε B: corr. Austin.

194 ἄγε καὶ suppl. Austin, μ]άγειρον ed.pr.

195 [ἃ δεῖ] suppl. Arnott (*exempli gratia*).

---

8 Purchases for the wedding. The 'beast to kill' (at a sacrifice

*goes to the door of his own house and calls for his slave
Parmenon, who obediently emerges at once. The ensuing
conversation implies that Parmenon is not very quick on
the uptake.)*

DEMEAS
Parmenon, boy, Parmenon!
[I want some (?)] garlands, sesame, a beast to kill.[8]   190
[Pick up a basket (?)], just [buy] all that's in
The market and come back with it!

PARMENON
All? Demeas,
[If one] leaves that to me—

*(Demeas is in a hurry to get the wedding under way, and
interrupts Parmenon before he has finished his sentence.)*

DEMEAS
Get moving! I mean *now*!
And [bring] a cook, [too]!

PARMENON
A cook, too? When I've bought
[What's needed]?

DEMEAS
(trying to be patient)
When that's bought.

during the wedding ceremonies: most commonly a sheep) would
be purchased live in the market from the cook hired for the wed-
ding. See vv. 74–75 and note, 123–5 and note, 159 and note, 211,
and Loeb Menander vol. I, pp. 38–39 n.2.

ΠΑΡΜΕΝΩΝ

ἀργύριον λαβὼν τρέχω.

ΔΗΜΕΑΣ

(353J) σὺ δ' οὐδ]έπω, Νικήρατ';

ΝΙΚΗΡΑΤΟΣ

εἰσιών, φράσας

πρὸς τ]ὴν γυναῖκα τἄνδον εὐτρεπῆ ποεῖν,
διώξομ' εὐθὺς τοῦτον.

ΠΑΡΜΕΝΩΝ

οὐκ οἶδ' οὐδὲ ἕν,

πλὴν προστέτακται ταῦτα, συντείνω τ' ἐκε[ῖ
200 ἤδη.

ΔΗΜΕΑΣ

τὸ πεῖσαι τὴν γυναῖκα πράγματα

(358J) αὑτῷ παρέξει· δεῖ δὲ μὴ δοῦναι λόγον
μηδὲ χ[ρ]όνον ἡ[μ]ᾶς. παῖ, διατρίβεις; οὐ δραμεῖ;
[   ]

196 Suppl. Austin.
197 Suppl. ed.pr.
199 Suppl. apogr., ed.pr.
202 Suppl. ed.pr.   δαραμει B: corr. Kassel.

9 For the wedding.
10 Parmenon, whom Nikeratos will shortly follow to market
(see below, comments after v. 204).
11 Nikeratos.

PARMENON

I'll get some cash, and run!   195

*(Parmenon goes off unhurriedly into Demeas' house.
Demeas now notices that Nikeratos is still on stage.)*

DEMEAS

Nikeratos, [not] gone yet?

NIKERATOS

I'll go in and tell
My wife to get things organised[9] inside.
I'll follow him[10] then promptly.

*(Nikeratos now departs into his own house, while from
Demeas' house Parmenon emerges with a basket and
money.)*

PARMENON

I'm completely in
The dark! Just given these orders. Now I'm off
There.

*(Parmenon points to the side entrance leading to the mar-
ket as he prepares to move unhurriedly in that direction.)*

DEMEAS

Trying to persuade his wife will give   200
Him[11] trouble, but we mustn't brook dispute
Or temporising. Boy, you're wasting time—
Get running! [   ]

*(As Parmenon now hurries off, Nikeratos reemerges from
his house, grumbling about the discussion he has just had
with his wife.)*

MENANDER

ΝΙΚΗΡΑΤΟΣ (?)

[περ]ί[ερ]γος ἡ γυνὴ
    ]. ἱκετεύω· τί οὖν;
    ]..[..]ς· ἡλίκον

205
205a [λαλεῖ(?)]

(After 205 there is a lacuna in B containing about 10 lines
of spoken text, as well as the sign ΧΟΡΟΥ to indicate the
break between Acts II and III.)

(ΜΕΡΟΣ Γ΄)

ΔΗΜΕΑΣ

206   ]. δρόμου καλο[ῦ
(376J) χει]μὼν ἀπ[ροσδ]όκητος ἐξαίφνης [μέγας
        ἐλθών. ἐκεῖνος τοὺς ἐν εὐδίᾳ ποτὲ
        θέοντας ἐξήραξε κἀνεχαίτισεν.
210   τοιοῦτο γὰρ καὶ τοὐμόν ἐστι νῦν· ἐγώ,
(380J) ὁ τοὺς γάμους ποῶν, ὁ θύων το[ῖ]ς θεο[ῖς,
        ᾧ πάντα κατὰ νοῦν ἀρτίως ἐγίν[ετο,

209 fr. 701 K-T (Favorinus, *Exil*. col. 23.27)

203 Suppl. Barigazzi.   205 ἡλίκον deciphered by De-
doussi.   205a λαλεῖ or βοᾷ suppl. Arnott.
206 E.g. ἐνέπεσε τοῖς πλέουσιν ἐ]κ ?   καλο[ῦ suppl.
ed.pr.   207 χει]μὼν suppl. Kassel, ἀπ[ροσδ]όκητος ed.pr.,
μέγας Sisti.   εξέφνης B: corr. Austin.   209 ἀνεχαίτισεν
Favorinus: ανεχεῖτισε B with the first ι crossed out.
211, 212 Suppl. ed.pr. (εγιγν[B).

NIKERATOS
                        The woman's[12] [nosy]—
[Quizzing me, saying] 'I beg [you]'. So what?   204
[   ] How she   205
[Goes on!]   205a

(After 205 there is a lacuna of about 10 lines in papyrus B. This would have contained the completion of Nikeratos' speech, his departure for market in the wake of Parmenon, and probably a short monologue from Demeas before he departed into his house at the end of Act II.)

(ACT III)

(The third act opens with Demeas returning to the stage in great distress, to deliver a long monologue whose opening lines—not more than two or three—are lost in the lacuna. When papyrus B resumes, he is comparing his own situation to that of travellers at sea hit by a storm.)

(DEMEAS)
                        ] after a good run, a [great]   206
And unexpected storm blows suddenly and [brings]
[Disaster], wrecking and capsizing men
Who sped in tranquil seas before. In fact my plight's
Just like that now—the organiser of   210
The wedding, sacrificing to the gods.[1]
Till now, I'd everything going to plan!

---

12 Nikeratos' wife.
1 As part of the wedding ceremonies.

οὐδ᾽ εἰ βλέπω, μὰ τὴν Ἀθηνᾶν, οἶδ[α νῦν

(383J) καλῶς ἔτ᾽. οὔκ, [ἀ]λλ᾽ εἰς τ[ὸ] πρόσθεν π[ροάγομαι,

215 πληγ]ήν τιν᾽ ἀνυπέρβλητον ἐξ[αίφνης λαβών.

(1Körte) ἦ ᾽στ[ὶ] πιθανόν; σκέψασθε πότερο[ν εὖ φρονῶ

ἢ μαίνομ᾽, οὐδέν τ᾽ εἰς ἀκρίβειαν [τότε

λαβών, ἐπάγομαι μέγ᾽ ἀτύχημα [νῦν ἐγώ.

(388J) ὡς γὰρ τάχιστ᾽ εἰσῆλθον, ὑπερεσπουδακὼς

220 τὰ τοῦ γάμου πράττειν, φράσας τὸ πρᾶγμ᾽ ἁπλῶς

(6K) τοῖς ἔνδον ἐκέλευσ᾽ εὐτρεπίζειν πάνθ᾽ ἃ δεῖ,

καθαρὰ ποεῖν, πέττειν, ἐνάρχεσθαι κανοῦν.

ἐγίνετ᾽ ἀμέλει πάνθ᾽ ἑτοίμως, τὸ δὲ τάχος

(393J) τῶν πραττομένων ταραχήν τιν᾽ αὐτοῖς ἐνεπόει,

225 ὅπερ εἰκός. ἐπὶ κλίνης μὲν ἔρριπτ᾽ ἐκποδὼν

(11K) τὸ παιδίον κεκραγός· αἱ δ᾽ ἐβόων ἅμα

"ἄλευρ᾽, ὕδωρ, ἔλαιον ἀπόδος, ἄνθρακας".

καὐτὸς διδοὺς τούτων τι καὶ συλλαμβάνων

(398J) εἰ[ς τ]ὸ ταμιεῖον ἔτυχον εἰσελθών, ὅθεν

213 οἶδ[α suppl. Austin, νῦν Lloyd-Jones.

214 καλωετουκ᾽ apparently B: corr. Austin. [ἀ]λλ᾽ suppl.
ed.pr., τ[ὸ] and π[ροάγομαι Austin. εἰς Sandbach: επι B.

215 πληγ]ήν suppl. Jacques, ἐξ[αίφνης ed.pr., λαβὼν Lloyd-
Jones. ανυπερβολητον B: corr. Austin.

216–45, 254–416 contained in B, 216–416 in C.

216 ἦ ᾽στ[ὶ] Sandbach: ηστ[apparently C (]πιθανον B).

217 τ᾽ Austin: γ᾽ B (ημαιν[C). τότε suppl. Austin.

218 Suppl. Sisti.

220 τατουγαμου C: τοτουσγαμους B with το crossed out.

222 ποειν C: ποιειν B. πεττειν C: τετ᾽τειν B corrected to
πετ᾽τειν, followed by an intrusive hasta that is probably an exten-
sion of the tail of the ρ in 221 (cf. 294–95, 381–82).

Yet—dammit—[at this moment] I don't know
If my eyes still see straight! No, out [I've come],
[The victim] of a sud[den] knock-out [punch].   215
Can one believe it? You decide whether [I'm sane]
Or crazy, whether [then] I got it wrong,
And [now] I usher in a great misfortune!
You see, as soon as I went in, too keen
To run this wedding, I explained the facts   220
Plainly to those inside, and told them to do all
That's needed—clean up, bake, prepare the basket.[2]
Of course it all went smoothly, though the rush
Of action did inject in them some panic,
As you'd expect. The baby'd been dumped screaming on   225
A couch out of the way. The women at
The same time yelled "Let's have flour—water—oil—
Charcoal!" I gave them some myself and helped,
And I'd just then gone in the pantry, and

[2] An important ritual before any sacrifice (cf. v. 211 and note)
was the preparation of a basket containing certain requisites:
grains of barley for sprinkling on the victim's head, the altar and
the ground; a garland; and a sharp knife. See P. Stengel, *Opfer-
bräuche der Griechen* (Leipzig and Berlin 1910) 47–49, J. Schelp,
Das Kanoun, der griechische Opferkorb (*Beiträge zur Archäolo-
gie* VIII, Würzburg 1975), and W. Burkert, *Homo Necans* (trans-
lated by P. Bing, Berkeley 1983) 4–5.

223 ἐγείνετ᾽ B, ἐγίγνετ᾽ C: corr. Austin.
225 ευθυσεκποδω C (with line over ω): ευθυς deleted by
Lefebvre (ερριπ] B with acute above first ρ).
229 ει[...]ταμιειον C,]οταμιειον B: suppl. Lefebvre.

MENANDER

230 πλείω προαιρῶν καὶ σκοπούμενος σ[χολῇ
(16K) οὐκ εὐθὺς ἐξῆλθον. καθ᾽ ὃν δ᾽ ἦν χρόνον ἐγὼ
ἐνταῦθα, κατέβαιν᾽ ἀφ᾽ ὑπερῴου τις γυνὴ
ἄνωθεν εἰς τοὔμπροσθε τοῦ ταμειδίου
(403J) οἴκημα· τυγχάνει γὰρ ἱστεών τις ὤν,
235 ὥσθ᾽ ἥ τ᾽ ἀνάβασίς ἐστι διὰ τούτου, τό τε
(21K) ταμεῖον ἡμῖν. τοῦ δὲ Μοσχίωνος ἦν
τίτθη τις αὕτη, πρεσβυτέρα, γεγονυῖ᾽ ἐμὴ
θεράπαιν᾽, ἐλευθέρα δὲ νῦν. ἰδοῦσα δὲ
(408J) τὸ παιδίον κεκραγὸς ἠμελημένον,
240 ἐμέ τ᾽ οὐδὲν εἰδυῖ᾽ ἔνδον ὄντ᾽, ἐν ἀσφαλεῖ
(26K) εἶναι νομίσασα τοῦ λαλεῖν, προσέρχεται
καὶ ταῦτα δὴ τὰ κοινὰ "φίλτατον τέκνον"
εἰποῦσα καὶ "μεγ᾽ ἀγαθόν· ἡ μάμμη δὲ ποῦ;"
(413J) ἐφίλησε, περιήνεγκεν. ὡς δ᾽ ἐπαύσατο
245 κλᾶον, πρὸς αὑτήν φησ[ι]ν "ὦ τάλαιν᾽ ἐγώ,
(31K) πρώην τοιοῦτον ὄντα Μοσχίων᾽ ἐγὼ
αὐτὸν ἐτιθηνούμην ἀγαπῶσα, νῦν δ᾽ [ἐπεὶ
248 παιδίον ἐκείνου γέγον[ε]ν, [ἤ]δη καὶ τόδ[ε

230 καισκοπουμενοσσ[C, καισυνκοπο[B with omitted σ
written above νκ.   σ[χολῇ suppl. Sudhaus.
231 ευθυς C,]θυσγ᾽ B with γ blotted.   233 τουμπροσθε
C: τουμπροσθεν B (with acute on μ).   ταμιειδίου Crönert:
ταμειῢου C (τα[B).   234 οικημα· C:]ματα B.   ιστεων C,
ειστιων B with ε crossed out.   235 το C: τ᾽ό B.   240 οντ᾽
C: ὁτ᾽ B.   244 περιενεγκ[B with the first ε crossed out and η
written above it.   246–48 C only (lacuna in B).
247 Suppl. Lefebvre.   248 [ἤ]δη deciphered and supple-
mented by Sudhaus.   τόδ[ε suppl. several.

66

Through getting more stuff out and pondering   230
[Unhurriedly], I didn't emerge at once.
While I was there, a woman climbed down from
A room upstairs into one opposite
The pantry—that's a weaving room,[3] you see,
So both our way upstairs and to the pantry   235
Goes through the room. This woman was our Moschion's
Old nurse, quite old. She then became
My maid, but now she's free. She saw the child
Ignored and screaming, unaware that I
Was in the house. Thinking it safe to speak   240
Out loud, she went right up to it[4] and said
The usual things, "My darling baby" and
"Great treasure—where's your mummy?" Then she
      kissed
And danced it round. When it stopped crying, she
Said to herself "Dear me, it's not so long   245
Ago that I nursed Moschion himself,
And loved him just like you, and now that his
Own baby's born, already it as well   248

*(Between vv. 248 and 249 there is a very short gap in which
apparently the nurse continued talking to herself. Then*

---

[3] The women in an Athenian family spun wool and wove from
it clothes and other textiles for daily use. See e.g. J. Forbes,
Studies in Ancient Technology 4² (Leiden 1964) 186–258, E.
Fantham and others, *Women in the Classical World* (New York
and Oxford 1994) 101–106, and S. R. Pomeroy's edition of Xeno-
phon's *Oeconomicus* (Oxford 1994), commentary on vii.6.

[4] The baby was a boy, and should be called 'he' throughout, but
I have used a colloquial but incorrect 'it' to avoid confusion with
other males mentioned.

(C has a lacuna of 2 or 3 verses between 248 and 249; B
does not resume until v. 254.)

(421J) 249   ]α καὶ

250   γεγο]νέναι."

(36K) .....].[....]... καὶ θεραπαινιδίῳ τινὶ

ἔξωθεν εἰστρέχοντι, "λούσατ', ὦ τάλαν,

τὸ παιδίον", φησίν, "τί τοῦτ'; ἐν τοῖς γάμοις

(426J) τοῖς τοῦ πατρὸς τὸν μικρὸν οὐ θεραπεύετε;"

255 εὐθὺς δ' ἐκείνη "δύσμορ', ἡλίκον λαλεῖς",

(41K) φήσ', "ἔνδον ἐστὶν αὐτός." "οὐ δήπου γε· ποῦ;"

"ἐν τῷ ταμιείῳ", καὶ παρεξήλαξέ τι,

"αὐτὴ καλεῖ, τίτθη, σε" καὶ "βάδιζε καὶ

(431J) σπεῦδ'· οὐκ ἀκήκο' οὐδέν· εὐτυχέστατα."

260 εἰποῦσ' ἐκείνη δ' "ὦ τάλαινα τῆς ἐμῆς

(46K) λαλιᾶς," ἀπῇξεν ἐκποδών, οὐκ οἶδ' ὅποι.

κἀγὼ προῄειν τοῦτον ὅνπερ ἐνθάδε

τρόπον ἀρτίως ἐξῆλθον, ἡσυχῇ πάνυ,

(436J) ὡς οὔτ' ἀκούσας οὐδὲν οὔτ' ᾐσθημένος.

265 αὐτὴν δ' ἔχουσαν αὐτὸ τὴν Σαμίαν ὁρῶ

(51K) ἔξω διδοῦσαν τιτθίον παριὼν ἅμα,

250 Suppl. Körte.
254–416 in both B and C.
255 δ' C: τ' or γ' B.   260 δ' C, omitted in B.
261 ἀπῇξ B, απηλθεν C.
262 καγὼπροῄειν B: κωγωπροηλθον C.   265 δ' C: τ' B.
266 So C: ἐξωκαθ'αυτηνδιδοῦσαντιθίον B with the omitted τ
written above ιθ.

SAMIA

from 249 only the word and *survives, from 250 only* to have
[become] *(or* been born*) at the close of what she said to
herself.)*

DEMEAS

(still speaking)

[That's roughly what she said (?)], and then she told a   251
     maid
Who ran in from outside[5] "You bath the baby!
Dear me, what's going on? Can't you look after
The little mite on daddy's wedding day?"
The maid at once retorted "You're pathetic! Not   255
So loud—our master's home!" "No, surely not?
Where is he?" "In the pantry," and then lowering
Her voice a bit "Nurse, mistress wants you. Go,
And hurry! He's[6] heard nothing. Luckily."
And with "My tongue gets me in trouble", off   260
The nurse scurried away, I don't know where,
And I came forward in the way that I
Emerged just now, quite calmly, just as if
I'd neither heard nor spotted anything.
I saw my Samian partner out of doors,[7]   265
The baby at her breast as I walked past.

---

[5] Presumably the courtyard of the house. See note on v. 265
below.   [6] Demeas.

[7] The houses of wealthy Athenians usually had an open air cen-
tral courtyard, through which one might pass on the way to the
front door and out onto the street. See especially H. A. Thompson
and R. E. Wycherley, *The Agora of Athens* (*The Athenian Agora*
14: Princeton 1972) 173–85, with its useful drawing of a similar
house in Menander's Athens (p.181 fig. 44), and M. Jameson in O.
Murray and S. Price, *The Greek City* (Oxford 1995) 171–95.

ὥσθ’ ὅτι μὲν αὐτῆς ἐστι τοῦτο γνώριμον
εἶναι, πατρὸς δ’ ὅτου ποτ’ ἐστίν, εἴτ’ ἐμὸν
(441J) εἴτ’—οὐ λέγω δ’, ἄνδρες, πρὸς ὑμᾶς τοῦτ’ ἐγώ,
270 οὐχ ὑπονοῶ, τὸ πρᾶγμα δ’ εἰς μέσον φέρω
(56K) ἅ τ’ ἀκήκο’ αὐτός, οὐκ ἀγανακτῶν οὐδέπω.
σύνοιδα γὰρ τῷ μειρακίῳ, νὴ τοὺς θεούς,
καὶ κοσμίῳ τὸν πρότερον ὄντι χρόνον ἀεὶ
(446J) καὶ περὶ ἔμ’, ὡς ἔνεστιν, εὐσεβεστάτῳ.
275 πάλιν δ’, ἐπειδὰν τὴν λέγουσαν καταμάθω
(61K) τίτθην ἐκείνου πρῶτον οὖσαν, εἶτ’ ἐμοῦ
λάθρᾳ λέγουσαν, εἶτ’ ἀποβλέψω πάλιν
εἰς τὴν ἀγαπῶσαν αὐτὸ καὶ βεβιασμένην
(451J) ἐμοῦ τρέφειν ἄκοντος, ἐξέστηχ’ ὅλως.
280 ἀλλ’ εἰς καλὸν γὰρ τουτονὶ προσιόνθ’ ὁρῶ
(66K) τὸν Παρμένοντ’ ἐκ τῆς ἀγορᾶς· ἐατέον
αὐτὸν παραγαγεῖν ἐστι τούτους οὓς ἄγει.

ΠΑΡΜΕΝΩΝ

μάγειρ’, ἐγώ, μὰ τοὺς θεούς, οὐκ οἶδα σὺ
(456J) ἐφ’ ὅ τι μαχαίρας περιφέρεις. ἱκανὸς γὰρ εἶ
285 λαλῶν κατακόψαι πάντα πράγματ’.

267 Corr. several: εστιτουτοαυτῆς BC (αυτης C).
268 ποτ’ C: τοτ’ B with ν written above o.   269 ειδ’ B.
270 ουχ’ B: ουθ’ C.   εισμεσον C: εσόμενον B.
272 μειρακείωι B with the second ε crossed out.
273 αἰει B with the ι crossed out.   276 ουσαν C: ὦσαν B.
280 τουτονϊπροσϊόνθ’ B: τουτονει[σ]ιονθ’ apparently C.
282 παραγαγειν C: παραγειν B.   284 ἵκανον B with the
second ν crossed out and a correcting ς written above it.

It's definite then that the baby's hers,
But who the father is—whether it's me,
Or whether—gentlemen,[8] no, I won't tell
You that! I've no suspicions, but I bring   270
The facts and what I've heard out in the open. I'm
Not angry, yet! I really know my boy—
That he was always well-behaved in days
Gone by, and showed the greatest possible
Respect to me. Again, when I consider that   275
The talker was his former nurse, and spoke
Not knowing I was there, then when I look
Again at her[9] love for the child, insisting it
Be raised, against my wishes—I'm completely
Incensed! But I see Parmenon—that's splendid!   280
Here he is, back from market. I must let
Him take inside the people that he's brought.

*(Parmenon now enters by the side entrance leading from
the city centre. He carries a basket loaded with his pur-
chases, and is accompanied by a cook[10] and one or more of
the cook's assistants. Parmenon and the cook are chaffing
each other, and do not notice Demeas, who may have re-
tired into the background.)*

PARMENON

I swear I don't know why you carry knives
Around with you, cook—by your talk alone
You can dismember every subject!

---

[8] Demeas here addresses the audience (cf. 329, 447, 683,
Dysk. 659), alternately hiding and revealing his suspicion that
Moschion and Chrysis are the baby's parents.
[9] Chrysis'.   [10] See n. 2 on *Aspis* 215–16.

MENANDER

ΜΑΓΕΙΡΟΣ

ἄθλιε

(71K) ἰδιῶτ᾽.

ΠΑΡΜΕΝΩΝ

ἐγώ;

ΜΑΓΕΙΡΟΣ

δοκεῖς γέ μοι, νὴ τοὺς θεούς.
εἰ πυνθάνομαι πόσας τραπέζας μέλλετε
ποεῖν, πόσαι γυναῖκές εἰσι, πηνίκα
(461J) ἔσται τὸ δεῖπνον, εἰ δεήσει προσλαβεῖν
290   τραπεζοποιόν, εἰ κέραμός ἐστ᾽ ἔνδοθεν
(76K) ὑμῖν ἱκανός, εἰ τοὐπτάνιον κατάστεγον,
εἰ τἆλλ᾽ ὑπάρχει πάντα—

ΠΑΡΜΕΝΩΝ

κατακόπτεις γέ με,
εἰ λανθάνει σε, φίλτατ᾽, εἰς περικόμματα,
(466J) οὐχ ὡς ἔτυχεν.

ΜΑΓΕΙΡΟΣ

οἴμωζε.

ΠΑΡΜΕΝΩΝ

καί σύ. τοῦτό γε
295   παντὸς ἕνεκ᾽. ἀλλὰ παράγετ᾽ εἴσω.

286 γε C, omitted in B.   290 εστ C, εστι B.
292 γε C, omitted in B.   293 φιλλατε B with the second
λ crossed out and a correcting τ written above it.
294 ετυχεν C: ετυχες B.   295 παραγετ᾽ C: παραγ᾽ B.

COOK

Oh,   285

Poor ignoramus!

PARMENON

Me?

COOK

I think so, yes!
If I enquire how many tables you intend
To set, how many women there will be,
When dinner will begin, if I shall need
To hire a waiter,[11] if your in-house crockery's   290
Sufficient, if the kitchen's got a roof,
If all the other things are there—

PARMENON

(interrupting the cook's flow)

You get
My goat—and cook it, darling, like an expert[12]—
Perhaps you hadn't noticed?

COOK

Damn you!

PARMENON

And the same
To you—on all counts! Go inside, though.

---

[11] See n. 3 on *Aspis* 232.
[12] The Greek here has a pun that defies literal translation:
literally, 'you chop me up (= also in contemporary slang 'irritate'
or 'bore') into mincemeat, darling, not in everyday fashion.'

ΔΗΜΕΑΣ

Παρμένων.

ΠΑΡΜΕΝΩΝ

(81K) ἐμέ τις κέκληκε;

ΔΗΜΕΑΣ

ναιχί.

ΠΑΡΜΕΝΩΝ

χαῖρε, δέσποτα.

ΔΗΜΕΑΣ

τὴν σφυρίδα καταθεὶς ἧκε δεῦρ᾽.

ΠΑΡΜΕΝΩΝ

ἀγαθῇ τύχῃ.

ΔΗΜΕΑΣ

τοῦτον γὰρ οὐδέν, ὡς ἐγῷμαι, λανθάνει

(471J) τοιοῦτον ἂν πραττόμενον ἔργον· ἔστι γὰρ

300 περίεργος, εἴ τις ἄλλος. ἀλλὰ τὴν θύραν

(86K) προϊὼν πέπληχε.

---

296 κεκληκε B: καλει C.   297 τηνφυριδα B with the
omitted σ added above νφ.   298 εγωμε B with the second ε
crossed out and αι written above.
299 λανθ[.]νοι B: λανθανει C.   300 ειτις C: κ᾽ειτις B
with κ᾽ written above the line in front of ει.

---

13 Parmenon's.

74

(The cook with his assistant or assistants goes off into Demeas' house.)

DEMEAS
(standing behind Parmenon)

Parmenon! 295

PARMENON
Someone's called me?

DEMEAS
Yes.

PARMENON
(now turning round)

Greetings, master.

DEMEAS

Take

Your basket in and come back here.

PARMENON

All right.

(Parmenon goes off with his basket into Demeas' house.)

DEMEAS
In my opinion, nothing would escape
His[13] notice, of the kind that's implicated
Here. He's uniquely nosy! But the door's 300
Creaked—out he comes!

(Parmenon enters from Demeas' house, but stays at first by the door with his back to Demeas in order to give instructions to Chrysis inside. Then he turns to address Demeas.)

ΠΑΡΜΕΝΩΝ

δίδοτε, Χρυσί, πάνθ᾽ ὅσ᾽ ἂν
ὁ μάγειρος αἰτῇ· τὴν δὲ γραῦν φυλάττετε
ἀπὸ τῶν κεραμίων, πρὸς θεῶν. τί δεῖ ποεῖν,

(476J)   δέσποτα;

ΔΗΜΕΑΣ

τί δεῖ ποεῖν; ‹ἴθι› δεῦρ᾽ ἀπὸ τῆς θύρας·
305   ἔτι μικρόν.

ΠΑΡΜΕΝΩΝ

ἤν.

ΔΗΜΕΑΣ

ἄκουε δή νυν, Παρμέν[ων.
(91K)   ἐγώ σε μαστιγοῦν, μὰ τοὺς δώδεκα θεού[ς,
οὐ βούλομαι διὰ πολλά.

ΠΑΡΜΕΝΩΝ

μαστιγοῦν; τί δὲ
πεπόηκα;

302 δὲ C: τε B.   φυλλάτετε B with the omitted τ written
above the first τε.

303 ποειν C: ποι[B.

304 ἴθι suppl. Leo, Mazon; it is omitted in B (Sudhaus' claim
to have detected in C traces of an omitted σε written after θυρας
is of uncertain validity).

305 νυν C: μου B.   -[ων suppl. Lefebvre: παρ[C,
παρμαιν[B with αι crossed out and correcting ε written above.

306 Suppl. Lefebvre: θ[C, θεου[B.

PARMENON

Give the cook everything
He asks for, Chrysis, and keep the old girl[14]
Away from the wine jars,[15] I beg you!—Master, what's
My task?

DEMEAS

Your task? [Come] here, out from the door—
A bit more!

(Parmenon follows Demeas' instructions.)

PARMENON

Here?

DEMEAS

Now listen, Parmenon.   305
I swear I've many reasons for not wanting to
Thrash you—

PARMENON

(taken aback)

Thrash me? What have I done?

---

[14] Possibly the old nurse described in vv. 236–61; cf. also
v. 373. Old women were commonly ridiculed in ancient comedy
for their love of strong drink. H. G. Oeri, *Der Typ der komischen
Alten in der griechischen Komödie* (Basel 1948) 13–19, 39–45 col-
lects the then known passages; see also my commentary on Alexis
(Cambridge 1996) pp.503–504.

[15] Part presumably of Parmenon's recent purchases in the
market.

MENANDER

ΔΗΜΕΑΣ

συγκρύπτεις τι πρός μ'· ἤ[σ]θημ'.

ΠΑΡΜΕΝΩΝ

ἐγώ;

(481J) μὰ τὸν Διόνυσον, μὰ τὸν Ἀπόλλω τουτονί,
  310   μὰ τὸν Δία τὸν Σωτῆρα, μὰ τὸν Ἀσκληπιόν—

ΔΗΜΕΑΣ

(96K) παῦ, μηδὲν ὄμνυ'· οὐ γὰρ εἰκάζων λέγω.

ΠΑΡΜΕΝΩΝ

ἦ μήποτ' ἆρ'—

ΔΗΜΕΑΣ

οὗτος, βλέπε δεῦρ'.

ΠΑΡΜΕΝΩΝ

ἰδού· βλέ[πω.

ΔΗΜΕΑΣ

τὸ παιδίον τίνος ἐστίν;

ΠΑΡΜΕΝΩΝ

ἤν.

308 Suppl. Wilamowitz: προσμ'η[apparently C with εγω beginning 309, πραγμ'η[.]θημ[B (B has the beginning of 309 cut or torn off, but there is space in the gap for a misplaced εγω). ἐγώ; assigned to Parmenon by Sudhaus, Dedoussi.
309 απολλον B with the ν crossed out and ω written above the second o.   312 Suppl. ed.pr. of B: βλε[B, ιδου[C.
313 ἤν Luck (*Rh. Mus.* 108, 1973, 20): ην BC.

SAMIA

DEMEAS

You are
Conspiring to hide something from me. That I know!

PARMENON
(averting his gaze from Demeas)
Me? No, by Dionysus, by Apollo here,[16]
By Zeus our Saviour, by Asclepius—   310

DEMEAS
Stop it—no oaths! My words aren't based on guesswork!

PARMENON
Or never[17]—

DEMEAS
You—look at me!

PARMENON
There. I'm looking.

DEMEAS
Whose is the baby?

PARMENON
(taken further aback)
Ah.[18]

---

[16] An altar or emblem of Apollo Agyieus stood outside
Demeas' front door. See n. 3 on *Dyskolos* 659.

[17] Presumably Parmenon intended to say something like 'Or
never may I prosper if I'm not speaking the truth,' before his re-
mark was cut off.

[18] On this translation of ἤν, a word not found in LSJ, see G.
Luck, *Rh.Mus.* 108 (1965) 269, and the Gomme–Sandbach com-
mentary on this line.

ΔΗΜΕΑΣ
                                        τὸ παιδίον
(486J)   τίνος ἐ[στ᾽, ἐρ]ωτῶ.

ΠΑΡΜΕΝΩΝ
Χρυσίδος.

ΔΗΜΕΑΣ
                                        πατρὸς δὲ τοῦ;

ΠΑΡΜΕΝΩΝ
315   σόν, φ[ησιν].

ΔΗΜΕΑΣ
ἀπόλωλας· φενακίζεις μ᾽.

ΠΑΡΜΕΝΩΝ
                                                        ἐγώ;

ΔΗΜΕΑΣ
(101K)   εἰδότα γ᾽ ἀκριβῶς πάντα καὶ πεπυσμένον
ὅτι Μοσχίωνός ἐστιν, ὅτι σύνοισθα σύ,
ὅτι δι᾽ ἐκεῖνον αὐτὸ νῦν αὕτη τρέφει.

ΠΑΡΜΕΝΩΝ
(491J)   τίς φησι;

ΔΗΜΕΑΣ
                        πάντες. ἀλλ᾽ ἀπόκριναι τοῦτό μοι·
320   ταῦτ᾽ ἐστίν;

        314 ἐστ᾽ suppl. Lefebvre, ἐρωτῶ Jensen: τινο[......]ωτω B,
τινοσε[.....]τω C.
        315 φ[ησιν] suppl. Sandbach: σον[.....]απολωλας B,

80

DEMEAS
                  I'm asking, who's

The parent?

PARMENON
          Chrysis.

DEMEAS
And the father?

PARMENON
                     You,

[She says. (?)]

DEMEAS
That's done for you. You've been deceiving me.   315

PARMENON

I have?

DEMEAS
    I know exactly all the facts. I've learnt
That Moschion's the father, that you're in
The know, and she's now nursing it for him!

PARMENON

Who says so?

DEMEAS
           All of them. But tell me, is

This true?

σο[.].[.......]λωλας C.   316 ειδοτ[....]ιβως B, ειδοταγα-
κριβω[apparently C.   320 εστιν (Demeas) C: εστι B.

ΠΑΡΜΕΝΩΝ

ἔστι, δέσποτ᾽, ἀλλὰ λανθάνειν—

ΔΗΜΕΑΣ

(106K)   τί "λανθάνειν"; ἱμάντα παίδων τις δότω
ἐπὶ τουτονί μοι τὸν ἀσεβῆ.

ΠΑΡΜΕΝΩΝ

μή, πρὸς θεῶν.

ΔΗΜΕΑΣ

στίξω σε, νὴ τὸν Ἥλιον.

ΠΑΡΜΕΝΩΝ

στίξεις ἐμέ;

ΔΗΜΕΑΣ

(496J)   ἤδη γ᾽.

ΠΑΡΜΕΝΩΝ

ἀπόλωλα.

ΔΗΜΕΑΣ

ποῖ σύ, ποῖ, μαστιγία;

324 ηδηγ᾽ B: ηληγ᾽ C.   μαστιγια C: γεμαστιγια B.

PARMENON
Yes, master, but concealment—

DEMEAS

(angrily interrupting)

What   320
"Concealment"? Servants, one of you give me
A strap to deal with this blackguard!

(Demeas goes to his own door to shout this last remark.)

PARMENON
Please, no!

*(At this point probably a slave emerges from Demeas'
house with a strap which he hands to Demeas. As Demeas
makes his next threat Parmenon begins to move to one side
of the stage.)*

DEMEAS
I'll brand you, yes I will!

PARMENON
You'll brand me?

DEMEAS
Yes—today!

PARMENON
I'm done for!

*(Saying this, Parmenon runs off by one of the side en-
trances.)*

DEMEAS
Where, where are you off to, you

325 λάβ' αὐτόν. — "ὦ πόλισμα Κεκροπίας χθονός,
(111K) ὦ ταναὸς αἰθήρ, ὦ —" — τί, Δημέα, βοᾷς;
τί βοᾷς, ἀνόητε; κάτεχε σαυτόν, καρτέρει·
οὐδὲν γὰρ ἀδικεῖ Μοσχίων σε. παράβολος
(501J) ὁ λόγος ἴσως ἐστ', ἄνδρες, ἀλλ' ἀληθινός.
330 εἰ μὲν γὰρ ἢ βουλόμενος ἢ κεκνισμένος
(116K) ἔρωτι τοῦτ' ἔπραξεν ἢ μισῶν ἐμέ,
ἦν ἂν ἐπὶ τῆς αὐτῆς διανοίας ἔτι θρασὺς
ἐμοί τε παρατεταγμένος. νυνὶ δέ μοι
(506J) ἀπολελόγηται τὸν φανέντ' αὐτῷ γάμον
335 ἄσμενος ἀκούσας. οὐκ ἐρῶν γάρ, ὡς ἐγὼ
(121K) τότ' ᾠόμην, ἔσπευδεν, ἀλλὰ τὴν ἐμὴν
Ἑλένην φυγεῖν βουλόμενος ἔνδοθέν ποτε·
αὕτη γάρ ἐστιν αἰτία τοῦ γεγονότος.
(511J) παρέλαβεν αὐτόν που μεθύοντα δηλαδή,
340 οὐκ ὄντ' ἐν ἑαυτοῦ. πολλὰ δ' ἐξεργάζεται
(126K) ἀνόητ' ἄκρατος καὶ νεότης, ὅταν λάβῃ

325–26 a fragment of Euripides' *Oedipus* (identified in the
right margin of B here): Οἰδίπους Εὐριπίδου (corr. Austin:
υριποδου or ιριποδου B)

325 χθονος B: χρονος C.
332 Suppl. several: ην[.]ν C, γενεν B.
334 φανεντ' B: φανενταδ' C.
336 τοτ' C: τόυτ' B.
337 ποτε C: ποθεν B.
340 Corr. Austin: εξερταζεται apparently B, ἐργαζεται C.
341 οταν C: εαν B.

Rogue? Catch him!

(The slave who brought the strap runs off in pursuit of Parmenon.)

DEMEAS

(now all alone on the stage)

      'O citadel of Cecrops' land,   325
O firmament outspread, O'[19]—Demeas, why shout!
Why shout, you fool? Control yourself, be strong—
For Moschion's not wronging you. That statement
Looks wild perhaps—it's true though, gentlemen![20]
If he'd done this intentionally or   330
Inflamed by passion or detesting me,
He'd still be of the same mind, impudent
And ranged against me. As it is, he's cleared
Himself before me by agreeing gladly to
The marriage planned for him. It wasn't love 335
That prompted him, as I then fancied,[21] but
A wish to break loose finally from my
Own Helen![22] She's the cause of what has happened.
It's clear she took him when he wasn't sober
Nor master of himself. Strong wine and youth 340
Commit a lot of foolish acts when they

[19] Demeas here quotes from Euripides' lost *Oedipus*.

[20] See note on v. 269.

[21] See vv. 165–66, referring to Moschion's confession at 146.

[22] Helen was regarded by the ancient Athenians as the prime example of a seductively unfaithful wife. Cf. e.g. Eur. *Andr.* 229, 630, *Electra* 1028, *Orestes* 99; L. B. Ghali-Kahil, *Les Enlèvements et le retour d'Hélène* (Paris 1955) I. 123–44.

MENANDER

τὸν συνεπιβουλεύσαντα τούτοις πλησίον.
οὐδενὶ τρόπῳ γὰρ πιθανὸν εἶναί μοι δοκεῖ
(516J) τὸν εἰς ἅπαντας κόσμιον καὶ σώφρονα
345 τοὺς ἀλλοτρίους εἰς ἐμὲ τοιοῦτον γεγονέναι,
(131K) οὐδ' εἰ δεκάκις ποιητός ἐστι, μὴ γόνῳ
ἐμὸς ὑός· οὐ γὰρ τοῦτο, τὸν τρόπον δ', ὁρῶ.
χαμαιτύπη δ' ἄνθρωπος, ὄλεθρος. ἀλλὰ τί;
(521J) οὐ γὰρ περίεσται. Δημέα, νῦν ἄνδρα χρὴ
350 εἶναί σ'. ἐπιλαθοῦ τοῦ πόθου, πέπαυσ' ἐρῶν,
(136K) καὶ τἀτύχημα μὲν τὸ γεγονὸς κρύφθ' ὅσον
ἔνεστι διὰ τὸν ὑόν, ἐκ τῆς δ' οἰκίας
ἐπὶ κεφαλὴν ἐς κόρακας ὦσον τὴν καλὴν
(526J) Σαμίαν. ἔχεις δὲ πρόφασιν, ὅτι τὸ παιδίον
355 ἀνείλετ'· ἐμφανίσῃς γὰρ ἄλλο μηδὲ ἕν,
(141K) δακὼν δ' ἀνάσχου, καρτέρησον εὐγενῶς.

ΜΑΓΕΙΡΟΣ
ἀλλ' ἆρα πρόσθεν τῶν θυρῶν ἔστ' ἐνθάδε;

342 τουτοις B: τοιτοις apparently C.
344]παντας C, απαντα B: originally suppl. Croiset.
346 Traces of letters in C written above νω and into the right margin remain undeciphered.
347 υιοσουγαρ C: υιοσυγαρ B.
351 κατατυχημα B (with circumflex over first τ), καιτατυμη C.
352 υον B: υιον C.   εκτησδ' C: εκδετης B.
353 επι B: επιτην C.
355 εμφ[.]νισησγαραλλο C: ενφανισασαλλογαρ B.
356 ευγενως C: δ'ευγενως B.
357 προσθεν C, προσθε B.

86

Find their collaborator[23] close at hand.
I do not find it credible at all
That one[24] who's well-behaved and self-controlled
With every stranger's[25] treated me like this—   345
Not though he were ten times adopted, not
My son by birth. It's not this that I look at, but
His character. That woman is a whore, a bitch!
So what? She'll not last long. Now, Demeas, you've got
To be a man. Forget your ardour, stop   350
Desiring her. Conceal the glitch that's happened
As best you can, for your son's sake. Eject
The lovely Samian woman from your house—
Headfirst to hell! You have just cause—she kept
The child. Make public nothing else. Bear up   355
Now, bite your lips, and bravely stick it out!

*(At this point the cook bustles out of Demeas' house in
search of Parmenon, unaware that the slave has panicked
and run away. The cook does not at first notice Demeas,
whom he has not previously met; his first question may be
voiced back to people inside the house.)*

COOK

But is he[26] here, outside the door? Boy! Parmenon!

---

[23] Demeas assumes that Chrysis had seduced Moschion when
he was drunk.

[24] Moschion; cf. Moschion's own words at v. 18.

[25] Literally 'anyone not belonging to the family.'

[26] The cook had been expecting the slave to help him with
the preparations for the meal, just like the cook in the *Dyskolos*
(vv. 419–24, 456–59, 546–51).

MENANDER

παῖ, Παρμένων. ἄνθρωπος ἀποδέδρακέ με,
(531J) ἀλλ' οὐδὲ μικρὸν συλλαβών.

ΔΗΜΕΑΣ

ἐκ τοῦ μέσου
360 ἄναγε σεαυτόν.

ΜΑΓΕΙΡΟΣ

Ἡράκλεις, τί τοῦτο; παῖ.
(146K) μαινόμενος εἰσδεδράμηκεν εἴσω τις γέρων,
ἢ τί τὸ κακόν ποτ' ἐστί; τί δέ μοι τοῦτο; παῖ.
νὴ τὸν Ποσειδῶ, μαίνεθ', ὡς ἐμοὶ δοκεῖ.
(536J) κέκραγε γοῦν παμμέγεθες. ἀστεῖον πάνυ,
365 εἰ τὰς λοπάδας ἐν τῷ μέσῳ μου κειμένας
(151K) ὄστρακα ποήσει· πάνθ' ὅμοια. τὴν θύραν
πέπληχεν. ἐξώλης ἀπόλοιο, Παρμένων,
κομίσας με δεῦρο. μικρὸν ὑπαποστήσομαι.

ΔΗΜΕΑΣ

(541J) οὔκουν ἀκούεις; ἄπιθι.

ΧΡΥΣΙΣ

ποῖ γῆς, ὦ τάλαν;

ΔΗΜΕΑΣ

370 ἐς κόρακας ἤδη.

359 δημ (as indication of speaker) crossed out in B after
συλλαβων·. 363 ποσιδω BC: corr. several.
364 κεκραγεγουν C: κεκραγενουν B. 366 Corr. Reeves,
West: ποιησαι BC. ομοια C: ετοιμ[B; punctuation and inter-
pretation here by Gronewald. 369 της B with τ crossed out
and a correcting γ written above it.

88

The fellow's run away from me, and not
Helped in the least!

DEMEAS
(shouting at the cook as he runs into his house.)
　　　　　Out of my way! Get back!

COOK
Heavens above, what's going on? Amazing!　　　　　360
A crazy greybeard's run inside. But what
The devil's going on? Yet what concern is it
Of mine? Amazing! Yes, he's crazy, that's
My view. At any rate he screamed out loud and clear.
Quite charming if he breaks my plates to smithereens—　　365
They're in the way. Always the same! He's rattled
The door. Oh, damn and blast you, Parmenon,
For bringing me here! I'll move back a little.

*(As the cook moves into the background, Demeas emerges
from his house, pushing before him the old nurse and
Chrysis with the baby.)*

DEMEAS
Then don't you hear? Be off!

CHRYSIS
　　　　　Where to? Oh dear!

DEMEAS
To hell—right now!

ΧΡΥΣΙΣ

δύσμορος.

ΔΗΜΕΑΣ

ναί, δύσμορος.

(156K) ἐλεινὸν ἀμέλει τὸ δάκρυον. παύσω σ᾽ ἐγώ,
ὡς οἴομαι—

ΧΡΥΣΙΣ

τί ποοῦσαν;

ΔΗΜΕΑΣ

οὐδέν. ἀλλ᾽ ἔχεις
τὸ παιδίον, τὴν γραῦν. ἀποφθείρου ποτέ.

ΧΡΥΣΙΣ

(546J) ὅτι τοῦτ᾽ ἀνειλόμην;

ΔΗΜΕΑΣ

διὰ τοῦτο, καὶ—

ΧΡΥΣΙΣ

τί "καί";

ΔΗΜΕΑΣ

375   διὰ τοῦτο.

ΜΑΓΕΙΡΟΣ

τοιοῦτ᾽ ἦν τὸ κακόν· ⟨νῦν⟩ μανθάνω.

371 ελεεινον BC: corr. van Herwerden.
372 ουδεν C: ουδεεν B.   373 ποτε B: ταχυ C.
375 μαγειρ᾽ (as indication of speaker) is crossed out in B after
διατουτο and added (]ειρ/) in the left margin.   ⟨νῦν⟩ suppl.
Barigazzi.   τοιουτ᾽ηντο C, τουτηντιτο B.

CHRYSIS

(beginning to weep)
> Poor me!

DEMEAS

> *(to Chrysis)* Oh yes—poor you!　370
(aside) Yes, tears that stir compassion. *(to Chrysis)* I be-
　lieve
I'll stop you—

CHRYSIS
> Doing what?

DEMEAS

> Oh, nothing—but you've got
The baby, the old woman.[27] Go to hell, and quick!

CHRYSIS
Because I kept this baby?

DEMEAS

> Through that, and—

CHRYSIS

> What else?

DEMEAS

Through that!

COOK

(from the background)
> So that's what caused the trouble! [Now]　375
I understand!

---

[27] Possibly the old nurse of 236–61 and 302–303.

MENANDER

ΔΗΜΕΑΣ

(161K) τρυφᾶν γὰρ οὐκ ἠπίστασ'.

ΧΡΤΣΙΣ

οὐκ ἠπιστάμην;

τί δ' ἐσθ' ὃ λέγεις;

ΔΗΜΕΑΣ

καίτοι πρὸς ἔμ' ἦλθες ἐνθάδε

ἐν σινδονίτῃ, Χρυσί—μανθάνεις;—πάνυ

(551J) λιτῷ.

ΧΡΤΣΙΣ

τί οὖν;

ΔΗΜΕΑΣ

τότ' ἦν ἐγώ σοι πάνθ', ὅτε

380 φαύλως ἔπραττες.

ΧΡΤΣΙΣ

νῦν δὲ τίς;

ΔΗΜΕΑΣ

μή μοι λάλει.

(166K) ἔχεις τὰ σαυτῆς πάντα. προστίθημί σοι

ἐγὼ θεραπαίνας, Χρυσί. ἐκ τῆς οἰκίας

ἄπιθι.

376 τρυφαν C: τρυφην B.   ηπιστασ' and ηπισταμην C:
επιστασο (with the second σ correcting a previously written let-
ter) and επισταμην B.   376–77 Dicola and paragraphi cor-
rectly placed in C: B has dicolon after -αμην, not after λεγεις, and
paragraphus only under 376.

380 μημοιλαλει C: μημοιδιαλεγου B.

382 Χρυσί Robert (χρυσί' Lefebvre): χρυσι C, χρυσι' B.

92

DEMEAS

You never knew how to enjoy

Our wealth.

CHRYSIS

I never knew? What *do* you mean?

DEMEAS

Yet you

Came here to me—remember?—in a quite
Plain linen dress.

CHRYSIS

Well?

DEMEAS

I was everything to you,

When you were poor then.

CHRYSIS

Who is now?[28]

DEMEAS

Don't talk   380

To me! You've got all your belongings. I
Can add some servants, Chrysis.[29] Leave my house!

---

[28] Sc. 'Who (else) is there (who means everything to me) now?'
In this scene Demeas refrains from accusing or even mentioning
Moschion, so that he does not respond to Chrysis' question here,
just as he stopped short of accusing Chrysis and his son of in-
fidelity at 374.

[29] The interpretation of these lines is disputed; the Greek
word translated here as 'Chrysis' can alternatively mean '(gold)
jewels.' See now especially R. F. Thomas, *ZPE* 83 (1990) 215–18.

ΜΑΓΕΙΡΟΣ

τὸ πρᾶγμ' ὀργή τις ἐστίν· προσιτέον.

(556J) βέλτισθ', ὅρα—

ΔΗΜΕΑΣ

τί μοι διαλέγει;

ΜΑΓΕΙΡΟΣ

μὴ δάκῃς.

ΔΗΜΕΑΣ

385 ἑτέρα γὰρ ἀγαπήσει τὰ παρ' ἐμοί, Χρυσί· νὴ
(171K) καὶ τοῖς θεοῖς θύσει.

ΜΑΓΕΙΡΟΣ

τί ἐστίν;

ΔΗΜΕΑΣ

ἀλλὰ σὺ

υἱὸν πεπόησαι· πάντ' ἔχεις.

ΜΑΓΕΙΡΟΣ

οὔπω δάκνει.

ὅμως—

383 μαγειρ' crossed out and rewritten straight above in B before τοπραγμ'.   384 τιμοι C: τιδημοι B.
385–90 Ends of lines also in O (O.16).
385 νη O: νυν BC.
386 τι C: τις B.   αλλασυ BC:]ατι O.
387 πεποησαι B: πεποηκας C.

30 Literally, 'she'll sacrifice to the gods': possibly a contempo-

COOK

(still in the background)
What's happened is a row. I must come forward.
Look here, sir—

(The cook has now gone up to Demeas.)

DEMEAS
Why accost me?

COOK

(retreating)

Don't lash out!

DEMEAS
(quietly turning to Chrysis)
Some other girl will love my home, and yes,   385
She'll thank the gods![30]

COOK
(in the background again)
What is this?

DEMEAS
(still quietly to Chrysis)

But you've had

A son. You've everything!

COOK
(being misled by Demeas' quiet tones, and approaching him again)

Now he's not lashing out.

Still,—

rary way of saying that she would show her gratitude to Demeas by
doing so.

95

ΔΗΜΕΑΣ

κατάξω τὴν κεφαλήν, ἄνθρωπε, σου

(561J) ἄν μοι διαλέγῃ.

ΜΑΓΕΙΡΟΣ

νὴ δικαίως γ'. ἀλλ' ἰδού,

390 εἰσέρχομ' ἤδη.

ΔΗΜΕΑΣ

τὸ μέγα πρᾶγμ'. ἐν τῇ πόλει

(176K) ὄψει σεαυτὴν νῦν ἀκριβῶς ἥτις εἶ.

αἱ κατά σε, Χρυσί, πραττόμεναι δράχμας δέκα
μόνας ἕτεραι τρέχουσιν ἐπὶ τὰ δεῖπνα καὶ

(566J) πίνουσ' ἄκρατον ἄχρι ἂν ἀποθάνωσιν, ἢ

395 πεινῶσιν, ἂν μὴ τοῦθ' ἑτοίμως καὶ ταχὺ

(181K) πρῶσιν. εἴσει δ' οὐδενὸς τοῦτ', οἶδ' ὅτι,
ἧττον σύ, καὶ γνώσει τίς οὖσ' ἡμάρτανες.
ἔσταθι.

ΧΡΥΣΙΣ

τάλαιν' ἔγωγε τῆς ἐμῆς τύχης.

389 νηδικαιωσγ' Β: καιδικαιως C (]ιδου O).
392 αικατα C: ουκατα Β.   393 ετεραι Β after correction
(second ε written above αι crossed out): εταιραι C.   διπνα Β
with omitted ε written above δι.   394 αχρισαν ΒC: corr.
Headlam.   η Β: και C (with correcting η written above).
395 πεινωσιν C: πινωσιν Β.   396 εισει C: εισι Β.
398 εγωγε Β: εγω C.

31 Demeas is assuming that Chrysis will now be forced to re-
turn to her old life as a *hetaira*.

96

DEMEAS
Mister, if you talk to me, I'll smash
Your head in.

COOK
Yes, and I'll deserve it. See,
I'm going in now.

(The cook goes back into Demeas' house.)

DEMEAS
(addressing Chrysis)
            Superstar! In town   390
You'll see exactly what you are! The others of
Your type dash to their parties, where they charge
A mere ten drachmas and knock back strong wine
Until they die—or else they starve, if what
They do's not quick and willing.[31] But I'm sure   395
You'll know this just as well as anyone.
You'll find out what you are and how you blundered!
Stay there.

(Demeas' command at the end of his speech is designed presumably to foil a final attempt by Chrysis to go back inside. Demeas now departs into his house and bolts his door. Chrysis, in tears, moves away from Demeas' house and stands in front of Nikeratos' door.)

CHRYSIS
Oh dear, how awful is my fate!

(At this point Nikeratos enters by the parodos that leads from the market. He pulls or carries a very scraggy sheep. At first he does not notice Chrysis and the nurse.)

MENANDER

ΝΙΚΗΡΑΤΟΣ

(571J) τουτὶ τὸ πρόβατον τοῖς θεοῖς μὲν τὰ νόμιμα
400 ἅπαντα ποιήσει τυθὲν καὶ ταῖς θεαῖς.
(186K) αἷμα γὰρ ἔχει, χολὴν ἱκανήν, ὀστᾶ καλά,
σπλῆνα μέγαν, ὧν χρεία 'στι τοῖς Ὀλυμπίοις.
πέμψω δὲ γεύσασθαι κατακόψας τοῖς φίλοις
(576J) τὸ κῴδιον· λοιπὸν γάρ ἐστι τοῦτό μοι.
405 ἀλλ᾿, Ἡράκλεις, τί τοῦτο; πρόσθε τῶν θυρῶν
(191K) ἕστηκε Χρυσὶς ἥδε κλάουσ᾿· οὐ μὲν οὖν
ἄλλη. τί ποτε τὸ γεγονός;

ΧΡΤΣΙΣ

                    ἐκβέβληκέ με
ὁ φίλος ὁ χρηστός σου. τί γὰρ ἄλλ᾿;

ΝΙΚΗΡΑΤΟΣ

                                    ὦ Ἡράκλεις.

(581J) τίς; Δημέας;

ΧΡΤΣΙΣ

ναί.

ΝΙΚΗΡΑΤΟΣ
διὰ τί;

ΧΡΤΣΙΣ
διὰ τὸ παιδίον.

---

400 ποιησαι B with α crossed out and correcting ε written
above.   θυθεν BC (-θὲν B): corr. van Leeuwen.
401 οστα C: ο[.]τεα B.   405 προσθετων[B: προστων C
with the omitted θε written above στ.   406 κααουσ᾿ B with
the first α crossed out and correcting λ written above: κλαιουσ᾿ C.

98

NIKERATOS

When sacrificed, this sheep will furnish all
The standard gifts for gods and goddesses.   400
It has some blood, an adequate gall bladder,
Fine bones, a large spleen, what the Olympians
Require.[32] I'll mince the fleece and send it to
My friends to taste. It's all that I've got left!
But heavens! What's up? Can that be Chrysis, standing   405
Outside my door, in tears? It's her, all right!
Whatever's happened?

CHRYSIS
                    It's your worthy friend—
He's thrown me out. Just that!

NIKERATOS
                    Good heavens! Who's done
It? Demeas?

CHRYSIS
        Yes.

NIKERATOS
        Why?

CHRYSIS
        It's through the baby.

[32] Nikeratos lists the portions for the gods, which would be
burnt on the altar as part of the sacrifice. The meat was then
cooked and shared by the participants. In this play Nikeratos is
portrayed as a poor man, unable to afford a sheep with plenty of
flesh.

---

407 ποτ᾿εστιτο BC: corr. several.

ΝΙΚΗΡΑΤΟΣ

410 ἤκουσα καὐτὸς τῶν γυναικῶν ὅτι τρέφεις
(196K) ἀνελομένη παιδάριον· ἐμβροντησία.
ἀλλ᾽ ἔστ᾽ ἐκεῖνος ἡδύς.

ΧΡΥΣΙΣ

οὐκ ὠργίζετο
εὐθύς, διαλιπὼν δ᾽, ἀρτίως· ὃς καὶ φράσας
(586J) εἰς τοὺς γάμους μοι τἄνδον εὐτρεπῆ ποεῖν,
415 μεταξύ μ᾽ ὥσπερ ἐμμανὴς ἐπεισπεσὼν
(201K) ἔξωθεν ἐκκέκλεικε.

ΝΙΚΗΡΑΤΟΣ

Δημέας χολᾷ.
ὁ Πόντος οὐχ ὑγιεινόν ἐστι χωρίον..
πρὸς τὴν γυναῖκα δεῦρ᾽ ἀκολούθει τὴν ἐμήν.
(591J) θάρρει. τί βούλει; παύσεθ᾽ οὗτος ἀπομανεὶς
420 ὅταν λογισμὸν ὧν ποεῖ νυνὶ λάβῃ.

ΧΟ Ρ ΟΥ

411 ανελλομενη B.
412–13 Change of speakers here indicated by Nicole,
Wilamowitz: BC signal the change in 413 by paragraphi, and
dicolon (C) or raised point (B) before ὅς.
417–546 survive only in B.
419 θαρσει B.

NIKERATOS

I personally heard the women say   410
You kept the child and rear it—lunacy!
But he's so kind![33]

CHRYSIS

At first he wasn't angry,
But later on, just now. He'd told me to
Arrange things indoors for the wedding, and
While I was busy, like a lunatic   415
He stormed in, locked me out.

NIKERATOS

Then Demeas
Is mad. The Black Sea's not a healthy place.[34]
Come with me to my wife, this way. Cheer up. What
    would
You like to do? When he's considered what
He's done, he'll stop and come back to his senses.   420

*(Nikeratos takes Chrysis with the baby and the nurse into
his house. When the stage is empty, the chorus give their
third entr'acte performance.)*

[33] Demeas.
[34] See note on v. 98.

MENANDER

ΜΕΡΟΣ Δ΄

ΝΙΚΗΡΑΤΟΣ

παρατενεῖς, γύναι. βαδίζω νῦν ἐκείνῳ προσβαλῶν.
οὐδ᾽ ἂν ἐπὶ πολλῷ γενέσθαι τὸ γεγονός, μὰ τοὺς
θεούς,
πρᾶγμ᾽ ἐδεξάμην. μεταξὺ τῶν γάμων ποουμένων

(596J)   συμβέβηκ᾽ οἰωνὸς ἡμῖν ἄτοπος. ἐκβεβλημένη
425   εἰσελήλυθεν πρὸς ἡμᾶς παιδάριον ἔχουσά τις.
δάκρυα γίνεθ᾽, αἱ γυναῖκες τεθορύβηνται. Δημέας
σκατοφαγεῖ. νὴ τὸν Ποσειδῶ καὶ θεούς, οἰμώξεται
σκαιὸς ὤν.

421 προσλαβων B with λ and β crossed out and correcting β and λ respectively written above.

424 συμβεβηκεναιωνος B with α crossed out and correcting ο written above.

425 Corr. Austin: εισεληλυθε B.

426 γινεσθ᾽ B with σ crossed out.   τεθορύβηται B: corr. Austin.

427 ποσιδῶ B: corr. Austin.

428 εων B with ε crossed out.

ACT IV

(After the chorus's performance, Nikeratos enters from his house. His opening words are addressed to his wife back in the house. The whole of this lively act is written in trochaic tetrameters.)

NIKERATOS

Wife, you'll wear me out with fussing! Now I'll go and
  challenge him.
I'd have never wanted this predicament to happen—no,
Not at any price! Right in the middle of the wedding a
Fearful omen has befallen us. A woman's been thrown
  out
And arrived in our house with a baby. Tears are flowing,   425
  and
Here the women are in turmoil. Damn it, Demeas is
  now
Acting like a callous brute. By God, I swear he'll pay for
  his
Crass behaviour!

(As Nikeratos moves in the direction of Demeas' door, Moschion now enters by the parodos leading from the town centre. After exiting at vv. 161–62 in order to get out of Demeas' way, he has been idling his time away in the baths and at the market (cf. 429–32), and he now returns in mid-afternoon, in order to fetch his bride and escort her to their new home together at the climax of the wedding ceremonies.)

MENANDER

ΜΟΣΧΙΩΝ

οὐ μὴ δύῃ ποθ᾽ ἥλιος. τί δεῖ λέγειν;
(601J) ἐπιλέλησθ᾽ ἡ νὺξ ἑαυτῆς. ὦ μακρᾶς δείλης. τρίτον
430 λούσομ᾽ ἐλθών· τί γὰρ ἔχοιμ᾽ ἂν ἄλλο ποιεῖν;

ΝΙΚΗΡΑΤΟΣ

Μοσχίων,

χαῖρε πολλά.

ΜΟΣΧΙΩΝ

νῦν ποοῦμεν τοὺς γάμους; ὁ Παρμένων
εἶπεν ἐν ἀγορᾷ περιτυχὼν ἄρτι μοι. τί κωλύει
μετιέναι τὴν παῖδά μ᾽ ἤδη;

ΝΙΚΗΡΑΤΟΣ

τἀνθάδ᾽ ἀγνοῶν πάρει;

ΜΟΣΧΙΩΝ

(606J) ποῖα;

ΝΙΚΗΡΑΤΟΣ

ποῖ; ἀηδία τις συμβέβηκεν ἔκτοπος.

ΜΟΣΧΙΩΝ

435 Ἡράκλεις. τίς; οὐ γὰρ εἰδὼς ἔρχομαι.

428 δυνη B with ν crossed out.
430 λευσομ᾽ B with ε crossed out and correcting ο written above.
434 ποια:ποιαφηις B: corr. Austin.

104

MOSCHION

(*not noticing Nikeratos*)

Will the sun now *never* set? What can I say?
Night's forgotten her vocation. How the afternoon drags
  on!
I shall go and take a third bath[1]—what else could I find   430
  to do?

NIKERATOS

(*going up to Moschion*)

Warmest greetings, Moschion.

MOSCHION

The wedding—are we getting on
With it? Parmenon's just told me, in the market where
  we met.
What's to stop me fetching now the bride?[2]

NIKERATOS

You're here, and haven't yet
Heard the news?

MOSCHION

What news?

NIKERATOS

You ask? A strange and nasty crisis has
Burst on us!

MOSCHION

My god, what's happened? I've come here   435
  without a clue.

---

[1] He had presumably taken the second one in public baths at
the town centre.

[2] See especially note on v. 159.

ΝΙΚΗΡΑΤΟΣ

τὴν Χρυσίδα
ἐξελήλακ᾽ ἔνδοθέν σου, φίλταθ᾽, ὁ πατὴρ ἀρτίως.

ΜΟΣΧΙΩΝ

οἷον εἴρηκας.

ΝΙΚΗΡΑΤΟΣ
τὸ γεγονός.

ΜΟΣΧΙΩΝ
διὰ τί;

ΝΙΚΗΡΑΤΟΣ

διὰ τὸ παιδίον.

ΜΟΣΧΙΩΝ

εἶτα ποῦ ᾽στι νῦν;

ΝΙΚΗΡΑΤΟΣ
παρ᾽ ἡμῖν, ἔνδον.

ΜΟΣΧΙΩΝ

ὦ δεινὸν λέγων
(611J) πρᾶγμα καὶ θαυμαστόν.

ΝΙΚΗΡΑΤΟΣ
εἴ σοι δεινὸν εἶναι φαίνεται,—

438 δεινονεγων B with omitted λ written above νε.

SAMIA

NIKERATOS

It's your father. He's just driven Chrysis from your
    house, dear boy!

MOSCHION

That's impossible!

NIKERATOS

It's happened.

MOSCHION

Why though?

NIKERATOS

Through the baby.

MOSCHION

Then
Where's she now?

NIKERATOS

She's come to our house, staying with us.

MOSCHION

Oh, this news
Is incredible and dreadful.

NIKERATOS

If it seems dreadful to you,—

*(Nikeratos breaks off in mid-sentence because Demeas now
bursts angrily out of his house. He first shouts back to some
slaves weeping inside, then turns and prays to the statue or
emblem of Apollo outside his door, interspersing remarks
to the audience. Nikeratos and Moschion retire quietly into
the background.)*

107

ΔΗΜΕΑΣ

440 ἂν λάβω ξύλον, ποήσω τὰ δάκρυ' ὑμῶν ταῦτ' ἐγὼ
ἐκκεκόφθαι. τίς ὁ φλύαρος; οὐ διακονήσετε
τῷ μαγείρῳ; πάνυ γάρ ἐστιν ἄξιον, νὴ τὸν Δία,
ἐπιδακρῦσαι· μέγα γὰρ ὑμῖν ᾤχετ' ἐκ τῆς οἰκίας

(616J) ἀγαθόν. αὐτὰ τἄργα δηλοῖ.—χαῖρ', Ἄπολλον
φίλτατε,

445 ἐπ' ἀγαθῇ τύχῃ τε πᾶσι τοὺς γάμους ⟨οὓς⟩
μέλλομεν
⟨νῦν⟩ ποεῖν ἡμῖν γενέσθαι δὸς σύ· μέλλω γὰρ
ποεῖν
τοὺς γάμους, ἄνδρες, καταπιὼν τὴν χολήν. τή[ρει δὲ
σύ,
δέσποτ', αὐτὸς ἵνα γένωμαι μὴ 'πίδηλος μηδ[ενί,

(621J) ἀλλὰ τὸν ὑμ[έν]αιον ᾄδειν εἰσανάγκασόν με σύ.

450 ἄρ]ξ[ομ' ο]ὐκ ἄριστ' ἐγὼ ⟨γὰρ⟩ ὡς ἔχω νῦν. ἀλλὰ
τί;
οὐκ ἂν ἐπα]νέλθοι.

440 ἐαν B: corr. Austin.

445, 446 ⟨οὓς⟩ and ⟨νῦν⟩ suppl. Austin.　　δοστι B with τι
crossed out and συ written above.

447 τή[ρει suppl. ed.pr., δὲ σύ Austin.

448 Suppl. Lloyd-Jones.

449 Suppl. ed.pr.　　αειδειν B with first ει crossed out and ι
written above.

450 ἄρ]ξ[ομ' suppl. Arnott (? αρομ' originally B, with omitted
ξ written above ρ or ρο), ο]ὐκ Barigazzi, ⟨γὰρ⟩ Roca-Puig.

451 Suppl. Jacques.

DEMEAS

If I grab a stick, I'll see that all those tears are beaten   440
out

Of you. What's this nonsense? Won't you give assistance
to the cook?

Yes indeed, you've every reason to lament and weep at
this,

For a mighty benefactor to you all has left the house!

Here the facts speak for themselves.[3]—All hail, Apollo,
dearest Lord![4]

Grant too that this wedding [which] we're now about to   445
celebrate

May confer good fortune on us all!—For, gentlemen,[5] I
mean

To conduct this marriage, swallowing my anger.—Keep
me, Lord,

From betraying my emotions to a single person, but

Force my lips to sing the wedding hymn,[6] I beg you,
[for] I shan't

[Start proceedings] all that well, the way that I now   450
feel!—but why

Worry? She[7] will [never] come [back]!

[3] Demeas implies that Chrysis was kind to, and loved by, the
slaves in his household.

[4] Demeas turns to the altar or emblem of Apollo outside his
house; see note on v. 309 and *Dysk.* 659, n. 3.

[5] See note on v. 269.

[6] See note on v. 127.

[7] Chrysis.

MENANDER

ΝΙΚΗΡΑΤΟΣ
σὺ πρότερος, Μοσχίων, πρόσελθέ μου.

ΜΟΣΧΙΩΝ
εἶέν, ὦ π]άτερ, τί ποιεῖς ταῦτα;

ΔΗΜΕΑΣ
ποῖα, Μοσχίων;

ΜΟΣΧΙΩΝ
ποῖ᾽, ἐρωτ]ᾷς; διὰ τί Χρυσὶς οἴχετ᾽ ἀπιοῦσ᾽; εἰπέ
μοι.

ΔΗΜΕΑΣ
(626J)   δηλαδὴ] πρεσβεύεταί τις πρός με· δεινόν.—οὐχὶ
σό[ν,
455   μὰ τὸν Ἀ]πόλλω, τοὔργον ἐστίν, ἀλλὰ παντελ[ῶς
ἐμόν.
τίς ὁ φλύ]αρος;—δεινὸν ἤδη. συναδικεῖ μ᾽ οὗτος—

ΜΟΣΧΙΩΝ
[τί φής;

452 εἶέν, ὦ suppl. Sandbach, π]άτερ ed.pr.
453 ποῖ᾽ suppl. Roca-Puig, ἐρωτ]ᾷς ed.pr.
454 δηλαδὴ suppl. Galiano.   εμε B: corr. Jacques.
σό[ν suppl. ed.pr.
455 μὰ τὸν Ἀ]πόλλω suppl. Roca-Puig, παντελ[ῶς ἐμόν
ed.pr.
456 Suppl. ed.pr.   Punctuation after ἤδη suggested by
Austin.

110

NIKERATOS

(still in the background, along with Moschion)

Moschion, you go to him

First, before me!

(Moschion goes up to Demeas, leaving Nikeratos on his own.)

MOSCHION

[Well then,] father, why do this?

DEMEAS

What, Moschion?

MOSCHION

Are you [asking what]? Just tell me, why has Chrysis upped and left?

DEMEAS

(to himself)

[It's quite plain!] A man here's come to parley with me! Awful! *(to Moschion)* This

Matter is not your concern, but [mine] entirely, that I   455
swear!

[What's this] claptrap? *(to self)* Really awful! He's joined her in wronging me—

MOSCHION

(not hearing what Demeas is saying to himself)

[What's that?]

ΔΗΜΕΑΣ

—περιφα]νῶς. τί γὰρ προσέρχεθ᾽ ὑπὲρ ἐκείνης;
ἀσ[μένῳ
χρῆν γὰρ αὐτῷ τοῦτο δήπου γε[γονέ‹ναι›.]

ΜΟΣΧΙΩΝ

[τί τ]οὺς φίλους

(631J) προσδοκᾷς ἐρεῖν πυθομένους;

ΔΗΜΕΑΣ

ο[ὐ προτιμ]ῶ, Μοσχίων,

460 τοὺς φίλους. ἔα μ᾽.

ΜΟΣΧΙΩΝ

ἀγεννὲς ἂν πο[οίη]ν ἐπιτρέπων.

ΔΗΜΕΑΣ

ἀλλὰ κωλύσεις μ᾽;

ΜΟΣΧΙΩΝ

ἔγωγε.

ΔΗΜΕΑΣ

τοῦθ᾽, ὁρᾷ[θ᾽, ὑ]περβολή.
τοῦτο τῶν δεινῶν ἐκείνων δεινό[τερο]ν.

457 περιφα]νῶς suppl. Lloyd-Jones, ἀσ[μένῳ Sandbach.
458 εχρην B: corr. Austin.   γε[γονέ‹ναι› suppl. Jacques,
τί Austin, τ]οὺς ed.pr.
459 Suppl. tentatively Arnott.
460 Supp. ed.pr.
461 ὁρᾷ[θ᾽ suppl. Oguse, ὑ]περβολή ed.pr.
462 Suppl. ed.pr.

DEMEAS

(still talking to himself)
            —[clearly]. Otherwise, why come in her
   support? He should
Surely have been [pleased] that this has [happened.]

MOSCHION

                              [What] do you expect
Friends will say when they find out?

DEMEAS

(to Moschion)
            [I'm not concerned about] my friends,
Moschion—leave that to me!

MOSCHION
                        I'd act ignobly if I did!   460

DEMEAS

Will you stop me?

MOSCHION
            Yes, I will!

DEMEAS

(probably here addressing the audience directly[8])
            This goes too far—[you all] see that!
This is worse than all the awful things before!

[8] This assumption is based on a plausible supplement of a
short gap in the papyrus text. An alternative supplement would
make Moschion the addressee and require the translation to be
amended to '[you must] see that!'

ΜΟΣΧΙΩΝ

[ο]ὐ πάντα γὰρ

ἐπιτρέπειν ὀργῇ προσήκει.

ΝΙΚΗΡΑΤΟΣ

Δημέα, κ[αλ]ῶς λέγει.

ΜΟΣΧΙΩΝ

(636J) ἀποτρέχειν αὐτῇ φράσον δεῦρ᾽ εἰσιών, Νικήρατε.

ΔΗΜΕΑΣ

465 Μοσχίων, ἔα μ᾽, ἔα με, Μοσχίων· τρίτον λέγω
τουτογί. πάντ᾽ οἶδα.

ΜΟΣΧΙΩΝ
ποῖα πάντα;

ΔΗΜΕΑΣ

μή μοι διαλέγου.

ΜΟΣΧΙΩΝ

ἀλλ᾽ ἀνάγκη, πάτερ.

ΔΗΜΕΑΣ
ἀνάγκη; τῶν ἐμῶν οὐ κύριος

ἔσομ᾽ ἐγώ;

ΜΟΣΧΙΩΝ
ταύτην ἐμοὶ δὸς τὴν χάριν.

463 Suppl. ed.pr.
465 Corr. Austin: ἐαμ᾽εαμ᾽ B.
466 Corr. Austin: τουτογε B.

114

MOSCHION

It isn't good

To give way to rage in all this!

NIKERATOS

(coming forward)

Demeas, he's right!

MOSCHION

(to Nikeratos)

Go in

And instruct her[9] to trot back here to our house,
   Nikeratos.

DEMEAS

Moschion, leave that to me—to me, yes, Moschion! I say   465
This a third time—I know all the facts!

MOSCHION

What facts?

DEMEAS

Don't talk to me!

MOSCHION

But I've got to, father!

DEMEAS

Got to? Shan't I be the master of

My possessions?

MOSCHION

Grant me this then as a favour.

[9] Chrysis.

115

MENANDER

ΔΗΜΕΑΣ

ποίαν χάριν;

(641J) οἷον ἀξιοῖς μ' ἀπελθεῖν αὐτὸν ἐκ τῆς οἰκίας
470 καταλιπόνθ' ὑμᾶς, δύ' ὄντας. τοὺς γάμους ἔα ποεῖν,
τοὺς γάμους ἔα με ποιεῖν, ἂν ἔχῃς νοῦν.

ΜΟΣΧΙΩΝ

ἀλλ' ἐῶ·

βούλομαι δὲ συμπαρεῖναι Χρυσίδ' ⟨ἡμῖν⟩.

ΔΗΜΕΑΣ

Χρυσίδα;

ΜΟΣΧΙΩΝ

ἕνεκα σοῦ σπεύδω μάλιστα τοῦτο.

ΔΗΜΕΑΣ

ταῦτ' οὐ γνώριμα,

(646J) οὐ σαφῆ; μαρτύρομαί σε, Λοξία, συνόμνυται
475 τοῖς ἐμοῖς ἐχθροῖς τις, οἴμοι, καὶ διαρραγήσομαι.

469 αξιος B with omitted ι inserted above ος.
471 ποειν εαν B: corr. Austin.
472 συνπαρειναι B: corr. Austin, who also supplied ⟨ἡμῖν⟩.
475 οιμαι B with α crossed out and ο written above it.
διαραγησομαι B: corr. Austin.

---

10 Moschion and Chrysis.
11 On this see note on 309 and *Dysk*. 659, n 3.
12 This epithet of Apollo (meaning 'the oblique one') most probably refers to the ambiguity and obscurity of his oracles; see especially W. Burkert, *Greek Religion* (English translation by J. Raffan, Oxford 1985), 147–8.

116

DEMEAS

Favour! What

Insolence! You might as well be asking me to quit the
house

On my own, and leave you two together!¹⁰ Let me now   470
get on

With the wedding, let me do that! If you're wise, you
will.

MOSCHION

I will!

Chrysis, though—I'd like her to be present [with us].

DEMEAS

(becoming apoplectic)

Chrysis?

MOSCHION

Yes—

It's for your sake mainly that I want this!

(Demeas is amazed and dismayed by Moschion's words.
He turns away from him, to address first the audience, then
Apollo's¹¹ statue or emblem.)

DEMEAS

Isn't it beyond

Question? Isn't it clear cut? I call you, Loxias,¹² as my

Witness—someone's¹³ plotting with my enemies—oh, I'll   475
lose

All control!

¹³ Demeas clearly means Moschion, but he hesitates to charge
him openly with having made love to Chrysis.

117

ΜΟΣΧΙΩΝ

τί δὲ λέγεις;

ΔΗΜΕΑΣ

βούλει φράσω σοι;

ΜΟΣΧΙΩΝ

πάνυ γε.

ΔΗΜΕΑΣ

δεῦρο δή.

ΜΟΣΧΙΩΝ

λέγε.

ΔΗΜΕΑΣ

ἀλλ᾽ ἐγώ. τὸ παιδίον σόν ἐστιν. οἶδ᾽, ἀκήκοα
τοῦ συνειδότος τὰ κρυπτά, Παρμένοντος. μηκέτι
(651J)   πρὸς ἐμὲ παῖζ᾽.

ΜΟΣΧΙΩΝ

ἔπειτά σ᾽ ἀδικεῖ Χρυσίς, εἰ τοῦτ᾽ ἔστ᾽ ἐμόν;

ΔΗΜΕΑΣ

480   ἀλλὰ τίς; σύ;

ΜΟΣΧΙΩΝ

τί γὰρ ἐκείνη γέγονεν αἰτία;

476 δή Austin: ηδη B.
478 ωστεμηκετι B: corr. Austin.
479 οι B with o crossed out and ε written above.
480 τισυ B with the omitted letter written above ις.

118

MOSCHION
(not hearing Demeas clearly)
What's that you say?

DEMEAS
You want to know?

MOSCHION
Yes!

DEMEAS
(pointing and moving to a spot further away from Nikeratos)
Over here!

MOSCHION
(following Demeas)
Speak!

DEMEAS
Well then, I will. The baby's yours. I know that,
  I've been told
By a man who knows your secrets—Parmenon. Stop
  playing your
Games with me!

MOSCHION
Then how does Chrysis wrong you, if this baby's mine?

DEMEAS
Who's to blame, then? You?

MOSCHION
How's she at fault, though?

119

ΔΗΜΕΑΣ

τί φής;

οὐδὲν ἐνθυμεῖσθε;

ΜΟΣΧΙΩΝ

τί βοᾷς;

ΔΗΜΕΑΣ

ὅ τι βοῶ, κάθαρμα σύ,
τοῦτ᾽ ἐρωτᾷς; εἰς σεαυτὸν ἀναδέχει τὴν αἰτίαν,
εἰπέ μοι, καὶ τοῦτο τολμᾷς ἐμβλέπων ἐμοὶ λέγειν;
(656J)   παντελῶς οὕτως ἀπεγνωκώς με τυγχάνεις;

ΜΟΣΧΙΩΝ

ἐγώ;

485   διὰ τί;

ΔΗΜΕΑΣ

"διὰ τί" φής; ἐρωτᾶν δ᾽ ἀξιοῖς;

ΜΟΣΧΙΩΝ

τὸ πρᾶγμα γάρ
ἐστιν οὐ πάνδεινον, ἀλλὰ μύριοι δήπου, πάτερ,
τοῦτο πεποήκασιν.

ΔΗΜΕΑΣ

ὦ Ζεῦ, τοῦ θράσους. ἐναντίον

481 ουδεν:ουδεν B: corr. Handley, Sandbach.
482–83 Corr. several: ειπὲμοι placed before εισεαυτον (with
the omitted σ added above ισ) in B.

SAMIA

DEMEAS
(amazed by this answer, and shouting)
                                    What is that you say?   480
Have you two no scruples?

MOSCHION
                        Why the shouting?

DEMEAS
(in a rage)
                                          Filthy rat, you ask
Why I'm shouting? Tell me, do you take the blame upon
    yourself?
Yet you dare to look me in the face and say those
    words![14]
Do you flatly turn your back on me like this?

MOSCHION
(amazed in his turn)
                                    Me turn my back?
Why do you say that?

DEMEAS
                    You wonder why? You dare to ask?

MOSCHION
                                          My crime   485
Isn't all that dreadful, father—millions have done the
    same,
Surely!

DEMEAS
            God in heaven, what a nerve! Before this audience

[14] At vv. 479 and 480.

δή σ' ἐρωτῶ τῶν παρόντων· ἐκ τίνος τὸ παιδίον
(661J) ἐστί σοι; Νικηράτῳ τοῦτ' εἶπον, εἰ μή σοι δοκεῖ
490 δεινὸν <εἶναι>.

MOΣXIΩN

νὴ Δί', ἀλλὰ δεινὸν οὕτω γίνεται
τοῦτο πρὸς τοῦτον λέγειν με· χαλεπανεῖ γὰρ
πυθόμενος.

NIKHPATOΣ

ὦ κάκιστ' ἀνδρῶν ἁπάντων· ὑπονοεῖν γὰρ ἄρχομαι
τὴν τύχην καὶ τἀσέβημα τὸ γεγονὸς μόλις ποτέ.

MOΣXIΩN

(666J) τέλος ἔχω τοίνυν ἐγώ.

ΔHMEAΣ

νῦν αἰσθάνει, Νικήρατε;

NIKHPATOΣ

495 οὐ γάρ; ὦ πάνδεινον ἔργον· ὦ τὰ Τηρέως λέχη

489 εμη B with the omitted ι written above εμ.
490 Suppl. Austin.
491–92 Corr. Austin: χαλεπαινει, πευθομενος and παντων B.
495 πα B with π crossed out and τ written above.   δελάχη
B with δ (but not ε) and α crossed out, and ε written above the α:
correction completed by Austin.

122

Seated here,[15] I ask you: who's the mother of your little
   child?
Give Nikeratos the information, if you don't believe
It'[s] so terrible!

MOSCHION
(terrified at being asked to confess now to Plangon's father)
            Indeed it *will* be terrible, if I   490
Have to talk to *him* about it in this way. He'll be in-
   censed,
When he learns the truth!

*(Nikeratos now rejoins Moschion and Demeas. He is just as
angry as Demeas.)*

NIKERATOS
(addressing Moschion)
          You vilest of mankind! I've just begun
Now to fathom this misfortune and the sinful act done
   here.

MOSCHION
That's me finished!

DEMEAS
       Well, Nikeratos, do you now understand?

NIKERATOS
(ranting as if he were a bad tragic actor)
Don't I then! O deed most dreadful! You have made the   495
   sexual crimes

[15] It is unusual for a character in Menander to bring the thea-
tre audience into the dramatic action: see especially D. Bain, *ZPE*
71 (1988) 9–10.

Οἰδίπου τε καὶ Θυέστου καὶ τὰ τῶν ἄλλων, ὅσα
γεγονόθ᾽ ἡμῖν ἐστ᾽ ἀκοῦσαι, μικρὰ ποιήσας—

ΜΟΣΧΙΩΝ

ἐγώ;

ΝΙΚΗΡΑΤΟΣ

τοῦτ᾽ ἐτόλμησας σὺ πρᾶξαι, τοῦτ᾽ [ἔ]τλης;
Ἀμύντορος
(671J) νῦν ἐχρῆν ὀργὴν λαβεῖν σε, Δ[η]μέα, καὶ τουτονὶ
500   ἐκτυφλῶσαι.

ΔΗΜΕΑΣ

διά σε τούτῳ γέγονε πάν[τ]α κα[τ]αφανῆ.

ΝΙΚΗΡΑΤΟΣ

τίνος ἀπόσχοι᾽ ἂν σύ; ποῖον οὐκ ἂν [αἰσχύνοις
λ]έχ[ος;

496 οιδιπους B with ς crossed out.
497 Corr. Kassel: γεγονασ᾽ B.   498–500 Suppl. ed.pr.
499 εχρην B with o crossed out and ρ written above.
500 τουτο B with second o crossed out and ω written above.
501 αποστιχοι B with τι crossed out.   [αἰσχύνοις λ]έχ[ος
tentatively suppl. Arnott.

---

16 Nikeratos makes an extravagant claim that Moschion's al-
leged affair with Demeas' partner Chrysis outdid the three most
blatant examples of incest and sexual misconduct in Greek my-
thology: Tereus' rape of his wife's sister Philomela, Oedipus' mar-
riage to his mother Jocasta, and Thyestes' double crimes of adul-
tery with his brother's wife Aerope and incest with his daughter
Pelopia. Attic tragedy kept these stories alive.

124

SAMIA

Of Thyestes, Oedipus and Tereus,[16] all those crimes
   we've heard
Were committed by the rest—you've made them all look
   trivial!

MOSCHION
(astonished by the violence of Nikeratos' attack)
I have?

NIKERATOS
(first to Moschion, then to Demeas)
         Did you dare to act thus, and hazard it? Demeas,
You should have adopted now Amyntor's[17] wrath, and
   blinded him!

DEMEAS
(to Moschion)
You're responsible for making all these things so clear to   500
   him![18]

NIKERATOS
(reviling Moschion)
Who'd be free from your attentions? Whose [bed (?)]
   would [you] not [defile]?

[17] Amyntor's son Phoenix was a further celebrated example of
(alleged) sexual misconduct. Phoenix was said to have made love
to his father's concubine, named either Clytia or Phthia, and then
to have been blinded by his father in punishment. Some versions
of the story make Phoenix the innocent victim of a lie dissemi-
nated by the concubine. See especially J. G. Frazer's note on
Apollodorus 3.13.8 in the Loeb edition (II.74–75, n. 2).
[18] Nikeratos.

125

εἶτ᾽ ἐγώ σοι δῶ γυναῖκα τὴν ἐμαυτ[οῦ θυγατέρα;
πρότερον—εἰς κόλπον δέ φασι· τὴν Ἀδ[ράστειαν
σέβω—

(676J) ἐπὶ Διομνήστῳ γενοίμην νυμφίῳ [νῦν πενθερός,
505 ὁμολογουμένην ἀτυχίαν.

ΔΗΜΕΑΣ

ταῦ[τ᾽ ἀκούσας, τὴν χολὴν
ἠδικημένος κατεῖχον.

ΝΙΚΗΡΑΤΟΣ

ἀνδράποδ[ον εἶ, Δημέα.
εἰ γὰρ ἐμὸν ἦσ[χυνε λέ]κτρον, οὐκ ἂν εἰς ἄλλον
ποτὲ
ὕβρισ᾽, οὐδ᾽ ἡ συγ[κλ]ιθεῖσα· παλλακὴν δ᾽ ἂν
αὔριον
(681J) πρῶτος ἀνθρώπ[ω]ν ἐπώλουν, συναποκηρύττων ἅμα

502 Suppl. ed.pr.   503 Suppl. Lloyd-Jones (with σέβων),
Austin.   504 διομνησποι B with ποι crossed out and τῶ writ-
ten above.   νῦν suppl. Arnott, πενθερός Austin.

505 τηνατυχιαν B: corr. Austin.   ταῦ[τα suppl. Austin, the
rest *exempli gratia* Arnott.

506 ἀνδράποδ[ον suppl. ed.pr., the rest Sandbach.

507 Suppl. Lloyd-Jones.

508 ουδ᾽ει B with ει crossed out and η written above.
Suppl. and corr. Austin: συν[κλε]ιθεισα apparently B.

509 Suppl. Austin.

---

19 The Greek proverb literally runs '(I spit) into my lap', al-
though Nikeratos omits 'I spit.' This act, and that of kowtowing
to the goddess Nemesis (see *Perikeiromene* 314 and my note b

Am I then to give my [daughter] as a wife to you? I'd
    first—
Touching wood,[19] the proverb goes, but [I bow down to
    Nemesis (?)]—
Rather have her marry Diomnestus[20] [and be *his* in-law
    (?)]—
An acknowledged tribulation!

DEMEAS
            [When I heard about] it,[21] though   505
I'd been injured, I suppressed [my wrath (?)].

NIKERATOS
                [You're acting, Demeas,]
Like a slave.[22] If he'd smirched *my* bed, never would he
    or his mate
Have outraged another! I'd have been the first man to
    sell off
Mistress on the morrow, and I'd auction son along with
    her!

there), were attempts to avert any evil consequences of intemper-
ate statements such as that made in v. 504.

   [20] Probably an otherwise unknown Athenian contemporary of
Menander who had become notorious as an adulterer or offender
in some other way against the institution of marriage. At least
six Athenians bore this name in the fourth century B.C.: see
Osborne–Byrne, *A Lexicon of Greek Personal Names*, 2 (Oxford
1994) 121. See also the introduction to this play.

   [21] The supplement here is very uncertain, but it is based on the
assumption that Demeas is referring to what he reported hearing
at vv. 245–50, and to his conclusion that Moschion and Chrysis
were the parents of the baby.

   [22] Sc. spinelessly.

510 υόν, ὥστε μηθὲ[ν εἶ]ναι μήτε κουρεῖον κενόν,
μὴ στοάν, κ[αθη]μένους δὲ πάντας ἐξ ἑωθινοῦ
περὶ ἐμοῦ λαλ[ε]ῖν, λέγοντας ὡς ἀνὴρ Νικήρατος
γέγον᾽, ἐπεξελθὼν δικαίως τῷ φόνῳ.

ΔΗΜΕΑΣ

ποίῳ φόνῳ;

ΝΙΚΗΡΑΤΟΣ

(686J) φόνον ἐγὼ κρίνω τὰ τοιαῦθ᾽ ὅστις ἐπαναστὰς π[ο]εῖ.

ΜΟΣΧΙΩΝ

515 αὖός εἰμι καὶ πέπηγα τῷ κακῷ, νὴ τοὺς θεούς.

ΝΙΚΗΡΑΤΟΣ

ἀλλ᾽ ἐγὼ πρὸς τοῖσιν ἄλλοις τὴν τὰ δείν᾽
εἰργασμένην
εἰσεδεξάμην μελάθροις τοῖς ἐμοῖς.

ΔΗΜΕΑΣ

Νικήρατε,
ἔκβαλ᾽, ἱκετεύω· συναδικοῦ γνησίως, ὡς ἂν φίλος.

ΝΙΚΗΡΑΤΟΣ

(691J) ὃς διαρραγήσομ᾽ οἰδῶν. ἐμβλέπεις μοι, βάρβαρε,

510–12 Suppl. ed.pr.   513 δικαιως originally omitted in
B, but then written in both above τωφο and in right-hand margin
(δικαιω[).   513 ποίῳ φόνῳ assigned to Demeas by Sandbach.
514 οσατις B: corr. Handley.
515 καιεπηγα B with the omitted π written above ε.
516 εργασαμην B with second α and ην crossed out, and ενη[
written above the ην: suppl. ed.pr.   519 διαραγησομ᾽ B:
corr. Austin.   οἰδῶν Gronewald: ἰδων B

128

Then no place would have been empty—barber's shop   510
   or colonnade[23]—
All the world would have been sitting in their seats from
   dawn's first light,
Gossiping about me, saying that Nikeratos had turned
Out a real man, rightly taking out a *murder* summons!

DEMEAS

                            How

Is this *murder*?

NIKERATOS

        In my view it's murder when men act like this,
As usurpers!

MOSCHION

(aside)

    This disaster's made me parched and numb with fear!   515

NIKERATOS

But on top of all the rest, I welcomed to my noble halls
The prime authoress of these appalling crimes!

DEMEAS

                     Nikeratos,

Throw her out, I beg you. Share my wrong sincerely, as a
   friend.

NIKERATOS

(moving to his door, but blocked at first by Moschion)

I'll swell out (?), explode in rage! You brute, you

---

[23] Two places where men habitually gathered and gossiped.
Cf. my n. 1 on Men. *Dysk.* 173 and N. Dunbar's commentary (Ox-
ford 1995) on Ar. *Birds* 1440–41.

520   Θρᾷξ ἀληθῶς; οὐ παρήσεις;

ΜΟΣΧΙΩΝ

πάτερ, ἄκουσον, πρὸς θεῶν.

ΔΗΜΕΑΣ

οὐκ ἀκούσομ' οὐθέν.

ΜΟΣΧΙΩΝ

οὐδ' εἰ μηδὲν ὧν σὺ προσδοκᾷς

γέγονεν; ἄρτι γὰρ τὸ πρᾶγμα κατανοῶ.

ΔΗΜΕΑΣ

πῶς μηδὲ ἕν;

ΜΟΣΧΙΩΝ

οὐχὶ Χρυσίς ἐστι μήτηρ οὗ τρέφει νῦν παιδίου,

(696J)   ἀλλ' ἐμοὶ χαρίζεται, τοῦθ' ὁμολογοῦσ' αὑτῆς.

ΔΗΜΕΑΣ

τί φής;

ΜΟΣΧΙΩΝ

525   τὰς ἀληθείας.

ΔΗΜΕΑΣ

διὰ τί δὲ τοῦτό σοι χαρίζεται;

521 νηδι'οὐδεν B: corr. Arnott.

Thracian goat[24] in truth,
Dare you look me in the eye? Just let me pass!

(After this onslaught Moschion allows Nikeratos to pass and exit into his own house. Moschion goes up to his father.)

MOSCHION

Do listen now,   520
Father.

DEMEAS
I'll hear nothing!

MOSCHION
Even if none of the things you fear
Has occurred? I understand this matter now.

DEMEAS
'None of those things'—
How's that?

MOSCHION
Chrysis isn't the mother of the baby she now feeds,
But she's doing *me* a favour, saying it's hers!

DEMEAS
What do you say?

MOSCHION
The plain truth!

DEMEAS
But why's she doing you this favour?

[24] Thracians had a reputation for lasciviousness.

MENANDER

ΜΟΣΧΙΩΝ

οὐχ ἑκὼν λέγω μέν, ἀλλὰ μείζον᾽ αἰτίαν φυγὼν
λαμβάνω μικράν, ἐὰν σὺ τὸ γεγονὸς πύθῃ σαφῶς.

ΔΗΜΕΑΣ

ἀλλ᾽ ἀποκτενεῖς πρὶν εἰπεῖν.

ΜΟΣΧΙΩΝ

ἔστι τῆς Νικηράτου
(701J) θυγατρὸς ἐξ ἐμοῦ. λαθεῖν δὲ τοῦτ᾽ ἐβουλόμην ἐγώ.

ΔΗΜΕΑΣ

530 πῶς λέγεις;

ΜΟΣΧΙΩΝ

ὥσπερ πέπρακται.

ΔΗΜΕΑΣ

μή με βουκολεῖς ὅρα.

ΜΟΣΧΙΩΝ

οὗ λαβεῖν ἔλεγχόν ἐστι; καὶ τί κερδανῶ πλέον;

ΔΗΜΕΑΣ

οὐθέν· ἀλλὰ τὴν θύραν τις—

526 λεγομεν (with ο crossed out and ω written above) and
αντιαν (with first ν crossed out and ι written above) B.
527 συντουτο B with ντου crossed out.

132

MOSCHION

I'll explain—   525

With reluctance—but in shrugging off more serious
  charges, I

Now plead guilty to a small one, once you clearly know
  the facts.

DEMEAS

Speak, before you kill me with suspense!

MOSCHION

The baby's parents are

Myself, and Nikeratos's daughter. That's what I desired

To keep secret.

DEMEAS

How d'you mean?

MOSCHION

That's what happened!

DEMEAS

Careful—no   530

Fooling!

MOSCHION

You can check the evidence. And what
  advantage would

I secure by lies?

DEMEAS

None. But the door—some one . . .

*(At this point Nikeratos rushes out of his house. He is in a
state of shock, and rants as if he were one of Greek trag-
edy's victims. Moschion and Demeas retire into the back-
ground.)*

ΝΙΚΗΡΑΤΟΣ

ὦ τάλας ἐγώ, τάλας·
οἷον εἰσιδὼν θέαμα, διὰ θυρῶν ἐπείγομαι
(706J)   ἐμμανής, ἀπροσδοκήτῳ καρδίαν πληγεὶς ἄχει.

ΔΗΜΕΑΣ

535   τί ποτ᾽ ἐρεῖ;

ΝΙΚΗΡΑΤΟΣ

τὴν θυγατέρ᾽ ἄ⟨ρτι⟩ τὴν ἐμὴν τῷ παιδίῳ
τιτθίον διδοῦσαν ἔνδον κατέλαβον.

ΔΗΜΕΑΣ

τοῦτ᾽ ἦν ἄρα.

ΜΟΣΧΙΩΝ

πάτερ, ἀκούεις;

ΔΗΜΕΑΣ

οὐδὲν ἀδικεῖς, Μοσχίων, ἐγὼ δέ σε,
ὑπονοῶν τοιαῦτα.

ΝΙΚΗΡΑΤΟΣ

πρός σε, Δημέα, πορεύομαι.

535 θυγατερατην B: suppl. Austin.
536 τιτθιον B with second τ wrongly crossed out.
536–37 Dicolon in B before τουτ᾽ and after ακουεις, but only
raised point after αρα; but in left margin of 537 μοσχ´ as indica-
tion of speaker. Part division here first suggested by Jacques,
Lowe.

NIKERATOS

(addressing the audience, but overheard by Demeas and Nikeratos)

Alas, alas—

What a sight befell my gaze! In frenzy through my por-
    tals I

Hasten out, with my heart stricken by an unexpected
    woe!

DEMEAS

(to Moschion)

What's he got to say?

NIKERATOS

(still to the audience)

[Just now] I found my daughter feeding the   535
Baby at her breast!

DEMEAS

(to Moschion)

So that's the explanation, then!

MOSCHION

You hear,

Father?

DEMEAS

Moschion, you do no wrong—but I did wrong to you,
With suspicions such as I had.

NIKERATOS

(now observing and approaching Demeas)

Demeas, I come to you!

MENANDER

ΜΟΣΧΙΩΝ

(711J) ἐκποδὼν ἄπειμι.

ΔΗΜΕΑΣ

θάρρει.

ΜΟΣΧΙΩΝ

τουτονὶ τέθνηχ᾽ ὁρῶν.

ΔΗΜΕΑΣ

540 τί τὸ πάθος δ᾽ ἐστίν;

ΝΙΚΗΡΑΤΟΣ

διδοῦσαν τιτθίον τῷ παιδίῳ
ἀρτίως ἔνδον κατέλαβον τὴν ἐμαυτοῦ θυγατέρα.

ΔΗΜΕΑΣ

τυχὸν ἔπαιζεν.

ΝΙΚΗΡΑΤΟΣ

οὐκ ἔπαιζεν. ὡς γὰρ εἰσιόντα μ[ε
εἶδεν, ἐξαίφνης κατέπεσεν.

ΔΗΜΕΑΣ

τυχὸν ἴσως ἔδοξέ [σοι.

544 Philostratus, *Vit. Apollon.* 7.22.

542–45 Suppl. ed.pr.

MOSCHION
(inching away from Nikeratos as he addresses Demeas)
I'll get off, out of the way!

DEMEAS
(seeing Moschion's panic)
> Be brave!

MOSCHION
(as he now darts off stage in the direction of the city centre)
> It's death, just seeing *him*![25]

DEMEAS
(to Nikeratos)
What's gone wrong?

NIKERATOS
(repeating to Demeas what he'd already told to the audience)
> Just now I came across my daughter feeding the   540
Baby at her breast indoors.

DEMEAS
> Perhaps she was pretending.

NIKERATOS
> No—
She was not pretending! When she saw me going in, you
    see,
She immediately fainted.

DEMEAS
> [You] perhaps imagined it.

---

[25] Nikeratos.

MENANDER

ΝΙΚΗΡΑΤΟΣ

(716J) παρατενεῖς "τυχόν" λέγων μοι πάντα.

ΔΗΜΕΑΣ

τούτων αἴτιος

545 εἴμ᾽ ἐγώ.

ΝΙΚΗΡΑΤΟΣ

τί φῄς;

ΔΗΜΕΑΣ

ἄπιστον πρᾶγμά μοι δοκεῖς λέγε[ιν.

ΝΙΚΗΡΑΤΟΣ

ἀλλὰ μὴ[ν] εἶδον.

ΔΗΜΕΑΣ

κορυζᾷς.

ΝΙΚΗΡΑΤΟΣ

οὗτος οὐκ ἔστιν λόγος.

(202K) ἀλλὰ πάλιν ἐλθών—

ΔΗΜΕΑΣ

τὸ δεῖνα· μικρόν, ὦ τᾶν—οἴχετ[αι.
πάντα πράγματ᾽ ἀνατέτραπται· τέλος ἔχει. νὴ τὸν
Δία,

(721J) οὑτοσὶ τὸ πρᾶγμ᾽ ἀκούσας χαλεπανεῖ, κεκράξεται.

547–686 B is joined again by C. 547 ταν C: ταλαν B.
Suppl. Lefebvre. 548 Corr. several: παντατα C,]τατα B.
:νηδια C (where presumably the dicolon indicates punctuation):
νητονδ[B. 549 ουτοσυ corrected to -σι B. καικραξεται
B with the omitted κε written above ικ.

138

SAMIA

NIKERATOS

Must you rile me, adding your "Perhaps" to all you say?

DEMEAS

(quietly, to himself)

This is
All my fault.

NIKERATOS
(overhearing Demeas, but not clearly)
What's that?

DEMEAS
I think that what you say's incredible!   545

NIKERATOS

But I *saw* her!

DEMEAS
Stuff and nonsense!

NIKERATOS

It's no fairy story, this!
Going back, though—

(Here Nikeratos rushes back into his house, presumably to check the reality of what he claimed to see.)

DEMEAS
(at first trying to address Nikeratos)
Tell you what—a moment, sir! He's disappeared!
Everything is topsyturvy. This has finished it, I'm sure.
Once he's heard the true position, he'll be furious and
scream.

550 τραχὺς ἄνθρωπος, σκατόφαγος, αὐθέκαστος τῷ
τρόπῳ.

(206K) ἐμὲ γὰρ ὑπονοεῖν τοιαῦτα τὸν μιαρὸν ἐχρῆν, ἐμέ.
νὴ τὸν Ἥφαιστον, δικαίως ἀποθάνοιμ᾽ ἄν.
Ἡράκλεις,
ἡλίκον κέκραγε τοῦτ᾽. ἤν, πῦρ βοᾷ. τὸ παιδίον

(726J) φησὶν ἐμπρήσειν, ἀπειλῶν. υἱδοῦν ὀπτώμενον

555 ὄψομαι. πάλιν πέπληχε τὴν θύραν. στρόβιλος ἢ

(211K) σκηπτὸς ἄνθρωπός τίς ἐστι.

ΝΙΚΗΡΑΤΟΣ

Δημέα, συνίσταται
ἐπί με καὶ πάνδεινα ποιεῖ πράγμαθ᾽ ἡ Χρυσίς.

ΔΗΜΕΑΣ

τί φής;

ΝΙΚΗΡΑΤΟΣ

τὴν γυναῖκά μου πέπεικε μηθὲν ὁμολογεῖν ὅλως,

(731J) μηδὲ τὴν κόρην, ἔχει δὲ πρὸς βίαν τὸ παιδίον,

551 μικρον B with κ crossed out and α written above.
553 Punctuation by van Leeuwen: (τουτ᾽ην B preceded by a
punctuating dicolon,]τουτ᾽ην C). βοατο C: αιτο B with
omitted τει written over ιτο. 554 εμπρησειναπειλων B:
α]πει[λων]εμπρησειν apparently C. υιωδουν BC: corr.
Richards.
555 οψωμαι B with ω crossed out and ο written above.
στροβειλ[..]η B, στροβιλος (with η omitted) C.
556 τις omitted by C. εστι C: εστιν B. συνισταται
C: νννισταται B. 557 επει B with second ε crossed out.
πανδειναποιει C: πανδειναάποει B. 558 μηθεν B: μηδεν C.

140

He's a bluff, vindictive creature, harsh and wilful in his   550
  ways.
I'm disgusting, I am—I should never have suspected
  things
Like that! Heavens, I deserve to have my throat cut. Oh,
  my god!

(*Here shouts and screams are heard, coming from
Nikeratos' house.*)

Hear the volume of his screaming! See, he calls for fire.
  He says
He'll cremate the baby, that's his threat. I'll see my
  grandson now
Being roasted! He's just clanged the door again. The   555
  man is a
Hurricane, a whirlwind!

(*During the last two verses the door has been squeaking
and clanging loudly, as Nikeratos opens it and rushes out to
Demeas again.*)

NIKERATOS
           Demeas, your Chrysis plots against
Me, and she is doing the most dreadful things!

DEMEAS
                 What do you say?

NIKERATOS
She's persuaded my wife not to admit to anything at
  all—
And my daughter. She's used force to grab the baby, and
  she vows

141

560 οὐ προήσεσθαί τε φησίν, ὥστε μὴ θαύμαζ᾽ ἐὰν
(216K) αὐτόχειρ αὐτῆς γένωμαι.

ΔΗΜΕΑΣ
        τῆς γυναικὸς αὐτόχειρ;

ΝΙΚΗΡΑΤΟΣ
πάντα γὰρ σύνοιδεν αὕτη.

ΔΗΜΕΑΣ
        μηδαμῶς, Νικήρατε.

ΝΙΚΗΡΑΤΟΣ
σοὶ δ᾽ ἐβουλόμην προειπεῖν.

ΔΗΜΕΑΣ
        οὑτοσὶ μελαγχολᾷ.

(736J) εἰσπεπήδηκεν. τί τούτοις τοῖς κακοῖς τις χρήσεται;
565 οὐδεπώποτ᾽ εἰς τοιαύτην ἐμπεσών, μὰ τοὺς θεούς,
(221K) οἶδα ταραχήν. ἔστι μέντοι τὸ γεγονὸς φράσαι
    σαφῶς
πολὺ κράτιστον. ἀλλ᾽, Ἄπολλον, ἡ θύρα πάλιν
    ψοφεῖ.

567 καρτιστον B.

---

26 Here Nikeratos is clearly threatening to kill Chrysis, not his
own wife, as some scholars have mistakenly believed; see espe-
cially the Gomme–Sandbach commentary, *ad loc.*

SAMIA

She won't hand it over, so don't be surprised if I become   560
Her[26] assassin!

DEMEAS

You assassinate *my* partner?

NIKERATOS

Yes—you see,
She's aware of all that's happened!

DEMEAS

Don't, Nikeratos!

NIKERATOS

But I
Wished to give you prior warning!

(Nikeratos now darts back inside his house.)

DEMEAS

This chap here's stark staring mad!
He's rushed off inside. How's one to deal with these
    calamities?
I have never known myself involved in such a mess   565
    before,
That I swear! It's far the best, however, for me to explain
Plainly what has happened. Heavens, there's the door
    creaking again!

*(The creaking of the door is followed by the emergence
from Nikeratos' house of Chrysis running with the baby,
pursued by Nikeratos waving his stick.)*

143

ΧΡΥΣΙΣ

ὦ τάλαιν᾽ ἐγώ, τί δράσω; ποῖ φύγω; τὸ παιδίον
(741J) λήψεταί μου.

ΔΗΜΕΑΣ

Χρυσί, δεῦρο.

ΧΡΥΣΙΣ

τίς καλεῖ μ᾽;

ΔΗΜΕΑΣ

εἴσω τρέχε.

ΝΙΚΗΡΑΤΟΣ

570 ποῖ σύ, ποῖ φεύγεις;

ΔΗΜΕΑΣ

Ἄπολλον, μονομαχήσω τήμερον,
(226K) ὡς ἔοικ᾽, ἐγώ. τί βούλει; τίνα διώκεις;

ΝΙΚΗΡΑΤΟΣ

Δημέα,
ἐκποδὼν ἄπελθ᾽. ἔα με, γενόμενον τοῦ παιδίου
ἐγκρατῆ, τὸ πρᾶγμ᾽ ἀκοῦσαι τῶν γυναικῶν.

ΔΗΜΕΑΣ

μηθαμῶς.

569 ἐσω B.
573 μαινομαι B with η θαμως written above αινομαι as cor-
rection: μαινεται C.

---

[27] On the possible relevance of this remark to the dating of the
play, see introduction.

144

CHRYSIS

Oh, dear me! What can I do? Where can I find asylum?
  He'll
Seize my baby!

DEMEAS

Chrysis, here!

CHRYSIS

(*still running and not turning her head yet to face Demeas*)
                    Who calls my name?

DEMEAS

                                  Just run inside!

(*Chrysis runs and now takes shelter behind Demeas.*)

NIKERATOS

(*to Chrysis*)
You, where are you going? Where?

DEMEAS

(*standing between Nikeratos and Chrysis*)
                    O God, I'll fight a duel,[27] it   570
Seems, today. What do you want? Who are you chasing?

NIKERATOS

                                  Demeas,
Move out of my way! Let me first take possession of the
  child,
And then hear the women's version of what's happened.

DEMEAS

(*keeping his ground and pushing Nikeratos back*)
                                  Never!

145

MENANDER

ΝΙΚΗΡΑΤΟΣ

(746J) ἀλλὰ τυπτήσεις μ';

ΔΗΜΕΑΣ
ἔγωγε. θᾶττον εἰσφθάρηθι σύ.

ΝΙΚΗΡΑΤΟΣ
575 ἀλλὰ μὴν κἀγώ σε.

ΔΗΜΕΑΣ
φεῦγε, Χρυσί· κρείττων ἐστί μου.

ΝΙΚΗΡΑΤΟΣ
(231K) πρότερος ἅπτει μοι σὺ νυνί· ταῦτ' ἐγὼ μαρτύρομαι.

ΔΗΜΕΑΣ
σὺ δ' ἐπ' ἐλευθέραν γυναῖκα λαμβάνεις βακτηρίαν
καὶ διώκεις.

ΝΙΚΗΡΑΤΟΣ
συκοφαντεῖς.

574 τυπησεις and εισφθαρητι B.   Dicolon in C after
εγωγε but not after συ.

575 καγωσε B: καγ[ω]γ[ε apparently C.   κριττων B.

576 C wrongly has a dicolon after νυνι, and B wrongly adds
δημεας in the right-hand margin as identification of the speaker.

---

28 By pushing Nikeratos back here, and so preventing him
from reaching Chrysis, Demeas technically strikes the first blow
in the brawl between him and Nikeratos; cf. v. 576. In Athenian
law the man who struck the first blow was deemed guilty of as-
sault. See especially D. M. MacDowell, *The Law in Classical Ath-
ens* (London 1978) 123–24, and D. Cohen, *Law, Violence and
Community in Classical Athens* (Cambridge 1995) 119–42.

NIKERATOS

Then
Will you strike me first?[28]

DEMEAS
(first facing up to Nikeratos, then shouting to Chrysis)
I will! You get to hell inside, and quick!

NIKERATOS

But I'll wallop you!

(As he says this Nikeratos now physically attacks Demeas, who fights back. Chrysis meanwhile dithers, clutching the baby.)

DEMEAS
Run, Chrysis! He's a stronger man than me.   575

(Chrysis now runs off with the baby into Demeas' house. With her departure the fight between Demeas and Nikeratos ends, and they resume their verbal dispute.)

NIKERATOS
You have struck me first today—I testify to that.[29]

DEMEAS

And you
Too have raised a stick against a woman of free birth,
    and chased
Her!

NIKERATOS
    You're lying![30]

[29] See note on v. 574.   [30] Literally 'You're making a vexatious (and probably false) accusation.'

147

ΔΗΜΕΑΣ
καὶ σὺ γάρ.

ΝΙΚΗΡΑΤΟΣ
τὸ παιδίον

(751J) ἐξένεγκέ μοι.

ΔΗΜΕΑΣ
γελοῖον· τοὐμόν.

ΝΙΚΗΡΑΤΟΣ
ἀλλ᾽ οὐκ ἔστι σόν.

ΔΗΜΕΑΣ
580 ἐμόν.

ΝΙΚΗΡΑΤΟΣ
ἰὼ ᾽νθρωποι.

ΔΗΜΕΑΣ
κέκραχθι.

ΝΙΚΗΡΑΤΟΣ
τὴν γυναῖκ᾽ ἀποκτενῶ

(236K) εἰσιών· τί γὰρ ποήσω;

ΔΗΜΕΑΣ
τοῦτο μοχθηρὸν πάλιν.
οὐκ ἐάσω. ποῖ σύ; μένε δή.

581 τιγαραν B.

---

31 Nikeratos' cry here is not addressed specifically to the audience, but to the world in general ('people' or 'men' literally). It

DEMEAS
And the same applies to you!

NIKERATOS
                                    Just bring the child
Out to me.

DEMEAS
You must be joking—it is *mine*!

NIKERATOS
                                    It's *not* yours, though!

DEMEAS
It is *mine!*

NIKERATOS
Oh, help me, anybody![31]

DEMEAS
                                    Bawl away!

NIKERATOS
                                              I'll go   580
In and kill your partner. What else can I do?

(*Nikeratos now tries to rush past Demeas in the direction
of Demeas' house, but Demeas raises his hand to prevent
him.*)

DEMEAS
                                    That's wicked, too!
I shan't let you. Where are you now going? Stop!

presumably echoed calls made in Athenian streets by people who
needed help and witnesses when they were being wronged. See
especially D. Bain, *ZPE* 44 (1981) 169–71 and 45 (1982) 27.

MENANDER

ΝΙΚΗΡΑΤΟΣ

μὴ πρόσαγε τὴν χεῖρά μοι.

ΔΗΜΕΑΣ

κάτεχε δὴ σεαυτόν.

ΝΙΚΗΡΑΤΟΣ

ἀδικεῖς, Δημέα, με, δῆλος εἶ,

(756J)   καὶ τὸ πρᾶγμα πᾶν σύνοισθα.

ΔΗΜΕΑΣ

τοιγαροῦν ἐμοὶ πυθοῦ,

585   τῇ γυναικὶ μὴ 'νοχλήσας μηδέν.

ΝΙΚΗΡΑΤΟΣ

ἆρ' ὁ σός με παῖς

(241K)   ἐντεθρίωκεν;

ΔΗΜΕΑΣ

φλυαρεῖς. λήψεται μὲν τὴν κόρην,
ἔστι δ' οὐ τοιοῦτον. ἀλλὰ περιπάτησον ἐνθαδὶ
μικρὰ μετ' ἐμοῦ.

ΝΙΚΗΡΑΤΟΣ

περιπατήσω;

586 Photius ε 1028 (s.v. ἐντεθριῶσθαι) has ἐντεθρίωκεν· τὸ
ἐσκεύακεν. ἔστι δὲ καὶ παρὰ Μενάνδρῳ; see Chr. Theodoridis,
ZPE 82 (1990) 42–43, and his edition, II p. 104.

583 σαυτον C (with no dicolon after it).   584 οισθα B.
585 την B with ν crossed out.   μηδεὲν B.
586 εντεθρειωκεν B.   587–88 μικρα (so B: μικρō =
μικρον C) misplaced at the end of 587 in BC: corr. several.

NIKERATOS

Don't lay your hand

On me!

DEMEAS
Now control yourself!

NIKERATOS
It's clear that you're ill-treating me,
Demeas, and you know all the facts in league with them!

DEMEAS

Well then,
Question me, and don't disturb at all my partner.

NIKERATOS

Has your son   585

Duped me?

DEMEAS
Nonsense! He will wed the girl, but circumstances are
Not what you imagine. Take a walk around here with me
   now—
Just a short one!

NIKERATOS

(*mystified*)

Must I?

ΔΗΜΕΑΣ

καὶ σεαυτόν γ᾿ ἀνάλαβε.

(761J) οὐκ ἀκήκοας λεγόντων, εἰπέ μοι, Νικήρατε,
590 τῶν τραγῳδῶν, ὡς γενόμενος χρυσὸς ὁ Ζεὺς ἐρρύη
(246K) διὰ τέγους, καθειργμένην τε παῖδ᾿ ἐμοίχευσέν ποτε;

ΝΙΚΗΡΑΤΟΣ

εἶτα δὴ τί τοῦτ᾿;

ΔΗΜΕΑΣ

ἴσως δεῖ πάντα προσδοκᾶν. σκόπει,
τοῦ τέγους εἴ σοι μέρος τι ῥεῖ.

ΝΙΚΗΡΑΤΟΣ

τὸ πλεῖστον. ἀλλὰ τί
(766J) τοῦτο πρὸς ἐκεῖν᾿ ἐστί;

ΔΗΜΕΑΣ

τότε μὲν γίνεθ᾿ ὁ Ζεὺς χρυσίον,
595 τότε δ᾿ ὕδωρ. ὁρᾷς; ἐκείνου τοὔργον ἐστίν. ὡς ταχὺ
(251K) εὕρομεν.

589 ακηκοασειπεμοιλεγον[C.
590 Corr. several: ὁζευσχρὺσος B, οζ[.]υ[.]χρ[. . .]s apparently C.   591 διατουτεγουσκατειργμενηνδε C.
593 τουτοτετους B with the second το and the fourth τ crossed out and a correcting γ written above that τ.
594 μενγαργεινεθ᾿ B.   595 οραιστ᾿ B.

32 Danae was locked by her father Acrisius, king of Argos, in a tower in order to preserve her virginity, but Zeus transformed himself into a shower of gold and ravished her, after which she

SAMIA

DEMEAS

                    Yes, and you must get a grip
On yourself! Nikeratos, just tell me, haven't you listened to
Our tragedians, who tell us how once Zeus turned into   590
    gold—
Dropping through a roof he ravished a young girl locked
    in a room.[32]

NIKERATOS

(*mystified even more*)
What of that, then?

DEMEAS

          We should be prepared for anything, perhaps—
Think—is any part of *your* roof leaking?

NIKERATOS

                          Most of it—but what's
That to do with what you said?

DEMEAS

          Zeus sometimes comes transformed to gold,
Sometimes, though, to rain—you follow? This is all *his*   595
    doing! How
Quickly now we've found the answer!

gave birth to Perseus. The story was popular in Greek drama.
Sophocles and Euripides each wrote a tragedy entitled *Danae*.
Aeschylus wrote a satyr play *Diktyoulkoi* (*The Netfishers*) dealing
with later events in the legend, when Danae and her baby were
shut in a chest and thrown into the sea by Acrisius; after floating to
the island of Seriphos they were rescued by the netfishers of
Aeschylus' title. Papyrus fragments from this play are printed in
volume II of the Loeb Aeschylus, pp. 531–41.

ΝΙΚΗΡΑΤΟΣ

καὶ βουκολεῖς με.

ΔΗΜΕΑΣ

μὰ τὸν Ἀπόλλω, 'γὼ μὲν οὔ.
ἀλλὰ χείρων οὐδὲ μικρὸν Ἀκρισίου δήπουθεν εἶ.
εἰ δ' ἐκείνην ἠξίωσε, τήν γε σὴν—

ΝΙΚΗΡΑΤΟΣ

οἴμοι τάλας.

(771J)   Μοσχίων ἐσκεύακέν με.

ΔΗΜΕΑΣ

λήψεται μέν, μὴ φοβοῦ

600   τοῦτο· θεῖον δ' ἐστ', ἀκριβῶς ἴσθι, τὸ γεγενημένον.
(256K)   μυρίους εἰπεῖν ἔχω σοι περιπατοῦντας ἐν μέσῳ
ὄντας ἐκ θεῶν· σὺ δ' οἴει δεινὸν εἶναι τὸ γεγονός.
Χαιρεφῶν πρώτιστος οὗτος, ὃν τρέφουσ'
ἀσύμβολον,

(776J)   οὐ θεός σοι φαίνετ' εἶναι;

ΝΙΚΗΡΑΤΟΣ

φαίνεται· τί γὰρ πάθω;

605   οὐ μαχοῦμαί σοι διὰ κενῆς.

596 τονεμου: B with the letters crossed out and γωμενου written above.

598 ειδ' C and (at first) B: ωσ B later.   γε C: τε B.

600 εστιν BC.   ικριβως B with first ι crossed out and α written above.   ἴσθι omitted in C.

603 πρωτιστ'ονς B with ν crossed out.

605 κεινης B.

NIKERATOS
　　　　　You are making fun of me!

DEMEAS
No, I'm not! You're every bit as noble as Acrisius,
Certainly. If Danaë deserved him, then your girl—

NIKERATOS
(distressed and interrupting)
　　　　　　　　　　　　　Oh dear!
Moschion has diddled me!

DEMEAS
　　　　　　　He'll wed her, have no fear of that.
What has happened is the work of higher powers, be　　600
　　quite, quite sure!
I can name for you so many sons of gods who walk
　　around
In our streets, and yet you think that our misfortune is
　　bizarre!
First there's Chaerephon,[33] who never pays his bill for
　　what he eats—
Don't you think that he's *divine*?

NIKERATOS
(puzzled about the relevance of Demeas' last remark)
　　　　　　　　I think so—oh, what can I do?
There's no point in fighting you there!

---

[33] A notorious Athenian parasite who had made a career of
dining out uninvited at other people's expense for ten years or
more. See especially my commentary (Cambridge 1996) on Alexis
fr. 213.1 K-A.

155

ΔΗΜΕΑΣ

νοῦν ἔχεις, Νικήρατε.

(261K) Ἀνδροκλῆς ἔτη τοσαῦτα ζῇ, τρέχει, πηδᾷ, πολὺ
πράττεται, μέλας περιπατεῖ. λευκὸς οὐκ ἂν
ἀποθάνοι,
οὐδ' ἂν εἰ σφάττοι τις αὐτόν. οὗτός ἐστιν οὐ θεός;

(781J) ἀλλὰ ταῦτ' εὔχου γενέσθαι [σ]υμφέροντα· θυμία·
610 σπένδε· τὴ]ν κόρην μέ[τε]ισ[ιν] οὑμὸς υἱὸς αὐτίκα.

ΝΙΚΗΡΑΤΟΣ

(266K) ἐξ ἀνάγκης ἐστὶ ταῦ[τ]α.

ΔΗΜΕΑΣ

πολλ[αχ]ῇ μ[ὲ]ν ν[ο]ῦν ἔχει[ς—

ΝΙΚΗΡΑΤΟΣ

εἰ δ' ἐλήφθη τότε—

ΔΗΜΕΑΣ

πέπαυσο· μὴ παροξύνου. πόει
τἄνδον εὐτρεπῆ.

606–11 omitted in B.
606 παιδα altered to πηδα apparently in C.
607 Punctuation after περιπατεῖ by Lefebvre.
609 Suppl. Lefebvre.
610 σπένδε suppl. Sudhaus, τὴ]ν Jensen (who deciphered κόρην), μέ[τε]ισ[ιν] van Leeuwen. υιος C.
611 ταῦ[τ]α and πολλ[αχ]ῇ μ[έ]ν suppl. Jensen (with part-division), ν[ο]ῦν Lefebvre, ἔχει[ς Körte.
612 B has one dicolon after τοτε and another (crossed out) before ποει.

DEMEAS

You show sense, Nikeratos. 605

Androcles[34] has lived a long time now. He runs, jumps,
   makes his pile,
Walks about with hair so dark—he'd never die with it
   turned grey,
No, not even if you cut his throat! So isn't he *divine*?
—You must pray, though, that this business turns out
   well. Let incense burn.
[Pour libations (?)]. Soon my son will come to take [his] 610
   bride away![35]

NIKERATOS

These things cannot be avoided.

DEMEAS

Frequently you talk good sense—

NIKERATOS

(*interrupting*)
If he'd[36] only then been caught—

DEMEAS

(*interrupting*)

Enough! Don't be upset! Make sure
Things are ready in your house.

---

[34] An otherwise unidentified Athenian. The references to
his running, jumping, and making his pile are obscure; he may
have been an athlete who had become rich as a usurer making
loans. The length of both his and Chaerephon's career (and the
fact that Androcles' hair remained dark in old age) are jokingly
cited by Demeas as evidence of immortality. See especially the
Gomme–Sandbach commentary *ad loc*.

[35] See especially note on v. 159.   [36] Moschion.

ΝΙΚΗΡΑΤΟΣ

ποήσω.

ΔΗΜΕΑΣ

τὰ παρ᾽ ἐμοὶ δ᾽ ἐγώ.

ΝΙΚΗΡΑΤΟΣ

πόει.

ΔΗΜΕΑΣ

(786J)   κομψὸς εἶ. χάριν δὲ πολλὴν πᾶσι τοῖς θεοῖς ἔχω,
615   οὐθὲν εὑρηκὼς ἀληθὲς ὧν τότ᾽ ᾤμην γεγονέναι.

XO P OY

ΜΕΡΟΣ Ε´

ΜΟΣΧΙΩΝ

(271K)   ἐγὼ τότε μὲν ἧς εἶχον αἰτίας μάτην
ἐλεύθερος γενόμενος ἠγάπησα, καὶ
τοῦθ᾽ ἱκανὸν εὐτύχημ᾽ ἐμαυτῷ γεγονέναι
(791J)   ὑπέλαβον· ὡς δὲ μᾶλλον ἔννους γίνομαι,
620   καὶ λαμβάνω λογισμόν, ἐξέστηκα νῦν

614 C has dicolon after ει.
615 ουδεν C.
617 B has a dicolon after γενομενος.
618 ετυχημ᾽ B with the omitted ν written above the τ.
619 εννο[C: ευνους B.

NIKERATOS
I'll do that.

DEMEAS
So shall I in mine.

NIKERATOS

Do that.

(Nikeratos turns away from Demeas and moves off stage into his house.)

DEMEAS
(addressing his opening words to the departing Nikeratos)
      You're a brick!—And many thanks to all the
  gods, because
I have found that none of my suspicions has in fact   615
  proved true!

(Demeas goes off into his own house. When the stage is empty, the chorus give their fourth entr'acte performance.)

ACT V

(After the chorus's performance, Moschion comes on stage by the side entrance leading from town, where he has been since his departure at v. 539.)

MOSCHION

When I was cleared of the false charge I had
To face, I felt quite happy at the time,
And thought that this had been for me good luck
Enough. The more I ponder this and take
Account of it, though, I'm beside myself   620

(276K) τελέως ἐμαυτοῦ, καὶ παρώξυμμαι σφόδρα
ἐφ' οἷς μ' ὁ πατὴρ ὑπέλαβεν ἡμαρτηκέναι.
εἰ μὲν καλῶς οὖν εἶχε τὰ περὶ τὴν κόρην
(796J) καὶ μὴ τοσαῦτ' ἦν ἐμποδών, ὅρκος, πόθος,
625 χρόνος, συνήθει', οἷς ἐδουλούμην ἐγώ,
(281K) οὐκ ἂν παρόντα γ' αὖθις ᾐτιάσατο
αὐτόν με τοιοῦτ' οὐδέν, ἀλλ' ἀποφθαρεὶς
ἐκ τῆς πόλεως ἂν ἐκποδὼν εἰς Βάκτρα ποι
(801J) ἢ Καρίαν διέτριβον αἰχμάζων ἐκεῖ.
630 νῦν δ' οὐ ποήσω διὰ σέ, Πλαγγὼν φιλτάτη,
(286K) ἀνδρεῖον οὐθέν· οὐ γὰρ ἔξεστ', οὐδ' ἐᾷ
ὁ τῆς ἐμῆς νῦν κύριος γνώμης, Ἔρως.
οὐ μὴν ταπεινῶς οὐδ' ἀγεννῶς παντελῶς
(806J) παριδεῖν με δεῖ τοῦτ', ἀλλὰ τῷ λόγῳ μόνον,
635 εἰ μηθὲν ἄλλ', αὐτὸν φοβῆσαι βούλομαι,
(291K) φάσκων ἀπαίρειν. μᾶλλον εἰς τὰ λοιπὰ γὰρ
φυλάξεθ' οὗτος μηθὲν εἴς μ' ἀγνωμονεῖν,
ὅταν φέροντα μὴ παρέργως τοῦτ' ἴδῃ.

621 παροξυμμαι B.   622 μ' after πατὴρ in B.
623 ἐχει B.   625 εδουλομην B with the omitted ν written
above ομ.   626 αυτις C.   627 αυτῶ B.
631 ουδεν C.   634 Corr. Austin: παρειδεῖν B, παρ[..]ε[ι]ν
C.   635 μηδεν C.
637 -θ'οὗτος B: -τ'αυτις or -τ'ουτος C.   μηδεν C.

---

[1] Plangon.   [2] Bactria, covering the area between the river
Oxus (now Amu-Darya) and the Pamir and Hindu Kush moun-
tains in what is now mainly north Afghanistan, was being devel-
oped and Hellenised from the 320's until well after Menander's

Now absolutely, and I'm most upset at what
My father thought that I'd done wrong. So if
There'd been no problems with the girl,[1] and if
There weren't so many obstacles—my oath,
Desire, time, our relationship, all things   625
Which fetter me, he'd not have charged me with
An outrage like this to my face, but I'd
Have left this city, off to Bactria[2]
Somewhere, or Caria,[3] living my life
There as a soldier. But I shan't do anything   630
Brave, darling Plangon, now—because of *you*!
I can't. Love, ruler of my heart now, won't
Allow me. Yet I mustn't feebly or
Ignobly disregard this altogether, but
Just by a trick, if nothing else, I want   635
To scare him.[4] I'll *pretend* to go abroad.
He'll be more careful in the future not to treat
Me harshly, when he sees me taking this

death, needing Greek mercenaries both to supervise these devel-
opments and to control an unruly native populace. See especially
S. Sherwin-White and A. Kuhrt, *From Samarkhand to Sardis*
(London 1993) 103–105 and A. B. Bosworth in *CAH* 6[2] (1994)
818–26, 863, 867, and cf. my introduction above.

   [3] Caria occupied the southwestern corner of Asia Minor. Mili-
tary activity there during Menander's career was virtually con-
tinuous. See especially A. Mastrocinque, *La Caria e la Ionia
meridionale in epoca ellenistica* (Rome 1979) 15–51, G. Bean, *Tur-
key beyond the Maeander* (1971[1] London and Totowa N.J., 1980[2]
London) and S. Hornblower, *Mausolus* (Oxford 1982) 1–105, and
in *CAH* 6[2] (1994) 214–16, 225–30; and cf. my introductions to
Samia and to *Sikyonioi*.

   [4] Demeas.

(811J) ἀλλ' οὑτοσὶ γὰρ εἰς δέοντά μοι πάνυ
640 καιρὸν πάρεστιν ὃν μάλιστ' ἐβουλόμην.

ΠΑΡΜΕΝΩΝ

(296K) νὴ τὸν Δία τὸν μέγιστον, ἀνόητόν τε καὶ
εὐκαταφρόνητον ἔργον εἴμ' εἰργασμένος.
οὐθὲν ἀδικῶν ἔδεισα καὶ τὸν δεσπότην
(816J) ἔφυγον. τί δ' ἦν τούτου πεποηκὼς ἄξιον;
645 καθ' ἓν γὰρ οὑτωσὶ σαφῶς σκεψώμεθα.
(301K) ὁ τρόφιμος ἐξήμαρτεν εἰς ἐλευθέραν
κόρην· ἀδικεῖ δήπουθεν οὐδὲν Παρμένων.
ἐκύησεν αὕτη· Παρμένων οὐκ αἴτιος.
(821J) τὸ παιδάριον εἰσῆλθεν εἰς τὴν οἰκίαν
650 τὴν ἡμετέραν· ἤνεγκ' ἐκεῖνος, οὐκ ἐγώ.
(306K) τῶν ἔνδον ὡμολόγησε τοῦτό τις τεκεῖν·
τί Παρμένων ἐνταῦθα πεπόηκεν κακόν;
οὐθέν. τί οὖν οὕτως ἔφυγες, ἀβέλτερε
(826J) καὶ δειλότατε; γελοῖον. ἠπείλησέ με
655 στίξειν. μεμάθηκας. διαφέρε[ι δ' ἀ]λλ' οὐδὲ γρῦ
(311K) ἀδίκως [πα]θεῖν τοῦτ' ἢ δικαίως· ἔστι δὲ
π]άντα τρόπον οὐκ ἀστεῖον.

639 ουτοσει B.   643 ουδεν C.
644 εμφυγον B with μ crossed out.   πεποιηκὼς B.
647–48 Dicola in B before αδικει and after αυτη with the top
point crossed out in both places.   650 ηνηγκ᾽ B followed by a
dicolon.   651 ωμολογηκε C.   652 πεποιηκεν C, πε[B.
653 ουδε[C.   εφυγεσουτως C, εφευγεσουτος B: corr.
several.   654 μοι C.

162

So seriously. But here, just at the right
Time, comes the man I wanted most to see.   640

(Parmenon enters at the end of the preceding speech by the same side entrance that he had used in running off at v. 324. Parmenon does not notice Moschion, who stays in the background during the following speech.)

PARMENON

I swear by mighty Zeus that I have done
A deed that's foolish and contemptible!
Though innocent, I quailed and ran away
From master. Yet what had I done to justify
This? Let's consider clearly, point by point, like this.   645
One: Moschion seduced a free young lady.
Presumably here Parmenon has done no wrong.
Two: she got pregnant. Parmenon was not to blame.
Three: baby was then brought into our house.
He[5] carried it, not I. Four: someone in   650
Our house[6] alleged she was the baby's mother.
What crime has Parmenon committed here?
None! So why did you run away like that,
You fool, you coward? Ludicrous! He threatened
To brand me.[7] Now you know. It doesn't matter   655
A scrap if punishments are right or wrong—
It isn't nice, in either case!

---

[5] Moschion.   [6] Chrysis.   [7] At v. 323.

---

656 Suppl. von Arnim.   το στιχθηναι in right margin of B, explaining τοῦτ'.   657 Suppl. Lefebvre.

ΜΟΣΧΙΩΝ

οὗτος.

ΠΑΡΜΕΝΩΝ

χαῖρε σύ.

ΜΟΣΧΙΩΝ

ἀφεὶς ἃ φλυαρεῖς ταῦτα, θᾶττον εἴσιθι
(831J) εἴσω.

ΠΑΡΜΕΝΩΝ

τί ποήσων;

ΜΟΣΧΙΩΝ

χλαμύδα καὶ σπάθην τινὰ
660 ἔνεγκέ μοι.

ΠΑΡΜΕΝΩΝ

σπάθην ἐγώ σοι;

ΜΟΣΧΙΩΝ

καὶ ταχύ.

ΠΑΡΜΕΝΩΝ

(316K) ἐπὶ τί;

ΜΟΣΧΙΩΝ

βάδιζε, καὶ σιωπῇ τοῦθ’ ὅ σοι
εἴρηκα ποίει.

ΠΑΡΜΕΝΩΝ

τί δὲ τὸ πρᾶγμ’;

659 ποιησων C.
661 πονθ’ B with π crossed out and τ written above it.

164

MOSCHION

(*coming forward*)

Hey, you!

PARMENON

(*turning to face Moschion*)
Hello!

MOSCHION

Drop all this nonsense. Go inside,
And quick!

PARMENON

To do what?

MOSCHION

Bring me out a cloak
And sword![8]

PARMENON

Bring you a sword?

MOSCHION

Yes, quickly, too!   660

PARMENON

What for?

MOSCHION

Just go, and carry out my orders
In silence.

PARMENON

What's it all about?

[8] Typical hallmarks of a soldier; cf. e.g. *Perikeiromene* 354–55.

---

662 ποιει B with the first ι wrongly crossed out, ποει C.

ΜΟΣΧΙΩΝ

εἰ λήψομαι

ἱμάντα—

ΠΑΡΜΕΝΩΝ

μηδαμῶς· βαδίζω γάρ.

ΜΟΣΧΙΩΝ

τί οὖν

(836J)   μέλλεις; πρόσεισι νῦν ὁ πατήρ· δεήσεται

665   οὗτος καταμένειν, δηλαδή. δεήσεται

(321K)   ἄλλως μέχρι τινός· δεῖ γάρ. εἶθ᾽, ὅταν δοκῇ,

πεισθήσομ᾽ αὐτῷ. πιθανὸν εἶναι δεῖ μόνον

ὅ, μὰ τὸν Διόνυσον, οὐ δύναμαι ποεῖν ἐγώ.

(841J)   τοῦτ᾽ ἐστίν. ἐψόφηκε προϊὼν τὴν θύραν.

ΠΑΡΜΕΝΩΝ

670   ὑστερίζειν μοι δοκεῖς σὺ παντελῶς τῶν ἐνθάδε

(326K)   πραγμάτων, εἰδὼς δ᾽ ἀκριβῶς οὐθὲν οὐδ᾽ ἀκηκοὼς

διὰ κενῆς σαυτὸν ταράττεις εἰς ἀθυμίαν τ᾽ ἄγεις.

664 προσεισιν B.   665 καταμενεινμου C.
666 αλλ᾽ως BC: corr. several.   667 πειθανον B.
668 ὁ C: ου B.   670 παντωντων B.
671 τ᾽ακριβως B.   ουδεν C.   ουτ᾽ακηκοως B.
672 εισθαυμιαν B with θ crossed out, the missing θ added
above αυ, and an incorrect τ added before and above θαυ.

---

9 Moschion faultily assumes that Parmenon's search for cloak
and sword would immediately lead to Demeas' appearance on
stage.

MOSCHION
If I

Must grab a whip—

PARMENON
(moving slowly towards Demeas' door)
Not that! I'm going—

MOSCHION
(threateningly approaching Parmenon)

Why

Delay then?

(Parmenon now sprints into Demeas' house.)

—Now my father will appear.
He'll beg me clearly to stay here, he'll beg   665
A while in vain—he's got to—then, when it
Seems right, I'll yield to him. Only it's got
To sound convincing—I cannot *really* be!

(Demeas' door is now heard creaking.)

That's it! The door creaked—*he*[9] is coming out.

(Out from Demeas' house comes not Demeas, as Moschion had expected, but an excited Parmenon without either cloak or sword. The metre now turns to trochaic tetrameters.)

PARMENON
You're not up to date at all, I think, with what is going on   670
Here. You know precisely nothing, you've not heard a
single thing.
You've no reasons to be worried or to sink into despair!

ΜΟΣΧΙΩΝ

οὐ φέρεις;

ΠΑΡΜΕΝΩΝ

ποοῦσι γάρ σοι τοὺς γάμους· κεράννυται,
(846J)   θυμιᾶτ᾽, ἐνῆρκτ᾽, ἀνῆπται θύμαθ᾽ Ἡφαίστου φλογί.

ΜΟΣΧΙΩΝ

675 οὗτος, οὐ φέρεις;

ΠΑΡΜΕΝΩΝ

σὲ γάρ, ⟨σὲ⟩ περιμένουσ᾽ οὗτοι πάλαι.
(331K) μετιέναι τὴν παῖδα μέλλεις; εὐτυχεῖς· οὐδὲν κακὸν
ἐστί σοι. θάρρει· τί βούλει;

ΜΟΣΧΙΩΝ

νουθετήσεις μ᾽, εἰπέ μοι,
ἱερόσυλε;

ΠΑΡΜΕΝΩΝ

παῖ, τί ποιεῖς, Μοσχίων;

ΜΟΣΧΙΩΝ

οὐκ εἰσδραμὼν
(851J) θᾶττον ἐξοίσεις ἅ φημι;

673 οινοσκεραν C with νυται added above κεραν.

674 θυμιατ᾽ ανηπτ᾽ανηρκαι᾽ B with κ crossed out and τ writ-
ten above, θυμιαματ᾽[.....]ατ᾽αναπτεται C: corr. Austin
(ἐνῆρκτ᾽) and Kassel (transposition to ἐνῆρκτ᾽ ἀνῆπται).
θυματ᾽ C: σπλαγχναθ᾽ B.   πυρι B with correcting φλογι
written above.   675 ⟨σὲ⟩ omitted by BC, added by Sudhaus.

678 π[.]ιεις C: ποεις B.

679 φηηι B with 2nd η crossed out and μ written above.

MOSCHION

Have you not brought them?[10]

PARMENON

      Your wedding's on—the wine is being mixed,
Incense smokes, rites have begun, the meat is lit by fire
  god's flame.[11]

MOSCHION

Hey, you—have you brought them?

PARMENON

          They've been waiting ages for   675
You! Why now delay to fetch the bride?[12] You're lucky!
  You've no more
Troubles, so cheer up!—What *do* you want?

MOSCHION

(losing his temper and striking Parmenon in the face)
              Shall *you* give *me* advice,
Tell me, wretch!

PARMENON

      Oh, Moschion, what are you doing?

MOSCHION

                Just run in
There, and bring out what I said! Quick now!

[10] The cloak and sword.

[11] Parmenon describes events at the wedding in poetically elevated language. Wine drunk on such occasions was always diluted with water. On the use of incense see notes on vv. 127 and 159.

[12] See note on v. 75 and cf. notes on vv. 127 and 159.

169

MENANDER

ΠΑΡΜΕΝΩΝ

διακέκομμαι τὸ στόμα.

ΜΟΣΧΙΩΝ

680   ἔτι λαλεῖς οὗτος;

ΠΑΡΜΕΝΩΝ

βαδίζω. νὴ Δί', ἐξεύρηκά γε

(336K)   τόδε κακόν.

ΜΟΣΧΙΩΝ

μέλλεις;

ΠΑΡΜΕΝΩΝ

ἄγουσι τοὺς γάμους ὄντως.

ΜΟΣΧΙΩΝ

πάλιν;

ἕτερον ἐξάγγελλέ μοί τι.—νῦν πρόσεισιν. ἂν δέ μου
μὴ δέητ', ἄνδρες, καταμένειν, ἀλλ' ἀποργισθεὶς ἐᾷ
(856J)   ἀπιέναι—τουτὶ γὰρ ἄρτι παρέλιπον—τί δεῖ ποεῖν;
685   ἀλλ' ἴσως οὐκ ἂν ποήσαι τοῦτ'. ἐὰν δέ; πάντα γὰρ
(341K)   γίνεται. γελοῖος ἔσομαι, νὴ Δί', ἀνακάμπτων πάλιν.

680 λαχεις B with χ crossed out and λ written above.
εξευρηκατε C.
    681 οντως:παλιν B: οντωσι C.   Punctuation after πάλιν
by Sandbach.
    682 εξαγγειλαι B.   μοιννν B with first ν written on
incompleted π (had the scribe misread τι in his source?).
    683 παροργισθεις B.   ειαι B with first ι crossed out.
    686 (341K) is the last verse extant in C.

PARMENON

(ruefully, feeling his lip)

My lip's split open!

MOSCHION

Still

Talking, are you?

PARMENON

(preparing to go, but still feeling his lip)

I am going—but I've found it's painful, this—   680

MOSCHION

Still not moving?

PARMENON

But your wedding's *really* on now!

*(After he has said this and heard Moschion's response, at
v. 682 Parmenon disappears into Demeas' house.)*

MOSCHION

That again?[13]

Tell me something different!—He'll[14] come now. If he
    doesn't beg

Me to stay here, gentlemen,[15] but blows his top and lets
    me go

Off abroad—I didn't think of that before—what must I
    do?

Yet perhaps he wouldn't do that—if he does, though—all   685
    things are

Possible—I'll look a fool if I backpedal, that's for sure!

---

[13] As at v. 673.   [14] Moschion is still expecting his father to
appear.   [15] See note at v. 269.

ΠΑΡΜΕΝΩΝ

ἤν· χλαμὺς πάρεστιν αὕτη καὶ σπάθη· ταυτὶ λαβέ.

ΜΟΣΧΙΩΝ

δεῦρο δός. τῶν ἔνδον οὐθείς σ᾽ εἶδεν;

ΠΑΡΜΕΝΩΝ

οὐθείς.

ΜΟΣΧΙΩΝ

οὐδὲ εἷς

(861J)   παντελῶς;

ΠΑΡΜΕΝΩΝ

οὔ φημι.

ΜΟΣΧΙΩΝ

τί λέγεις; ἀλλά σ᾽ ὁ Ζεὺς ἀπολέσαι.

ΠΑΡΜΕΝΩΝ

690   πρόαγ᾽ ὅποι μέλλεις· φλυαρεῖς.

(At this point Parmenon reenters from Demeas' house, furtively checking that he hasn't been seen. He carries a soldier's cloak and sword, presumably in its scabbard, along with a belt or baldric.)

PARMENON

See—I have a cloak here and a sword too. Take them now.

MOSCHION
(hoping that Demeas had in fact seen Parmenon and would follow him out)
Give them here. Did no one in there see you?

PARMENON
(handing everything over but still unaware of Moschion's real intentions)

No one!

MOSCHION
(disappointed and becoming irritated)

No one at All?

PARMENON

I tell you, none!

MOSCHION

What's that you say? God damn and blast you now!

PARMENON
(assuming—or pretending to assume—that Moschion really intends to go abroad and serve as a mercenary soldier)
You go off where you intend. You're blathering!

173

ΔΗΜΕΑΣ

εἶτα ποῦ 'στιν, εἰπέ μοι;

παῖ, τί τοῦτο;

ΠΑΡΜΕΝΩΝ

πρόαγε θᾶττον.

ΔΗΜΕΑΣ

ἡ στολὴ τί β[ούλετα]ι;

τί τὸ πάθος; μέλλεις ἀπαίρειν, εἰπέ μ[οι, σύ,

Μοσχίων;

ΠΑΡΜΕΝΩΝ

ὡς ὁρᾷς, ἤδη βαδίζει κἄστιν ἐν ὁδῷ. [νῦν δὲ δεῖ

(866J)   κἀμὲ τοὺς ἔνδον προσειπεῖν· ἔρχο[μ᾿ εἴσω.

ΔΗΜΕΑΣ

[Μοσχίων,

695   ὅτι μὲν ὀργίζει, φιλῶ σε, κοὐχ[ὶ μέμφομαί τί σοι.

εἰ λελύπησαι γὰρ ἀδίκως, αἰτίαν ἔ[γωγ᾿ ἔχω.

ἀλλ᾿ ἐκεῖν᾿ ὅμως θεώρει· τίνι πικρὸ[ν τὸ πρᾶγμ᾿;

ἐμοί.

691 προαγεϊθϊθαττον B: corr. Austin.   β[ούλετα]ι suppl.
ed.pr.   692 μ[οι suppl. ed.pr., the rest Austin.
693 Suppl. West (νῦν δὲ also several).   694 εἴσω suppl.
Barigazzi, the rest ed.pr.   695 οττι B with first τ crossed out.
695–96 Suppl. Austin *exempli gratia*.
697 Suppl. Rossi (ἐμοί also Sisti).

16 Whether Parmenon is serious here or play-acting, as a slave
he is committed to look after Moschion whatever he decides to do.

174

(Demeas now comes out of his house, looking for Moschion. His first remark is addressed back to people in his house, but then he sees Moschion, who has presumably been putting on his cloak, fastening the belt or baldric and attaching the sword to it.)

DEMEAS

                    Then tell me, where   690

Is he? Oh! What's this?

PARMENON

              Quick, off you go!

DEMEAS

                      What does this fancy dress

[Mean]? What's happened? Tell [me, Moschion], do you
   plan to decamp?

PARMENON

As you see, he's marching now, he's on his way. I too
   [must now]

Say goodbye to those indoors.[16] I'm going [in now].

(Parmenon goes off into Demeas' house.)

DEMEAS

(alone with Moschion)

                      [Moschion],

I love you for being angry, and I don't [blame you]. If   695
   you've

Been unfairly wounded, [I accept] responsibility.

Yet you must consider this too. Who's been hurt by [this
   affair]?

MENANDER

εἰμὶ γὰρ πατήρ. ἐ[γώ ποτ᾽ ἀν]αλαβών σε παιδίον

(871J) ἐξέθρεψ᾽. εἴ σοι [χρόνος τι]ς γέγονεν ἡδὺς τοῦ βίου,
700 τοῦτόν εἰμ᾽ ὁ δοὺς [ἔγωγε], δι᾽ ὃν ἀνασχέσθαι σε
    δεῖ

καὶ τὰ λυπήσαντα [παρ᾽ ἐ]μοῦ, καὶ φέρειν τι τῶν
    ἐμῶν

ὡς ἂν ὑόν. οὐ δικαί[ως] ἡτιασάμην τί σε.

ἠγνόησ᾽· ἥμαρτον· ἐμάνην. ἀλλ᾽ ἐκεῖν᾽ ὀρ[θῶς
    σκόπει,

(876J) εἴς γε τοὺς ἄλλους ἁμαρτών, σοῦ πρόνοιαν ἡλίκη[ν
705 εἶχον, ⟨ἐν⟩ ἐμαυτῷ τ᾽ ἐτήρουν τοῦθ᾽ ὃ δή ποτ᾽
    ἠγνόουν·

οὐχὶ τοῖς ἐχθροῖς ἔθηκα φανερὸν ἐπιχαίρειν. σὺ δὲ
τὴν ἐμὴν ἁμαρτίαν νῦν ἐκφέρεις, καὶ μάρτυρας
ἐπ᾽ ἐμὲ τῆς ἐμῆς ἀνοίας λαμβάνεις. οὐκ ἀξιῶ,

(881J) Μοσχίων. μὴ μνημονεύσῃς ἡμέραν μου τοῦ βίου
710 μίαν ἐν ᾗ διεσφάλην τι, τῶν δὲ πρόσθεν ἐπιλάθῃ.
πόλλ᾽ ἔχων λέγειν, ἐάσω. καὶ γὰρ οὐ καλῶς ἔχει
πατρὶ μόλις πείθεσθ᾽, ἀκριβῶς ἴσθι, τὸ δ᾽ ἑτοίμως
    καλόν.

698 Suppl. Lowe (ἐ[γὼ…ἀν]αλαβών also Webster).

699 ση[B with η crossed out and ο[ι (?)] written above.
χρόνος suppl. Barigazzi, τι]ς several.   700 Suppl. several
(ἐγώ σοι Handley, Barigazzi).   701–702 Suppl. ed.pr.

703 Suppl. Austin.   704 γε Sandbach: τε B.   Before
σοῦ B has a crossed-out dicolon.   ἡλίκη[ν suppl. ed.pr.

705 εἶχον Arnott: εσχον B.   ἐν om. B, suppl. several.

712 πείθεσθαι Arnott, Mette: πιθεσθαι B.

[*I have!*] I'm your father. I adopted you [once] as a child.
I have brought you up. If [any moment] in your life's
   been sweet,
I provided this for you, and that's why you should toler-   700
   ate
Acts [of] mine that may distress you, and put up with all
   my faults,
As a son should. I accused you wrong[ly], didn't know
   the facts,
Made an error. I was crazy. But [take due account of]
   this:
How I favoured your own wishes when I'd acted badly to
Others, how I always kept my false suspicions [to] my-   705
   self.
I have never publicised them for my enemies to crow
Over. Now, though, you have advertised my blunder, you
   create
Witnesses against me of my folly! I don't think that's
   right,
Moschion. Don't just remember one day in my life when
   I
Made a slip, and overlook the times that came before. I   710
   could
Add much more, but I'll stop there. Do realise, it isn't
   good
To obey a father grudgingly—no, *cheerfully* is best!

(*Nikeratos now enters from his house. His opening re-
marks are addressed back to his wife inside. Then he sees
Moschion, dressed as a soldier.*)

177

MENANDER

ΝΙΚΗΡΑΤΟΣ

μὴ 'νόχλει μοι. πάντα γέγονε· λουτρά, προτέλει', οἱ
  γάμοι·
(886J) ὥστ' ἐκεῖνος, ἄν ποτ' ἔλθῃ, τὴν κόρην ἄπεισ' ἔχων.
715 παῖ, τί τοῦτ';

ΔΗΜΕΑΣ

οὐκ οἶδ' ἔγωγε, μὰ Δία.

ΝΙΚΗΡΑΤΟΣ

πῶς οὐκ οἶσθα σύ;
χλαμύς· ἀπαίρειν οὑτοσί που διανοεῖται.

ΔΗΜΕΑΣ

φησὶ γοῦν.

ΝΙΚΗΡΑΤΟΣ

φησὶν οὗτος; τίς δ' ἐάσει, μοιχὸν ὄντ' εἰλημμένον,
ὁμολογοῦντ'; ἤδη σε δήσω, μειράκιον, οὐκ εἰς
  μακράν.

ΜΟΣΧΙΩΝ

(891J) δῆσον, ἱκετεύω.

713 fr. 903 K-T.

716 χαμυς B with omitted λ written above the α.

178

NIKERATOS

Don't you fuss me! Everything's *done*!—Baths. First
  rites. The wedding. So
If that fellow ever turns up, he can take his bride away![17]
Oh! What's this?

DEMEAS

(teasing Nikeratos by playing along with Moschion)
       I swear I've no idea!

NIKERATOS

          You must have, though! A cloak!   715
This young puppy's planning to decamp, I think!

DEMEAS

                 That's what he says.

NIKERATOS

(angrily)
He says? Who'll allow him? He's a self-confessed
  seducer, who's
Been caught in the act! Young man, I'll tie you up
  directly now!

MOSCHION

*(drawing his sword when Nikeratos approaches him
threateningly)*
Tie me up, please!

[17] Nikeratos refers to two aspects of the wedding ceremony
that have been completed (the prenuptial baths of the womenfolk
and the 'first rites,' i.e. the προτέλεια or preliminary sacrifice) and
to one that remains to be accomplished (the bridegroom's taking
the bride from her parent's house to his). See notes on vv. 75 and
125.

ΝΙΚΗΡΑΤΟΣ

φλυαρεῖς πρός μ' ἔχων. οὐ καταβαλεῖς
720 τὴν σπάθην θᾶττον;

ΔΗΜΕΑΣ

κατάβαλε, Μοσχίων· πρὸς τῶν θεῶν,
μὴ παροξύνῃς.

ΜΟΣΧΙΩΝ

ἀφείσθω· καταλελιπαρήκατε
δεόμενοί μου.

ΝΙΚΗΡΑΤΟΣ

σοῦ δεόμενοι; δεῦρο δή.

ΜΟΣΧΙΩΝ

δήσεις μ' ἴσως;

ΔΗΜΕΑΣ

μηδαμῶς. ἔξω κόμιζε δεῦρο τὴν νύμφην.

ΝΙΚΗΡΑΤΟΣ

δοκεῖ;

ΔΗΜΕΑΣ

(896J) πάνυ μὲν οὖν.

720 καταβε B: corr. several.
721 παροξυνος B: corr. several.
722 δευροηδη B: corr. several.
723 μηδαμως originally omitted in B but added in left margin.

180

NIKERATOS
(nonplussed)
> Keeping up this nonsense with me? Won't you put
Up your sword, without delay?

DEMEAS
> Do put it up. Don't badger him,   720
Moschion, for heaven's sake!

MOSCHION
(sheathing his sword and letting it fall to the ground)
> I'll drop it. Your appeals to me
Have succeeded.

NIKERATOS
(again angry)
> My appeals to you? Come here!

MOSCHION
(pretending to be afraid of Nikeratos)
> He's going to
Tie me up, perhaps?

DEMEAS
(ending the banter and addressing Nikeratos)
> No, never! Bring the bride out here!

NIKERATOS
(looking at both Demeas and Moschion)
> Agreed?

DEMEAS
Certainly!

(Nikeratos accordingly goes off into his own house.)

ΜΟΣΧΙΩΝ

εἰ τοῦτ᾽ ἐποίεις εὐθύς, οὐκ ἂν πράγματα
725 εἶχες, ὦ πάτερ, φιλοσοφῶν ἄρτι.

ΝΙΚΗΡΑΤΟΣ

πρόαγε δὴ σύ μοι.
—μαρτύρων ἐναντίον σοι τήνδ᾽ ἐγὼ δίδωμ᾽ ἔχειν
γνησίων παίδων ἐπ᾽ ἀρότῳ, προῖκα τἀμὰ πάνθ᾽—
ὅταν
ἀποθάνω γ᾽· ὃ μὴ γένοιτ᾽, ἀλλ᾽ ‹εἰσ›αεὶ ζῴην.

ΜΟΣΧΙΩΝ

ἔχω,
(901J) λαμβάνω, στέργω.

ΔΗΜΕΑΣ

τὸ λοιπόν ἐστι λουτρὰ μετιέναι.
730 Χρυσί, πέμπε τὰς γυναῖκας, λουτροφόρον,
αὐλητρίδα.

724 εποισεις and 725 εχεις B: corr. several.
725 συνδευρομοι B: corr. Austin.
727 τωνπαιδων B: corr. several.   ταμανθ᾽ B: corr.
Handley.
728 τομη B: corr. several.   αλλ᾽αει B: corr. Sandbach,
West.

MOSCHION

If you had done that straight away, you wouldn't have
Had to bother, father, just now with this moralising!

*(Nikeratos now returns, bringing Plangon with him. She
eventually stands by Moschion.)*

NIKERATOS
(first to Plangon, then to Moschion)

Go   725
Forward, please.—In front of witnesses I give this girl to
    you
As your wife, to harvest lawful children.[18] And a
    dowry—all
My possessions—when I die. I hope this won't occur,
    and I'll
Live for ever![19]

MOSCHION
(taking Plangon's hand)

Thus I hold, take, cherish her.

DEMEAS
(eventually going to his door to address Chrysis inside)

One thing remains—
We must fetch the holy water.—Chrysis, send the   730
    women, the

---

[18] Nikeratos uses the standard formula of betrothal, with its
quaintly agricultural wording; see note 1 on *Dyskolos* v. 843.

[19] The announcement of the dowry was an integral part of the
betrothal ceremony. Here Nikeratos, a poor man, breaks the nor-
mal rule by not promising to hand the dowry over at the time of
the wedding.

MENANDER

δεῦρο δ' ἡμῖν ἐκδότω τις δᾷδα καὶ στεφάνους, ἵνα
συμπροπέμπωμεν.

ΜΟΣΧΙΩΝ

πάρεστιν ὅδε φέρων.

ΔΗΜΕΑΣ

πύκαζε σὺ
κρᾶτα καὶ κόσμει σεαυτόν.

ΜΟΣΧΙΩΝ

ἀλλ' ἐγώ.

ΔΗΜΕΑΣ

παῖδες καλοί,
(906J) μειράκια, γέροντες, ἄνδρες, πάντες εὐρώστως ἅμα
735 πέμψ[α]τ' εὐνοίας προφήτην Βακχίῳ φίλον κρότον.
ἡ δὲ κα]λλίστων ἀγώνων πάρεδρος ἄφθιτος θεὰ
737 εὐμε]νὴς ἕποιτο Νίκη τοῖς ἐμοῖς ἀεὶ χοροῖς.

731 B may have an incorrect dicolon before ἵνα.
734 μιρακια B: corr. several.   735–37 Suppl. ed.pr.

20 The bridegroom has arrived late, and still needs to take his ritual prenuptial bath, for which water from a sacred spring (Callirrhoe in Athens) was needed. A young relative of the bridegroom (as 'water bearer') was sent to fetch it in a special vase (also called 'water bearer'); he would be accompanied by womenfolk. The piper mentioned was a female slave who would play for the procession accompanying Moschion when he escorted his bride to his own house. See note on v. 127 and the works cited there, along with the introduction and notes to *Fabula Incerta* 9.

21 The Greek here has 'Bacchus,' one of the names of Dionysus.   22 Demeas closes the play with a variant (in the trochaic-

Bearer, and the piper.[20] Some one give us torch and gar-
    lands here,
Then we can escort them home.

*(A slave enters from Demeas' house, carrying torches and
garlands, which he distributes to the characters on stage.)*

MOSCHION
He's got them here.

DEMEAS
(to Moschion)

Now crown your head,
Put your best clothes on!

MOSCHION
I'll do that!

DEMEAS
(turning to the audience)

Handsome boys, young men and old,
Gentlemen, now all together loudly give applause that's
    prized
By our god of theatre,[21] as evidence of your goodwill!   735
May [the] patron of our noblest games, immortal Vic-
    tory,
Visit too my cast and chorus with her favour evermore![22]

tetrameter metre used throughout the scene) of the iambic-
trimeter formula that ends other plays by Menander (*Dyskolos*
965–69, *Misoumenos* 993–96 Arnott = 463–66 Sandbach, *Sikyo-
nioi* 420–23) and other playwrights of the New Comedy such as
Posidippus (fr. 6.11–13 K-A); cf. also *P.Oxyrhynchus* 1239 (as-
signed doubtfully to Menander by Kassel–Austin, *PCG* VI.2 fr.
903).

MENANDER

Two Fragments Doubtfully Attributed to the Play

1 *P.Berlin* 8450

This scrap of papyrus, containing the middle letters of 21 iambic trimeters, was attributed to the *Samia* by its original editors, W. Luppe and W. Müller, because v. 2 mentions a character named Chrysis. The editors suggested that the scrap could have fallen in one of B's gaps during an early monologue: either Moschion's prologue (between vv. 29 and 31 or between 57 and 59), his slightly later speech (between vv. 85 and 86), or Chrysis' entrance monologue (between 57 and 59). The attribution and placings are conceivable, but the Chrysis of *Samia* was not the only character with this name in Menander (the *hetaira* in his *Eunouchos* had this name: see Σ Persius, Sat. 5.161), and it turns up also in the Roman adaptations of New Comedy (Plautus *Pseudolus* 659, Terence *Andria* 85, Trabea fr. I. 3 Ribbeck). A different source for this fragment is possible and perhaps likely; Kassel–Austin consign it to their adeswere (*PCG* VIII fr. 1131). Yet see also my comments on the opposite page.

$$] \ \pi\rho\grave{o}s \ \grave{\epsilon}\mu\alpha\upsilon\tau\grave{o}\nu \ [$$
$$]\eta\nu \ X\rho\upsilon\sigma\acute{\iota}\delta' \ [$$
$$] \ \tau o\hat{\upsilon}\tau o\nu \ \epsilon\iota[$$
$$]. \ \grave{\epsilon}\kappa\epsilon\acute{\iota}\nu\eta\nu \ [$$

Supplements by ed.pr.
3 Or] τοῦτο νει[.

SAMIA

*Two Fragments, One On Papyrus and the Other
an Ancient Quotation, Have Been Assigned to This
Play On Doubtful Grounds.*

1

*A papyrus scrap containing a few letters from each of 21
lines. A few words can be made out:* to myself *1,* Chrysis *2,*
this *3,* that *or* her *4,* you see, what *or* you see, whom *5,* he *or*
she is free *6,* she (?) was tearing her (?) hair *7,* the other day
8, and that *9,* for . . . came down *(or* back) *10,* fine (?) *12,* for
there *13,* unlucky *14,* and (?) *16. The mention of Chrysis
and a scenario in which the free girl Plangon came down
from the roof tearing her hair after her violation would fit
well into Samia, best perhaps in the gap between vv. 57 and
58, where Chrysis on her first entrance could have added
details about Plangon's violation which Moschion either
did not know or had been too ashamed (cf. vv. 47–48) to
mention. Even so, the name Chrysis was not unique to this
one play by Menander (see opposite), and Plangon's viola-
tion had not taken place* the other day.

5
```
              ]ν· τίνα γὰρ α[
           ]εστ' ἐλευθ[ερ
      τὰς τρ]ίχας τ' ἔτιλ[λ
           ]ν πρώ[η]ν ε[
           ]ε καὶ τ[.]δε[
```
10
```
           ]ι γὰρ κ[α]τῆλ[θ
           ]αναν[.]ασ[
           ]σκαλο[.]δε[
           ] γὰρ ἐκ[ε]ῖ δ[
           ]ατυχει[.]τα[
```
15
```
           ]τωσ[..]λ.[
           ]και[..]ο[
           ]ουτω[
           ]ετο[
           ]νλε[
```
20
```
           ]πα[
           ]σσ[
```

2 (437 Kock, unnumbered in Körte and Sandbach)

Phrynichus, *Eclogae* 157 Fischer (p.75.78–81): λίβανον
λέγε τὸ δένδρον, τὸ δὲ θυμιώμενον λιβανωτόν . . .
ἄμεινον δὲ Μένανδρος ἐν τῇ Σαμίᾳ φησίν·

φέρε τὸν λιβανωτόν· σὺ δ' ἐπίθες τὸ πῦρ, Τρύφη.

fr. 1, line 8 Or θ[.   9 τ[ό]δε [, τ[ό]δ' ε[, τ[ά]δε [, or τ[ά]δ' ε[.
11 Or [.]σο[.   14]α τυχεῖν or ἀτυχεῖ[ν (or -χεῖ[ς).
15 Or]γωσ[.

fr. 2 τὸν mss. Uc: τὴν b.

188

2

Phrynichus: Use λίβανος for the (frankincense-)tree and λιβανωτός (incense) for the material that is burnt . . . Menander in the *Samia* says more correctly,

Bring incense. Tryphe, place the fire on top.

In distinguishing between the Greek words for the tree that produces frankincense (various species of Boswellia) and the aromatic gum (olibanum or frankincense) that the tree exudes, Phrynichus cites a puzzling trimeter. One possibility is that this line has been mistakenly attributed to the Samia, because of confusion with the very similar v. 158 of the play. Another is that the line comes from one of the gaps in the papyrus text: either (i) between vv. 57 and 58, with Chrysis on her first entrance preparing to burn incense and to pray for Demeas' safe return; or (ii) between vv. 119a and 119b, with Demeas at the end of Act I making a thank-offering after his safe return; or (iii) between vv. 205 and 206, with Demeas at the end of Act II making the offering in connection with his son's proposed marriage. Tryphe would be a slave in Demeas' house, called out and appearing as a mute, or simply addressed through the house door. The fire in a portable hearth would be placed 'on top' of an altar visible on the stage or imagined inside Demeas' house.

SIKYONIOI OR SIKYONIOS

(THE SICYONIANS
OR THE MAN FROM SICYON)

INTRODUCTION

Manuscripts

S = *P.Sorbonne* 72, 2272 and 2273, parts of 21 columns from a papyrus roll written in the last third of the third century B.C., and later, after much use, cut up and glued to form cartonnage for mummy wrappings. Seven fragments (= *P.Sorbonne* 72) were discovered in 1901–2 during excavations at the Ptolemaic cemeteries of Ghoran and Medinet-en-Nahas and published (with an attribution to Menander that most scholars at the time contested) by P. Jouguet, *Bulletin de Correspondance Hellénique* 30 (1906) 103–23 and pl. III (photograph of lines 280–321); these fragments contained lines 52–61, 63–8, 75–109, 205–13, 280–322, 382–6 and 405–10 whole or in part. Five further fragments (= *P.Sorbonne* 2272) in 1962, and two more (= *P.Sorbonne* 2273) in 1963, were recovered from mummy cartonnages in the Institut de Papyrologie at the Sorbonne, and identified as belonging to the same papyrus roll as the Jouguet fragments, by A. Blanchard and A. Bataille, who published them with photographs of both their and the Jouguet fragments in *Recherches de Papyrologie* 3 (1964) 103–76; the new fragments, which include a colophon identifying the play as 'Menander's Men (*sic*: see below) from Sicyon', supplement those of Jouguet so that 422 complete or partial lines of this play can now be read on this papyrus. Whether it originally contained just the one play or more is now uncertain.

In addition, fragments 1 to 3 here are three scraps of papyrus assigned to this play with some confidence:

1 (*P.Oxyrhynchus* 1238), dating from the first century A.D., contains the beginnings of nine lines. It was first published by A. Hunt, *The Oxyrhynchus Papyri* 10 (1914) 95–7, with a photograph (pl. V) and a tentative attribution to Menander; two speakers are identified on it as Ther(on) and Malth(ake), and this enabled Blanchard and Bataille to assign it to *Sikyonioi*.

2 (*P.Oxyrhynchus* 3217) is a tiny scrap containing the middle parts of seven lines, first published by Susan A. Stephens, *The Oxyrhynchus Papyri* 45 (1977) 26, with a photograph (pl. IV), and attributed by her to the same scene of *Sikyonioi* as fr. 1 because (i) its handwriting appeared to be identical, and (ii) the same abbreviation Π—for Π(υρρίας), P(yrrhias) ?—was used to identify a speaker in v. 3 as was used on fr. 1 to indicate a third speaker there.

3 is a further fr. from Oxyrhynchus (inv. 33 4B 83E 8–11), from a roll written at the end of the first or beginning of the second century A.D. It contains the ends of 29 comic verses and was first published by E. W. Handley, *BICS* 31 (1984) 25–36, with a photograph (between pp. 26–27), and assigned by him to *Sikyonioi* because of references in it to a Malthake (v. 21) and to bitter exile (v. 15).

Fragments 4 to 13 finally are quotations from the play by later authors, 4 to 11 being firmly, 12 to 13 only conjecturally, assigned thereto (see introduction to Volume 1, pp. xxiv f.).

All these 13 fragments are printed after the end of S's text, together with four testimonia containing supplementary evidence relating to the play.

Pictorial Evidence

A wall painting of the late second century A.D. from a house in the centre of Ephesus, in the same room as one portraying a scene from Menander's *Perikeiromene* (see volume II pp. 369–370). It has the plural title ΣΙΚ-ΤΩΝΙΟΙ (*The Sicyonians*: see below) clearly inscribed at the top in white paint, and presents two male figures against a plain red background. On the left stands a man whose mask and dress (a knee-length tunic fastened so as to leave the right shoulder and breast visible) indicate a slave. He is gesticulating with his left arm extended and his right one half raised. To his right stands a young, unbearded man whose mask and costume (a cloak on top of a tunic) suggest that he is free and (if a soldier) wearing civilian clothes. He turns toward the slave with his right arm extended in a gesture of either entreaty or dismissal. His left hand appears to be clutching his cloak or some object which it is now impossible to specify owing to a patch of damage at this point. The painting indicates neither the act of the play nor the names of the characters involved; this fact, combined with our loss of two thirds of the play text, makes any identification of the scene portrayed highly uncertain. The slave may be Dromon or Pyrrhias, the free young man Stratophanes (out of uniform) or Moschion;

the one incident in the extant portions of *Sikyonioi* that
seems to correspond with the picture is the meeting of
Pyrrhias and Stratophanes when the slave hands over to
the soldier recognition tokens and a letter from Strato-
phanes' foster mother (141–44: so first E. W. Handley in
Ginouvès and others, *Les Mosaïques* 100). Authoritative
publication of the painting: V. M. Strocka, *Die Wand-
malerei der Hanghäuser in Ephesus* (*Forschungen in
Ephesus* VIII/1, Vienna 1977) 48, 54–55 and colour plates
62 and 64; the latter plate is reproduced on the front cover
of A. M. Belardinelli's edition of the play (Bari 1994). The
painting is listed in T. B. L. Webster's *Monuments Illus-
trating New Comedy*, 3rd edition revised and enlarged by
J. R. Green and A. Seeberg (*BICS* supplement 50, London
1995) as XZ 32 = 6DP 1.1, 1.93 and 2.472 respectively.

The title of the play is problematical.[1] It is normally
quoted as Σικυώνιος in the masculine singular (*The Man
from Sicyon*) by those excerptors who quoted phrases or
short passages of the play (certainly Aelius Dionysius,
Harpocration, Photius, the *Suda*, probably Pollux: see frs.
1, 3–5, 7–9 below).[2] The plural title Σικυώνιοι (*The Sic-*

---

[1] See especially A. M. Belardinelli, *Corolla Londiniensis* 2
(1982) 15-20 and her edition of *Sik.* (Bari 1994) 56-59.

[2] Manuscripts of two citers, however (Stobaeus, a scholiast on
Plato's *Symposium*: see frs. 2, 6), present the title as Σικυωνία in
the feminine singular (*The Girl* or *Woman from Sicyon*). This is
most plausibly explained as either a scribal error or a faulty expan-
sion of a title that had been abbreviated in an earlier manuscript or
on a didascalic inscription. See e.g. R. L. Hunter's edition of
Eubulus (Cambridge 1983) 95, my commentary on Alexis (Cam-
bridge 1996) p. 108, and *ZPE* 116 (1997) 1-3. Certainly in the sur-

yonians), however, appears in the colophon of the Sorbonne papyrus (written within ninety years of Menander's death) and on the Ephesus wall painting, and a corrupt variant of it (Σικνωλιοι) is found on a papyrus apparently listing some titles of plays by Menander (testimonium I). Both forms can be defended. The plural could be best interpreted as denoting Stratophanes (who at the beginning of the play believed himself Sicyonian: cf. *vv*. 125–45, 246 f.) and his Sicyonian foster parents, even though both of these had died before the events of the play begin. The singular form, referring to Stratophanes on his own, makes equally good dramatic sense. It is noticeable that either Stratophanes, the play's main character, or his foster father is identified as ὁ Σικυώνιος . . . ἡγεμών in the prologue (vv. 13 f.), and sometimes Menander thus includes his chosen title in the wording of an opening scene or a prologue speech (cf. *Aspis* 16, 72, 109, *Dyskolos* 6, *Samia* 13, perhaps also v. 22 of *P.Antinoopolis* 15, if this comes from a comedy entitled Δακτύλιος).[3]

Since the evidence for both forms of the title seems so well based, it may be that the play in antiquity went under both titles—an original title Σικυώνιοι attached to the play's production and recorded in the Sorbonne papyrus, and later perhaps Σικυώνιος too, taking its alternative title

viving portions of *Sikyonioi* there seems to be no one Sicyonian woman who plays a dramatically effective part (Stratophanes' Sicyonian foster mother, who sent an important letter and recognition tokens to him on her deathbed, vv. 130ff., can hardly be so construed).

[3] See my paper in *Drama* 2 (1994) 29. *P.Antinoopolis* 15 is printed in this volume of the Loeb Menander as *Fabula Incerta* 6.

from the chief character, like many other second titles in later Greek comedy.[4]

This edition hesitantly retains for the play the line numbering suggested first by R. Kassel in his edition (Berlin 1965) and followed later by F. H. Sandbach (Oxford 1972[1], 1990[2]) and A. M. Belardinelli (Bari 1994). Kassel thus arranges the Sorbonne papyri fragments in an order that is generally accepted as dramatically correct (with reservations about the placing of lines 52–71 and 72–109 relative to each other). However, this numbering, which is consecutive from 1 to 423, takes no account of the lacunae (often of incalculable length) between separate pieces of the Sorbonne papyri. Although portions of some 470 lines of the play survive from these and the other sources listed above, only about 180 of them are preserved in a state achieving or approaching completeness; the remainder range from tantalisingly meaningful scraps to odd letters. The original length of Sikyonioi was probably greater than 1000 lines,[5] and the fragmentation of what is still pre-

---

[4] So first A. Guida, *Studi Italiani di Filologia Classica* 46 (1974) 233-234. See also the Gomme–Sandbach commentary on Menander pp. 129 f., O. Taplin, *JHS* 95 (1975) 185, Hunter's edition of Eubulus pp. 146-148 and my commentary on Alexis p. 51.

[5] In the colophon of S appended to the end of the play the scribe seems to have written a number between 1000 and 1099, presumably indicating the number of lines that he had copied (which may have included prefatory matter such as we find prefixed to the Bodmer papyrus of *Dyskolos* and to the Cairensis text of *Heros*). In act four of the papyrus the stichometric numbers H (700) and Θ (800) appear opposite lines 151 and 244, but such scribal calculations of lines are regularly inexact. See Blanchard–

served leaves us with a lot of puzzles about the plot, especially in the play's first three acts. Even so, the extant remains teach us three interesting lessons about Menander's technique. The first is that the dramatist here is clearly aiming at a kaleidoscopic variation of a series of conventional motifs. In two other plays from which extensive fragments survive, *Misoumenos* and *Perikeiromene*, our attention is similarly focused on a sympathetic and sensitive soldier who is in love with a girl whom at the beginning of the play he is unable to marry, because he is unaware that he is a free citizen, and she the legitimate daughter of a free citizen, of the same city. This they discover by the end of each play through recognition scenes which reunite the girl with a lost parent. Yet the details and circumstances are imaginatively varied in each play; thus in two of them the soldier has a rival also in love with the girl: one rival turns out to be the girl's brother (*Perikeiromene*), the other to be the soldier's brother (*Sikyonioi*).

Secondly, *Sikyonioi* has a scene in which Theron attempts for a ruse to persuade Kichesias into pretending to be the father of a girl who in fact really is his own daughter (343–376). There is a closely parallel treatment of the same motif in Plautus' *Poenulus*, which appears to have been adapted from Alexis' *Karchedonios*.[6] In the Latin play (1099–1173) it is a shifty slave who seeks to persuade an elderly Carthaginian to impersonate the father of two girls whose parent he really is. This is one of several passages which at first sight appear to endorse an ancient suggestion

---

Bataille 162 and R. Kassel, *Eranos* 43 (1965) 12 f. = *Kleine Schriften* (Berlin and New York 1991) 283.

[6] See especially my commentary on Alexis pp. 284-287.

that Alexis was Menander's dramatic tutor, although in this and some other cases we have no means of testing whether Alexis wrote his passage before or after Menander.[7]

Thirdly, *Sikyonioi* contains a long narrative (176–271) in which a messenger describes the discussion at an informal assembly in Eleusis about the status of Philoumene after she and Dromon had taken refuge there at an altar. Here Menander owes a clear debt to the messenger's speech in Euripides' *Orestes* (866–956), narrating the trial of Orestes at an assembly in his native Argos. Menander echoes or modifies phrases from the Euripidean scene (*Sik.* 176–177, 182, 188, 215 ~ *Or.* 866–867, 920, 871, 918 respectively), but he transforms and modernises the tragic situation by substituting something contemporary and bourgeois for the distanced past of myth.[8]

No hypothesis, didascalic notice or cast list is preserved for *Sikyonioi*. Although its date of production is nowhere recorded, the extant portions of the play include several references to events and circumstances which may have been intended to provide a realistic historical background to the staged action. At vv. 3–15 and 354–357 we learn that Philoumene and Dromon had been seized by pirates at

---

[7] See my commentary on Alexis pp. 5 (testimonium 2), 11–13 and 26–28.

[8] The relation between the Euripidean and Menandrean scenes has been much discussed. See especially A. G. Katsouris, *Tragic Patterns in Menander* (Athens 1975) 29–54, and my paper in *Studies in Honour of T. B. L. Webster* 1 (Bristol 1986) 3–6.

Halae on the Attic coast,[9] when Philoumene was only four years old, about eleven or twelve years before the scenic date of the play. V.137 implies that Stratophanes had been fighting, presumably as a mercenary, in or around Caria. In the acrimonious political duel of vv. 150–168 one speaker is presented as a supporter of the oligarchs, the other as a convinced democrat. Unfortunately, however, none of these references can be tied with any certainty to any one datable event. Menander's dramatic career extended from the 320's to the 290's. During this period piracy was a continual hazard, warfare in and around Caria was virtually uninterrupted, and dissension between oligarchs and democrats was a repeated ingredient of political life.[10]

The text of this play is in places badly mutilated, and its exegesis, together with the identification of speakers and of speech beginnings and ends, is often difficult and some-

---

[9] One of the two coastal areas in Attica with this name: see my note on v. 355.

[10] On piracy at this period see H. A. Ormerod, *Piracy in the Ancient World* (Liverpool 1924) 120–126, M. M. Austin, *The Hellenistic World from Alexander to the Roman Conquest* (Cambridge 1981) pp. 69, 98, 157–160, 162, 175, 282–283, and W. K. Pritchett, *The Greek State at War* 5 (Berkeley, Los Angeles, Oxford 1991) 312–348; cf. also F. Marx's commentary (Berlin 1928) on Plaut. *Rudens* 39. On Caria see the references in my note on *Samia* 629. On the changes in Athenian government during Menander's career, with its swings between democracy and oligarchy in 322, 318, 317, 307, 301 and 294 see especially W. S. Ferguson, *Hellenistic Athens* (London 1911) chapters 1 to 4.

times impossible. Inevitably the text, translations and interpretations given below are at times speculative; defences in detail of the more controversial decisions can be found in three articles published in *ZPE* 116 (1997) 1–10, 117 (1997) 21–34 and 118 (1997) 95–103.

Dramatis Personae, presented in alphabetical order, since the extant fragments do not allow us to determine the order of their first appearances in the complete play:

Dromon, slave formerly of Kichesias but owned at the beginning of the play by Stratophanes

Eleusinios, a messenger

A god or goddess as speaker of the prologue: perhaps one worshipped particularly at Eleusis (e.g. Persephone)

Kichesias, father of Philoumene

Malthake, probably originally a *hetaira*, but now in Stratophanes' entourage

Moschion, son of Smikrines, in love with Philoumene

An old man portrayed as a keen democrat, possibly identical with one of the other old men in this play (but not Smikrines)

Pyrrhias, slave of Stratophanes

Smikrines (if that is his name[11]), father of Stratophanes and Moschion

The wife of Smikrines (if that is his name)

[11] In the extant portions of the papyrus he seems to be addressed just once (156), and there only the first two letters of his name survive; see ad loc.

Stratophanes, a soldier, son of Smikrines, in love with
    Philoumene
Theron, a parasite and intriguer in Stratophanes' entou-
    rage, in love with Malthake

In the extant fragments a slave named Donax has a mute
role, but Philoumene, the girl loved and at one stage
owned by Stratophanes, makes no certain appearance (but
see below on lines 25–51, where one of the two speakers
may be either Philoumene or an otherwise unknown fe-
male slave of Stratophanes). There was presumably also
a conventional chorus of tipsy revellers, to perform the
entr'actes.

ΣΙΚΥΩΝΙΟΙ

(SCENE: A street in a part of Attica that is not specifically identified in the preserved portions of the prologue or elsewhere in the play, but passing references indicate that it was most probably Eleusis or a neighbouring deme. In lines 176–271 one character describes events that he has just witnessed at Eleusis, and the same deme is mentioned at 57 in a puzzlingly mutilated context which may or may not imply that it was the dramatic setting. Two houses at least are visible; Smikrines owns one, Stratophanes lodges in the other.)

(The first two fragments (III, IV.A) of the Sorbonne papyrus contain portions of a divine prologue (vv. 1–19, 20–34), followed by the opening lines of a scene introducing in all probability Malthake and another woman. It is uncertain whether this divine prologue opened the play (like Pan's in the Dyskolos) or whether it was preceded by one or more scenes involving human characters (as e.g. in Aspis, Heros, Perikeiromene). The identity of the prologue speaker is also uncertain, but in a play highlighting incidents at Eleusis and mentioning its priestess (v. 258) the most appropriate divinity would be one of the local cult goddesses. Demeter and Calligeneia have been suggested,[1] but in a

[1] See e.g. H. Lloyd-Jones, *Greek, Roman and Byzantine*

204

SIKYONIOI

*play whose heroine was kidnapped as a young girl (vv. 2,
354–357) an apter choice might perhaps be Persephone,
herself the victim of a celebrated abduction.*

*It is impossible to say how much of the prologue has been
lost before v. 1; part only of the play's exposition survives,
and the extensive gaps and severe mutilation in the papy-
rus throughout the first half of the play make much of the
earlier dramatic action unknown and undivinable. In view
of this it may be useful to prefix to text and translation a
brief account of the known dramatic antecedents and the
problems that the textual gaps cause.*

*Kichesias' daughter Philoumene was kidnapped when
four years old, along with the slave Dromon and an elderly
woman (probably the girl's nurse), by pirates at Halai
in Attica (Sik. 354–57, cf. 2–3); this could have been
either Halai Aixonides or perhaps more probably Halai
Araphenides.[2] The extant text does not reveal whether this
was Philoumene's home, or whether she was on her way to*

Studies, 7 (1966) 155 (reprinted in Greek Comedy, Hellenistic
Literature, Greek Religion, and Miscellanea, Oxford 1990, 74–
75), A. Guida, Studi Italiani di Filologia Classica, 46 (1974) 211
n.1.

[2] On these two demes, see note on v. 355 below.

or from a festival such as the Tauropolia, held at Halai, or the Brauronia, held nearby only three kilometres away.[3] *Philoumene and Dromon were taken to Mylasa in Caria, where they were sold as slaves to a wealthy Sicyonian officer (5–15) who was campaigning in the area. This could have been Stratophanes himself or perhaps more plausibly his foster father. The abduction and enslavement occurred ten to twelve years before the play's dramatic present; Philoumene has meanwhile grown up to sexual maturity.*

When the play begins Stratophanes has himself just returned from a Carian campaign. He turns out to be one of the two sons of Smikrines, another Athenian, who for some reason (most probably poverty) brought Moschion up himself but handed Stratophanes as a baby over to a Sicyonian woman who wanted children (281–82). Whether she and her husband, identified provisionally above as the officer who bought Philoumene, lived and died in their native Sicyon or as metics in Athens is not made clear in the surviving fragments, but the latter alternative seems likelier. It makes many of the antecedent and ongoing events in the

[3] Both festivals, in which young girls danced wearing attractive costumes, might well have attracted a little child such as Philoumene. On these events see especially A. Brelich, *Paides e parthenoi* (Rome 1969) 229–311; L. Kahil in J. N. Coldstream and M. A. R. Colledge (edd.), *Greece and Italy in the Classical World: Acta of the XI International Congress of Archaeology* (London 1978) 73–87; H. Lloyd-Jones, *JHS* 103 (1983) 91–98 (= *Greek Comedy etc.*, 313–23); E. Simon, *Festivals of Attica* (Madison, Wisc. 1983) 83–88, W. Burkert, *Greek Religion* (tr. J. Raffan, Oxford 1985) 151–52, R. Osborne, *Demos* (Cambridge 1985) 154–74, and J. P. Vernant, *Mortals and Immortals* (Princeton 1992) 200–02, 214–19.

play more credible: Smikrines' choice of Sicyonian foster parents for Stratophanes, the presence of Philoumene and Dromon in Attica (resident presumably in the foster parents' house while these latter were still alive, during Stratophanes' absence in Caria), Stratophanes' decision to lodge in Attica on his return to Greece, and his despatch of Pyrrhias 'home' (120) to his foster mother's house. Before the action of the play begins Stratophanes' foster parents had both died. The father had fallen seriously into debt to an unidentified Boeotian (133–35) after a lawsuit, and the mother had died leaving written and other evidence which proved Stratophanes was not their natural son but the legitimate offspring of an Athenian marriage: information which might absolve Stratophanes from responsibility to repay his foster father's debt (138–40).[4]

At the age of 15 or 16 Philoumene was now of marriageable age, and apparently both Stratophanes and Moschion had become enamoured of her (200–66, 397–99). In the fourth act of the play Philoumene and Dromon had fallen into some danger which had induced them to leave their home and seek refuge as suppliants at the entrance to the sanctuary of Demeter and Persephone at Eleusis (189–90, cf. the comments linking 52–71 with 72–109). The nature of that danger is not made perfectly clear in what survives of the play, but one explanation may have been Philou-

---

[4] But contrast the situation in Menander's *Heros*, where Athenian twins are compelled to work off a foster parent's debt as employees of the creditor. It is possible that in *Sikyonioi* Menander was reproducing or assuming a difference between the laws of Sicyon and Athens. Cf. the Gomme–Sandbach commentary on *Heros* 36 and my Loeb edition, II pp. 4 and 19 note c.

mene's fear that Stratophanes was going to force her into what in her opinion would have been an unlawful marriage (see on vv. 72–109 below). There are, however, other possibilities, which need not be mutually exclusive. Philoumene could have feared from Moschion too an amorous approach which would have been harder for a slave to resist, and would have handicapped her (just as would an unlawful union with Stratophanes) from securing an honourable marriage if she regained her freedom. Or the Boeotian could have come to Athens with the intention of seizing Philoumene and Dromon, together with the house of Stratophanes' foster parents, in payment of the debt he was owed.

Two other characters, whose roles appear to have been highly acclaimed in antiquity (see testimonia III and IV), were involved at least peripherally in some of these actions: Malthake and the parasite Theron. The latter was an Athenian (cf. 144) who acted unscrupulously as Stratophanes' agent; after Stratophanes discovered his Athenian citizenship, Theron resorted to perjury (possibly 52–68, certainly 343–67) in an effort to prove that Stratophanes and Philoumene were born free Athenians and so able to marry each other. Theron's presentation thus closely resembles that of the parasite in Terence's Phormio, who similarly used perjury in order to achieve the marriage his young patron desired. Theron, however, has two further interests which the loss of more than half the play makes more difficult to link with the remainder of the plot. He is somehow involved with donkeys and their drivers (395, cf. 411); did he perhaps continue in Athens an earlier employment by Stratophanes on campaign as his officer in charge of baggage animals? Theron also wishes to marry Malthake

(145), and both fr. 12, if correctly assigned to this play, and vv. 411–23 seem to imply that he succeeds in his objective. This requires Malthake also to have been free and Athenian, and the name was borne by many such girls in Menander's Athens.[5] In comedy, however, this name is associated only with hetairai,[6] but if that was her role in Menander's Sikyonioi, no sexual relationship with Theron or any other character in the play can be identified.)

[5] See M. J. Osborne and S. G. Byrne, *A Lexicon of Greek Personal Names*, 2 (Oxford 1994) 296, where Menander's Malthake is included among 27 Athenian women with this name, at least eight of them demonstrably free. Cf. also my comments below on frs. 3 and 4 of *Sikyonioi*.

[6] So Theophilus fr. 11.5; the one surviving fragment (146) of Antiphanes' *Malthake* concerns *hetairai*; Lucian, *Rhet. Praec.* 12 links the character Malthake with *hetairai* like Thais and Glykera. The word ἑταίρα occurs once in a mutilated line of Menander's *Sikyonioi* (409), possibly with reference to Malthake.

(The opening fragment of S, which begins with the divine
prologue in mid-speech.)

ΘΕΟΣ (? ΦΕΡΡΕΦΑΤΤΑ)

].[..]..[.].[

....γ]ὰρ εἶναί φημι τούτου θυγάτριον.
ὡ[ς δ'] ἐγκρατεῖς ἐγένοντο σωμάτων τρ[ιῶν,
τὴν γραῦν μὲν οὐκ ἔδοξε λυσιτελεῖν ἄ[γειν
5 αὐτοῖς, τὸ παιδίον δὲ καὶ τὸν οἰκέτην
τῆς Καρίας ἀγαγόντες εἰς τὰ Μύλασ', ἐ[κεῖ
ἐχρῶντ' ἀγορᾷ, καθῆτό τ' ἐπὶ τῆς ἀγκ[άλης
ἔ]χων ὁ θεράπων τὴν τροφίμην. πωλ[ουμένοις
π]ροσῆλθεν ἡγεμών τις· ἠρώτα "πόσ[ου
10 ταῦτ' ἐστίν;" ἤκουσεν· συνεχώρησ'· ἐπ[ρίατο.
παλίμβολος δὲ τῷ θεράποντι πλησίο[ν
τ]ῶν αὐτόθεν τις ἕτερος ἅμα πωλουμ[ένων
"β]έλτιστε, θάρρει," φησίν, "ὁ Σικυώνιος

11 fr. 379 K-T.

In the apparatus to this play, those corrections and supple-
ments whose author is not identified were made by A. Blanchard
and A. Bataille (hereafter BB), editing the Sorbonne papyrus (S)
in *Recherches de Papyrologie* 3 (1964) 103–176.

1–19 Fragment III (BB) of S.   1 First letter has a long
sublinear vertical (ρ, τ, ν, φ).   2 Suppl. several, but
π]αρεῖναι and] ἄρ' εἶναι also possible.   3 ὡ[ς δ'] and
τρ[ιῶν suppl. several.   4 Suppl. several.   5 τὸν Kassel:
τιν apparently S.   6 καιριας S: corr. several.   μυλασσ[or
μυλασε[S.   ἐ[κεῖ suppl. several.   8 ἔ]χων suppl. several,
πωλ[ουμένοις Austin, Handley.   9 πόσ[ου suppl. several.
10 ἐπ[ρίατο suppl. Handley.   11 Suppl. several.

SIKYONIOI

(The opening of the prologue is lost. When the text becomes legible at line 2, the speaker is describing how eleven or twelve years ago pirates kidnapped Kichesias' four-year-old daughter Philoumene, the family slave Dromon and an old woman, probably Philoumene's nurse.)

DIVINE PROLOGUE (? PERSEPHONE)

... for [she[1]] was, I emphasise, his[2] little girl.   2
Now that they'd overpowered [three] people, they
Reckoned it wouldn't pay [to take] the old
Woman; the child though and the slave they took   5
To Mylasa in Caria,[3] [where] they found
Their market, and the slave sat holding his
Young mistress on one arm. [They were] for sale.
An officer[4] approached. He asked 'How much
Are they?' He was informed, agreed, and [bought]   10
Them. Near the slave another of the men
On sale there (he'd been through this hoop before)
Said 'Sir, cheer up! This man from Sicyon
Who's bought you is a colonel, very fine

---

[1] Philoumene.   [2] Kichesias'.

[3] The old capital of Caria, about halfway between Miletus and Halicarnassus, where several Macedonian colonies were established in Hellenistic times. The modern town of Milas now covers the site, obliterating most of its remains; the site of the ancient market is unknown. See especially G. E. Bean, *Turkey beyond the Maeander* (London 1980) 13–24 with plates 1–5, and S. Hornblower, *Mausolus* (Oxford 1982) 68–70, 313–14.

[4] Either Stratophanes himself as a very young man, or (more probably) Stratophanes' foster father from Sicyon.

---

12 πωλουμ[ένων suppl. Austin, Gallavotti.

ἠ]γόρακεν ὑμᾶς, ἡγεμὼν χρηστὸς σφόδρα
15 κ]αὶ πλούσιός γ’, οὐ τῶν [τ]υχόν[των
   ἐ]κ τοῦ παραχρῆμ[
   τ]ῷ παιδίῳ τὴν πατ[ρίδα
   .]εον προσάγων οἰκεῖον εἰς τ[
19 πρὶ]ν εἰδέναι δοκεῖν τ[ι

(After v. 19 there is a gap in the Sorbonne papyrus (see
ZPE 116, 1997, 4–5) of either between 5 and 15 lines if the
next fragment of S (IV) begins in the column immediately
following fr. III, or between 26 and 40 lines if a lost column
intervenes between these two fragments. The speaker is
still the divine prologue.)

20   ] δ’ ἔδοξεν οὗτινος
                ] γὰρ ποιοῦσί τε
                ].αν[.] ἔτι.
   ταῦτ’ ἐστὶ τὰ κεφάλαια, τὰ] καθ’ ἕκαστα δὲ
   ὄψεσθ’ ἐὰν βούλησθε· βουλή]θητε δέ.

15 πλουσιοστουτων[.]υχον[S: corr. and suppl. Arnott (see
ZPE 116, 1997, 4).   17 πατ[ρίδα suppl. Handley.
   18 αγων S with προσ written above.   19 Deciphered
and suppl. Austin.   20–51 Fr. IV (BB) of S: column A 20–35,
col. B 36–51.   20]δειδοξενουντινος unmetrically S: corr. sev-
eral (with]δε δ’ ὁ ξένου τινὸς a less plausible alternative).
   23–24 Suppl. several exempli gratia, after Dyskolos 45–46.

5 This is argued with fuller detail in ZPE 116 (1997) 5–6.

And wealthy too—he's someone special (?) [15
Immediately [
Her home[land] for the child (?) [
Taking [her (?)] as family (?) [
Apparently [not] knowing [yet] wh[at (?)   19

(Lines 16–19 are too mutilated for assured interpretation
and plausible supplementation. The 'home[land]' in v. 17 is
clearly the young girl's, but it is uncertain whether the
girl's native Attica or a possible future home in Sicyon is in-
tended. After v. 19 there is a short gap of uncertain length;
when the papyrus text resumes, the speaker appears to be
approaching the end of her prologue.)

           ] it seemed [   ] of no[body (?)   20
           ] for they do *(or* make*)*
           ] still. (?)
[That's the synopsis. Now you're going to see]
[The] details, [if you like:] you'd [better like!]   24

(At this point probably, if the mutilated remains of vv. 23–
24 contain the formula used towards the end (vv. 45–46) of
the Dyskolos prologue, the prologue speaker of Sikyonioi
will leave the stage. What happens next is uncertain, but
the most likely hypothesis[5] is that two human characters
then enter, probably in mid-conversation; their dialogue
seems to continue up to and perhaps beyond v. 51. One of
them is certainly female (addressed as ma'am *in v. 32, and*
see notes on vv. 34–35), and the references to male calcula-
tion *25,* a woman's cohabitation *32,* trembling *35,* you'll be
feeding *39,* a man's excessive fondness for food *43, 44, 46,*

ΜΑΛΘΑΚΗ (?)

25
    λ]ογισμὸν ἀνδρικὸν
    ]τεραν ἰδεῖν
    τοῖ]ς ὄνοις, ὡς γίγνεται
    ].ενη δεύτερον
    ] οὑτοσὶ

30
    ]ν μου πυθοῦ
    ]....[..το]ύτῳ τῷ κακῷ
    ] με καὶ συνοικίζειν, γύναι.

ΓΥΝΗ ΑΛΛΗ (?)

    ]ν οὐδεμία, μὰ τὼ θεώ,
    ]ν ἄπεστι. τούτῳ γάρ, τάλαν,

35
    ]. φασιν, ὁ δὲ τρόμος πολὺ

(After v. 35 there is a gap in the papyrus of between 5 and 9 lines.)

25–35 Assigned to Malthake tentatively by Sandbach, but it seems just as likely that her companion intervened, perhaps with 33–35. 27 Or] πονοις S.
33 Corr. several: τωιθεωι S.
35]ε,]ν or]ς S: ? ὤ]ς φασιν.

---

[6] The Greek text here may alternatively be interpreted as 'toils.'

[7] If this translation is correct, and the reference is to Theron, the implication will be that the speaker points to Stratophanes' house, with Theron inside it. See also ZPE 116 (1997) 6.

[8] Demeter and Persephone. This oath was used only by women.

and perhaps donkeys 27, *if that word is rightly deciphered,
all seem to imply that the subject of their conversation was
the desire of a parasite to marry or cohabit with a woman
who recoils from any future maintenance of him and (?) his
donkeys. This makes it likely that Malthake herself was one
of the two speakers, and the other a second woman (?
Philoumene or some other slave in Stratophanes' house-
hold) introduced here for just the one scene, who listens
and responds while Malthake outlines expository details
about the parasite Theron's amorous pursuit of her. These
presumably would not have been mentioned in the divine
prologue.)*

MALTHAKE (?)

] male calculation   25
] more [   ] to see
[the] donkeys,[6] as it happens (?)
] second
] this [man (?)] here[7]
] find out from me   30
[with (?)] this trouble
] me, ma'am, and set up house with me.

SECOND WOMAN (?)

not any [   ], by the pair divine,[8]
] is far off, for this, oh dear,[9]
]as they say, and greatly does the trembling   35

*(After v. 35 there is a short gap. When the papyrus re-
sumes, the same two characters seem still to be conversing.*

[9] τάλαν, translated here as 'oh dear,' was an expression used
only by women.

36 [
[
ημ[

ΓΥΝΗ ΑΛΛΗ (?)

θρέψεις μο[
40 μᾶλλον δετ[
τέχνην α.[
κτῆμ᾽ ἐστὶ σ[
ἄπληστος ε[
πάντ᾽ ἐσθίει.[
45 οὕτω γὰρ ἡ γα[στὴρ
ἀνὴρ ἄπληστ[ος
γυναικὶ παν[

ΜΑΛΘΑΚΗ (?)

τοῦτ᾽ ηὐχόμη[ν
ἐγώ. τὸ ποῖον.[
50 πρὸς ταῦτα ν[ῦν
51 δίδωμι προ[

36, 37, 38 have paragraphi under them in S.

39–47 assigned to this speaker (and 48–50 to Malthake) tentatively by Arnott.　　41 δ[, ε[, or σ[S.　　45 Suppl. tentatively Lloyd-Jones.　　46 ἀνήρ West, but ἀνὴρ is also possible.
ἄπληστ[ος suppl. several.　　47, 51 have paragraphi under them in S.　　50 Suppl. Austin.

---

10 Or 'To eat.'　　11 Or 'prayed that this'
12 This reference clearly places vv. 52–71 some time before vv. 176–271, in which events at that town meeting are described.

Nothing is intelligible before v. 39.)

SECOND WOMAN (?)

You'll feed [	39
But rather [	40
A skill [	
Is a possession [	
Insatiable[	
Eats[10] everything[	
For that's the way one's belly (?) [	45
The (?) man's insatiable[	
To a woman every [	

MALTHAKE (?)

I prayed for this[11] [	
What kind of [	
In face of this n[ow (?)	50
I give[	51

(After the mutilated and unfathomable remains of vv. 48–51 there is a gap of uncertain length before the next two portions (VIII and VII) of the Sorbonne papyrus. Both of these almost certainly derive from the first half of the play, with VIII (vv. 52–71 here) in all probability coming earlier than VII (vv. 72–109). In vv. 52–71 two characters seem to be involved, discussing a stratagem to find somebody in a town meeting at Eleusis[12] who could be suborned into swearing that a person unspecified in the unsupplemented part of the text (but presumably Philoumene) was a free Athenian. Since the parasite Theron later in the play (vv. 343–60) is portrayed as a miscreant attempting to persuade Kichesias to perjure himself by pretending to be

217

MENANDER

(At v. 51 fr. IV of the Sorbonne papyrus breaks off. Frs.
VIII and VII also seem to come from an early stage in the
action of the play, but which of the two comes first, and
how many lines are missing between v. 51 and either fr.
VIII or VII, it is impossible to say.)

ΣΤΡΑΤΟΦΑΝΗΣ (?)

52   ]ων ἀπολεσάντων παιδίον
ἐκ]δόντων τρέφειν ἢ τὸν τόπον
]γεγραμμένων ἄλλως ἐκεῖ.

ΘΗΡΩΝ (?)

55 τί δὴ τὸ κακ]όν ποτ᾽ ἐστίν; οὕτω μαρτυρεῖν
μάρτυρα] τοιοῦτον ἄν τις εὕροι πολλαχοῦ
ἐνταῦθ᾽ ἐ]ν ἄστει τοῦδ᾽· Ἐλευσίς ἐστι, καὶ
πανήγ]υρίς που. τίς νοήσει, πρὸς θεῶν;
εἰ συνδρα]μεῖται δῆμος, εἷς τις οὐ ταχὺ
60 τὴν παῖδ᾽] ἀφελκύσαιτ᾽ ἄν. εἰ δὲ περιμένω
ἐνθάδε, γένοιτ᾽ ἄν] ἔτι λέγοντος ἑσπέρα
62   ]τ[..].[

52–71 Fr. VIII (BB) = fr. VII Jouguet (hereafter J) of S (52–62
col. A, 63–71 col. B), placed before fr. VII (BB) by Barigazzi,
Kassel; Arnott tentatively identified speakers (Theron after
Jacques) and speech division (after Schröder).   53 Suppl.
Blass.   54 Or ἀλλ᾽ ὡς.   55 Suppl. *exempli gratia* Arnott.
56 Suppl. Schröder.   57 ἐνταῦθ᾽ suppl. Schröder, ἐν
Jouguet.   τουδεελευσις S.   58 Suppl. Jouguet.   59 εἰ
suppl. Page, συνδρα]μεῖται Austin (-δραμεῖται also Barigazzi).
60 Suppl. and corr. Sandbach: αφειλκυσαις S.
61 ἔνθαδε suppl. Arnott, γένοιτ᾽ ἄν Blass.

218

SIKYONIOI

*Philoumene's father, it is likely that he is the man proposing
a similar scheme in vv. 55–61, and his companion may
well be Stratophanes, the soldier whose plan to marry
Philoumene depended on her being a free woman. Even
so, the identifications, assignments of speeches and text-
ual supplements given here are all speculative.*[13] *If
Stratophanes spoke vv. 52–54, his references to people
'having lost a child' and 'placed out for rearing' leave us
in some doubt whether here he is thinking more about
Philoumene (who was not 'placed out') than about himself.
His (if they are his) final references to 'the scene' and things
(?) 'written there' are a mystery; was Stratophanes per-
haps raising hypothetical objections to Theron's perjurious
scheme?)*

STRATOPHANES (?)

   [people (?)] having lost a child   52
          ] placed [out] for rearing, or the scene
          ] written there in vain (?).

THERON

[What]ever is [the problem]? Such [a witness]   55
You could find [here] to testify to it
All over town. This is Eleusis, and
I think there's a town meeting. Heavens, who
Will notice? [If] folk [crowd together], one
Man couldn't drag [the girl] off quickly. Yet if I   60
Stay [here], darkness [could fall] while I'm still talking!   61

(At this point or shortly afterwards Theron presumably

---

13 For a fuller discussion see *ZPE* 116 (1997) 7.

(After v. 62 there is a gap in the papyrus of between 10 and 14 lines.)

63 πεζῆ͗ σ[
    αὖθις λα[
65 ἀκη[
    τε[
    λ[
    σ[
    [
70 [
71 [

(After v. 71 there is a gap whose length is uncertain.)

69, 70, 71 have paragraphi under them in S.

---

14 See *ZPE* 116 (1997) 7–9.

15 In Menander's time a free Athenian girl could contract a legal marriage only with a free Athenian man; see A. R. W. Harrison, *The Law of Athens: the Family and Property* (Oxford 1968) 24–29, D. M. MacDowell, *The Law in Classical Athens* (London 1978) 87, S. C. Todd, *The Shape of Athenian Law* (Oxford 1993) 177–79.

departs. There is now a short gap in the papyrus, and then a few letters and paragraphi preserved from nine further lines (63–71). These yield two intelligible Greek words (on foot 63, again 64) and indications that vv. 69–71 were split between two speakers. Someone else must have joined Theron's companion.

We cannot be certain exactly what happened after v. 71, but one plausible but tentative hypothesis[14] is a sequence of events in which (i) Theron prevailed upon Stratophanes to give him money (cf. vv. 92, 97), so that he might bribe a witness to swear that Philoumene was a free Athenian girl; (ii) as a result of this Philoumene feared that Stratophanes, who at this point was still believed to be a Sicyonian, might now attempt to force her into a union with him that would not count as a legal marriage in Athenian law;[15] (iii) finally she, accompanied by the slave Dromon (still presumably her personal attendant), ran away and sought refuge as suppliants at the entrance to the sanctuary of Demeter and Persephone in Eleusis (cf. 189–90). If this hypothesis is correct, vv. 72–109 can be interpreted as part of one or more scenes portraying a result of such developments. Stratophanes, distraught over Philoumene's and Dromon's flight and believing Theron to be its prime cause, vents his anger on the parasite and orders him to go on an errand to bring Philoumene back. While Stratophanes and Theron wrangle, a third character apparently listens unseen in the background. He is most plausibly identified as Moschion, Stratophanes' rival for Philoumene's hand. We do not know when or by what route (the door of Smikrines' house, or one of the parodoi?) he originally came on stage.

Of the very mutilated vv. 72–79 only a few words and expressions can safely be deciphered. They are perhaps best

221

ΣΤΡΑΤΟΦΑΝΗΣ (?)

72   ]ει
                                  ]δ...
                                  ]
75   ]..υπερβ..ω
                         ]..αλ' ἤθ[ε]λον
                      ] εἴπερ ἐγενόμην
                      οἰ]κότριψ Δρόμων
                      ]ς εὐεργέτην
80   ὁ] Διόνυσος ἀπολέσαι
             οὐδὲν ὑγ]ιὲς οὐδ' ἁπλοῦν φρονῶν
                    ]ην ἀνήρηκάς με νῦν
                    ]τ' ἐπυθόμην ὅτι
                    τ]ὸ παιδίον χάριν
85   ]ν φιλανθρώπων κακῶς
             ]ωσολ..τι τὴν μὲν παρθένον
87   ] νῦν οἶδεν ἐνδεέστερον

(Line 88 may follow directly on v. 87, or there may be a gap

72–109 Fr. VII (BB) of S = II and IV (J): 72–87 col. A, 88–109
col. B; at 81–83, 85–87 tiny scraps of text on the left edge of S
were originally read by Jouguet and Blass, but are now missing.
Speakers tentatively identified by Marzullo (Stratophanes), Ar-
nott (after Post: Theron) and Barigazzi (Moschion).
72, 75 deciphered by Coles (ἀνυπερβάτῳ Lloyd-Jones).
76 Suppl. Austin.   77 deciphered by Coles, Lloyd-Jones.
78 Suppl Schröder (ᾧ]κότριψ Wilcken).
80, 81 Suppl. Blass.
82 Corr. Blass: ανειρηκας S.

*interpreted as part of one long speech addressed to Theron
by Stratophanes. At v. 75 there may be a reference to some-
one or something as not transgressing bounds; 76 may have
I or they were willing. 77 yields if I'd become or been born;
78 Dromon, a or [the] menial slave, 79 benefactor. Was
Stratophanes here mentioning the flight of Philoumene and
Dromon and complaining that he had always acted as their
benefactor? At v. 80, however, for a few lines the sense is a
little less disjointed, although its general message remains
speculative.)*

STRATOPHANES (?)

(? in mid speech)

] may Dionysus strike [you (?)] down!   80
you have]n't [a single] sound or honest thought!
] you've destroyed me now!
] I discovered that
the] child [   ] gratitude
] humane, wickedly   85
] the maiden
] now less adequately knows   87

*(I interpret 80–82 as invective against Theron, and 84–87
as references partly at least involving Philoumene, al-
though any decoding of v. 85 is bedevilled by our ignorance
whether it is 'things' or 'people' that are humane.*

*In vv. 88–91 only two expressions can be made out: my-
self not 89 and quite smooth-shaven 91, the latter perhaps
a reference to Moschion, who is so described at v. 201.
Lines 92–109 generally reveal more connected sense, open-
ing perhaps with a reference to money from Stratophanes*

223

of up to three lines between them. The speaker at 88 is
probably still Stratophanes.)

88 .].[.........].π[
   ἐμαυ[τὸ]ν οὐδω[
90 .]υσ[......].αυται καὶ [
   ὑπόλειον [.........]ω...ρα...[
   ἔδωκας ἂν δίς· οὐκ ἀγαθά;

ΘΗΡΩΝ (?)

κάλ᾽, ὦ θ[εοί.

ΣΤΡΑΤΟΦΑΝΗΣ (?)

καὶ νῦν δραμὼν τὴν παῖδα παρ[ακάλει
ἔσται γὰρ ὥσπερ...........ἐμο[
95 ὡς ἔστιν.

ΘΗΡΩΝ (?)

οὐκ ἐᾷς με κοινῶσαι λ[όγον.

ΣΤΡΑΤΟΦΑΝΗΣ (?)

τίς δ᾽] οὐκ ἐᾷ σ᾽; ἔδωκ᾽, ἐδέξω. νῦ[ν δ᾽ ἴθι.

ΜΟΣΧΙΩΝ (?)

δ]έδοικε, φησί, δεσπότην ξένο[ν

89 Suppl. Jouguet.   91 ὑπόλειον deciphered by Coles,
Handley.   92 Suppl. Austin, with speech division.
93 Suppl. Kassel.   95, 96, 97 in S have uncertain traces of
paragraphi under them, and 95 has a one-letter space indicating
change of speaker.   95 Suppl. Austin.   96 Corr. and
suppl. Arnott (εαιδεδωκ S) after Gronewald (τίς σ᾽] οὐκ ἐᾷ δ᾽;
ἔδωκ᾽) and Austin (νῦ[ν]).   97 Suppl. Blass (ξε[now S, with
the scrap lost that contained the νο read by Jouguet).

*that Theron had used in order to bribe a perjurious wit-
ness.)*

STRATOPHANES (?)

You could have offered twice as much—isn't *that* good?

THERON (?)

[Yes,]   92

That's fine.

STRATOPHANES (?)

Now run along and [fetch (?)] the girl [
It'll be just like [to] me
That's how it is (?).

THERON (?)

You won't let me explain!   95

STRATOPHANES (?)

[Who] won't let [you]? I gave, you took![16] Now [go!

*(If my interpretation of these lines is correct, Theron now
goes off in search of Philoumene, and Moschion speaks
aside, at first presumably unheard by Stratophanes.)*

MOSCHION (?)

He says[17] she's scared of him—her owner, who's

---

[16] The reference here is uncertain, but possibly Stratophanes
is alluding to money that he may have given to Theron in order to
bribe a witness to manufacture evidence for an Athenian court
that Philoumene was an Athenian citizen.

[17] Presumably a reference to something that Stratophanes had
said (and Moschion overheard) in a part of his speech now lost.

τρίτον τ᾽ ἐρῶντ᾽, ἐγγύς τε τω[..]ρ.[
λέγοντα τούτους τοὺς λόγους ἐπει[
100 ἐμοὶ δὲ καὶ τούτῳ τί πρᾶγμ᾽ ἐστ[
μὴ τοῦτον ἡμῖν τὸν τρόπον λαλει[
τολμητέον γάρ ἐστιν, ἀλλ᾽ ει[..].[
τούτων ἀληθὲς ὁ θεράπων τι.[
ἅπασιν ἦ[ν] .[..]α τοῖς πολίταις ἡ κ[όρη
105 οὐκ ἀλλοτρία· πρῶτον μὲν αὐτηστ[
προσῆν ἔ[πει]τα ...εκαδ..τει[
οὐκ οἶδ᾽ ὅ τι λέγω· τῷ θεράπ[οντι
κἀμοὶ τ[

ΣΤΡΑΤΟΦΑΝΗΣ (?)

109 μειρακιο[ν, .].[.]οντι[.].πορνη[

98 ερωντα S.
100 Corr. Blass: τουτων S.   ἐστ[ὶν suppl. Jouguet.
104 ἦ[ν] suppl. Barigazzi, κ[όρη Schröder.
106 Suppl. tentatively Jacques.
107 Suppl. Austin.
108 in S has a paragraphus under it.
109 Assigned tentatively to Stratophanes by Arnott.

---

18 Presumably a further reference to part of the lost preceding conversation between Stratophanes and Theron, in which the parasite had warned the soldier about Moschion's rival pursuit of Philoumene, and been ordered not to open his mouth on that subject.

19 These disconnected remarks seem to imply that Philoumene and the slave Dromon had already been involved in a public meeting of the citizens of Eleusis, presumably in connection with their request for sanctuary.

An alien, [too], what's more, in love—and near [
Saying these words when [
'Now what concern is that of him and me? [100
Don't talk to us this way!'[18] [
You see, I must be bold, but [
The servant [   ] any part of this that's true.
The [girl   ] to all the citizens
[Did] not [seem] out of place.[19] First, she's [105
[Then] there's additionally (?) [
I don't know what I'm saying. For (?) the slave[
And me [   ] whore [

*(At this point Stratophanes may have noticed Moschion
and addressed him.)*

STRATOPHANES (?)

Young man, [109

*(Here this portion of the Sorbonne papyrus breaks off, and
a gap of unknown length ensues before the next section of
text, which is much more extensive, although in places still
badly mutilated (vv. 110–279, with a seven-line lacuna be-
tween vv. 192 and 193). It is pointless to speculate in any
detail about what might have happened between vv. 109
and 110, although some comments made in the scene di-
rectly after this gap may possibly point to one part of the
lost preceding action. At v. 110 we are 40 lines from the end
of the third act, and Stratophanes and Theron, identified
here by name in the text (the former at 135 and 142, the lat-
ter at 146), are on stage. They are in the middle of a dis-
cussion about a situation which will make a third person
furious (112), involve one of the speakers (presumably
Stratophanes) profiting from what he owns (118), and re-*

227

(After v. 109 there is a gap of incalculable length. The next fragment of papyrus S begins 40 lines before the end of the third act.)

ΘΗΡΩΝ

110   ]κες διαμένει, μηδὲ σαυτὸν ἀξίου
τ]ούτου ποτ᾽ ἔσται καιρός.

ΣΤΡΑΤΟΦΑΝΗΣ

εὖ γε, νὴ Δία.

ΘΗΡΩΝ

] γὰρ αὐτόν, ἐπιπαροξυνθήσεται.
εἴτε ....]ασιν οὕτως εἴτε μή, πεπράξεται
πάντα νῦν. ἔστ]ω, δεδόχθω.

110–77 Fr. X of S (BB): 110–32 col. A with the first 10–12 letters of each line cut off, 133–54 col. B, 155–77 col. C. Part division and assignment of speakers in 110–19 are uncertain (the assignments here are tentatively suggested by Arnott, the part division in 111 by Blanchard–Bataille, 111–112 and 117–18 Mette, 114 several, 115, 117, 118–19 Arnott).

110 Or]σες.

113 First εἴτε suppl. Arnott, second εἴτε Handley correcting ειτα S.   πεπραζεται S.

114 πάντα νῦν suppl. Arnott *exempli gratia*, ἔστ]ω Jacques (comparing [Aristaenetus] 1.21.1).

sult in more than one person being preserved (121). These
remarks in a passage of regrettably mutilated text may
partly link up with, partly presage, information given
more clearly in the final scene of this act (vv. 125–49),
when the slave Pyrrhias brings news that Stratophanes
was not the offspring of his Sicyonian foster parents but an
Athenian citizen, and thus arguably not responsible for the
repayment of the debt that his foster father had died owing.
It is possible that at some point before v. 110 either the
Boeotian creditor or more probably some Athenian acting
on his behalf had turned up (like Crito in Terence's Andria
796ff.) with the intention of seizing Stratophanes' Athe-
nian property (including slaves such as Philoumene and
Dromon) as part payment of his foster father's debt. Such a
person would naturally be furious if Stratophanes' claim to
Athenian citizenship had been used in order to evade an
obligation to repay a Sicyonian debt.

Vv. 110–49 are composed in trochaic tetrameters. Muti-
lation in vv. 110–32 makes speech division, supplemen-
tation of gaps and interpretation often difficult and some-
times impossible.)

THERON (?)
] persists. Don't think yourself   110
] one day there'll be time for that.

STRATOPHANES (?)
                                        That's fine!

THERON (?)
] him, you see; he'll be more furious.
[Whether they   ] in this way or not, [it all (?)] will have
[Now (?)] been settled. [Let's accept it] and agree.

ΣΤΡΑΤΟΦΑΝΗΣ

νῦν δοκεῖ μοι, νὴ Δία,

115 ταῦτα γοῦν.]

ΘΗΡΩΝ

οὐκ ἐ]νθάδ᾽ ἦσθα, διαλογισμὸν οὐθενὸς

,] μὰ τὴν Ἀθηνᾶν. πρῶτον εὐφρονέστερον

τοῦτ᾽ ἂν ἦν ποεῖν.]

ΣΤΡΑΤΟΦΑΝΗΣ

Ἄ]πολλον· εὖ γε, νὴ τὸν Ἥλιον.

ΘΗΡΩΝ

] τῶν σῶν ὄνασθαι μηθέν᾽ ἄλλον, ἀλλὰ σέ.

ΣΤΡΑΤΟΦΑΝΗΣ

]ον εἶπον οὐδὲ προὐνόησά ‹γ᾽› οἵτινες

120   ]

ΘΗΡΩΝ

ὁ] ποῖος;

ΣΤΡΑΤΟΦΑΝΗΣ

Πυρρίας, ὃν οἴκαδε

115 Suppl. Arnott *exempli gratia* (ἐ]νθάδ᾽ already Blanchard–Bataille).   116 πρωτοτευφθονεστερον S.   117 Suppl. Arnott *exempli gratia*.   119 ‹γ᾽› added by Arnott.
120 Suppl. Barigazzi, Kassel.   Part division suggested by several.

---

20 The mutilated remains of vv. 110–23 are difficult to interpret and impossible to supplement with any confidence.

230

STRATOPHANES (?)

Yes, I agree

Now, [at least to that]!

THERON (?)

You were[n't (?)] here, [so you]   115
never [made a (?)] list
Of a single [thing you owned (?)], I'll swear to that!
    More sensibly
[You'd have seen to that (?)] at first!

STRATOPHANES (?)

Good heavens! Yes, that's really good!

THERON

] no one else but you should profit from
your worldly goods.

STRATOPHANES (?)

] I (?) did[n't] say or plan for who[20]
]

(The slave Pyrrhias now approaches by one of the parodoi, apparently walking very quickly and seeming to be in the doldrums.)

THERON

Who's he?

STRATOPHANES

It's Pyrrhias, whom [I sent (?)] home[21]   120

---

[21] Presumably to the house of Stratophanes' foster parents, whether that was in Athens or (less probably: see my comments at beginning of play) Sicyon.

MENANDER

].. ἑαυτόν, ἵνα φράσῃ σεσωμένους
]ντες ὀλίγων.

ΘΗΡΩΝ
οἶδα· πρὸς τὴν μητέρα
τόνδ' ἐπέμψα]μεν.

ΣΤΡΑΤΟΦΑΝΗΣ
τί οὖν δεῦρ' ἔρχεται μαθὼν πάλιν
καὶ διὰ σπουδῆς] βαδίζων;

ΘΗΡΩΝ
καὶ σκυθρωπὸς ἔρχεται.

ΣΤΡΑΤΟΦΑΝΗΣ
125 ἦ τι συμβέβη]κεν ἡμῖν, Πυρρία, νεώτερον;

ΠΤΡΡΙΑΣ
ἤ γε σὴ μήτηρ] τέθνηκε· πέρυσιν.

ΣΤΡΑΤΟΦΑΝΗΣ
οἴμοι.

ΠΤΡΡΙΑΣ
γραῦς σφόδρ' ἦν.

121 Corr. several: τεσωμενους S.

122 ολιων S, with one-letter space afterwards.

122–23 οἶδα—ἐπέμψα]μεν assigned to Theron by Perusino (one-letter space after but not before S's τιουνν).

123 τόνδ' supplied *exempli gratia* by Arnott, ἐπέμψα]μεν by Mette.   124 Supplied *exempli gratia* by Arnott (καὶ μάλα σπουδῇ already Sandbach).   βαδίζων several: βαδιζω S with space after it.   125 ἦ τι suppl. Gallavotti, Oguse–Schwartz, συμβέβη[κεν several.

232

] himself, to say that [they've] been saved[22]
] a few.

THERON
I know—we (?) [sent him] to your mother's house
.]

STRATOPHANES
So what's he learnt to make him come back here,
Moving [hell for leather (?)].

THERON
Yes, and he comes sunk in gloom!

(By now Pyrrhias has reached centre stage.)

STRATOPHANES
Pyrrhias, has [something happened]? Have you got some   125
news for us?

PYRRHIAS
[Yes, your mother]'s died—last year.

STRATOPHANES
That's dreadful!

PYRRHIAS
She was very old.

---

[22] It is uncertain whether the 'they' here refers to people
(members of the Sicyonian family?) or things (the property of
Stratophanes' foster parents?).

---

126 Suppl. Arnott (ἤ γε μήτηρ σου Barigazzi).   πυρυσιν
corrected to περ- in S, with space after (but not before it, nor after
οἴμοι); part divisions and assignments suggested by several.
γρανσφοδρην S.

ΣΤΡΑΤΟΦΑΝΗΣ

φιλτάτη δ᾽ ὅμω]ς ἐκείνη γέγονεν.

ΠΥΡΡΙΑΣ

ἀλλ᾽ ἐν πράγμασιν,

Στρατοφάνη, κ]αινοῖς ἔσει σὺ σφόδρα τ᾽
ἀνελπίστοις τισίν.
οὐ γὰρ αὐτῆς ἦσ]θας υός, ὡς ἔοικεν.

ΣΤΡΑΤΟΦΑΝΗΣ

ἀλλὰ τοῦ;

ΠΥΡΡΙΑΣ

130   ]ο τελευτῶσ᾽ ἐνθαδὶ τὸ σὸν γένος
ἐ]γραψεν.

ΘΗΡΩΝ

ἀποθνήσκων οὐ φθονεῖ
οὐδενὸς τοῖς ζ]ῶσιν ἀγαθοῦ· τοὺς σεαυτοῦ σ᾽
ἀγνοεῖν
οὐκ ἐβούλετ᾽.

ΠΥΡΡΙΑΣ

οὐ μόνον δ᾽ ἦν τοῦτο· καὶ δίκην δέ τω
ὦφλεν ὁ πατήρ, ὡς ἔοικε, ζῶν ὁ σὸς Βοιωτίῳ.

ΣΤΡΑΤΟΦΑΝΗΣ

135   ἐπυθόμην.

127 Suppl. Austin.   εμπραγμασιν S.
128 Suppl. several.   συφοδρα S.
129 Suppl. several.   ωις S: corr. several.
131 Space after]γραψεν in S.

SIKYONIOI

STRATOPHANES
[All the same,] she's been [most precious]!

PYRRHIAS
Even so, [Stratophanes],
You'll be in a new position, one that's unexpected, too—
Very much so! You [were not her] son, it seems.

STRATOPHANES
Whose am I, then?

(*Pyrrhias now reveals a letter, written on a wooden tablet, that he has been carrying.*)

PYRRHIAS
[   ] here's where she wrote down details of your family   130
On her deathbed [   ].

THERON
(*sententiously*)
People, when they die, don't grudge
[Any] boon to [those] surviving. She'd no wish to hide from you
Knowledge of your kin.

PYRRHIAS
It wasn't just that—when your father was
Still alive, he lost a suit with some Boeotian, so it seems.

STRATOPHANES
So I heard.

---

132 Suppl. Mette.   τουσεαυτου S: corr. Handley, Papatho-
mopoulos.

134 in S has paragraphus under it.   ωφελεν S: corr. several.

MENANDER

ΠΙΤΡΡΙΑΣ

πολλῶν ταλάντων, Στρατοφάνη, κατὰ σύμβολα.

ΣΤΡΑΤΟΦΑΝΗΣ

ἦλθε περὶ τούτων ἁπάντων μοι τότ᾽ εὐθὺς γράμματα
τήν τε τοῦ πατρὸς τελευτὴν ἅμα λέγοντ᾽ εἰς Καρίαν.

ΠΙΤΡΡΙΑΣ

ὄντ᾽ ἀγώγιμόν σε τούτῳ πυθομένη τῶν τοὺς νόμους
εἰδότων τήν τ᾽ οὐσίαν σου, τοῦτο προὐνοεῖτό σου
140 καὶ τελευτῶσ᾽ ἀπεδίδου σε τοῖς σεαυτοῦ γ᾽ εὐλόγως.

ΣΤΡΑΤΟΦΑΝΗΣ

δὸς τὸ γραμματείδιόν μοι.

137 and 140 in S have paragraphi under them.
137 καιριαν S: corr. several.
138 αγωγομον S.   τουτων S: corr. Kassel.
139 πουνοειτο S: corr. several.
140 Corr. Arnott (after σεαυτοῦ Papathomopoulos, ἑαυτοῦ γ᾽ several): εαυτων S.
141, 142, 143, 144, 145 and 146 in S have paragraphi under them.
141 γραμματιδιον S: corr. several.   S has a space after μοι.

---

[23] Such 'interstate agreements' (σύμβολα in the Greek) were made by two independent states allowing their respective nationals to fight legal actions in either territory: see especially Kahrstedt in *RE* IVa.1 (1931) s.v. Συμβολή, σύμβολον 1, 1088–90, A. W. Gomme, *A Historical Commentary on Thucydides,* I (Oxford 1945) 237–39, P. Gauthier, *Symbola: Les étrangers et la*

236

PYRRHIAS

     Stratophanes, by interstate agreements[23] his   135
Debt was many talents.

STRATOPHANES

       At the time a letter quickly reached
Me in Caria about all that, with news too of the death
Of my father.

PYRRHIAS

    When she learnt from legal experts that this man[24]
Could distrain you and your goods, she planned ahead
   for you, and tried
Shrewdly at her death to give you back to your own   140
   family.

STRATOPHANES

Let me have the letter.

(Pyrrhias hands the letter to Stratophanes, and then produces a bundle of other items.)

justice dans les cités grecques (Nancy 1972), D. M. MacDowell, *The Law in Classical Athens* (London 1978) 220–21, and S. C. Todd, *The Shape of Athenian Law* (Oxford 1993) 63, 333–34. Menander here must imagine that such an agreement was in force between Sicyon and the Boeotian's city, enabling the Boeotian to distrain property belonging to Stratophanes' foster father in payment of the latter's debt. If Stratophanes could prove that he was a free Athenian, however, he would not be liable for that debt after his foster father's decease, since any judgement based on an agreement between Sicyon and a Boeotian city would not apply to Athens.

24 The Boeotian creditor.

MENANDER

ΠΥΡΡΙΑΣ

καὶ ταδὶ χωρὶς φέρω
τῶν γεγραμμένων ἐκείνοις, Στρατοφάνη,
γνωρίσματα
καὶ τεκμήρι᾽, ὡς ἐκείνην ἔφασαν οἱ δόντες λέγειν
ζῶσαν.

ΘΗΡΩΝ

ὦ δέσποιν᾽ Ἀθηνᾶ, τουτονὶ σαυτῆς πόει,
145 ἵνα λάβῃ τὴν παῖδ᾽, ἐγὼ δὲ Μαλθάκην.

ΣΤΡΑΤΟΦΑΝΗΣ

βαδίζετε.

δεῦρο, Θήρων.

ΘΗΡΩΝ

οὐ λέγεις μοι;

ΣΤΡΑΤΟΦΑΝΗΣ

πρόαγε· μηθέν μοι λάλει.

ΘΗΡΩΝ

ἀλλ᾽ ὅμως—κἀγὼ βαδίζω.

141 φέρω Kassel: λεγω S.
144–45 S has a space after ζωσαν, and a dicolon after
μαλθακην.   βαδίζετε several: βιαζετε S.
146 πρόαγε Barigazzi, Evangelinos: πραγε S.
146–47 Speech divisions and assignments uncertain; here as
suggested by Barigazzi, Kassel (in *Eranos* 43, 1965, 6 = *Kleine
Schriften*, Berlin and New York 1991, 277) and Webster.
147 and 149 in S have paragraphi under them.

PYRRHIAS

And I've *these* here, in addition to
What they[25] wrote—they're evidence and tokens of
  identity.
That's what those who gave them claimed she said,
  Stratophanes, when she
Was alive.

THERON

O Lady Athena, make this man your countryman,[26]
So that he may win the girl, and I gain Malthake!

STRATOPHANES
(addressing both Theron and Pyrrhias as he moves off)
                                          Come on—   145
This way, Theron.

THERON
Can't you tell me—

STRATOPHANES
                  Forward—stop your chattering!

THERON
Even so—

*(As Theron disobediently lingers, Stratophanes makes a
threatening gesture.)*

          I'm really coming.

[25] 'They' (ἐκείνοις) are presumably the people mentioned in
v. 143 as 'those who gave' (οἱ δόντες) the tokens to Pyrrhias and
wrote down the foster mother's dying words.
[26] I.e. a free Athenian, and so able to marry Philoumene.

MENANDER

ΣΤΡΑΤΟΦΑΝΗΣ

         καὶ σὺ δεῦρο, Πυρρία·
τῶν ἐμῶν λόγων γὰρ οἴσεις εὐθέως τὰ σύμβολα
καὶ παρὼν δείξεις ἐάν τις αὐτὰ βούληται σκοπεῖν.

ΧΟΡΟΥ

ΜΕΡΟΣ Δ΄

ΣΜΙΚΡΙΝΗΣ (?)

150 ὄχλος εἶ, φλυάρου μεστός, ὦ πονηρὲ σύ,
δίκαια τὸν κλάοντα προσδοκῶν λέγειν
καὶ τὸν δεόμενον· τοῦ δὲ μηδὲ ἓν ποεῖν
ὑγιὲς σχεδὸν ταῦτ᾽ ἐστὶ νῦν τεκμήριον.

150 The speaker's name is conjectural, but plausibly based on the supplement at 156.   οχλος corrected from εχλος in S.

151 In the left-hand margin of S the scribe has written H (= 700), presumably as a rough calculation of the number of lines written; see the introduction to this play, n. 5, and app. crit. at vv. 252–53.   τογκλαοντα S.

153 υγιεσχεδον S: corr. several.

---

[1] One possibility, suggested to me by Professor J.-M. Jacques in a letter, is that this democrat was none other than the parasite Theron.

240

STRATOPHANES

Pyrrhias, you too, this way!
You can take the tokens now, these are the proofs of
    what I'll say.
You'll be there to bring them out if someone wants to in-
    vestigate.

(*Stratophanes hands Pyrrhias the bundle and leads him
and Theron off by one of the side entrances in the imagined
direction presumably of the civic centre of Eleusis. When
the stage is empty, the chorus give their third entr'acte per-
formance.*)

ACT IV

(*After the entr'acte two old men enter, probably by the
parodos imagined to lead from the centre of Eleusis. They
are in mid-conversation. One—a supporter of oligarchy—
has a name beginning with Sm (v. 156), and the only
known character name in Greek New Comedy beginning
with these two letters is Smikrines. The other—a keen dem-
ocrat—is not identified by name; he seems to be an ac-
quaintance of Smikrines, appears to be poor while
Smikrines is rich, and may well have appeared in one or
more lost earlier scenes.[1] The metre now reverts to iambic
trimeters.*)

SMIKRINES (?)

Riff-raff—that's what you are, stuffed full of drivel,   150
You rogue, expecting that a man who weeps
And begs will tell the truth! Today that's normally
A sign of total lack of probity.

οὐ κρίνεθ᾽ ἀλήθεια τοῦτον τὸν τρόπον,
155 ἀλλ᾽ ἐν ὀλίγῳ πολλῷ γε μᾶ[λλον συνεδρίῳ.

ΔΗΜΟΤΗΣ
ὀλιγαρχικός γ᾽ εἶ καὶ πονηρός, Σμ[ικρίνη,
νὴ τὸν Δία τὸν μέγιστον.

ΣΜΙΚΡΙΝΗΣ (?)
οὐδέν [μοι μέλει.

ΔΗΜΟΤΗΣ
ὦ Ἡράκλεις, ἀπολεῖτέ μ᾽ οἱ σφόδ[ρ᾽ ἄθλιοι
ὑμεῖς.

ΣΜΙΚΡΙΝΗΣ (?)
τί γάρ μοι λοιδορεῖ; βαρύς [τις εἶ·

ΔΗΜΟΤΗΣ
160 μισῶ σε καὶ τοὺς τὰς ὀφρῦς ἐπη[ρκότας
ἅπαντας. ὄχλος ὢν δ᾽ ὁμολογῶ, [πιστός γε μήν.

ΣΜΙΚΡΙΝΗΣ (?)
οὐκ ἂν γένοιτο τοῦτ᾽.

ΔΗΜΟΤΗΣ
ἐγώ σε .[
τὸν πλούσιον κλέπτοντα σ.[

154 ηαληθεια S.

155, 156, 157, 159 and 161 in S have paragraphi under them.

155 ολιωι S.   μα[λλον suppl. several, συνεδρίῳ Lloyd-Jones, Sandbach.   156 ολιαρχικος S.   Σμ[ικρίνη suppl. several.   157 Suppl. Austin.   158 Suppl. Arnott.

159 S has a space before τι.   λοιδορεῖ several: λοιδορεις S. τις εἶ suppl. Sandbach.   160 Suppl. Chantraine.

That's not the way that truth's decided—no,
It's reached far [better] in a small [committee].   155

SMIKRINES [DEMOCRAT]

DEMOCRAT

You're an elitist,[2] Sm[ikrines], upon
My oath—a rogue, too!

SMIKRINES (?)
     [I] don't [give a damn! (?)]

DEMOCRAT

You lot are too [contemptible (?)], you'll be
The death of me, I swear!

SMIKRINES (?)
     Why call me names?

[You're] poison!

DEMOCRAT
     You and all your snooty friends—   160
I loathe them. I admit I'm riff-raff, [but
I'm honest. (?)]

SMIKRINES (?)
     That could never be!

DEMOCRAT
       I [   ] you
With all your riches stealing [

---

[2] Literally, 'oligarchic supporter.' On the struggles between
oligarchs and democrats at the time of Menander's play, see also
the introduction to this play.

---

161 Suppl. Arnott.   162, 166, 167 and 168 in S have
paragraphi under them.   162 ? e.g. ἐγὼ σὲ ν[ῦν ὁρῶ Arnott.
163 τομπλουσιον S.

σκεύη τε καὶ τούτων απot.[

165 ἀργύριον. οὐκ ἐξ οἰκίας ἴσως φ[
τῶν ἀγομένων ἐκεῖσε προ[

ΣΜΙΚΡΙΝΗΣ (?)

οἴμωζε.

ΔΗΜΟΤΗΣ

καὶ σύ.

ΣΜΙΚΡΙΝΗΣ (?)
νοῦν ἔχεις φ[εύγων· σκάφης
ἐγὼ γὰρ ἄν σ᾽ ἐπόησα συστο[μώτερον.

165 Punctuation by Marzullo.   φ[έρειν suppl. Barigazzi, φ[έρεις Kassel.
167 One letter space before and after καισυ in S. φ[εύγων suppl. Kassel.   σκάφης suppl. Kassel, Barigazzi.
168 Suppl. Kassel, Barigazzi, Gallavotti.   συνστο[S.

3 These mutilated lines are difficult to interpret and supplement, but the democrat seems to be accusing Smikrines of stealing property and money. These charges *may* have been wild and unsubstantiated, but it would make better dramatic sense if they could be linked in some way to previous statements or actions in the plot. Could Smikrines have acted as the Boeotian creditor's representative in Athens, and have threatened or attempted to distrain Stratophanes' property in a lost earlier scene? If so, the 'property' and 'money' (164–65) would have belonged to Stratophanes, and it is at least feasible that 'those being taken there' (166) were slaves (including Philoumene and Dromon?) being taken to Smikrines' house. There would also be an attractive irony if Smikrines was presented as a man who in ignorance of his blood ties intended to destrain his own son's goods; an obvious

Both property and their [
Money! Not from a house perhaps [165
Those being taken there[3] [

SMIKRINES (?)

To hell with you!

DEMOCRAT

You too!

(After saying this, the democrat angrily departs, but whether into one of the stage houses or by a side entrance, is unknown.)

SMIKRINES (?)

      [Gone!] You've shown sense—
Else I'd have closed your mouth tight [like a clam]![4]

parallel is provided by *Epitrepontes*, where another Smikrines acted as the arbitrator of his own grandson's future in similar ignorance of the relationship.

[4] This is perhaps as near as modern English can approach to the original Greek, which runs literally 'For otherwise I'd have made you tighter-lipped than a (metic's) tray.' This was an Athenian saying, based on the fact (see Theophrastus fr. 654 Fortenbaugh = 103 Wimmer) that in state processions metics (non-citizens registered as residents in Attica) carried a tray or bowl, and so were nicknamed 'tray carriers' or just 'trays.' Metics were denied any share in political life in Athens, and were commonly expected to comply in silence with decisions made by the Athenian government: cf. e.g. Aesch. *Suppl.* 202, Soph. *O.C.* 12–13, Eur. *Med.* 222–24 and *Suppl.* 893–95 (with C. Collard's commentary on 891b–95 in his edition, Groningen 1975). See D. Whitehead, *The Ideology of the Athenian Metic = PCPhS* suppl. 4, Cambridge 1977, especially 6–7, 69–71, 89–97, 164, and *PCPhS* 32 (1986) 145–58.

245

ΕΛΕΤΣΙΝΙΟΣ

γεραιέ, μεῖνον ἐμπαραστὰ[ς ἐνθάδε.

ΣΜΙΚΡΙΝΗΣ (?)

170 μένω· τίνος δὲ τοῦτο θωύσ[σεις χάριν;

ΕΛΕΤΣΙΝΙΟΣ

ὡς ἂν σὺ μικρὸν καὶ καπν[ῷ φέρῃς ὕδωρ.

ΣΜΙΚΡΙΝΗΣ (?)

βουλόμεθ' ἀκοῦσαι τὰ περὶ τ[οῦ καπνοῦ, γέρον.
καλ..υ....φαίνει δὲ ..[

ΕΛΕΤΣΙΝΙΟΣ

εἰδώς γ' ἃ πυν[θάνει

ΣΜΙΚΡΙΝΗΣ (?)

175 ἅπασαν ἡμῖν εἰ[πὲ τήν γε συμφοράν.

169, 170, 171, 173 and 174 in S have paragraphi under them.
169 ωγεραιε S: corr. and suppl. Arnott.
170 Suppl. several.
171–72 Suppl. tentatively and *exempli gratia* Arnott.
174 Corr. and suppl. Sandbach: ειδωστα S.
175 εἰπὲ suppl. several, τήν γε συμφοράν Arnott (τὴν κατάστασιν Handley).

SIKYONIOI

(After this remark Smikrines moves towards his own house, but his exit is stopped by the sudden arrival of Eleusinios, via the side entrance opposite to that just used by the departing democrat, if the latter used a parodos for his exit. From v. 169 to v. 171 the speakers clearly ape the language and rhythms of tragedy, and Eleusinios' extraordinarily long speech from 176–271 at times echoes phrases from the messenger's speech in Euripides' Orestes 866–956 (see the introduction to this play). For convenience those echoed phrases are printed in Greek and translation at the foot of each relevant page.)

ELEUSINIOS

Old man, stay [where you are], stand by the door!

SMIKRINES (?)

I stay, but [why] do you shout this command?   170

ELEUSINIOS

That you may [bring (?)] a little [water to a smoking fire (?)].[5]

SMIKRINES (?)

We wish to hear about the [smoke, old man (?)].
[   ] but you seem [

ELEUSINIOS

Yes, knowing what [you] learn (?) [

SMIKRINES (?)

Give us [a] full account [of this event].   175

---

[5] Interpretation and supplementation of the mutilated text here are very uncertain.

ΕΛΕΤΣΙΝΙΟΣ

ἐτύγχανον μὲν οὐ[
βαίνων, μὰ τὸν Δί, οὔτε τ[
    (15–17 letters)]ε τοῦτ᾿ ἐμοί, καλῶς ποῶν
    (11–13)   ] καὶ τῶν ἄλλων κακὰ
180   (8–10)]μαι φοβερὸς εἰς τριώβολον
    (4–6)].ε κοινὸν μέγα βοῶν οἷς ἂν τύχω
δημο]τικός, οἵπερ καὶ μόνοι σῴζουσι γῆν,
ἐξ] ἄστεως δ᾿ ἥκων ἵν᾿ ἐντύχοιμι τῷ
τ]ῶν δημοτῶν μέλλοντι λεπτὸν βοΐδιον
185 νέμειν ἀκούειν θ᾿ ὅσα πρόσεστ᾿ αὐτῷ κακὰ
ὑπὸ τῶν λαβόντων μερίδα. τούτων δ᾿ αὐτὸς ἦν·
τοῦ τῆς θεοῦ δήμου γὰρ ἦν ἐπώνυμος—
βλέπ᾿ εἰς μ᾿—Ἐλευσίνιος. ἐπέστην ὄχλον ἰδὼν
πρὸς τοῖς προπυλαίοις, καὶ "πάρες μ᾽" εἰπὼν ὁρῶ

176–77 Euripides *Orestes* 866–67 (opening words of messenger's speech) ἐτύγχανον μὲν ἀγρόθεν πυλῶν ἔσω / βαίνων.
182 *Or.* 920 αὐτουργός—οἵπερ καὶ μόνοι σῴζουσι γῆν.
188 *Or.* 871 ὁρῶ δ᾿ ὄχλον στείχοντα.

177 βαίνων several: βαινω with β erased and rewritten above the α S.   Either οὔτε τ[or οὔτ᾿ ἔτ[.
178–213 Fr. V of S (BB): 178–92 col. A, 193–213 col. B; 205–13 = fr. III J).
178 ποιων S.   180 ? σαφῶς πέπυσ]μαι Arnott.
182 Suppl. Handley.
183 Suppl. several.   Either τῷ or τῳ.
184 μελοντι S with the omitted λ written above the o.
188 βλέπ᾿ εἶς μ᾿ tentatively Arnott: βλεπηις S.

ELEUSINIOS

I was just walking, not [
By Zeus, no!—nor [
        ] this for me, as a favour
       ] and other people's troubles
[I like to know (?)]—a terror for the details![6]   180
And [   ] normal. Loudly greeting all I met
—A common man, me—they alone preserve
Our land—I'd come from town to meet the head
Man of the deme,[7] who planned to share with us
A skinny little bullock, and got from   185
The sharers all the insults he deserved. I too
Was one of them. My name comes from Our Lady's[8]
    deme—
Look at me!—Eleusinios. I saw a crowd
Just by the gates,[9] and stopped. I shouted "Let me
    through"

176–77 Euripides, *Orestes* 866–67 I was just walking from the country to / The gates.

182 *Or.* 920 A farmer—they alone preserve our land.

188 *Or.* 871 I saw a crowd proceeding.

[6] Mutilation of the papyrus makes this and the next line hard to fathom. 180 means literally 'terrible' (or 'timorous') 'down to a three-obol coin' (= half a drachma), a small coin that is elsewhere used as a symbol of something insignificant.

[7] A deme was one of the 139 districts into which Attica was politically divided; see especially D. Whitehead, *The Demes of Attica* (Princeton 1986).

[8] Demeter, the principal goddess worshipped at Eleusis.

[9] The Propylaea, at the northeastern entrance to the precinct of Demeter and Persephone in Eleusis.

190 καθημένην παῖδ', ἔκ τε τούτων τῶν κύκλῳ
γενόμενος εὐθὺς δῆμος ἦν, καὶ κύριον
εὑρεῖν ἐπεθύμει τ]ῆς καθημένης κόρης

(Between vv. 192 and 193 there is a gap in the Sorbonne
papyrus of between 6 and 8 lines.)

οὔπω πέπυσμαι π[
ὁ κύριος κακὸν ποήσῃ κ.[
195 καὐτὸς μεθ' ὑμῶν ἐνθαδὶ κα[θίζομαι."
ἐπόησε τοῦτο καὶ μέγ' ὠρεχθή[σαμεν
ἡμεῖς "πολῖτίς ἐστιν ἡ παῖς", καὶ μόλι[ς
οὖν τῷ κύκλῳ πάλιν κατεσβέσθη π[ολὺς
ἦχος. σιωπῆς γενομένης προσίσταται
200 μειράκιον ἐγγὺς τῷ θεράποντι λευκόχρω[ν
ὑπόλειον ἀγένειόν τι, καὶ μικρὸν λαλεῖν
ἐβούλετ'· οὐκ εἰάσαμεν. "μεῖζον λέγε"
εὐθύς τις ἀνεβόησε καὶ "τί βούλεται;

196 Or. 901–02 ἐπερρόθησαν δ' οἱ μὲν ὡς καλῶς λέγοι, / οἱ
δ' οὐκ ἐπήνουν.

190 ἐκ Handley: εις S.   192 Suppl. tentatively Sandbach
(τ]ῆς Blanchard–Bataille).   194 κακομ S.   195 Suppl.
Handley.   196 Corr. and suppl. several: ωροχθη[S.
197 ηταις S.   198 οὖν τῷ Kassel, Oguse: ουτωι S.
κατεσβέσθη Chantraine: κατεσβεσθην S.   π[ολὺς suppl.
several.   199 προσιστασαι S.   201 λαλεῖν Oguse, Web-
ster: λαθυ S.   202–03 S has offset of ναλ from 271 after λεγε,
and offset of π (in παρην) from 270 after βουλεται.

250

And saw a girl[10] sat there. Those standing round   190
At once formed an assembly, [trying to (?)]
[Find out (?)] to whom that seated girl belonged.   192

*(There is a short gap in the papyrus between vv. 192 and
193. It seems to have introduced the slave Dromon into
the narrative, for a speech that he was making is being
described when the text resumes. In the lost lines he must
already have alleged Philoumene's free Athenian birth,
to which a consequential reference is made in v. 197.)*

("")I've not yet learnt [193
My master do some ill [
And I myself with you here [take my seat (?)]."   195
He[11] did this, and we loudly roared "The girl's
A free Athenian," and it was hard
To quench anew the [noisy] clamour all
Around. When silence came, a pale, smooth-faced
And beardless lad[12] appeared just by the slave.   200
He wished to have a quiet word. We would
Not let him. Someone promptly shouted out
"Speak up!" and "What's he want? Who's he? What are

196 *Or.* 901–02 They growled, some that his speech was fine, /
But some did not approve.

[10] Philoumene.
[11] The slave Dromon.
[12] Moschion.

τίς ἐστι; τί λέγεις;" "οἶδέ μ' οὗτος ὁ θεράπων"
205 φησίν, "πάλαι γὰρ οὖν βοηθῶ, κἄν τινος
δέητ', ἐρωτ[ῶ" κ]αὶ "τὰ πόλλ' ἀκήκοα
αὐ]τοῦ λέγοντος ἄρτι πρὸς τὸν δεσπότην."
κα]ὶ κόκκινος γενόμενος ὑπανεδύετο.
κοὐ] παντελῶς ἦν βδελυρός, οὐ σφόδρ' ἤρεσεν
210 ἡ]μῖν δέ, μοιχώδης δὲ μᾶλλον κατεφάνη.
μέ]γ' ἐγκραγόντες εἰς.....[.]........[
νῦ]ν τοῦτον. εἰς θ' ἡμῶν γενόμενος ἔβλεπ[εν
εἰς] τὴν κόρην, ἐλάλε[ι] τε τοῖς ἐγγὺς συχν[ά.
]ον πεφευγυῖ' ἡ κόρη
215 ὄ]ψει τις ἀνδρικὸς πάνυ
]μως, νὴ τὸν Δί', ἐγγὺς ἵσταται
ἄ]νθρωπος ἕτερος, καὶ τρίτος
θεράπων τις α]ὐτῶν· ὡς δ' ἐνέβλεψ' ἐγγύθεν

215 Or. 918 ἀνδρεῖος δ' ἀνήρ.

204 οἶδέ μ' Sandbach: οιδεν S.
205 οὖν Barigazzi: ον S.
206 ἐρωτ[ῶ supplied by Sandbach, κ]αί by Barigazzi, Lloyd-Jones, inverted commas by Jacques.   πολλαακηκοα S.
208 Suppl. Austin, Kassel.
209 Suppl. Blass.
210 ἡ]μῖν Schröder:]μειν S.
211 μέ]γ' suppl. Blass, εἰς deciphered by Coles.
212 νῦ]ν suppl. Austin, ἔβλεπ[εν Jouguet.
213 εἰς] suppl. Blass (but S has space only for ες), ἐλάλε[ι] Jouguet, συχν[ά Schröder.
214–79 Fr. VI (BB) of S (214–35 col. A, 236–57 col. B, 258–79 col. C), joining on to the end of fr. V.

You saying?" He replied "This slave knows who I am.
I've long been helping, and I'm asking if   205
He needs some aid. I've heard him recently
Conversing with his master[13] quite a lot."
And blushing scarlet he withdrew a little.
He wasn't totally repulsive, but
We didn't like him much—he rather seemed   210
A libertine. We shouted out and [then we pushed (?)]
Him [back (?)]. He joined us, but kept looking [at]
The girl, and spoke at length to those nearby
          ] having fled from [him (?)],[14] the girl
          ] someone quite manly in appearance[15]   215
              ] I swear he stood nearby
              ] a second man, and then a third—
[A slave] of theirs. But as he looked upon

215 *Or.* 918 A manly fellow.

[13] Stratophanes.
[14] From Moschion, presumably.
[15] A description of Stratophanes, presumably. The second man
would then be Theron, the third perhaps Pyrrhias.

---

214 ομπεφευγυηι S (πεφευγυῖ correction of Austin, Kassel).
215 Suppl. Kassel, Barigazzi.
218 Suppl. Sandbach *exempli gratia*.

τὴν παρθένον τή]νδ᾽, ἐξαπίνης ποταμόν τινα
220 δακρύων ἀφίησ᾽ ο]ὗτος, ἐμπαθῶς τε τῶν
τριχῶν ἑαυτοῦ λα]μβάνεται βρυχώμενος.
ἔπειτα δ᾽ οἶκτος] ἔλαβε τοὺς ἑστηκότας,
πάντες δ᾽ ἐβόησαν "σὺ δ]ὲ τί βούλει; λέγε, λέγε."
"ἡ παῖς ἐμή 'στι," φησί]ν, "οὕτως ἡ θεὸς
225 δοίη τὸ λοιπόν, ἄνδρες,] ὑμῖν εὐτυχεῖν.
τὴν γὰρ κόρην ἐκτέ]τροφα, μικρὸν παιδίον
                ] αὐτῷ φαίνεται
                ] πρώτιστα μὲν
                ὑ]μῶν ἀξίως
230   ]ησηθ᾽ ὅσ᾽ ἂν
                πατ]ὴρ
                ]ιων ὄχλον
                ]ειν
                ].
235   οἰκέτης ἦν τοῦ πα]τρὸς
αὐτῆς, ἐμὸν δ᾽ ὄντ᾽ ἀποδίδωμι τῇ κόρῃ.

219–22 Or. 949–51 πορεύει δ᾽ αὐτὸν ἐκκλήτων δ᾽ ἄπο / Πυλάδης δακρύων· σὺν δ᾽ ὁμαρτοῦσιν φίλοι / κλαίοντες, οἰκτίροντες.

219 Suppl. Austin exempli gratia (]νδ or]ιδ S).
220–1 Suppl. Austin, Sandbach (λα]μβάνεται already Blanchard–Bataille).
222 Suppl. Arnott (οἶκτος already Kumaniecki, Marzullo).
223 Suppl. Austin exempli gratia (σὺ δ]ὲ already several).
224 Suppl. Arnott (φησί]ν already Kassel).
225 Suppl. Kassel (δοίη already several).

[This girl] so close to him, he suddenly [let flow]
A stream [of tears], and passionately ran   220
His fingers through [his hair (?)], groaning the while.
[Now pity (?)] gripped the people standing there,
[And they all shouted (?)] "What's your wish? Speak!
   Speak!"
[He answered] "May the goddess[16] [grant] you luck,
[Good sirs, in future (?)]—but [the girl is mine (?)]!   225
I've brought [her] up. When still a tiny child   226

*(Lines 227–35 are so badly mutilated that they yield only a
few unconnected scraps of sense:* appears to him (?) 227,
first of all 228, just as you deserve 229, [fath]er (?) 231 *and*
crowd *or* people 232. *The final word preserved in* 235
[fa]ther's *then introduces a well-preserved section of
Eleusinios' speech.)*

         [He][17] was her fa]ther's [slave].   235
He's mine now, but I give him back to her.

219–22 *Or.* 949–51 Pylades in tears / escorts him (Orestes)
from the meeting, and his friends / come with them, weeping,
pitying.

16 Demeter.
17 Dromon, presumably introduced into Stratophanes' re-
marks in the mutilated lines that precede.

---

226 Suppl. Arnott (τέ]τροφα already Blanchard–Bataille).
229, 231 Suppl. Kassel.
235 Suppl. Handley (τοῦ πα]τρὸς already Gallavotti, πα]τρὸς
several).

MENANDER

τροφεῖ ἀφίημ'· οὐδὲν ἀξιῶ λαβεῖν.
εὑρισκέτω τὸν πατέρα καὶ τοὺς συγγενεῖς·
οὐκ ἀντιτάττομ' οὐθέν." "εὖ γ'." "ἀκούσατε

240 καὶ τἀμὰ δ', ἄνδρες. ὄντες αὐτοὶ κύριοι
ταύτης—ἀφεῖται τοῦ φόβου γὰρ ὑπό γ' ἐμοῦ—
πρὸς τὴν ἱέρειαν θέσθε, καὶ τηρησάτω
ὑμῖν ἐκείνη τὴν κόρην." πολλήν τινα
τοῦθ', ὡς προσῆκ', εὔνοιαν εἵλκυσ'· ἀνέκραγον

245 "ὀρθῶς γε" πάντες, εἶτα "λέγε" πάντες πάλιν.
"Σικυώνιος τὸ πρότερον εἶναι προσεδόκων
κἀγώ. πάρεστι δ' οὑτοσί μοι νῦν φέρων
μητρὸς διαθήκας καὶ γένους γνωρίσματα·
οἶμαι δὲ καὐτός, εἴ τι τοῖς γεγραμμένοις

250 τούτοις τεκμαίρεσθαί με πιστεῦσαί τε δεῖ,
εἶναι πολίτης ὑμέτερος. τὴν ἐλπίδα
μήπω μ' ἀφέλησθ', ἀλλ', ἂν φανῶ τῆς παρθένου
κἀγὼ πολίτης, ἣν ἔσωσα τῷ πατρί,
ἐάσατ' αἰτῆσαί με τοῦτον καὶ λαβεῖν.

237 Corr. several: τρεφεισαφιημι S.   238 τομπατερα S.
239 ενγε S.   240 Corr. several: ανδρασοντας S.
242 τηρησατωι S.   243 Corr. several: εκεινηντηγκορην
S.   245 παντασειτα S.   246 Corr. several: προσεδοκουν
S.   247 Corr. several: ουτοσοιμοι S.   249 Corr. several:
οιμοιδε and τισοις S.   252 Corr. Barigazzi, Reeve, Handley:
αφελης S.   253–54 In the left-hand margin of S the scribe
has written a coronis, and to its left Θ (= 800), presumably as a
rough calculation of the number of lines written; see n. 5 on the
introduction to this play, and app. crit. at v. 151.   254 Corr.
Chantraine: εασας S.

I cancel charges for her rearing, I don't claim
A penny. Let her find her father and
Her relatives. I've no objections." "Fine," we cried.
"Hear my proposals, gentlemen," he said.   240
"*You* are her guardians, I've removed that fear[18]
From her, so place her with the priestess.[19] She can guard
The girl for you." This won great favour, as
Was proper. They all cried "That's fair!" and then
Again "Go on!" He said "I formerly assumed   245
That I too[20] hailed from Sicyon, but this fellow
Who's standing by me now[21] has brought my mother's will
And indications of my ancestry.
If I'm to judge by what is written here,
And place my faith in it, I think that I   250
Too am your fellow citizen.[22] Don't dash
My hopes now, but if I as well am shown
To share my citizenship with this girl,
Whom I protected for her father, let me ask

[18] Philoumene need no longer fear any possible ill-treatment (such as sexual harassment) from Stratophanes now that he has acknowledged her free status and proposed that the citizens of Eleusis become her guardians in place of himself.

[19] The priestess of Demeter.

[20] That is, as well as his foster parents.

[21] Pyrrhias.

[22] Sc. an Athenian, like the free men participating in the assembly.

MENANDER

255　τῶν ἀντιπραττόντων δ' ἐμοὶ τῆς παρθένου
　　μηθεὶς γενέσθω κύριος πρὶν ἂν φανῇ
　　ἐκεῖνος." "ὀρθῶς καὶ δίκαι', ὀρθῶς." "ἄγε
　　πρὸς τὴν ἱέρειαν, ἄγε λαβών." ὁ λευκόχρω[ς
　　ἐκεῖνος ἐξαίφνης τε παραπηδᾷ πάλ[ιν
260　καὶ φησι "ταυτὶ συμπέπεισθ', ὡς οὑτοσὶ
　　νῦν ἐξαπίνης εἴληφε διαθήκας ποθέ[ν,
　　ἐστί τε πολίτης ὑμέτερος, τραγῳδίᾳ
　　κενῇ τ' ἀγόμενος τὴν κόρην ἀφήσε[ται;"
　　"ἆρ' οὐκ ἀποκτενεῖς τὸν ἐξυρημένον;"
265　"μὰ Δί', ἀλλά σ', ὅστις—οὐ γάρ;" "οὐκ ἐκ τοῦ
　　μέσ[ου,
　　λάσταυρε;" "πόλλ' ὑμῖν γένοιτο κἀγ[αθά."
　　ἐκεῖνος "ἄγε, βάδιζ' ἀναστάσ'." ὁ θερά[πων
　　"ὑμῶν κελεόντων βαδιεῖται" φη[σί, καὶ
　　"κελεύετ', ἄνδρες." "ναί, βάδιζ'." ἀνίστ[ατο,

　　　　256 πριναμφανη S.
　　　　257 δικαια S.　　　259 παραπηδαις S.
　　　　260 συμπέπεισθ' Arnott, Gallavotti: συμπεποιθ S.
　　　　262 τραγωιδια[S.　　　264 αιρουκαποτεινεις with the omit-
　　　　ted κ written above οτ S: corr. several.
　　　　265 σ', ὅστις Handley: σοιτις S.　　　μέσ[ου suppl. several.
　　　　266 Suppl. several.　　　267 βαδιζε S.
　　　　268 Suppl. several.　　　269 βάδιζ' several: βαδιζο S.

---

23 The girl's father. Athenian marriages were arranged by
the male suitor and the girl's father or guardian; cf. e.g. Men.
Asp. 290–93, *Dysk.* 751–2, 759–63, 827–44; A. R. W. Harrison,
The Law of Athens, I (Oxford 1968) 1–9, 17–21, D. M.

Him[23] for her hand in marriage. None of my   255
Opponents[24] must take charge of her before
He's found!" We cried "That's right and fair, that's right!"
And he, "Now take her to the priestess, take
Her!" Instantly that white-faced lad jumped in
Once more, and said "Do you believe that suddenly   260
He's found a will from somewhere, and is now
Your fellow citizen? That he will take the girl
With this inane performance, then release her?"
A voice: "Won't you get rid of smoothface?" "No—
Get stuffed, whoever you are!" "Out you go,   265
You queer!" "Best wishes to you all!"[25] The goody to
The girl: "Up now, do come!" The slave cut in:
"She'll come, if you all tell her to," [and] "Sirs,
Tell her!" "Yes, come!" She rose and then began

MacDowell, *The Law in Classical Athens* (London 1978) 86–89,
C. B. Patterson in S. B. Pomeroy (ed.), *Women's History and Ancient History* (Chapel Hill, N.C. and London 1991) 49–50, and S.
C. Todd, *The Shape of Athenian Law* (Oxford 1993) 210–16.

[24] The 'opponents' (in the plural) were Moschion, in love with
Philoumene and so Stratophanes' rival (cf. vv. 199–207, 258–64,
397 ff.), and presumably also the Boeotian creditor (? with an
Athenian representative: cf. nn. on 135, 138, 166, 271–72, and
comment between vv. 109 and 110), wishing to gain possession
of Philoumene as a slave in part payment of the debt owed by
Stratophanes' foster father.

[25] Lines 264–69 require a talented actor to imitate a series of
different voices: an unnamed participant in the assembly and
Moschion in an angry exchange, ending with Moschion's sarcastic
good wishes to the assembly (264–66); Stratophanes, Dromon and
the assembly (the "Sirs" addressed at 268) responding with "Yes,
come!" in the following line (267–69).

270 ἐβάδιζε. μεχρὶ τούτου παρῆν. τ[ὰ δ᾽ ὕστερα
οὐκέτι λέγειν ἔχοιμ᾽ ἄν, ἀλλ᾽ ἀπ[έρχομαι.

ΜΟΣΧΙΩΝ

τοὺς ἀνδραποδιστὰς ἀπαγαγεῖ[ν ὑμᾶς θέλω.

ΣΤΡΑΤΟΦΑΝΗΣ

ἡμᾶς σύ;

271 *Or.* 956 (closing words of messenger's speech) ἀλλ᾽
ἀπώλεσεν.

270 Suppl. Austin.
271 in S has a paragraphus under it.   Suppl. Austin,
Handley.
272, 273, 274, 275, 276 and 277 in S have paragraphi under
them.
272 Suppl. Austin.

---

271 *Or.* 956 (closing words of messenger's speech) But he
finished (Orestes) off.

[26] Given the limitation to three speaking actors in Menander's
plays, the actor playing Eleusinios would have had to make a quick
change before reentering in the role of Moschion. The time taken
for the change could have been easily covered by stage business,
with Stratophanes and companion(s) seeking to establish which
was Smikrines' house. See F. H. Sandbach, *PCPS* 13 (1967) 39–40.

[27] Moschion must have believed that his family legally owned
Philoumene (? because Smikrines, Moschion's father, had been
acting as the Boeotian creditor's representative: see n. on v. 256),
so that when Stratophanes placed the girl under protection of the
priestess, this was equivalent to an act of kidnapping. Kidnapping

To move. I stayed till then. [What happened after]   270
I couldn't now report, [but off I went.]

*(At the end of his long speech Eleusinios departs along the
parodos from which he originally entered. Smikrines may
have stayed on stage as a silent witness of the opening of the
next scene, but more probably he went off into his own
house. Along the same parodos as Eleusinios eventually
Stratophanes enters, probably accompanied by Theron
and/or Pyrrhias (here played by a mute or mutes). They
must be imagined to have left Philoumene with the priest-
ess of Demeter and to have come on stage in search of
Smikrines' house, acting on information provided by the
documents and tokens that Stratophanes has received, to
the effect that Smikrines is Stratophanes' real father.
Moschion[26] then enters by the same parodos, eager to
arrest Stratophanes and his companion(s) for allegedly
kidnapping[27] Philoumene, the girl that he too loves.)*

MOSCHION
(going up to Stratophanes)
[I wish] to apprehend [you—you are] kidnappers!

STRATOPHANES
(taken aback)
You? Apprehend us?

was one of the offences for which in Athens a citizen's arrest
($\dot{\alpha}\pi\alpha\gamma\omega\gamma\acute{\eta}$) was legally permitted. See especially F. H. Sandbach,
PCPhS 13 (1967) 41–44, A. R. W. Harrison, *The Law of Athens*, II
(Oxford 1971) 222–29, and H. M. Hansen, *Apagoge, Endeixis and
Ephegesis against Kakourgoi, Atimoi and Pheugontes* (Odense
1976).

ΜΟΣΧΙΩΝ

νὴ τὸν Ἥλιον.

ΣΤΡΑΤΟΦΑΝΗΣ

κορυ[βαντιᾷς,

μειράκιον.

ΜΟΣΧΙΩΝ

ἐξαίφνης πολίτ[ης ἀναφανείς;

275 γενναῖον.

ΣΤΡΑΤΟΦΑΝΗΣ

οὐκ ἔξεστι πο[

ΜΟΣΧΙΩΝ

πῶς; ἀγνοῶ τὸ τοιοῦτο[

ΣΤΡΑΤΟΦΑΝΗΣ

ὁρᾷς; βάδιζ᾽ εἰς ἐξετα[σμὸν

πρᾶγμ᾽ ἐξεταζε[

279 παρὰ τῆς ἱερεία[ς

(Between vv. 279 and 280 there is a gap in the Sorbonne
papyrus of most probably 2, 3 or 4 complete columns, i.e.
approximately 46, 69 or 92 lines.)

273 Space before and after τονηλιον in S.　κορυ[βαντιᾷς
suppl. several.

274 μιρακιον S with space after it.　πολίτ[ης ἀναφανείς
suppl. Arnott (π. ἀνεφάνης Sandbach).

275 Space after γενναιον in S.

277 ἐξετα[σμὸν or ἐξέτα[σιν: suppl. Kassel.

279 ιερεα[S.

MOSCHION
Yes indeed.

STRATOPHANES
                              Young man,
[You're] crazy!

MOSCHION
(*sarcastically*)
                    Suddenly [appearing as]
A citizen! That's rich!

STRATOPHANES
          [I (?)] can't [275

MOSCHION
How? I don't know about a thing like this [

STRATOPHANES
You see? Go now to scrutinise [
To scrutinise a matter [
[Get (?)] from the priestess [279

(*Although mutilation in vv. 275–79 prevents an assured interpretation, they seem to have included a suggestion that the dispute between Moschion and Stratophanes could be settled by a visit to the priestess and an examination in her presence of the evidence for Philoumene's free Athenian birth. After 279 there is a sizable gap in the papyrus, in which Moschion apparently made his exit into Smikrines' house. If in the lost part of his conversation with Moschion (between 279 and 280) Stratophanes told Moschion that he was searching for Smikrines, Moschion could have promised to send Smikrines out to Stratophanes, without necessarily revealing that he was Moschion's father. At v. 280*

ΣΜΙΚΡΙΝΟΥ ΓΥΝΗ (?)

280 πτέρυξ χιτωνίσκου γυναικείου διπλῆ·
ἔ]κρυπ[τε γὰ]ρ σῶμ' ἡνίκ' ἐξεπέμπομεν
πρὸς τὴ]ν ξένην σε τὴν τότ' αἰτοῦσαν τέκνα
].νεστιν ἀλλὰ τῷ βεβαμμένῳ
]τ' ἔχουσα χρώματος φύσιν
285 πέριξ ἰώ]δους, τοὐν μέσῳ δὲ πορφύρας.

ΣΜΙΚΡΙΝΗΣ (?)

ἤ]δη καὐτὸς ἐμβλέπω σε, παῖ,
]ηται καιρὸς ὡς παρ' ἐλπίδας
φ]ημὶ λαμπαδηφόρου
]ντος ὑπεραγωνιῶν.

ΣΤΡΑΤΟΦΑΝΗΣ

290]τι, μῆτερ, ἀλλὰ τί
ὀνόμα]τος ὃ νομίζω καλεῖν

(It is impossible to be certain who speaks what in vv. 292–
304, but Smikrines' wife may have spoken what remains of
293, 296 and 297.)

280–322 Fr. XII (BB) = fr. I (J) of S (280–304 col. A, 305–22
col. B.   280 Corr. Jouguet: διπληι S.   280–90 Part divi-
sion by Barigazzi (after Jouguet, Blass).   281–82 Suppl.
Schröder.   282 Corr. Schröder: αισουσαν S.   283]ον or
]εν.   285 Suppl. Schröder.   τουμμεσωι S.   πορφύρας
(paroxyton) Evangelinos.   286 Suppl. Jouguet.
288 Suppl. Schröder.   291 Suppl. Sudhaus.

SIKYONIOI

Smikrines and his wife are on stage with Stratophanes, ex-
amining the tokens of identity which prove that Strato-
phanes is Smikrines' son. From v. 280 to the end of the act,
the rhythms and style approximate closely to those of trag-
edy, just as in the recognition scene of Perikeiromene,
vv. 779–827.)

SMIKRINES' WIFE (?)

Half of a woman's dress that's folded double—   280
It cloaked your body when we sent you [to]
[That] foreign lady who then wanted children.[28]
    ] is [   ], but with the dyed
         ] having a shade (?) [of green]
[Around each side,] and crimson in between.   285

SMIKRINES (?)

    ] now I too look at you, my son.
    ] time has [   ] beyond our dreams.
    I [say (?)], a torch bearer
      ] being in great distress.

STRATOPHANES

      ] mother, but what   290
    name (?)] that I usually call   291

(Lines 283–91 are too mutilated to provide continuous
sense. In 283–85 the description of the garment in which
Stratophanes was wrapped as a baby appears to continue.
In 286–89 Smikrines' opening words clearly reveal his
pleasure at this unexpected reunion, but the references to a
torch bearer (v. 288) and being in great distress (289) are

---

[28] Stratophanes' Sicyonian foster mother.

].εις τὸν χρόνον
] ἐλπίσασά τε
]ν ἡ τύχη
295   σύ]μβολον
τἀτύ]χημα, παῖ,
γ]αμουμένη
]λα γνωρίσῃ
ἐκβά]λλων τέκνα
300   ]ας φανεὶς
]λαβεῖν .[
]α παιδίο[
]καλω.[
]κ[

ΣΜΙΚΡΙΝΟΥ ΓΥΝΗ

305 ἴωμεν εἴσω δεῦρ[ο· καὶ γὰρ Μοσχίων,
ἄνερ, ἐνθάδ᾽ ἐστι.

ΣΜΙΚΡΙΝΗΣ

.[

ἡμῖν τε ποιήσειν ἕτοιμο[
ἔφη προελθὼν ἐχθὲς εἰς ὁμ[

292]ν or]μ (ἡ]μεῖς or ὑ]μεῖς Coles).
295 Suppl. Jouguet.
296 Suppl. Sudhaus.
297 Suppl. Blass.   299 Suppl. tentatively Arnott.
304 So Jouguet, from a minuscule scrap of S now detached and lost.   305 Suppl. Blass.
306, 308 and 309 in S have paragraphi under them.
307 ετοιμο[on a scrap of S now lost.

puzzling. Races with young men holding lit torches were a feature of night events in festivals like the Panathenaea (cf. e.g. Ar. Ran. 1087–97),[29] and under cover of darkness on such occasions—in New Comedy at least—drunken young men habitually raped young women. Could Smikrines here have been confessing his guilt over committing when young such a rape which led to Stratophanes' conception?[30]

Lines 292–302 yield only odd expressions at line ends: 292 we or you (?) . . . the time, 293 and having hoped (spoken by Stratophanes' mother?), 294 chance, 295 token, 296 [the mis]fortune, son, 297 a girl about to marry (Smikrines' rape victim and future wife?), 298 [to (?)] recognise, 299 [discard]ing children, 300 appearing, 301 to take, 302 child.)

SMIKRINES' WIFE

(moving to her door)
Let's go inside here. [Moschion, you see, (?)]   305
My dear, is there.

SMIKRINES

    [
And when he went out yesterday to [
He said he'd have [   ] brought into effect.

[29] See especially J. Jüthner in *RE* XII.1 (1924) s.v. λαμπαδηδρομία, 569–77, H. W. Parke, *Festivals of the Athenians* (London 1977) 45–46, 171–73, D. S. Kyle, *Athletics in Ancient Athens* (*Mnemosyne* suppl. 95, Leiden 1987) 190–93 and 240 (index s.v. Torch race), and N. V. Sekunda, *ZPE* 83 (1990) 149–82.

[30] On this and some other references in this passage (vv. 305–22) see my paper in *ZPE* 117 (1997) 31–34.

MENANDER

ΣΤΡΑΤΟΦΑΝΗΣ

ὁ Μοσχίων ἀδελφὸς ἐμός ἐσ[τιν, πάτερ;

ΣΜΙΚΡΙΝΗΣ

310 ἀδελφός· ἀλλὰ δεῦρο πρὸς [τὴν οἰκίαν·
ἡμᾶς γὰρ ἔνδ[ον] προσ.[

ΧΟ Ρ [ΟΥ]

ΜΕΡΟΣ Ε΄

ΚΙΧΗΣΙΑΣ

ἐμοὶ τί σὺ σπουδαῖο[ν, ὦ βέλτιστ᾽, ἔχεις;
ὥστ᾽ ἄξιον ταύτης φ[ανῆναι τῆς ὁδοῦ
ἣν κεκόμικάς με, δεό[μενός μου συντόνως
315 ἀεί τι μικρὸν ἔτι προε[λθεῖν· νῦν δ᾽ ἐμοὶ
ἄξιον, ἀκριβῶς ἴσθι, γιν[ώσκειν τίς εἶ.

ΘΗΡΩΝ

τίς εἰμι; μὰ τὸν Ἥφαιστ[ον, οὐ πεύσῃ τόδε.

309 Suppl. Blass.   310 Suppl. tentatively Schröder.
After 311 ΧΟ Ρ [ΟΥ] suppl. Blass.   312 Suppl. *exempli gra-
tia* Arnott (ἔχεις already Lloyd-Jones, ἂν . . . ἔχοις Barigazzi).
     313 αχιον S with χ corrected to ξ.   Suppl. Lloyd-Jones
(τῆς ὁδοῦ already Blass).   314 δεό[μενός suppl. Blass, μου
Sudhaus, συντόνως tentatively Arnott.   315 προε[λθεῖν
suppl. Blass, νῦν δ᾽ ἐμοὶ tentatively Arnott.
     316 and 317 in S have paragraphi under them.
     316 Corr. Blass: ισοι S.   γιν[ώσκειν suppl. Sudhaus, τίς εἶ
Page (after a supplement by Sudhaus in 316).
     317 τόδε suppl. Arnott, the rest Blass.

268

SIKYONIOI

STRATOPHANES

Father, is Moschion my brother?

SMIKRINES

Yes,

Your brother, but let's go here to [my house (?)].   310
Inside, you see, [   ] us.   311

(What Moschion intended to effect in vv. 307–08 is uncertain. After 311 Smikrines and Stratophanes go off into Smikrines' house, along with Smikrines' wife, unless she had already left the stage at v. 306. When the stage is empty, the chorus give their fourth entr'acte performance.)

ACT V

(After the entr'acte Kichesias and Theron enter in mid-conversation. Theron is hurrying the other man along.)

KICHESIAS

What [have] you [got (?)] for me, [sir], that's important,   312
And [seems] to merit this [long trail], on which
You've led me, [sharply] beg[ging me push] on
Always a little further still! [Now I've] a right,   315
I'd have you know, to learn [just who you are]!

THERON

Who *I* am? [That], in heaven's name, [you'll never learn (?)]!

ΚΙΧΗΣΙΑΣ

σπουδαῖον ἂν δέξῃ μ[
λαλοῦντα γάρ σε, θηρί[ον
320   πρὸς τὸν τελώνην λιθι[νο
σπασάμενον εὐθὺς ἡμ[ι-
322   ]..[ ]ρισμο[

(Between vv. 322 and 323 there is a gap in the Sorbonne papyrus of 4 lines. Of the next column only a few letters at the end of some lines are preserved.)

323]ριον, 326].ον, 327]ιωι, 328 ο]υς, 330]ιωι, 331]ν, 332]ιων, 333]., 334].γένους, 335 ἀπ]ολέσαι, 336]σα, 340].ν.

319–22 εθηρι[, ηνλιοι[(corr. and suppl. to λιθι[ν by Blass), ευθυσημ[, ρισμο[on a scrap of S now lost.
321 ἡμ[ι- Arnott.
322 χά]ρις μο[ι suppl. Schröder, ἀναγνω]ρισμο[Merkelbach.
323–410 Fr. XI (BB: 323–42 col. A, 343–62 col. B, 363–86 col. C, 387–410 col. D); 382–86 and 405–10 incorporate frs. V and VI (J).
323 θη]ρίον, ποτή]ριον or τεκμή]ριον suppl. Arnott tentatively.

---

[1] Literally 'animal.' Could this be clever word play on Menander's part? Kichesias has been denied knowledge of the name Θήρων, and two lines later appears to compare his companion unwittingly to a θηρίον.
[2] Or perhaps:] recognition [. It is difficult to link the quirky remarks in vv. 318–22 into a meaningful context. Kichesias is clearly

SIKYONIOI

KICHESIAS

If you expect me [   ] important—
You chatterbox, you monkey,[1](?) [
More heartless than (?) the tax-collector [320
At one go quaffing half [a litre (?)   ]
[   ] thanks to me[2][322

(There is then a short gap, followed by a column of text in which the only preserved or guessable words are: v. 323 cup (?: if the Greek word is thus correctly supplemented, perhaps a hint that the conversation in the preceding gap was about drinking or drunkenness), 334 family and 335 may [   ] strike [you (?)] down as in v. 80 (perhaps a hint that Theron here was turning the conversation to Philoumene and her parentage, and being cursed by Kichesias for doing so). About 12 lines after this, an intelligible text is once more preserved. Kichesias and Theron are still the only characters on stage. The dialogue that follows allows us to infer that in the gap before v. 343 Theron had asked Kichesias to help him in a plan concerning Philoumene and her lost father. Theron must already have mentioned the father's name to Kichesias, and then asked his companion to impersonate Kichesias in total ignorance of that companion's real identity.)

angry at his treatment by Theron, and the translation given here (which is highly speculative) assumes that Kichesias delivers a string of insults. Tax collectors were objects of universal loathing in Athens; see W. Schwan in *RE* V.A.i (1924) s.v. τελῶναι, 418–25 and H. Michell, *The Economics of Ancient Greece* (Cambridge 1940) 356–57.

MENANDER

(After v. 340 there are traces of two further lines in the column, then a gap of either 4 or less probably 5 lines.)

ΚΙΧΗΣΙΑΣ

343 οὐκ εἰς τὸν ὄλεθρον—

ΘΗΡΩΝ

χαλεπὸς ἦσθ'.

ΚΙΧΗΣΙΑΣ

—ἀποφθερεῖ

ἀπ' ἐμοῦ; Κιχησίαν σὺ τοιοῦθ' ὑπέλαβες
345 ἔργον ποήσειν ἢ λαβεῖν ἂν παρά τινος
ἀργύριον—

ΘΗΡΩΝ

ἀδίκου πράγματος.

ΚΙΧΗΣΙΑΣ

—Κιχησίαν,

Σκαμβωνίδην γενόμενον;

343–57 The speakers here are limited to Kichesias and Theron, but it is sometimes uncertain who speaks what.

343 χαλεπὸς ἦσθα given to Theron by Sandbach; S has a small space before χαλεπος but none after ησθα.
ησθααποφθαρει S.   344 απομου S.

345 λαμπρα S: corr. to ἂν (or ἂμ) παρά by several.

346 in S has a paragraphus under it.   ἀδίκου πράγματος given to Theron by Arnott.   347, 349, 352 and 353 in S have paragraphi under them.   347 σαμβωνιδην S with omitted κ written above the α.   γενομενος S.

SIKYONIOI

KICHESIAS

Damn you!

(*Theron is irritated, but still tries to cajole Kichesias, perhaps by trying to lay a friendly arm on Kichesias' shoulder*)

THERON

You're trouble!

KICHESIAS

Get to hell away   343
From me! Did you suppose Kichesias
Would do a job like that, or take a bribe   345
From anyone—

THERON

(*ironically*)

A wicked crime!

KICHESIAS

Kichesias,
Born a Skambonides![3]

---

[3] Athenians often added the name of their deme (here Skambonidai, a deme of the Leontis tribe) to the individual name that they were given at birth. Skambonidae was located in Athens itself, almost certainly north of the Agora and inside the city walls. See especially W. Judeich, *Topographie von Athen* (2nd edition, Berlin 1931) 172–73; D. Whitehead, *The Demes of Attica* (Princeton 1980) 370–71 and 476 (index s.v. Skambonidai); J. S. Traill, *Demos and Trittys* (Toronto 1986) 130.

ΘΗΡΩΝ

εὖ γ᾽· ἆρ᾽ ὑπέλαβες;
τούτου με πρᾶξαι μισθὸν αὐτοῦ, μηκέτι
ὧν ἔλεγον ἄρτι.

ΚΙΧΗΣΙΑΣ
τοῦ τίνος;

ΘΗΡΩΝ
Κιχησίας

350 Σκαμβωνίδης γε—πολὺ σὺ βέλτιον λέγεις.
νοεῖν τι φαίνει τὸν τύπον τοῦ πράγματος.
οὗτος γενοῦ· καὶ σιμὸς εἶ γὰρ ἀπὸ τύχης
καὶ μικρός, οἷον ἔλεγεν ὁ θεράπων τότε.

ΚΙΧΗΣΙΑΣ
γέρων ὅς εἰμι γέγονα.

ΘΗΡΩΝ
πρόσθες "θυγάτριον

355 Ἀλῆθεν ἀπολέσας σεαυτοῦ τετραετές—"

ΚΙΧΗΣΙΑΣ
Δρόμωνά τ᾽ οἰκέτην ἀπολέσας.

352 Corr. several: γονου S.
354 S has a dicolon after γεγονα.
355 σεαυτοῦ Arnott: εαυτου S.   τετταρας S: corr. Lloyd-
Jones, who also explained S's αληθεν.
356, 358 and 360 in S have paragraphi under them.
356 τεοικετην S.
356–57 S has spaces after απολεσας and ληιστων.

THERON
                    Splendid! You thought
That up? Demand your pay for that alone—
And not for what I said before!

KICHESIAS
                            What's that?

THERON
"Kichesias Skambonides"—your words are far   350
More pat! You've clearly got the picture. You
Must change into the fellow. Luckily you're short
And snub-nosed, as the slave described before.[4]

KICHESIAS
I've changed into the old man that I am.

THERON
                                Just add,
"Your daughter, lost at Halai,[5] four years old—"   355

KICHESIAS
(interrupting)
My slave Dromon, lost too!

---

[4] Dromon, presumably on an earlier occasion which was
staged or reported in a lost portion of the play.

[5] Here (unlike vv. 3–5) there is no mention of the nurse. There
were two coastal demes in Attica named Halai. One was Halai
Aixonides, 16 kilometres southeast of Athens (see especially C. W.
J. Eliot, *Coastal Demes of Attica*, *Phoenix* suppl. 5, Toronto 1962,
25–34, R. Osborne, *Demos*, Cambridge 1985, 22–26, and J. S.
Traill, *Demos and Trittys*, 136); the other was Halai Araphenides,
on the east coast 25 kilometres from the city (see especially Traill
128). Menander here is perhaps more likely to have referred to
Halai Araphenides: see the introduction to this play.

MENANDER

ΘΗΡΩΝ
εὖ πάνυ·

"ἁρπασθὲν ὑπὸ λῃστῶν."

ΚΙΧΗΣΙΑΣ
ἀνέμνησας πάθους
τὸν ἄθλιόν με καὶ φθορᾶς οἰκτρᾶς ἐμοί.

ΘΗΡΩΝ
ἄριστα· τοῦτον διαφύλαττε τὸν τρόπον
360   τό τ᾽ ἐπιδακρύειν. ἀγαθὸς ἄνθρωπος σφόδρα.

ΔΡΟΜΩΝ
ἡ μὲν τροφίμη 'στιν ἀσφαλῶς τηρουμένη—

ΘΗΡΩΝ (?)
362   π]άτερ.

(Between vv. 362 and 363 there is a gap of either four or
just possibly five lines.)

358 φθορᾶς Oguse–Schwartz: θυρας S.
359 Corr. Austin, Thierfelder: αριστε S.
360 ανθρωπος S: correctly interpreted as ἄν- by Blanchard–
Bataille.
362 π]άτερ assigned to Theron by Lloyd-Jones.

---

[6] See vv. 2–6 and the introduction to this play.

[7] See D. Bain, *Actors and Audience* (Oxford 1977) 185–207.

[8] See D. Bain, 205 n.1, and E. Dickey, *Greek Forms of Address*
(Oxford 1996) 77–81.

THERON
                That's very good—
Add "snatched by pirates."[6]

KICHESIAS
(now in tears)
                You've reminded me—
Oh dear—of my distress and bitter loss!

(Theron, who all along has been unaware that the man he is bribing to impersonate Kichesias is the real Kichesias, takes these tears to be a convincing bit of play-acting.)

THERON
Splendid! Continue just like that, and with
Those tears! *(aside)* This fellow's absolutely great!   360

(Dromon now enters by the parodos imagined to lead from the Eleusis sanctuary. He is presumably on his way back from there to Stratophanes' house after the arrangements for Philoumene's temporary lodging with the priestess had been made.)

DROMON
Young mistress is being safely tucked away.   361

THERON (?)
[   ], father.   362

(In v. 361 Dromon addresses either the audience or himself.[7] It is likely that he is then noticed by Theron, who addresses Kichesias as πάτερ ('father'[8]) after drawing his attention to Dromon's arrival in the lost part of the mutilated

ΔΡΟΜΩΝ

363 ζῇ καὶ πάρεστιν. μὴ πέσῃς. ἀνίστασο,
Κιχησία. Θήρων, ὕδωρ, ὕδωρ· ταχύ.

ΘΗΡΩΝ

365 οἴσω γε, νή Δί᾽, εἰσδραμὼν καὶ Στρατοφάνην
ἔνδοθεν ἀποστελῶ πρὸς ὑμᾶς.

ΔΡΟΜΩΝ

οὐκέτι

ὕδατος δεήσει.

ΘΗΡΩΝ

τοιγαροῦν αὐτὸν καλῶ.

ΔΡΟΜΩΝ

ἀναφέρεται γὰρ οὑτοσί. Κιχησία.

ΚΙΧΗΣΙΑΣ

τί ἐστι; ποῦ γῆς εἰμι; καὶ τίνος λόγου
370 ἤκουσα φήμην;

ΔΡΟΜΩΝ

ἔστι σοι καὶ σῴζεται

τὸ θυγάτριον.

363 Corr. Handley, Page: ανιστασαι S.
364, 366, 367, 368, 371 and 372 in S have paragraphi under them.
367 S has a space after δεησει.   αυτοι S.
368 Corr. several: ουτοσοι S.

v. 362. After 362 there is a short gap in the papyrus, during which Kichesias and Dromon must have been reunited and Kichesias have asked Dromon about Philoumene's fate. When Dromon answers, Kichesias swoons at the news.)

DROMON

She is alive, and here! You mustn't faint! Get up,   363
Kichesias! Some water, water—quick,
Theron!

THERON

(making for Stratophanes' house)
      I'll run in, yes, and bring some, I'll   365
Send out Stratophanes to you.

(Kichesias now regains consciousness.)

DROMON

          We shan't
Need water any more—

THERON

(interrupting)
        I'll call him then.

DROMON

—He's coming round, you see. Kichesias!

KICHESIAS

What happened? Where on earth am I? What tale
Did I hear told?

DROMON

      Your daughter is alive,   370
And safe, as well.

MENANDER

ΚΙΧΗΣΙΑΣ

καλῶς δὲ σῴζεται, Δρόμων,
ἢ σῴζετ᾽, αὐτὸ τοῦτο;

ΔΡΟΜΩΝ

παρθένος γ᾽ ἔτι,
ἄπειρος ἀνδρός.

ΚΙΧΗΣΙΑΣ

εὖ γε.

ΔΡΟΜΩΝ

σὺ δὲ τί, δέσποτα;

ΚΙΧΗΣΙΑΣ

ζῶ· τοῦτ᾽ ἔχοιμ᾽ ἂν αὐτό σοι φράσαι, Δρόμων·
375   τὰ δ᾽ ἄλλ᾽, ὅταν γέροντα καὶ πένητ᾽ ἴδῃς
καὶ μόνον, ἀνάγκη πάντ᾽ ἔχειν οὕτω κακῶς.

ΣΤΡΑΤΟΦΑΝΗΣ

σκεψάμενος ἥξω ταῦτα, μῆτερ.

ΔΡΟΜΩΝ

Στρατοφάνη,
πατὴρ Φιλουμένης.

372 S has a space after τουτο.
373, 376, 377, 378 and 379 in S have paragraphi under them.
376 αναγη S with the omitted κ written above γη.   κακῶς
Sandbach: καλως S.
378–79 S has a dicolon after φιλουμενης and spaces after
ποιος and πατερ.

SIKYONIOI

KICHESIAS
Decently safe, Dromon,

Or *just* safe?

DROMON
She's a virgin still—no man
Has touched her.

KICHESIAS
Good.

DROMON
But, master, how are you?

KICHESIAS
Alive. That's all, Dromon, that I can tell
You. When you see a poor old man alone,   375
All else must then be bleak.

(*Stratophanes now enters from Smikrines' house. His
opening remark is addressed to Smikrines' wife unseen in-
side the house.*)

STRATOPHANES
Mother, I'll see

To this[9] and then be back.

DROMON
(*presenting Kichesias to Stratophanes*)
Stratophanes,
The father of Philoumene.

---

[9] Sc. the summons he has just received from Theron (v. 367).

MENANDER

ΣΤΡΑΤΟΦΑΝΗΣ
ὁ ποῖος;

ΔΡΟΜΩΝ
οὑτοσί.

ΣΤΡΑΤΟΦΑΝΗΣ
χαῖρε, πάτερ.

ΔΡΟΜΩΝ
οὗτός σοι σέσῳκε τὴν κόρην.

ΚΙΧΗΣΙΑΣ
380 ἀλλ᾽ εὐτυχὴς γένοιτ᾽.

ΣΤΡΑΤΟΦΑΝΗΣ
ἐάνπερ σοι δοκῇ,
ἔσομαι, πάτερ, καὶ μακάριός γε.

ΔΡΟΜΩΝ
Στρατοφάνη,
πρὸ]ς τὴν Φ[ιλουμένην βαδί]ζωμεν ταχύ,
πρὸς τῶν] θεῶν.

ΣΤΡΑΤΟΦΑΝΗΣ
ἡγοῦ μ[όνος σύ]· κατὰ πόδας
ἐγὼ δι]ώκω, μικρὰ το[ῖς γ᾽ ἔνδο]ν φράσας.

380 and 381 in S have paragraphi under them.
380 γενοιτο εαμπερ S with a space after γενοιτο.
381 S may have a space after γε.
382–86 Frs. V and VI (J), which preserve the ends of 382–86
and middles of 383–86 respectively, were incorporated in fr. XII
(BB) by Blanchard and Bataille.

282

SIKYONIOI

STRATOPHANES
(*somewhat taken aback*)
Who?

DROMON
This man here!

STRATOPHANES
Hello, sir.

DROMON
(*to Kichesias*)
He's the man who's kept your daughter safe!

KICHESIAS
(*to Dromon*)
I wish him then good fortune.

STRATOPHANES
Sir, with your consent   380
I'll have that, and be blessed!

DROMON
Stratophanes,
Let's [fetch Philoumene] without delay,
[In] heaven's [name]!

STRATOPHANES
You start [without me]—I'll be close
Behind, but I've a few words first to say
To those [indoors].

---

382 πρὸ]ς suppl. several, Φ[ιλουμένην Barigazzi, βαδί]ζω-
μεν Barigazzi, Gallavotti.

383 πρὸς τῶν suppl. Barigazzi, Kassel, μ[όνος σύ Arnott
(μόνον σύ already Lloyd-Jones).

384 ἐγὼ suppl. Kassel, δί]ωκω Blass, το[ῖς γ᾽ ἔνδο]ν Handley.

ΔΡΟΜΩΝ

385 προάγ]ωμεν ἡμεῖ[ς, ὦ Κ]ιχησία.

ΣΤΡΑΤΟΦΑΝΗΣ

Δόναξ

παῖ, παῖ] Δόναξ, φράσον εἰσιὼν πρὸς Μαλθάκην
εἰς γειτόνων ἅπαντα δεῦρ[ο μεταγαγεῖν,
τοὺς κανδύτανας, τοὺς ἀόρτ[ας, τὰ πλόκανα
ἅπαντα, τοὺς ῥίσκους ἅπαντ[ας οἰκόθεν·

390 καὶ μηκέθ' εὕρισκ' ὄντας ἐνθά[δ' ὕστερον·
αὐτήν τ' ἀπιέναι δεῦρο πρὸς [τὴν μητέρα
κέλευε τὴν ἐμὴν μεθ' ὑμῶ[ν, τῶν δ' ἐμῶν
τοὺς βαρβάρους παῖδας καταλ[είπειν βούλομαι
ἐνταῦθα καὶ Θήρωνα τούς τ' ὀ[νηλάτας

395 καὶ τοὺς ὄνους. ταῦτα λέγ'· ἐγὼ [δ' αὐτῇ ταχὺ
ἐντεύξομ' αὐτός· τἄλλα τῷ τ.[

<hr />

385 προάγ]ωμεν ἡμεῖ[ς, ὦ suppl. Barigazzi, Κ]ιχησία several.   S has a space before δοναξ.   386 Suppl. Handley.

387 The space in S after απαντα was caused by a fault in the papyrus and does not indicate change of speaker.
μεταγαγεῖν suppl. Austin, Kumaniecki.

388 Suppl. Handley (cf. Gallavotti at 387); alternatively ἀόρτ[ας, τἄπιπλα Arnott.

389 οἰκόθεν suppl. Arnott.

390 μηκέθ' εὕρισκ' Arnott: μη.ρ (or ι) ευρησκ S.
ὕστερον suppl. Arnott.

391 Suppl. Oguse, Webster.

392 τῶν δ' ἐμῶν suppl. exempli gratia Arnott.

393 Suppl. Arnott (other parts of καταλείπω suppl. several).

394 Suppl. Gallavotti, Kassel.

SIKYONIOI

DROMON
Let's [go], Kichesias.   385

(*Dromon leads Kichesias off by the parodos, in the direc-
tion of the Eleusis sanctuary. Stratophanes now goes to the
door of Smikrines' house, opens it, and shouts to a slave
inside.*)

STRATOPHANES
Donax, Donax [boy]! Go, tell Malthake
[To move] all her possessions here next door—
Her cases, shoulder bags, all of [her baskets],
All her portmanteaux, [out of my old house]!
And see they're here no longer (?) [after that]!   390
And order her to go to [mother's house]
With you here, [but I'd like to leave] behind
At home the foreign slaves [of mine], with Theron,
The [donkey men] and donkeys. That's what you
Must say. I'll talk [to her] myself [quite soon].   395
The rest [is] for the [

(*Stratophanes finishes speaking in v. 396, and then makes a
quick exit by the parodos in the direction of Eleusis, in pur-
suit of Dromon and Kichesias. The slave Donax then comes
out from Smikrines' house and enters that of Stratophanes,
in order to give Stratophanes' instructions to Malthake.
Moschion then emerges from Smikrines' house onto the
empty stage.*)

---

395 Suppl. Arnott (δ' ὑμῖν ταχὺ Kassel).

396 Paragraphus underneath in S, which originally had
εντευξομεντος with the second ν crossed out, a correcting α writ-
ten under that ν, and υ written above the second ντ.

ΜΟΣΧΙΩΝ

νῦν οὐδὲ προσβλέψαι σε, Μοσχίω[ν, ἔτι
πρὸς τὴν κόρην δεῖ. Μοσχίων, [κακοδαιμονεῖς.
λευκή, σφόδρ᾽ εὐόφθαλμός ἐστιν· οὐδὲ[ν εἶ.
400 ἀδελφὸς ὁ γαμῶν, μακάριος κα[ὶ πλούσιος.
οἷον γὰρ οὗτος ἔτι λέγεις· ὃν ἄντ[ικρυς
πρᾶγμ᾽ ἐστ᾽ ἐπαινεῖν, χάριν ενο[
ἀλλ᾽ οὐκ ἐρῶ γε· μὴ γάρ, ὦ τᾶν, ὅσον [
παροχήσομαι δηλονότι καὶ κ[
405 τρίτος με[τ]᾽ αὐτῶν. ἄνδρες, οὐ δυ[νήσομαι
αν..[
οὐκ ..[
ἕτερος [..].......[
αὐτῆς θ᾽ ἑταίρας ἡ κακ[
410 ἀλλ᾽ ἔργον ἀρέσαι· νῦ[ν] ἔδ[ει

397 ἔτι suppl. Kassel, Oguse.   398 Suppl. Barigazzi.
399 σφοδρεστευφαλμος S with θ written above the α:
εὐόφθαλμος Blanchard and Bataille, ἐστ᾽ transposed by Handley,
Lloyd-Jones, οὐδὲ[ν εἶ suppl. Arnott (οὐδὲ[ν λέγεις Handley).
400 μακαριος S after correction from εακ- or οακ-.   κα[ὶ
πλούσιος suppl. Arnott (κα[tentatively deciphered by Coles).
401 Or λέγει σ᾽?   ἄντ[ικρυς suppl. Austin.
403 ὦ τᾶν Austin, Barigazzi: οταν S.
405–10 Fr. V (J), which preserves τριτο[in 405 and 406–10,
was incorporated in fr. XII (BB) by Blanchard and Bataille.
405 [μετ᾽] suppl. Barigazzi, Gallavotti before με[.] was deci-
phered by Austin.   δυ[νήσομαι Coles.
408 ἕτερος deciphered by Coles.
410 νῦ[ν] ἔδ[ει suppl. Austin, after decipherment of traces by
Schröder and Coles.

SIKYONIOI

MOSCHION

No [more] may you so much as eye the girl
Now, Moschion. [You've no luck], Moschion.
She's pale,[10] she's lovely eyes. [You're] no[body].
Your brother is the groom, blissful and [rich].   400
What tosh you're babbling still! I'll have to praise
Him face [to face,   ] thanks (?) [
But I won't speak—don't you, sir!—all [
Of course I'll be best man, and [
The gooseberry beside them.[11] Gentlemen, I'll [not]   405
[Be able]

(*Here the papyrus' increasing mutilation makes less intel-
ligible the remarks of Moschion about Stratophanes'
and Philoumene's future wedding procession, in which
Philoumene will be seated with her husband and best man
as they drive to Stratophanes' house. Lines 406–10 are too
damaged for continuous translation: 407 yields only* not,
408 (the) other, *409* the bad [   ] *of a courtesan herself,*

---

[10] In ancient Athens a pale complexion was considered an
essential element of female beauty. See K. Jax, *Die weibliche
Schönheit in der griechischen Dichtung* (Innsbruck 1933) 82–83,
186–88, and the commentaries of R. L. Hunter on Eubulus
fr. 34.2 K-A (35.2 Kock) and myself on Alexis fr. 103, vv. 17 and
18 K-A.

[11] In an ancient Athenian wedding, after the bride's parents
had entertained the bridegroom in their house, the bridegroom
usually drove the bride, seated between him and the best man, in
a mule cart to the bridegroom's house. See especially R. Garland,
The Greek Way of Life (London 1990) 217–25 and J. H. Oakley
and R. H. Sinos, *The Wedding in Ancient Athens* (Madison, Wisc.
and London 1993) 26–34 and figs. 72–95.

MENANDER

(Between v. 410 and v. 411 there is a gap of between one and three columns in the papyrus: i.e. c.23, c.46 or c.69 lines. Of the column immediately before v. 411 in the Sorbonne papyrus (XXI.A) only a few letters from a few line ends in its first column are preserved; Kassel does not include these in his continuous sequential line numbering, but for convenience here they are numbered 410e]ει, f]σει, m]ει, n].ιμοι, p].οι, u]ε.)

ΜΑΛΘΑΚΗ (?)

411 φέρουσα κριθῶν τοῖς ὄνοι[ς καθ' ἡμέραν
ἐν ταῖς πορείαις, ὡς παν[

ΘΗΡΩΝ (?)

ἀεὶ τοιαύτην εὐχόμην ἔ[χειν τύχην.

ΜΑΛΘΑΚΗ (?)

εὔχου τοιαύτην; τί δ' ἀδικε[ῖς; οἷς ὤμοσεν
415 οὐκ ἐμμεμένηκεν ὁ βαθύ[πλουτος οὑτοσί.

ΘΗΡΩΝ (?)

ἄνθρωπον ἐλπίσαντα δεο[

410e–423 Fr. XXI (BB: 410e–u col. A, 411–23 and colophon col. B).   411 καθ' ἡμέραν suppl. *exempli gratia* Arnott.

412, 413, 415, 416, 417, 418 and 419 have paragraphi under them in S.   413–14 Suppl. Lloyd-Jones (ἔ[χειν 413 also Barigazzi).   415 εμμεμνηκεν S.   βαθύ[πλουτος οὑτοσί suppl. Lloyd-Jones.

---

12 Presumably marriage to Malthake.

*possibly with reference to Malthake, and 410 it's hard to
please, however—now I had to [. There follows a gap of
about 23, 46 or 69 lines before the final papyrus fragment,
which contains the last thirteen lines of the play, also
somewhat mutilated. Moschion has now apparently disap-
peared from the scene, and two characters—most plausi-
bly identified as the parasite Theron and Malthake, the
woman he wants to marry—are presented in the middle of
a puzzling dialogue that leads to the traditional coda of
a Menandrean play. The interpretation of that dialogue
given below is inevitably speculative.)*

MALTHAKE (?)

(*in mid-speech*)

        [There I was, in Caria, (?)]
Bringing the donkeys [every day (?)] some barley,   411
When on our marches all [

THERON (?)

I always longed [to have a break] like this![12]

MALTHAKE (?)

You longed for one like this? Why do [you] wrong me?
[This money]bags hasn't kept [his promises]![13]   415

THERON (?)

[You're turning down (?)] a man who hoped and [pleads
   (?)] . . .

[13] What lies behind Malthake's remarks here is uncertain. It is
possible that she was an Athenian woman without kinsfolk, living
in Stratophanes' house and regarding him as the head of the fam-
ily. Can Stratophanes have offered her money as an inducement to
marry Theron, and then reneged?

ΜΑΛΘΑΚΗ (?)

καὶ τὴν δέησίν ἐστί σου δρ[
πῶς δ' ἂν διακόψαις;

ΘΗΡΩΝ (?)
δᾳδά [μοί τις ἐκδότω.

ΜΑΛΘΑΚΗ (?)

πρὶν ὁμολογῆσαι;

ΘΗΡΩΝ (?)
καὶ στεφάν[ους. πείσθητί μοι.

ΜΑΛΘΑΚΗ (?)

420   δράσω.

418–19 Suppl. Handley (418 τις νῦν ἐκδότω Barigazzi).
420 δρασω or δωσω S (*pace* Coles, *Emerita* 34, 1966, 137).

---

14 Garlands were worn in bridal processions, and torches also played an important role, not only because the procession took place at dusk, but because torches carried by the bride's mother brought fire from her hearth to light and protect the bride until the groom's mother received the bride with blazing torches lit from fire in the bride's new home. See especially J. H. Oakley and R. H. Sinos, *The Wedding in Ancient Athens* (Madison, Wisc. and London 1993) 26–34 figs. 72–95.

MALTHAKE (?)

[You've got to make (?)] your pleading [more effective
   (?)].
How could you twist my arm?

THERON (?)
           [Bring me] a torch, [someone]!

MALTHAKE (?)

Before consenting?

THERON (?)
           Garlands, too! [Say yes!]

(Lines 418–20 are puzzling. Torches and garlands are conventionally requested at the end of Menander's comedies (cf. Dysk. 963–64, Mis. 989–90 Arnott, Sa. 730–31), but when here Theron shouts his request for them presumably through the opened door of Stratophanes' house, he apparently intends to use them as important elements in a bridal procession,[14] with himself the groom and Malthake the bride. Hence when a slave emerges with torch and garlands, Malthake assumes that Theron is acting prematurely. She finally gives way, however, in v. 420. Whether at this point Theron changes his costume and puts on the white clothes appropriate to a bridegroom, or whether he has presumptuously worn wedding costume throughout this scene, is uncertain; see further my comments on fr. 9 below.)

MALTHAKE (?)

I'll do it!

ΘΗΡΩΝ (?)

κατάνευσον. μειράκ[ι', ἄνδρες, παιδία,
πρωράσατ' ἐκτείναντες, ἐπ[ικροτήσατε.
ἡ δ' εὐπάτειρα φιλόγελώς τε [παρθένος
423   Νίκη μεθ' ἡμῶν εὐμενὴ[ς ἕποιτ' ἀεί.

(Beneath the final line of the play the scribe has added his colophon.)

Σικυώνιοι
Μενάνδρου

ἀριθμὸς

μὴ καταγελᾶτε τῆς γραφῆς [
τοῦ κα[τ]αγελῶντος τὸ σκέλο[ς
οὐ]κ ἀνέπαυσα τοῦ στρε[βλ

420 Suppl. Kassel.

421 πρωράσατ' Lloyd-Jones (cf. Quincey, *Phoenix* 20, 1966, 116): πρωιρασετ S.   ἐπ[ικροτήσατε suppl. several.

Colophon: after ἀριθμὸς S has a numeral sign: see note 16 opposite.

SIKYONIOI

THERON (?)
Show me!

(Malthake shows her consent with a nod.)

                  Youths, [men, boys], stretch out   420
Your arms, cry out,[15] [applaud]! May Victory,
That merry [virgin], born of noble line,
[Attend] us with her favour [all our days]!   423

(Theron and Malthake depart in their bridal procession, wearing garlands and lit with torches.)

(Below the last line of the play the scribe has added the following information and warning.)

THE SICYONIANS
OF MENANDER

number (of lines written) 10[16

Don't mock the writing [
The mocker's leg [
I didn't stop from [being] sprain[ed

15 Cf. A. M. Belardinelli, *Eikasmos* 2 (1991) 193–96.
16 The right-hand end of the number is torn off, but the original figure must have been between 1000 and 1099. This was probably an inexact calculation, and may have included prefatory matter (cf. e.g. *Dyskolos*, *Heros*) as well as the lines of the play.

MENANDER

Fragments 1 to 3 Are Three Scraps of Papyrus Which Do Not Overlap Any Known Part of This Play, but Have Been Assigned to It With Some Confidence

1 (*P.Oxyrhynchus* 1238 = fr. 11 Kassel, Sandbach, Belardinelli)

This papyrus fragment was first assigned to the play by A. Blanchard and A. Bataille, *Recherches de Papyrologie* 3 (1964) 159–60, because the names of its three speakers, added by a hand different from that of the play text in the papyrus—Θηρω(ν) v. 2 suprascript; Μαλθ(ακη) 4 suprascript, 5 left-hand margin; Π[(? = Π[υρριας]) 9 suprascript—correspond with characters who all feature in *Sikyonioi*, but not together in any other known play of Menander.

ΜΑΛΘΑΚΗ (?)

μὴ ζηλοτυπῶν μ[
ἑτέρα παροῦσα.

ΘΗΡΩΝ

τ[

τουτὶ τετόλμηκε[
πεισθεῖσ᾽.

ΜΑΛΘΑΚΗ

ἐμοὶ π[   ]

ΘΗΡΩΝ (?)

[

294

SIKYONIOI

*Fragments 1 to 3 Are Three Other Scraps of
Papyrus Plausibly Attributed to This Play*

1

*Fr. 1 contains the openings of nine iambic trimeters.
Theron the parasite and Malthake appear to be involved in
a lively discussion before a third character (whose name
begins with P) intervenes. If that is Pyrrhias (no other
character with this initial is known to have featured in the
play), the scrap comes in all probability from a lost scene in
the second half of the play (i.e. some time after v. 123, when
Pyrrhias makes his first appearance). None of the
Sorbonne papyrus fragments appears to bring these three
characters together on the stage.*

MALTHAKE (?)

Not he in jealousy [1
Another woman being there [

THERON

This she (?: *or* he) has dared to [
She, being induced . . .

MALTHAKE

     By me (?) [   ]

THERON

                [

ΜΑΛΘΑΚΗ

5 κακὸς κακῶς ἀπόλ[οιο
   ταύτη λελ[ά]ληκ᾽ αν[
   τὸ[ν ἄ]νδρ᾽. ἄ[π]ειμ᾽ εἰς [
   ....]ο παρέ[χ]ετε το[
   ....]σιν.

ΠΤΡΡΙΑΣ (?)
   [οἴ]μωζε [

2 (*P.Oxyrhynchus* 3217 = fr. 12 Belardinelli)

This papyrus scrap was assigned to this play by its ed. pr.,
S. Stephens, because it is written in the same hand as fr. 1.
The name Π[, which appears suprascript in v. 3 as
identification of a speaker, can perhaps be supplemented
to Π[υρρίας as in fr. 1, but whether the scrap comes from
the same scene as fr. 1 or from elsewhere in the play
remains an open question.

(?)
1   ]νεαθ[
                     ]εαν αυτο[
                     ]τιν.
             Π[ΤΡΡΙΑΣ] (?)
                     ..[
                     ]ποδων .[
5   ].ερ[
                     ].ερουσ[
7   ]με.[

MALTHAKE

Oh, go to hell, [you] villain [5
She's *or* He's *or* I've talked to her [
The man. I'll go off in [
    ] you supply the [
    ]

PYRRHIAS (?)

    Be damned to you [9

*The mutilation of this fragment and the loss of most of the
first half of the play combine to make the subject matter
here a mystery. The* he *of v. 1 may be Stratophanes, the
other woman of 2 Philoumene, and the act of daring in 3
just possibly Philoumene's flight from her house to Eleusis
(cf. v. 214); yet the nature and extent of Theron's and
Malthake's involvement in these affairs of Stratophanes
and Philoumene remain uncertain. It seems probable,
however, that Malthake makes her departure at v. 9, and
that Pyrrhias enters directly afterwards. His opening curse
could be directed at Theron if the parasite remains on
stage, but it is just as likely to have been an apostrophe or
an address back into the house from which he has entered.*

2

*A tiny scrap containing a few mid-verse letters of seven
successive lines. Two speakers seem to be involved; the
name of the second can perhaps be supplemented as
P[yrrhias]. V.2 may yield* if it *or* if him, *4 perhaps of* feet.

Fr. 1 5–8 Suppl. A. S. Hunt.
5 Or ἀπόλ[οιτο.   6 Or λελ[ά]ληκα ν[.

3 (*P.Oxyrhynchus* inv. 33 4B 83E 8–11 = fr. 13 B)

This papyrus scrap was assigned to this play by its ed. pr.,
E. W. Handley, because (i) it mentions Malthake (v. 21),
who is known to have been a character of *Sikyonioi* but not
of any other known Menandrean play (cf. above on fr. 1),
and (ii) its reference to a πικρᾶς ἐκδημίας ('grievous
absence from home,' 16) agrees with what we learn about
Stratophanes' situation in the earlier part of this play's plot.
Neither reason on its own would be compelling, but their
conjunction adds plausibility, though not certainty, to
Handley's attribution.

ΣΤΡΑΤΟΦΑΝΗΣ (?)

1
   ἀπολέ]σαι κακῶ[ς
    ] τῶν ὅλων
    ]γήσομαι
    ]την.

ΘΗΡΩΝ (?)

     ἐρῶ

5
    ]ρε
    ].[ ].ησμένος
    ]αι μεμνήσομαι

ΣΤΡΑΤΟΦΑΝΗΣ (?)
    ἄπε]λθ'.

All supplements by Handley.
4 Dicolon before ερω.
8 απελθε (so papyrus) followed by dicolon.

SIKYONIOI

3

The ends of some 29 lines, either iambic trimeters or tro-chaic tetrameters. Dicola in vv. 4 and 8 indicate dialogue in the earlier lines of the fragment. Scraps of sense can be de-ciphered: v. 1 may [he *or* she perish] vile[ly, *2* all the *or* all them, *3* I shall, *4* I shall say *or* I love *spoken by a character different from the one speaking immediately before, 7* I'll remember, *8* Go [off]! *spoken by the first character, with the addressee responding* I'm off, *9* no longer, *10* clear or (?) to say, *11* no longer, *12* comes, *13* mother, *14* he's *or* she's mad, *15* grievous absence from our home, *16* it (?) be-ing wretched, *17* a phrase that's said, *18* with one's friends, *19* but her I see, *20* she's (*or* he's) been doing coming there, *21* to Malthake, *22* by birth *or* by nature, *23* you evil-minded swine, *24* I know, *25* master (nominative, not voca-tive).*

If this fragment comes from Sikyonioi, it must belong to a scene in the first half of the play probably involving Theron, the character who is elsewhere disparaged (in ab-sentia: 43–44, 46; in his presence: 414) by Malthake and treated peremptorily by Stratophanes (145–47, ? 95–96). In this fragment he is the man most likely to have been addressed by Malthake as evil-minded (23) and ordered away by Stratophanes but not immediately obeying (8). The fragment will then begin in the middle of a discus-sion between Stratophanes and Theron, ending with Stratophanes ordering Theron to depart on some mission. Stratophanes then himself leaves, and Theron remains on stage to muse possibly on the soldier's unhappiness (13–16), which might have arisen from ignorance about the fate of his foster mother, of which Stratophanes was unaware

ΘΗΡΩΝ (?)

ἀπέρχομαι.

(?)

] οὐκέτι

10   φ]ανερῶν ἢ λέγειν

]αν οὐκέτι

]τος ἔρχεται

τὴ]ν μητέρα

μ]ελαγχολᾷ

15   ] πικρᾶς ἐκδημίας

ἀθ]λίως ἔχον

λεγ]όμενος λόγος

] σὺν τοῖς φίλοις

ἀλ]λὰ τήνδ' ὁρῶ

20   πε]πόηκ' ἐλθοῦσ' ἐκεῖ

]τι πρὸς τὴν Μαλθάκην

]ηρ τῇ φύσει

ΜΑΛΘΑΚΗ (?)

]. βάσκανε

]σετ', οἶδ' ὅτι

25   ]......ον δ[ε]σπότης

]νν[ ].

].[.]εταν

]......[

29   ].[

before v. 126, from a love for Philoumene at this point unreturned, or from homesickness (the grievous absence from home of 15 would most probably be a reference to Stratophanes' and Theron's recent campaigning in Caria voiced on return to Greece at the beginning of the play). Theron then sees Malthake come on stage (19) from an unexpected quarter (? Smikrines' house), which leads him to wonder what she's been doing coming there (20). At the end of the fragment he appears to be in conversation with her, but the word master *(25) raises a problem. It is slaves who habitually refer to masters, but Theron and Malthake are apparently free Athenians; could Malthake have originally been a slave bought (cf. fr. 4 below) and later set free by Stratophanes, or did a slave such as Dromon enter at the end of the fragment?*

MENANDER

Eight Other Fragments of Σικυώνιοι *or*
Σικυώνιος, *Quoted With Attribution to This Play*
by Ancient Authors

4 (Fr. 1 Kassel, Sandbach and Belardinelli,
371 Körte–Thierfelder)

Photius s.v. ἄβραι (α 50 Theodoridis), *Suda* s.v. ἄβρα (α
68 Adler), Eustathius 1854.17ff. (citing Aelius Dionysius α
6 Erbse) : ἄβραι· νέαι δοῦλαι. οἱ δέ φασιν (so Photius:
these six words replaced simply by the heading ἄβρα in
Ael. Dion. and *Suda*) οὔτε ἁπλῶς ἡ θεράπαινα ἄβρα
λέγεται οὔτε ἡ εὔμορφος, ἀλλ᾽ ἡ οἰκότριψ γυναικὸς
κόρη καὶ ἔντιμος, εἴτε οἰκογενὴς εἴτε μή. Μένανδρος
Ψευδηρακλεῖ (fr. 411 K-A) . . . καὶ Σικυωνίῳ (so Ael.
Dion.: καὶ misplaced after Σικυωνίῳ in Phot., *Suda*)·

ἄβραν γὰρ ἀντωνούμενος,
Φιλουμένην ταύτῃ μὲν οὐ παρέδωκ᾽ ἔχειν,
ἔτρεφε δὲ χωρὶς ὡς ἐλευθέρᾳ πρέπει.

Fr. 4, lines 1–2 αὐτωνούμενος and ταύτην mss. b, z of Photius.
2 Φιλουμένην Arnott: ἐρωμένην all mss. of citers.
3 τρέφειν mss. of *Suda*.

---

[1] On the word and its history see E. D. Francis, *Glotta* 53
(1975) 43–66.

Eight Fragments Quoted by Ancient Authors

4

Photius, the *Suda* and Eustathius (citing Aelius Diony-
sius), s.vv. ἄβραι ('lady's maids') and ἄβρα ('lady's maid'):
young slave girls. They say neither a female slave nor a
good-looking girl is called simply a 'lady's maid,' but only a
woman's maid working in the house and valued highly,
whether born in the house or not. Menander in *False
Heracles* (fr. 411 K-A = 453 K-T) . . . in *Sikyonios* (*sic*),

> Buying instead a lady's maid[1]
He didn't entrust Philoumene to her, but brought
Her up apart, as fits a girl who's free.

*This fragment almost certainly derives from the prologue,
coming originally in the gap between lines 19 and 20, and
describing the arrangements made by Stratophanes or his
foster father for Philoumene after she was purchased along
with Dromon in the slave market at Mylasa (5–10). A
simple correction in v. 2 restores sense to an otherwise
puzzling line, but lack of quoted context prevents us from
knowing whom or what the lady's maid replaced, and
whether she played any further role in the plot. Could she
perhaps have been Malthake? If so, it would explain how
she came to be in Stratophanes' household, but at the same
time require us to assume that her devoted services to that
household—whether sexual as would befit a hetaira or ex-
hetaira, or purely as a lady's maid—had led to her being
given her freedom.*

5 (2 Ka, S, B, 372 K-T)

Stobaeus, *Eclogae* 4.12.4 (ψόγος τόλμης στρατείας καὶ ἰσχύος): Μενάνδρου Σικυωνίᾳ (-ωνί with α suprascript ms. M: title abbreviated to -ῶνὶ S, -ω A)·

εὐλοιδόρητον, ὡς ἔοικε, φαίνεται
τὸ τοῦ στρατιώτου σχῆμα καὶ τὸ τοῦ ξένου.

6 (3 Ka, S, B, 375 K-T)

Photius s.v. Στρατοφάνη (p. 542 Porson)· τὴν κλητικὴν πτῶσιν· Μένανδρος Σικυωνίῳ·

Στρατοφάνη,
λιτόν ποτ᾽ εἶχες χλαμύδιον καὶ παῖδ᾽ ἕνα.

καὶ ἀεὶ οὕτως λέγει.

Fr. 5, line 2 τοῦ before στρατιώτου omitted by ms. A.
Fr. 6, line 2 παῖδα corr. Toup: πέλα ms. g. The fr. may be construed either as above in iambic trimeters or as a single trochaic tetrameter.

5

Stobaeus ('Censure of military daring and brawn'): in Menander's *Sikyonia* (*sic*),

The dress of soldiers and of foreigners
Is easy to deride, apparently.

Clearly a response to an attack on Stratophanes, but now impossible to place; it could have been uttered by Stratophanes or a member of his entourage to an unknown assailant in one of the lost early scenes, or by Stratophanes to Moschion in the gap after 279.

6

Photius, s.v. Στρατοφάνη: the vocative case of Στρατοφάνης (Stratophanes). Menander in *Sikyonios* (*sic*),

                             Stratophanes,
You once owned one plain cloak and one male slave!

Menander always uses this form (of the vocative).

A reference to the days when Stratophanes was poor at the beginning of his military career. It implies that his foster father had lost the wealth he had gained in Caria (v. 4), perhaps as a result of the lawsuit with the Boeotian (133–35), and that Stratophanes went off himself to Caria as a mercenary in order to restore the family fortunes. Speaker, scene and metre cannot be securely identified, but since the tone does not seem unduly aggressive or unfriendly, we could have here a member of Stratophanes' entourage reminding him of earlier days (Theron perhaps in the gap before 110, if the metre is a trochaic tetrameter).

305

7 (4 Ka, S, B, 373 K-T)

Photius (α 95 Theodoridis), *Suda* (α 165 Adler) and
Eustathius 1854.27 ff. (citing Aelius Dionysius α 16 Erbse)
s.v. ἄγγαροι· οἱ ἐκ διαδοχῆς γραμματοφόροι. οἱ δὲ
αὐτοὶ καὶ ἀστάνδαι. τὰ δὲ ὀνόματα Περσικά (so
Photius, *Suda*: ἡ δὲ λέξις Περσική Ael. Dion.) . . . καὶ
ἀγγαρεύεσθαι καλοῦσιν, ὥσπερ ἡμεῖς νῦν, τὸ εἰς
φορτηγίαν καὶ τοιαύτην τινὰ ὑπηρεσίαν ἄγεσθαι.
Μένανδρος καὶ τοῦτο ἐν τῷ Σικυωνίῳ παρίστησιν·

ὁ πλέων κατήχθη. κρίνεθ᾽ οὗτος πολέμιος.
ἐὰν ἔχῃ τι μαλακόν, ἀγγαρεύεται.

8 (5 Ka, S, B, 374 K-T)

Photius (κ 81 Theodoridis) and *Suda* (κ 149 Adler) s.v.
κακὴ μὲν ὄψις· κόμμα παροιμίας (παροιμίας most mss.
of *Suda*: παροιμία mss. I of *Suda*, g of Photius)·

κακὴ μὲν ὄψις, ἐν δὲ δείλαιαι φρένες.

Μένανδρος Σικυωνίῳ (Σικυννίῳ ms. F of *Suda*).

Fr. 7, line 1 κρίνεθ᾽ ms. M of *Suda*: κρίνεσθ᾽ GIT of *Suda*,
κρίνε A of *Suda*, κρῖναι θ᾽ mss. b and z of Photius.

---

[2] See Sandbach's commentary on *Sik.* 135.

SIKYONIOI

*Photius cites the fragment to illustrate Menander's use of
the vocative form Στρατοφάνη, which, though strictly an
irregular substitute for Στρατόφανες, was in widespread
use throughout the Greek world in Menander's time and
before.*[2]

7

Photius, the *Suda* and Eustathius (citing Aelius Diony-
sius), s.v. ἄγγαροι (mounted couriers): postmen working
in relay; the same people are also called ἀστάνδαι. The
nouns are (so Photius, *Suda;* Aelius Dionysius has 'The
word is') Persian. They use the verb ἀγγαρεύεσθαι (liter-
ally, 'to be drafted into service as a mounted courier') too,
just as we do now, in the sense 'to be pressed into carrying
loads and any similar service.' Menander introduces this
word also into his *Sikyonios (sic),*

A sailor lands—he's judged an enemy.
If he has gear, he's sentenced to hard labour!

*The relevance of this comment to any words or situation in
what remains of this play is unknown.*

8

Photius and the *Suda*, s.v. κακὴ μὲν ὄψις (an evil face):
part of a proverb.

An evil face, a craven heart within.

Menander in *Sikyonios (sic).*

*It is uncertain whether Menander introduced the whole
line or just the first three words into the play. The words*

307

9 (6 Ka, S, B)

A scholiast on Plato, *Symposium* 195b s.v. ὅμοιον ὁμοίῳ (p. 61 Greene)· "ὡς αἰεὶ τὸν ὅμοιον ἄγει θεὸς ὡς τὸν ὅμοιον", ἐπὶ τῶν τοὺς τρόπους παραπλησίων καὶ ἀλλήλοις ἀεὶ συνδιαγόντων, ἐξ Ὁμήρου (*Od.* 17.218) λαβοῦσα τὴν ἀρχήν. μέμνηται δὲ αὐτῆς Πλάτων καὶ ἐν τῷ Λύσιδι (214b) καὶ ἐν Συμποσίῳ, καὶ Μένανδρος Σικυωνίᾳ.

10 (7 Ka, S, B)

Photius s.v. ἐμπρίσασα (ε 770 Theodoridis; cf. E. W. Handley, *BICS* 12 (1965) 61–62 n.15, and K. Tsantsanoglou, *New Fragments of Greek Literature from the Lexicon of Photius*, Athens 1984, p. 131 no. 162)· ἀντὶ τοῦ ὀργιζομένη.

<ἐμπρίσασά σε>

ἀπῆλθε, φασίν, ἀπολιποῦσα,

ὡς Μένανδρος Σικυωνίῳ.

Fr. 10, lemma ἐμπριάσασα z: corr. Tsantsanoglou. Thereafter z writes ἀντὶ τοῦ ἀπῆλθε φασὶν ἀπολίπουσα ὡς ὀργιζομένην. Μένανδρος Σικυωνίῳ: transposed and corrected by Arnott (ὀργιζομένη Tsantsanoglou).

---

[3] Two lines of Menander cited by Stobaeus, *Eclogae* 2.33.4 (the section headed ὅτι ἡ ὁμοιότης τῶν τρόπων φιλίαν ἀπεργάζεται, 'That similarity of character produces friendship') from an unnamed play, ἡ τῶν ὁμοίων αἵρεσις μάλιστά πως / τὴν τοῦ βίου σύγκρασιν ὁμόνοιαν ποεῖ ('Choice of like-minded comrades turns life's blend / Best, I imagine, into harmony,' fr. 697

may have been a description of Moschion (cf. 199–202), but it is uncertain when and by whom they were said.

9

A scholiast on Plato's *Symposium,* explaining the phrase ὅμοιον ὁμοίῳ ('like to like'): "for god always leads like to like," with reference to those with similar characters and always spending their time together; the expression originates in Homer (*Od.* 17.251). It is also mentioned by Plato in his *Lysis* and in *Symposium,* and by Menander in *Sikyonios (sic).*

There is no way of establishing who were the like-minded couple in Menander's play (? Eleusinios and the democrat) nor how the expression was used in it.[3]

10

Photius, s.v. ἐμπρίσασα (gnashing): instead of 'being angry':

[Gnashing her teeth],
They say, she's left you, gone away,

as Menander in *Sikyonios (sic)* writes.

This entry in the Zavorda manuscript of Photius is gravely

K-A = 376 K-T), were identified by A. Nauck, *Mélanges Gréco-romains* 6 (1894) 114, as the scholiast's source here, but there is very little connection between these lines and the expression "like to like," and the suggestion is now wisely rejected; see C. W. Müller, *Rhein. Mus.* 107 (1964) 285–87.

11 (8 Ka, S, B, 378 K-T)

Harpocration s.v. ἀναίνεσθαι (a 113 Keaney p. 22)·
κοινῶς μὲν τὸ ἀρνεῖσθαι, ἰδίως δὲ ἐπὶ τῶν κατὰ τοὺς
γάμους καὶ τὰ ἀφροδίσια λέγεται. Δημοσθένης ἐν τῇ
ὑπὲρ Φορμίωνος παραγραφῇ (36.31), Πλάτων Φάωνι
(fr. 197 Kassel–Austin), Μένανδρος Σικυωνίῳ.

Two Other Fragments Quoted by Ancient Authors,
Whose Attributions to Menander's Σικυώνιοι or
Σικυώνιος Are in Varying Degrees Uncertain

12 (9 Ka, S, B, 377 K-T)

Pollux 4.119: καὶ πορφυρᾷ δ᾽ ἐσθῆτι χρῶνται (ἐχρῶντο
mss. BC) οἱ νεανίσκοι, οἱ δὲ παράσιτοι μελαίνῃ ἢ φαιᾷ,

corrupt, and we cannot be certain where the Menander
quotation begins and ends. The text printed here, however,
fits snugly into what we know of the plot of Sikyonioi; a
character such as Theron could have spoken these words
(? in the fractured text or gap between 69 and 74) to
Stratophanes, reporting what the house slaves had told
Theron about Philoumene's departure with Dromon from
Stratophanes' house to the precinct at Eleusis.

11

Harpocration, s.v. ἀναίνεσθαι: in general it means 'to re-
ject/deny,' but it is specifically applied to cases involving
marriages and sexual relations. Demosthenes uses it in his
speech of counter-prosecution defending Phormio, (the
comic poet) Plato in his *Phaon,* and Menander in *Sikyonios*
(sic).

Although Harpocration does not add any quotation from
Menander's play, the word is most likely to have been used
in a lost passage either by Malthake rejecting Theron's ad-
vances or by Philoumene (probably in somebody else's re-
port of her action rather than by her personally on stage)
rejecting Stratophanes'.

Two Other Fragments Quoted by Ancient Authors,
Whose Attributions to Menander's Sikyonioi or
Sikyonios Are in Varying Degrees Uncertain

12

Pollux: young men (sc. in New Comedy) wear crimson, but
parasites black or grey, except in *Sikyonios (sic),* where the

πλὴν ἐν Σικυωνίῳ λευκῇ, ὅτε (ὅταν A) μέλλει γαμεῖν ὁ
παράσιτος (B omits πλὴν—ὁ παράσιτος).

On the assignment of this reference to Menander's
Sikyonioi see the facing page.

13 (10 Ka, S, B, 698 K-T)

(a) Eustathius 998.31f.: ἡ δὲ χρῆσις τῆς λέξεως καὶ
παρὰ Παυσανίᾳ, ὅς φησιν ὅτι ῥινᾶν τὸ ἐξαπατᾶν.
Μένανδρος·

ἔγωγ' ἐπίσταμαι

ῥινᾶν.

Here παρὰ Παυσανίᾳ is probably a slip by Eustathius for
παρὰ Αἰλίῳ Διονυσίῳ; cf. Eustathius 1822.44f., φέρει δὲ
χρῆσιν τῆς λέξεως (sc. the use of ῥινᾶν in the sense
of ἐξαπατᾶν) ἐκ Μενάνδρου Αἴλιος Διονύσιος (ρ 10
Erbse), τὸ ἔγωγ' ἐπίσταμαι ῥινᾶν.

(b) Aelian, *De Natura Animalium* 9.7: καὶ ὁ μὲν τοῦ
Μενάνδρου Θήρων μέγα φρονεῖ, ὅτι ῥινῶν ἀνθρώπους
φάτνην αὐτοὺς ἐκείνους εἶχε.

---

[4] Eustathius' error here for Aelius Dionysius.

parasite wears white when he is going to be married.

Plays with the title Sikyonios are recorded only from Alexis and (? as a secondary title: see the introduction to this play) Menander, but Pollux here is more likely to be referring to Menander's play, which was more celebrated in antiquity (see testimonia III and IV) and is known to have included the parasite Theron among its characters. The scene in which Theron will have worn (or changed to) his wedding garment will have been 411–23, as discussed above. Bridegrooms regularly wore a white cloak (Plutarch Mor. 771d, cf. Eur. Alc. 922–23, Plautus Casina 446; see W. Erdmann, Die Ehe im alten Griechenland, Munich 1933, 255 n.25, and my commentary on Alexis, Cambridge 1996, p. 601 n.1).

13

(a) Eustathius, on the verb ῥινᾶν (*literally* to nose, *i.e.* to lead by the nose): The word is also found in Pausanias,[4] who says that ῥινᾶν is 'to swindle.' Menander,

> I know how
> To lead men by the nose.

Eustathius writes elsewhere: Aelius Dionysius cites the use of the word from Menander, 'I know how to lead men by the nose'.

(b) Aelian writes: And Menander's Theron thinks well of himself because by leading men by the nose he used people themselves as his meal ticket.

MENANDER

Four Testimonia about Σικυώνιοι or Σικυώνιος

I (Menander, testimonium 42 in Kassel–Austin, PCG VI. 2)

P. British Museum 2562 (first published by H. J. M. Milne, *Greek Shorthand Manuals*, London 1934, 21–56) is a shorthand manual of the third or fourth century A.D., with a tetrad of four usually linked words chosen to illustrate each symbol. J. Stroux, *Philologus* 90 (1935) 88–89 first noted that tetrads 330–333 and the first word of tetrad 334 were titles of Menandrean plays, and M. Gronewald, *ZPE* 33 (1979) 6–7 later showed that two further tetrads (509, 510) also appeared to correspond with other Menandrean titles, although corruptly written down.

509 Καρχηδονιοι (*sic*), Περινθιοι (*sic*), Βοιωτια, Ιμβριοι.
510 Καρινη, Ξενολογος, Μηλια, Σικυωλιοι (*sic*).

The papyrus misspells Καρχηδόνιος, Περινθία (509), and Σικυώνιοι (510).

See also *Phasma,* test. III.

*Although Menander's Sikyonioi is not identified as the
source in any of these extracts, the Theron of that play was
a celebrated parasite (see test. III below), and no other
character with that name is recorded for Menander. It ap-
pears therefore that these extracts are referring to a single
speech in a lost portion of the play when Theron said some-
thing like* I know how to lead men by the nose—when so
acting I use them as my meal ticket.

Four Testimonia about Sikyonioi or Sikyonios

I

*A shorthand manual from late antiquity tests its pupils
with exercises that contain four words at times related to
each other in various ways. One of the two series where the
theme is titles of Menander's plays runs as follows:*

Tetrad 509

Karchedonioi *(The Men from Carthage: an error for*
   Karchedonios: *Loeb II.81–107),*
Perinthioi *(The Men from Perinthos: an error for*
   Perinthia: *II.471–501),*
Boiotia *(The Girl from Boeotia),*
Imbrioi *(The Men from Imbros).*

Tetrad 510

Karine *(The Carian Girl),*
Xenologos *(The Man Who Enlisted Mercenaries),*
Melia *(The Girl from Melos),*

II (Menander, testim. 20 K-A)

Alciphron 4.19.19 (a letter headed Γλυκέρα Μενάνδρῳ):
ὥστε πειρῶ μᾶλλον, ἐμὴ φιλότης, θᾶσσον εἰς ἄστυ
παραγενέσθαι, ὅπως . . . ἔχῃς (so the Aldine edition:
ἔχοις most mss., ἔχεις ms. Δ) εὐτρεπισμένα τὰ δράματα
⟨καὶ⟩ (suppl. Reiske) ἐξ αὐτῶν ἃ μάλιστα ὀνῆσαι
δύναται Πτολεμαῖον καὶ τὸν αὐτοῦ Διόνυσον . . . εἴτε
Θαΐδα (corr. Meineke: Θαΐδης Φ, Θαίδης Vat.2, Flor.,
Θαΐδες the other mss, Θαΐδας Aldine) εἴτε Μισούμενον
εἴτε Θρασυλέοντα εἴτε Ἐπιτρέποντας (-τες Flor., -τος
Φ, Vat.2) εἴτε Ῥαπιζόμενον εἴτε Σικυών⟨ιον or
Σικυων⟨ίους, εἴθ᾽ ὁτι⟩οῦν (Σικυών⟨ιον⟩ suppl. Bergler,
Σικυων⟨ίους Fernández Galiano, the rest Meineke: here
ms. O has a lacuna of 9, mss. ΠΔ one of 20 letters) ἄλλο.

III

Three entries in the *Suda*:
    (a) s.v. δεινόν (δ 340 Adler)· . . . καὶ αὖθις· ἀνθρώπους

Sikyolioi (*an error for either* Sikyonioi *or perhaps even* Sikyonios).

On the the alleged relevance of Sikyolioi *here to the correct form of Menander's title, see the introduction to this play, and ZPE 116 (1997) 1–3. See also Phasma, test. III.*

II

Alciphron (in a fictional letter imagined to have been written by 'Glykera to Menander'): So, my darling, do try rather to come quickly to Athens, so as to . . . have your plays all ready, [including] those of them that may particularly delight Ptolemy and his Dionysus . . . whether *Thais* or *Misoumenos* or *Thrasyleon* or *Epitrepontes* or *Rhapizomene* or *Sikyon[ioi* or any other] at all.

Alciphron bases this letter on two beliefs current in his time: one (almost certainly false) that a woman called Glykera was Menander's real-life mistress; the other (quite possibly true) that Menander had been invited to Alexandria by Ptolemy I, then king of Egypt: see my Loeb Menander I pp.xvi–xvii. Alciphron adds his selection of Menandrean masterpieces. Thais (a hetaira), Thrasyleon (a soldier) and Rhapizomene (The Girl Who Has Her Jaw Slapped) are now lost; for Misoumenos see Loeb Menander II 245–363, for Epitrepontes volume I 379–526.

III

Three entries in the *Suda*:

(a) s.v. δεινόν (formidable): . . . and further, men with

MENANDER

ἐσθίειν βλέποντας καὶ δεινοὺς κατὰ (καὶ κατὰ mss. GI)
γαστέρα. λέγω δὴ Κλεισόφους τε καὶ Θήρωνας καὶ
Στρουθίας καὶ Χαιρεφῶντας.

(b) s.v. διώνυμοι (δ 1244 Adler)· ἐν τοῖς Ἕλλησι
διώνυμοι κόλακες καὶ (καὶ om. GI) κεκηρυγμένοι
περιηχοῦσιν ἡμᾶς, Κλείσοφοί τε καὶ Στρουθίαι
(Στρινθία mss. AGI) καὶ Θήρωνες.

(c) s.v. Κλείσοφος (κ 1762 Adler)· ἐπεὶ οἱ Ἕλληνες
Κλεισόφους τε ᾄδουσι καὶ Θήρωνας καὶ Στρουθίας καὶ
Χαιρεφῶντας, ἀνθρώπους ἐσθίειν (before ἐσθίειν ms.
G writes ἢ ἐσθίειν ἔχοντας τέχνην, words which mss.
VM add in the margin with the note γρ(άφεται)) εἰδότας
εἰς κόρον, καὶ δεινοὺς γαστέρα δέ, φέρε καὶ ἡμεῖς καί
τι παίσωμεν, παρασίτου μνημονεύσαντες ἡμεδαποῦ.

---

5 Aelian, who was born in Italy, goes on here to talk about
Iortius, a toady of Maecenas.

the light of dinner in their eyes and formidable of belly—I
mean men like Kleisophos and Theron and Strouthias and
Chairephon.

(b) s.v. διώνυμοι (well-known): The names of parasites
well-known and celebrated among Greeks still resound
with us: men like Kleisophos and Strouthias and Theron.

(c) s.v. Κλείσοφος (Kleisophos): When the Greeks
glorify people like Kleisophos and Theron and Strouthias
and Chairephon, men who know about eating to excess
and are also formidable of belly—come on, let us too have
a little sport by mentioning one of our own parasites.[5]

The Suda's selection here of four paradigmatic gormandis-
ing parasites from antiquity is taken from Aelian (= frs.
107, 108 Hercher). Two of the parasites are real-life Athe-
nians of the fourth century B.C.; Kleisophos was a lackey of
King Philip II of Macedon, famous for his witty comments
and for the way that when Philip was twice wounded he
immediately copied the king's eye-bandage and limp
(Athenaeus 6.248d–f, Aelian, De Natura Animalium 9.7,
with O. Ribbeck, Kolax, Abhandlung Leipzig 9, 1884, 51);
Chairephon won a reputation for gatecrashing feasts
towards the end of the century and was frequently
mentioned by contemporary writers (Men. Sam. 603, cf.
Athenaeus 4.135d, 164f–165a, 6.242f–244a, with my com-
mentary (Cambridge 1996) on Alexis fr. 213.1 K-A, p. 610).
The other two were characters in Menander's plays (on
Strouthias, one of the two parasites in Kolax, see Loeb
Menander II, 153–203).

IV

Lucian, *Rhetorum praeceptor* 12: φαίη τοιγαροῦν ἂν (ἂν om. γ group of mss.) πρὸς σὲ ὧδέ πως ἐπισπασάμενος ὁπόσον ἔτι λοιπὸν τῆς κόμης καὶ ὑπομειδιάσας τὸ (τὸ om. β group of mss.) γλαφυρὸν ἐκεῖνο καὶ ἁπαλὸν οἷον εἴωθεν, Αὐτοθαΐδα (αὐτὸς· Θαΐδα β) τὴν κωμικὴν ἢ Μαλθάκην ἢ Γλυκέραν τινὰ μιμησάμενος τῷ προσηνεῖ τοῦ φθέγματος.

SIKYONIOI

IV

Lucian, *Professor of Public Speaking:* For this reason he (sc. the professor) would address you in some fashion like this, tossing back what still remained of his hair and faintly smiling in that refined and tender way so typical of him, imitating Thais herself of comic fame or Malthake or Glykera in the seductiveness of his voice.

Lucian picks out three names of celebrated women in Menander: on Thais, see test. II above; on Glykera, the name of a hetaira in at least three plays: Glykera, Misogynes and Perikeiromene, cf. test. II above and volume II, 365–469.

SYNARISTOSAI

(WOMEN LUNCHING TOGETHER)

INTRODUCTION

Possible Manuscripts

H = *P. Heidelberg* 175 (= fr. adesp. 1074 K-A), a tiny scrap of papyrus from the 1st century A.D. It contains the ends of 12 lines (probably iambic trimeters) from a comedy which has been provisionally identified as Menander's *Synaristosai*. First edition: G. A. Gerhard, *Veröffentlichungen aus den badischen Papyrussammlungen* 6 (Heidelberg 1938) 18–19. It was first ascribed to *Synaristosai* by T. B. L. Webster, *An Introduction to Menander* (Manchester 1974) 187 n.105; cf. W. G. Arnott, *ZPE* 72 (1988) 23–25 = *Alexis, The Fragments: A Commentary* (Cambridge 1996) 830–33.

O = *P. Oxyrhynchus* 4305 (= fr. adesp. 1155 K-A), two tattered fragments of a papyrus roll written in the 3rd century A.D. The larger scrap contains (i) the ends of the top 13 lines in a column with an act break signalled after the third, and (ii) the opening letters of the top 10 lines in the next column. The other scrap has some letters from near the ends of the top 15 lines of either a new column or of the second column in the first scrap. First edition, with tentative ascription to the *Synaristosai*: E. W. Handley, *The Oxyrhynchus Papyri* 62 (1995) 14–21, with a photograph (plate VI).

Fragments 1–10 are certainly, and frs. 11 and 12 may be, ancient quotations from the play (see my introduction to volume I of the Loeb Menander, pp.xxiv–xxv).

Pictorial Evidence

A mosaic of (probably) the late fourth century A.D. from the 'House of Menander' at Mytilene in Lesbos. It is inscribed ΣΥΝΑΡΙΣΤΩΣΩΝ ΜΕ(ΡΟΣ) Α (*Synaristosai*, Act I), and portrays the scene which almost certainly opened the play and gave it its title. Three women are seated behind a small three-legged table. On the left an old, white-haired woman (identified as ΦΙΛΑΙΝΙΣ, Philainis) sits on a high-backed chair with her head turned towards her two companions. Dressed in a blue gown topped by a pink wrap, she holds a wine cup in her right hand and rests her left on her knees. The other two women are young, and sit together on a couch to the right of Philainis. The left-hand one (identified as ΠΛΑΓΓΩΝ, Plangon) turns slightly to her left and raises her right arm in an animated gesture, while her left hand rests on her knee. She wears a yellow and purple gown over a mainly white tunic. To her right the other young woman (identified as ΠΥΘΙΑΣ, Pythias) turns slightly to face Philainis and Plangon; the positions of her hands match those of Plangon's. She too has a mainly white tunic, under a brick-coloured gown. On the extreme left behind Philainis' chair a youngster's head is visible. This was presumably the slave who served the meal and poured the drinks as a mute extra while the other three conversed; Menander's *Synaristosai* (here fr. 4) implies that this slave was female, but in neither this mosaic nor the famous un-

titled Dioscurides mosaic of the same scene is the figure's
sex clearly defined. The relation of this picture to (i) the
Dioscurides mosaic, (ii) the papyrus fragment of
Synaristosai, and (iii) the opening scene of Plautus'
Cistellaria, is discussed below. Standard publication of
the mosaic: S. Charitonidis, L. Kahil, R. Ginouvès, *Les
Mosaïques de la Maison du Ménandre à Mytilène* (*Antike
Kunst*, Beiheft 6, Berne 1970), 41–44 and colour plate 5
(featuring both the Mytilene and the Dioscurides mosa-
ics); colour plates of the two appear also in R. Green and E.
W. Handley, *Images of the Greek Theatre* (London 1995)
pp.78–79. Cf. also T. B. L. Webster, *Monuments Illus-
trating New Comedy* (3rd edition, revised and enlarged by
J. R. Green and A. Seeberg, London 1995), I.94 (XZ 37)
and II.186 (3DM1) and 469 (6DM 2.3); and L. Berczelly,
BICS 35 (1988) 119–27.

As long ago as 1916 B. Prehn[1] identified Menander's
Synaristosai as the Greek model for Plautus' *Cistellaria*,
while fifteen years later F. Marx[2] identified the Dioscu-
rides mosaic of the three seated women as a portrayal of
the opening scene of the Greek play, yet at first both sug-
gestions were generally disbelieved. It took further argu-
mentation from later scholars[3] and the lucky discovery of
the Mitylene mosaic to convince scholars of the correct-

[1] *Quaestiones Plautinae* (Diss. Breslau 1916) 10 and n.1.
[2] *Rh.Mus.* 79 (1930) 197–208.
[3] Especially E. Fraenkel, *Philologus* 87 (1932) 117–20 =
Kleine Beiträge zur klassischen Philologie 2 (Rome 1964) 33–36.
For a brief account of that scholarship see Dorothy K. Lange,
Class. Journ. 70/2 (1974–75) 30–32.

ness of Prehn's and Marx's theories.

In the opening scene of Plautus' *Cistellaria* (vv.1–119) an elderly bawd converses with two young women at the end of a lunch party. One is her daughter Gymnasium, a young courtesan. The other is Selenium, a foundling from Lemnos in love with a young man named Alcesimarchus; she is giving the lunch party in the house that she has been sharing with Alcesimarchus. The equivalent scene in the Menandrean model gave the play its Greek title, and several fragments from it which were cited by ancient authors (frs. 337, 335, 343 K-A = 382, 385, 389 K-T = 1, 4, 8 in this edition) appear to provide the Greek source of passages in the Plautine scene (vv.89–93, 19 and 48–49 respectively). To these can be added the lines in *P.Heidelberg* 175, if these are correctly identified as the source of *Cistellaria* 95–103. It seems very likely that the lunch scene opened Menander's play just as it opened that of Plautus.

The Mytilene mosaic names the bawd Philainis and the two young courtesans Pythias and Plangon; Plangon is sitting next to Philainis and thus more likely to be her daughter. Plautus thus renamed Plangon Gymnasium and Pythias Selenium; if he gave a name to Menander's Philainis, it is not preserved in the now mutilated version of his text.[4]

An abbreviation of the name Pythias may have been written to indicate the speaker in the right-hand margin of v.9 of *P.Oxyrhynchus* 4305, and this is one of three admittedly treacherous foundations for any tentative attribution of this papyrus to *Synaristosai*. The second is a possible

---

[4] Those editors who call her Syra are misinterpreting two passages of Festus (390.8, 480.23 Lindsay), as the paper of Fraenkel cited above clearly shows.

reference in the papyrus (v.4) to that play's opening scene, when Pythias is accused apparently of "partying just now". Finally, there appears to be a similarity in dramatic action between *P.Oxy.* 4305 and *Cistellaria* 305–17. The opening of the Plautine passage is mutilated, but here Alcesimarchus' father enters with the intention of finding Selenium and detaching her from his son. It is Gymnasium (= Pythias in *Synaristosai*), however, who appears now out of Selenium's house; Alcesimarchus' father mistakes her for Selenium, and accuses her of corrupting his son. *P.Oxy.* 4305 begins with one unidentified character giving a warning to another just before an act-break; the next act begins with a conversation between a man possibly named Demeas (and so likely to be old) and a girl possibly called Pythias; the papyrus is too mutilated for us to follow their speeches clearly, but in addition to the partying reference there are allegations that the girl "carried off" somebody (8), and that a marriage was involved (9). If Handley's attribution of *P.Oxy.* 4305 to *Synaristosai* is correct, we should have to assume that Menander ended one of his acts with a conversation between an unknown character and a man possibly named Demeas (in that event presumably Menander's name for Alcesimarchus' father), and the latter's departure into Plangon's (= Selenium's) house three lines before a choral entr'acte; and that the new act began with Pythias (= Gymnasium) and Demeas entering in conversation, with Demeas referring to Plangon's lunch party at the beginning of the play before he went on to accuse the girl whom he had misidentified as Plangon of corrupting his son and perhaps of trying to persuade him to marry her. In that case Plautus would have cut out an act break in his Greek model, and reorganised his dramatic structure

329

so that Gymnasium entered from Selenium's house directly after Alcesimarchus' father had completed his entry monologue. This is clearly one way in which Plautus treated his Greek originals, as the *Dis Exapaton* has made clear.[5] Even so, as Handley himself admits, the ascription of *P.Oxy.* 4305 to *Synaristosai* remains a high-risk speculation.

The Mytilene mosaic of *Synaristosai*, like the one in the same villa of *Theophoroumene*, reverses the artistically superior version of Dioscurides, who places the old bawd on the right and the two younger women on her left. Dioscurides' young servant is shown in profile from the top of the head down to below the waist, but despite the delicacy of the drawing, it is still impossible to define the servant's sex.

Menander's *Synaristosai* appears also to have been adapted for the Roman stage by Caecilius Statius.[6]

Apart from the characters portrayed and named on the Mytilene mosaic, and the one possible further name in *P.Oxy.* 4305, we do not know either the names or the number of characters featured in Menander's play. The cast-list of Plautus' *Cistellaria* numbered at least the twelve characters identifiable in the preserved portions of its text; most of their counterparts doubtless had roles in Menander's play. No information survives about the date and place of production for *Synaristosai*, but its imaginary scene was Sicyon, the annual Dionysiac festival of that city

[5] See the comments in Volume I of my Loeb Menander, pp.164–67.

[6] See O. Ribbeck, *Comicorum Romanorum Fragmenta*[3] (Leipzig 1898) 79.

played an important role in its plot, and Sicyon's hippo-drome was mentioned in Plautus' adaptation (549–51). This has led to a plausible but unverifiable suggestion that *Synaristosai* had its first production in Sicyon rather than Athens.[7]

[7] See W. Ludwig in *Entretiens de la Fondation Hardt* 16 (1970) 47.

ΣΥΝΑΡΙΣΤΩΣΑΙ

P. Heidelberg 175 (H)

ΦΙΛΑΙΝΙΣ (?)
```
        ]τινοσ[
        ]υσαθ' ἡ κ[όρη
      ]ς τὴν μητ[έρα
      ]ελειν τὰ πολ[
5     ]ον ὅτι χαρ[
      ]καν προσλαβ[
     ]τ' ἔρως ἐρρωμ[έν
     ]ς.
```

ΠΛΑΓΓΩΝ (?)
```
       —ἆ ποίας, τάλαν,
      ]κειν τῆς Λημνία[ς
10    ]τι γειτνιᾷ γέρων
      ]τρέφων γὰρ θυγατ[έρα
      ]ε κωλύσειν γαμεῖν
```

Supplements whose author is not named were made by the ed.pr. of H, G. A. Gerhard.
3 πρὸ]ς Gerhard.   6] κἂν προσλάβ[ῃ Edmonds.
7]τ' ἔρως ἐρρωμ[ένος or -νως Arnott.

SYNARISTOSAI

The Heidelberg Papyrus

The twelve lines of the Heidelberg papyrus are too badly damaged for any attempt at continuous translation, but the following words and phrases can be made out: v. 1 of whom or of some(one), 2 the [girl], 3 the mother, 4 most, 5 that, 6 take as well (?), 7 love powerful or powerfully, all probably spoken by Plangon's mother Philainis to Pythias; 8 ah what, poor thing, 9 the Lemnian (? girl), 10 old man lives next door, 11 for, bringing up a daughter, 12 to stop [him (?)] marrying.

Despite this mutilation, the twelve lines of this scrap link up remarkably closely with the passage in Plautus' Cistellaria which treats the imagined rivalry for Alcesimarchus' affections between Selenium and 'the relation born in Lemnos'; words and phrases where there is verbal contact between the papyrus and Plautus' adaptation are printed in capitals in both the English translation below and the Latin septenarii opposite:

---

8 ς· with the lower point of a dicolon perhaps lost in a lacuna (so Austin).

MENANDER

This scrap seems to come from the Greek original adapted by Plautus at *Cistellaria* 95–103:

95   *o mea Selenium,*
adsimulare amare oportet. nam si AMES, *extempulo*
melius illi multo, quem AMES, *consulas quam rei tuae.*

SELENIUM

at ille conceptis iurauit uerbis apud matrem meam,
me uxorem ducturum esse; ei nunc alia ducendast
  domum,
100 *sua cognata* LEMNIENSIS, *quae* HABITAT HIC IN
  PROXUMO.
nam eum pater eius subegit. nunc mea mater iratast
  mihi,
quia non redierim domum ad se, postquam hanc rem
  resciuerim,
103 *eum uxorem* DUCTURUM ESSE *aliam.*

  95 *selenium* A: *selenium quid est* or *quidem* P (the Palatine group of mss.)
  96 Corr. Camerarius: *extemplo* all mss.
  97 *quem* P: *qui* or *que* A.
  101 *eius* P: *us* A.
  102 *quia* P: *que* A. *hanc* A: *eam* P.

BAWD

O my dear Selenium,   95

You must just pretend to love, for if YOU really LOVE,
  you will
Put the man YOU LOVE far, far before what's in your
  interest.

SELENIUM

But he swore the solemnest of oaths to my own mother
  that
He would marry me, and now he's got to wed another
  GIRL,
Some relation BORN IN LEMNOS who's now LIVING   100
  HERE NEXT DOOR!
It's his father who has forced him. Now my mother's mad
  at me,
All because I've not gone back to her, when I found out
  about
This—his MARRYING another woman.   103

*Plautus is not an exact translator of his models, as the frag-
ments of Menander's Δὶς ἐξαπατῶν clearly show, and this
fact, when added to the incoherence of a tiny mutilated
scrap of papyrus, makes it impossible to prove beyond all
shadow of doubt that P.Heidelberg 175 derives from
Menander's Συναριστῶσαι. Even so, the ties between the
Plautine scene and the papyrus go substantially beyond
circumstances that could be explained as casual coinci-
dence.*

*In the papyrus there are almost certainly two speakers,
although the lower part of the dicolon in v. 8 has vanished,
perhaps in a lacuna. Of these speakers the one who speaks*

*after the dicolon is certainly a woman, for the interjection
τάλαν (poor thing) in that verse is confined to females.[1] At
the beginning of the papyrus one speaker refers to* mother
(v. 3) in the accusative just after mentioning the girl *(v. 2)
in the nominative, if Gerhard's supplement is accepted. In
the passage of* Cistellaria *immediately preceding the one
quoted, Selenium three times mentions her own mother
and herself in the same phrase (83–85, 90, 92), and al-
though in the Latin text at 95–97 the bawd says nothing
about a mother or her daughter, her Greek counterpart
might well have done so in this context. At v. 7 the speaker
makes a remark (if I interpret the line correctly) about* love
powerful *(or* powerfully); *the effect of sexual passion is pre-
cisely what the bawd talks about at* Cist. 95–97. *The words
and phrases uttered by the woman who speaks after the
change of speaker in v. 8 tie remarkably closely with Sele-
nium's speech at* Cist. 98–103. *After her initial* 'poor thing'
(8) she mentions the Lemnian (? girl) *(v. 9), then says* old
man lives next door *(v. 10), adds (as a reason:* note for *in
v. 11) a reference, possibly to that same* old man *bringing
up* a daughter *(v. 11), and finally, before the scrap breaks
off, talks of somebody or something being about to* stop
[him] (γαμεῖν *is active)* marrying *(v. 12). At* Cist. 98–103
Selenium refers to Alcesimarchus' female *relation born in*
Lemnos *(100), who* lives next door *(100: sc. next door to the
old man Demipho, who turns out to be Selenium's father);*

[1] See especially Christina Dedoussi, *Hellenika* 18 (1964) 1–10,
Sandbach's commentary on Men. *Epitr.* 434, D. Bain, *Antichthon*
18 (1984) 33–35, and A. H. Sommerstein in *Lo spettacolo delle
voci* 2 (Bari 1995) 70 (edited by F. De Martino and him).

she does not actually say in the Plautine version that Demipho had been 'rearing a daughter' in Lemnos, but this is the fact that lies behind the subterfuge of the Lemnian relation, and the determination of Alcesimarchus' father that the young man should marry the girl from Lemnos (Cist. 101, cf. 103) would at this stage appear to be a barrier that would prevent (the male) Alcesimarchus from marrying Selenium.

The links are sufficient in number and detail to make the identification of the papyrus scrap as Menander's Συναρι-στῶσαι highly probable. These links come in the same sequence in both Cist. and the Heidelberg papyrus. In Menander's play the bawd was named Philainis and Selenium's counterpart Plangon. We may therefore tentatively attach names to the speakers in this papyrus scrap.)

The Oxyrhynchus Papyrus

Although the first 8 lines of the Oxyrhynchus papyrus are badly mutilated, it is possible to provide a partial, provisional translation. In the opening three lines the speaker addresses a man who is either already on his way off stage or about to leave with the speaker when he has finished his speech. If this papyrus does derive from Synaristosai, that man would be the Greek counterpart of Alcesimarchus' father, probably called Demeas, and he would make his exit into Plangon's (= Selenium's) house.

P. Oxyrhynchus 4305 (O)

Fragment 1, column i

1
        μ]ὴ οὐ φθάσῃς· ἂν δὲ φθάσῃς,
        εὖ] ἴσθι. χρησμόν σοι λέγω·
        ]ιζε τοῦτον συμβαλών.

XO]   P   Oϒ

ΔΗΜΕΑΣ
]ας σὺ πίν[ο]υσ᾽ ἀρτίως;

ΠϒΘΙΑΣ

5 [   ]

ΔΗΜΕΑΣ
] αἰτιᾷ, δ᾽, ἐπεί σ᾽—

ΠϒΘΙΑΣ

                ἐγώ;

ΔΗΜΕΑΣ
νὴ τὸν Δία τὸν Σ]ωτῆ[ρ]α, νὴ τὸν Ἥλιον,
νὴ τὸν Ποσειδῶ, ν]ὴ τ[ὸν Ἀ]πό[λ]λ[ω] τουτονί,
        ]φήμ᾽ ἐγώ σε κατα[λα]βεῖν

[   ]

All the supplements here were made by the ed.pr. of O, E. W.
Handley.

SYNARISTOSAI

UNIDENTIFIED CHARACTER

] don't anticipate, but if you do,   1
] be sure, here's my prediction—
] figuring it out.

(Here the play's second, third or fourth act ends, and the chorus perform their entr'acte. Afterwards two characters enter and converse; if this papyrus is from Synaristosai, they will be Demeas and Pythias emerging from Plangon's house.)

DEMEAS (?)
[   ] you [   ] when partying just now?

PYTHIAS (?)
[   ]

DEMEAS (?)
But don't you blame (?) [yourself (?)], when you—

PYTHIAS (?)
                                                    When I?   5

DEMEAS (?)
Swearing [by Zeus the] Saviour, by the Sun,
[And by Posidon], by Apollo here,[2]
[   ] I declare you carried off
[My boy (?)]!

---

[2] Demeas points to an altar or emblem (usually a pointed pillar) erected to Apollo Agyieus that was placed by one of the stage house doors. See the note on *Dyskolos* 659 (Loeb volume I pp. 290–91, n.3).

MENANDER

ΠΥΘΙΑΣ

ἤδ]η Δ[η]μέα, γάμον λ[
10   ]... μὰ τὼ θ[εώ
]κες ἐξέκρα[ξε] τε[
]δε[.]δενη[..]κ.[
13   ] [.]ορμ[..]δι[

(Between columns i and ii of fragment 1 there is a gap of
unknown length. The placing of fragment 2 is uncertain:
see the introduction to this play.)

Fragment 1, column ii

14 κ.[, 15 ποτ[, 16 οργ[, 17 .[, 18 κ[, 19 π[with para-
graphus, 20 τ[, 21 πρ[, 22 κα[with paragraphus, 23 .[.

Fragment 2

24]αστε.[, 25]προσω[, 26]γω (line end), 27]θυρα.[,
28]στοφ[, 29]ον (line end), 30]ωτισ[, 31]ετε (line end),
32]εγχε[, 33 συ]μποτ[, 34]..ι..[, 35].φοδ[, 36]..[,
37]ει[, 38]..[.

This scrap may possibly come from the Greek original
transformed by Plautus at *Cistellaria* 306–17:

ALCESIMARCHI PATER
306 *mulierculam exornatulam [   ] quidem hercle scita.*
quamquam uetus cantherius sum, etiam nunc, ut ego
     opinor,
adhinnire equolam possum ego hanc, si detur sola soli.

340

PYTHIAS
[   ] marriage, Demeas, [

[   ] no, by the Ladies!³   10

Thereafter only occasional words can be deciphered:
shouted *v. 11,* anger *or* angry (?) *16,* forwards (?) *25,* door
27, pour (*or* pouring) *in 32,* fellow drinker *or* drinkers (?)
*33. Despite its mutilation, however, the papyrus passage
can (but not necessarily must) be read in a way that allows
one to see it as the original adapted, expanded and trans-
formed by Plautus in Cistellaria vv. 306–17. An English
translation of this part of the Roman play appears below;
only one verbal link between it and the papyrus is discern-
ible; it is printed in capital letters in both Plautus' Latin
opposite and the English version.*

Plautus, *Cistellaria* 306–17

*(Alcesimarchus' father is on stage. Gymnasium now enters
from Selenium's house.)*

FATHER
A well-dressed girly [   ] in fact damned pretty!   306
Though I'm an old decrepit hack, I think I can still
  whinny
To this wee filly even now, if one to one's the contest!

³ A woman's oath, by the goddesses Demeter and Persephone,
as at *Dysk.* 878 and elsewhere.

---

9 In the right-hand margin the name of the speaker seems to
be given as π[υ]θ(ιας).
306 A's text between *exornatulam* and *quidem* is unreadable.

GYMNASIUM

nimis opportune mi euenit rediisse Alcesimarchum;
310 *nam sola nulla inuitior solet esse.*

ALCESIMARCHI PATER

me uocato,
ne sola sis: ego tecum [ero, uolo] ego agere, ut tu agas
   aliquid.

GYMNASIUM

nimis lepide [ex]concinnauit hasce aedis Alcesimarchus.

ALCESIMARCHI PATER

ut quo[m Ven]us adgreditur, [place]t; lepidumst amare
   semper.

GYMNASIUM

Venerem meram haec aedes olent, quia amator expoliuit.

ALCESIMARCHI PATER

315 *non mo[do i]psa lepidast, commode quoque hercle*
   fabulatur.
sed cum dicta huius interpretor, HAEC HERCLEST, *ut ego*
   opinor,
meum QUAE CORRUMPIT *filium.*

311–12 Suppl. Studemund.
313 Suppl. Leo.
315 Suppl. Studemund.

SYNARISTOSAI

GYMNASIUM
(not noticing Alcesimarchus' father)
It's been a very lucky break for me, Alcesimarchus
Returning here. No girl hates her own company more   310
   than I do!

FATHER
(aside)
Call me, you won't be lonely! [I'll be] with [you, I should
   like to]
Ensure you're on the go.

GYMNASIUM
(still unaware of Alcesimarchus' father)
                              Alcesimarchus did this house up
So nicely!

FATHER
(still aside)
         Like when [Ven]us enters, [I approve]. Love always
Is nice.

GYMNASIUM
(still unaware)
    Pure love's the perfume of this house, because a lover's
Embellished it!

FATHER
(still aside)
              It's not just her that's nice, she also speaks well!   315
But when I spell out what she says, I'm sure that this is
   really
The GIRL THAT'S RUINING my son.   317

343

MENANDER

Ten Fragments of Συναριστῶσαι
Quoted by Ancient Authors

Fragment 1 (337 K-A, 382 K-T)

[Hermogenes], *de Inventione* IV.11 (pp. 200–201 Rabe):
ὅπου δ᾽ ἂν ὁ νοῦς αἰσχρὸς ᾖ, ἐκεῖ (so V group of mss.:
τότε P group of mss.) χρεία τῆς σεμνότητος τοῦ λόγου,
ἵνα τὸ νοούμενον αἰσχρῶς οὕτως ἐξενέγκῃ τις τῷ
λόγῳ εὐφυῶς, ὄνομα ἀντ᾽ ὀνόματος (so P: ὄνομα
ὀνόματι V) ἀμείβων, ὡς μὴ δόξαι τισὶν αἰσχρὸν εἶναι
τὸ πρᾶγμα διὰ τὴν τοῦ λόγου σεμνότητα, ὡς παρὰ τῷ
Μενάνδρῳ. πυθομένου γάρ τινος κόρης, πῶς εἴη
διεφθαρμένη, σεμνῶς ἀφηγήσατο πρᾶγμα αἰσχρὸν
ὀνόμασι βελτίστοις·

Διονυσίων ⟨γὰρ⟩ ἦν

πομπή. ⟨   ⟩
ὁ δ᾽ ἠκολούθησεν μέχρι τοῦ πρὸς τὴν θύραν·
ἔπειτα φοιτῶν καὶ κολακεύων ⟨ἐμέ τε καὶ⟩
5 τὴν μητέρ᾽, ἔγνω μ᾽.

Verse 1 of fragment: ⟨γὰρ⟩ suppl. Clericus.
2 Quoter's omission of most of this verse noted by Dobree.
3 ὁ δ᾽ Herwerden: ὁ δέ με or ὁ δέ μοι mss.   τοῦ ms. Sc: τὰ
PV.
4 Suppl. Dobree from Plaut. *Cist.* 92.
The whole fragment is spoken by Plangon.

---

4 Pausanias 2.7.5–7 informs us that in Sicyon (the scene of the
Synaristosai) the Dionysia festival was an annual event, with a

SYNARISTOSAI

*Ten Fragments of Synaristosai
Quoted by Ancient Authors*

Fragment 1

An anonymous treatise titled *On Invention,* falsely attributed to the rhetorician Hermogenes: Where the meaning is indecent, the language there requires dignity, in order that one may thus express the indecent idea by a skilful use of language, replacing one word with another in such a way that the subject matter will not seem indecent to anybody because the language is dignified, as in Menander. For there, when someone asked a girl how she had been sexually assaulted, she described a disgusting event with dignity by using the most choice vocabulary:

PLANGON
⟨For⟩ the Dionysia had a
Procession[4] ⟨........................⟩[5]
He followed me right to the door, and then
With always dropping in and flattering
⟨Me and my mother⟩ he knew me too well.   5

torchlit procession in which hymns were sung and two images of Dionysus were carried to his temple situated behind the theatre. See now Audrey Griffin, *Sikyon* (Oxford 1982), especially 8–19, which in effect updates Frazer's still useful translation and commentary (vol. 3, London 1898, 49–51).

[5] The rhetorical treatise does not quote the speech of Pythias in full; it omits any reference to Pythias' mother taking Pythias to see the procession and Pythias' return home (v. 2), as well as the mention of "my mother and me, too" (v. 4), as the Plautine adaptation reveals.

τὸ γὰρ διεφθάρθαι (so ms. Pc: ἐφθάρθαι or ἐσχίσθαι
other mss.) καὶ ὑβρίσθαι σεμνῶς "ἔγνω με" εἰπὼν
ἐκόσμησε πρᾶγμα αἰσχρὸν σεμνοτέρᾳ λόγου συν-
θέσει (so P: συνθήκῃ V).

Plautus' adaptation, *Cistellaria* 89–93:

89   *per Dionysia*
90   *mater pompam me spectatum duxit. dum redeo domum*
     conspicillo consecutust clanculum me usque ad fores.
     inde in amicitiam insinuauit cum matre et mecum simul
93   *blanditiis, muneribus, donis.*

   92 conspicillo BVEJ: conspicio[apparently A.

By describing seduction and sexual assault in a dignified way as "he knew me too well," he glossed over a disgusting act by the greater dignity of his language.

As long ago as 1576 Lambinus in the commentary attached to his edition of Plautus identified the above quotation as the Menandrean original of a short speech by Selenium in the opening scene of Plautus' Cistellaria, which runs as follows:

	During the Dionysia	89

Mother took me to see the procession. As I went back home,   90

He caught sight of me and followed secretly right to my door.

Then he charmed his way to friendship with my mother and me, too,

By his sweet talk, favours, presents.   93

The combined evidence of the Menander fragment and the Cistellaria passage is one of several indicators that a scene involving Philainis, Plangon and Pythias began Menander's play just as its Roman counterpart began the Cistellaria, while it demonstrates that here Plautus followed his original closely in setting down the dramatic antecedents of the staged action, with the Greek counterpart of Plautus' Alcesimarchus pursuing Plangon and eventually seducing her.

MENANDER

Fr. 2 (339 K-A, 383 K-T)

Stobaeus, *Eclogae* 4.20.15 (περὶ Ἀφροδίτης), with the
heading Μενάνδρου Συναριστώσαις·

Ἔρως δὲ τῶν θεῶν
ἰσχὺν ἔχων πλείστην ἐπὶ τούτου δείκνυται·
διὰ τοῦτον ἐπιορκοῦσι τοὺς ἄλλους θεούς.

Fr. 3 (340 K-A, 384 K-T)

Athenaeus 6.247f–248a: καλεῖται δ᾽ οἰκόσιτος ὁ μὴ
μισθοῦ, ἀλλὰ προῖκα τῇ πόλει ὑπηρετῶν . . .
Μένανδρος . . . ἰδίως δ᾽ ἐν Συναριστώσαις ἔφη·

ἀστεῖον τὸ μὴ
συνάγειν γυναῖκας μηδὲ δειπνίζειν ὄχλον,
ἀλλ᾽ οἰκοσίτους τοὺς γάμους πεποηκέναι.

SYNARISTOSAI

Fr. 2

Stobaeus ('On Aphrodite'), with the heading 'Menander in *Synaristosai*':

               Among the gods Love has
The greatest power. It's shown by this: because
Of him, oaths sworn by all the other gods are false!

This remark does not appear in the extant portions of Plautus' Cistellaria. It either came in a lost portion of the Roman play, or was cut out by Plautus in a context where Love's faithlessness (e.g. Cist. 72), Love's unfairness (e.g. Cist. 103) or the unreliability of lovers' oaths (e.g. Cist. 471–72) was being mentioned, or perhaps where one or more characters were indulging in a string of oaths (e.g. Cist. 512–22).

Fr. 3

Athenaeus: the expression οἰκόσιτος (fed at home) is applied to a man serving his city not for pay but at his own expense . . . but Menander uses it in a special way in *Synaristosai:*

            It's clever, not inviting women
Or entertaining crowds, but limiting
The wedding feast to those who're fed at home.

Athenaeus implies that Menander here uses the word οἰκόσιτος in a slightly unusual way by applying it, either seriously or ironically, to a tight-fisted father who wishes to restrict the number of people invited to his son's or daughter's wedding. There is nothing remotely similar in what survives of Cistellaria, but Plautus has cut out virtually all

Fr. 4 (335 K-A, 385 K-T)

The Συναγωγὴ λέξεων χρησίμων (Bekker, *Anecdota
Graeca* 1.358.4–18), Photius (α 648 Theodoridis) and the
Suda (αι 299 Adler) s.v. αἴρειν (mss. of Phot., *Suda*: αἶρε
Bekker ms.)· . . . ἐτίθεσαν δὲ τὴν λέξιν καὶ ὡς ἡμεῖς ἐπὶ
τοῦ παρακειμένην ἀφελεῖν τὴν τράπεζαν. Μένανδρος
. . . Συναριστώσαις (mss. of Phot., *Suda*: σναριστώσαις
Bekker ms.)·

ἂν ἔτι πιεῖν μοι δῷ τις· ἀλλ' ἡ βάρβαρος
ἅμα τῇ τραπέζῃ καὶ τὸν οἶνον ᾤχετο
ἄρασ' ἀφ' ἡμῶν.

? Plautus' adaptation, *Cistellaria* 18:

raro nimium dabat quod biberem, id merum infuscabat.

Fr. 5 (341 K-A, 386 K-T)

Stobaeus, *Eclogae* 4.34.53 (περὶ τοῦ βίου, ὅτι βραχὺς
καὶ εὐτελὴς καὶ φροντίδων ἀνάμεστος), and the *Corpus
Parisinum* 759 Elter,* with the heading Μενάνδρου
Συναριστώσαις (so mss. MA of Stobaeus: play title
omitted by ms. S of Stobaeus and *Corp. Paris.*)·

τρισάθλιόν γε καὶ ταλαίπωρον φύσει
πολλῶν τε μεστόν ἐστι τὸ ζῆν φροντίδων.

Fr. 4, line 1 πιεῖν Photius, Bekker ms., mss. GV of *Suda*:
ποιεῖν mss. AIFM of *Suda*.

Fr. 5, line 2 μεστὸν mss. of Stobaeus: μεστῶν *Corp. Paris.*

* On this collection and its manuscript, see O. Hense's edition
of Stobaeus, 4 (Berlin 1909) pp. xxxviii–ix.

*of Menander's original ending to this play (cf. 782–86), and
the above remark could have been made by a character
commenting on the guest list suggested by Alcesimarchus'
father for the wedding of his son to Selenium in the fifth act
of the play.*

Fr. 4

Three lexica, discussing αἴρειν (to lift): . . . and they ap-
plied this word as we also do to removing the little table
that was placed by (sc. people dining). Menander . . . in
Synaristosai:

. . . If someone gives me more to drink! The foreign
Girl's gone and shifted, though, the table and
The wine away from us!

*This may be Menander's version of the tipsy bawd's remark
in Plautus, Cistellaria 19:*

She very rarely gave me aught to drink—she spoiled the
  wine, too!

*The winebibber here implies that mixing wine with water
(the normal procedure at Greek parties) spoiled the wine.*

Fr. 5

Stobaeus ('On life, that it is short and cheap and full of
care'), with the heading 'Menander in *Synaristosai,*' and
an anonymous collection of gnomes, with the heading
'Menander':

Life's utterly grim, miserable and
Brim full of many cares. That's natural.

MENANDER

Fr. 6 (338 K-A, 387 K-T)

The Συναγωγὴ λέξεων χρησίμων (Bekker, *Anecdota Graeca* 1.324.27–30), Photius (α 123 Theodoridis) and the *Suda* (α 152 Adler) s.v. ἀγαπησμός (heading omitted by Phot.)· ἀγαπησμὸν (so mss. of *Suda*: ἀγαπισμὸν mss. of Phot., word omitted by Bekker ms.) λέγουσιν Ἀττικοὶ καὶ ἀγάπησιν τὴν φιλοφρόνησιν (φιλοφροσύνην most mss. of *Suda* and written above -φρόνησιν in ms. b of Phot.). Συναριστώσαις Μένανδρος·

καὶ τὸν ἐπὶ κακῷ
γινόμενον ἀλλήλων ἀγαπησμὸν οἷος ἦν

Fr. 7 (342 K-A, 388 K-T)

Stobaeus, *Eclogae* 4.26.7 (ὁποίους χρὴ εἶναι τοὺς πατέρας περὶ τὰ τέκνα), with the heading (in mss. MA) Μενάνδρου Συναριστώσαις·

πατὴρ δ' ἀπειλῶν οὐκ ἔχει μέγαν φόβον.

Fr. 6, line 2 ἀγαπησμὸν Bekker ms, mss. of *Suda*: ἀγαπισμὸν mss. of Phot.

Fr. 7 μέγαν SA: μέγα M.

There is nothing parallel in what survives of Cistellaria, but both Selenium (e.g. 59–61, 76) and Alcesimarchus (e.g. 205–29, 459–60) dwell on their miseries.

Fr. 6

Three lexica, discussing ἀγαπησμός (affection): Attic writers use ἀγαπησμός also in the sense of friendliness. Menander in *Synaristosai*:

> And mutual
> Affection of some kind, on evil based . . .

Again, there is nothing similar in the surviving portions of Cistellaria. Could Alcesimarchus' father have criticised the relationship of his son and Selenium with such a remark when he came on stage after v. 304, either in an initial monologue or in conversation with Gymnasium?

Fr. 7

Stobaeus ('How fathers should behave to their children'), with the heading 'in Menander's *Synaristosai*':

A father's threats don't generate great fear.

Again, there is nothing like this in what survives of Cistellaria. The father in question is doubtless Alcesimarchus'. He himself could have made the remark in a monologue, or some other character (Gymnasium? Alcesimarchus? a slave?) could have so commented at virtually any point in the play.

MENANDER

Fr. 8 (343 K-A, 389 K-T)

P.Oxyrhynchus 1803, lines 1–7, a fragment of an anonymous glossary from which some words beginning with sigma are preserved: στιφρόν· ὃ οἱ πολλοὶ στριφνόν, ὡς . . . Μένανδρος ἐν Συναριστώσαις·

ὡς ἀεὶ
στιφρὰς ἐσομένας καὶ νέας, ταλάντατος.

? Plautus' adaptation, *Cistellaria* 48–49:

nam si quidem ita eris ut uolo, numquam hac aetate fies,
semperque istam quam nunc habes aetatulam optinebis.

Fr. 9 (344 K-A, 390 K-T)

Pollux 10.18 καὶ μὴν εἰ γυναικείαν ἀγορὰν τὸν τόπον, οὗ τὰ σκεύη τὰ τοιαῦτα πιπράσκουσιν, ἐθέλοις καλεῖν, εὕροις ἂν ἐν ταῖς Συναριστώσαις Μενάνδρου τὸ ὄνομα.

Fr. 8, line 1 O has αει with the alpha cancelled.
2 Corr. Hunt: στεφρας O.
This fragment could also be construed as a single trochaic tetrameter.
Cist. 48 Corr. Seyffert: *et haec ate* VE and before correction B, *haecate* B after correction.

354

Fr. 8

An entry in an anonymous glossary: στιφρόν (sinewy/
firm), a word which the majority now spell στριφνός. . . .
Menander in *Synaristosai:*

>   . . . girls who will
> Always be sinewy and young—poor fellow . . .

*The glossary here contrasts the correct Attic (στιφρός)
and the contemporary Koine (στριφνός) spellings of the
adjective. The quotation from Menander is syntactically
incomplete, but may have belonged to a sentence adapted
by Plautus in Cistellaria 48–49, where the bawd is address-
ing her daughter Gymnasium:*

> For if you turn out as I want you, never will you age like
>   me,
> You will always keep that youthful bloom that you pos-
>   sess today.

Fr. 9

Pollux: If indeed you wanted to call the place where they
sell women's things the 'women's market,' you would find
that expression in Menander's *Synaristosai.*

*The one reference to a market in Plautus' Cistellaria comes
when Demipho, the natural father of Selenium, says that
the slave Lampadio had apparently been searching for him
'in foro' (in the market: 775–76), but it seems unlikely that
either of these two males would have been described by
Menander at this point as visiting the women's market. The
reference in Synaristosai more probably came in the open-*

MENANDER

Fr. 10 (336 K-A, 391 K-T)

Pliny, *Nat. Hist.* 23.159 *myrtus satiua candida minus utilis medicinae quam nigra. semen eius medetur sanguinem excreantibus, item contra fungos in uino potum. odorem oris commendat uel pridie commanducatum. ita apud Menandrum Synaristosae hoc edunt.*

Two Further Fragments Speculatively Attributed to Συναριστῶσαι

Fr. 11 (Fr. Adesp. 479 K-A)

[Hierocles and Philagrius], *Philogelos* 226 λιμόξηρος κωμῳδίας ὑποκριτὴς τὸν ἀγωνοθέτην πρὸ τοῦ εἰσελθεῖν ἄριστον ᾔτει. τοῦ δὲ ἐπιζητοῦντος διὰ τί προαριστῆσαι θέλει, "ἵνα" ἔφη "μὴ ἐπιορκήσω λέγων (corr. Thierfelder: λέγω ms. A)·

<ἐγὼ> μὲν ἠρίστησα, νὴ τὴν Ἄρτεμιν,
μάλ᾽ ἡδέως.

Fr. 10 *utilis* mss. TXg: *utile* L, *inutilis* Vd.   *ita* conj. Mayhoff: *item* mss.   *edunt* EXg: *adeunt* V, *edant* d.
Fr. 11, line 1 <ἐγὼ> suppl. Cobet.   Ἄρτεμιν Mynas: ἄρτεμην ms. A.

---

6 The black myrtle is the common myrtle (*Myrtus communis*), with bluish black berries; the white myrtle is a rare variety (var. *leucocarpa*) with white berries. An oil (*Eau d'anges*) is still made from various parts of the tree for use in perfumery.

*ing scene, perhaps when the bawd was expatiating to
Plangon and Pythias on the different experiences of courte-
sans and high-born women (22–41, 47–50).*

Fr. 10

The elder Pliny's *Natural Histories:* The cultivated white
myrtle is less useful to medicine than the black.[6] Its berries
treat those spitting blood, and also, taken in wine, they act
against fungi. Even when chewed the day before, they
give fragrance to the mouth. Thus in Menander the
Synaristosai ('Women lunching together') eat them.

*A reference to the women eating myrtle berries must have
come, most probably from the bawd, in the opening scene
of the Greek play, and been omitted by Plautus.*

*Two Further Fragments Speculatively Attributed
to Synaristosai*

Fr. 11

An ancient joke book entitled *Philogelos:* A starving comic
actor asked the festival organiser for lunch before he went
on stage. When the organiser asked why he wanted an ad-
vance lunch, he replied "It's to stop me committing perjury
when I say:

I swear by Artemis, the lunch I've had
Was most agreeable!"

*The punch line in this joke is the scrap of quoted verse,
whose metre and style, combined with the fact that it is
voiced by an actor, indicate that it came from an unnamed*

MENANDER

? Plautus' adaptation, *Cistellaria* 10–11 or 15:

GYMNASIUM

10   *ita in prandio nos lepide ac nitide*
accepisti apud te.

LENA

15 *ecastor ad te, ita hodie hic acceptae sumus suauibus*
modis.

Fr. 12 (Menander Fr. 643 K-A, 763 K-T)

Scholiast on Aristophanes, *Acharnians* 202 (ΕΓ = older mss.; Lh = Triclinian) ἄξω τὰ κατ᾽ ἀγρούς· . . . ἔνθα (ἔνθεν ms. E) καὶ ὁ ἐπιλήναιος ἀγὼν (ἀγ. ἐπιλ. Lh) τελεῖται τῷ Διονύσῳ (αὐτῷ Lh). Λήναιον γάρ ἐστιν (ἐστιν omitted by Lh) ἐν ἀγροῖς (ἀγρῷ Lh) ἱερὸν τοῦ (τοῦ om. Lh) Διονύσου . . . · Μένανδρος·

Cist. 10 *ac* VE: *atque* B.   15 *hic* omitted by B.

---

7 See especially G. Anderson, *BICS* 23 (1976) 59–60.

8 *Stud. Urbin.* 35 (1961) 113–15; cf. his edition of the *Philogelos* (Munich 1968) 271. Thierfelder's guess that this scrap may have opened the play cannot be dismissed, although the two equivalent remarks in Plautus' *Cistellaria* come slightly later than the very opening.

9 *The Philogelos* (Amsterdam 1983) 104–105.

10 On the scholiast's remarks here, which imply a false interpretation of the passage of Aristophanes, see especially L. Deubner, *Attische Feste* (Berlin 1932) 124 and n.7, A. Pickard-Cambridge, *The Dramatic Festivals of Athens* (2nd edition, revised by J. Gould and D. M. Lewis, Oxford 1968) 26 and 37–39,

358

comedy by an unnamed author. Quoted scraps of this kind most commonly derive from the opening pages of a popular work,[7] *and A. Thierfelder's suggestion*[8] *that here we have an early—perhaps even the opening—remark in the first scene of Synaristosai deserves serious consideration, since it tallies closely with remarks made in the Plautine adaptation by the two guests at the lunch party: Gymnasium's (vv. 10–11)*

> In fine and handsome fashion you've entertained us
> At your home to lunch like this!

and the bawd's (v. 15)

> Truly here with you today we've been so nicely enter-
>   tained!

Gymnasium's remark seems closer in expression to the Greek fragment. However, as B. Baldwin notes in his translation of the Philogelos,[9] *"Eating is too staple a feature of Greek New Comedy . . . to allow assigning these verses to any particular play."*

Fr. 12

Scholiast on Aristophanes, *Acharnians* 202: 'I'll celebrate the Rural (Dionysia)': there also the Lenaean contest is held in honour of Dionysus. The Lenaeum is a temple of Dionysus in the country[10] . . . Menander:

and F. Kolb, *Agora und Theater: Volks- und Festversammlung* (Berlin 1981) 26–27 with nn. 49 and 50.

MENANDER

τραγῳδὸς ἦν ἀγών, Διονύσια.

? Plautus' adaptation, *Cistellaria* 156:

fuere Sicyoni iam diu Dionysia.

It was the tragic contest at the Dionysia.

T. B. L. Webster[11] *suggested that this quotation from an unnamed play of Menander in fact derives from Synaristosai, because it appears to be translated by Plautus at Cistellaria 156:*

In Sicyon it was the Dionysia, long ago.

The link seems real, but the Greek scrap is perhaps too short for any certain attribution.

---

[11] *An Introduction to Menander* (Manchester 1974) 188 n.106.

PHASMA

(THE APPARITION)

INTRODUCTION

Manuscripts

P = *Membrana Petropolitana* 388, one damaged leaf of a parchment codex from which two leaves of the *Epitrepontes* also survive (see volume I p. 381 of my Loeb Menander); it is dated to the fourth century A.D. It was originally found in the monastery of St. Catherine on Sinai and is now in the Saltikov-Schedrin Public Library, St. Petersburg. The *Phasma* leaf contains on one side vv. 1–27 and on the other 31a–56, both mutilated; the fractured remains of vv. 25–27 coincide with the beginning of a previously known fragment of Menander cited without play title by Clement of Alexandria and containing vv. 25–31. First edition of vv. 1–27, based on an apograph of P made by K. von Tischendorf: C. G. Cobet, *Mnemosyne* 4 (1876) 285–93 = *Miscellanea Critica* (Leiden 1876) 438–46; first edition of vv. 1–27 and 32–56 based on the original manuscript: V. Jernstedt, *Zapiski ist.-fil. S.-Petersburgskago Univ.* 26 (1891) 54, 148–53. A photograph of vv. 1–27 is printed as plate II by Körte in his first two Teubner editions of Menander (Leipzig 1910 opposite p. lviii, 1912 opposite p. lxiv); one of vv. 31a–56 appears as pl. I in *ZPE* 123 (1998). Jernstedt provides facsimiles (carefully handwritten) of 1–27 opposite p. 54 (= I.a), and of 31a–56 opposite

p. 152 (pl. I.b); these are reproduced in *ZPE* 123 (1998) 35. The present edition uses photographs of P originally in the possession of E. G. Turner, and kindly loaned to me by the Oxyrhynchus Archive in Oxford, where they are now deposited.

O = *P.Oxyrhynchus* 2825, fragments of four columns from a papyrus roll written early in the first century A.D. and containing vv. 57–98 and 193–208 (in my numbering: see below) and two other minute scraps (here vv. 99–107). First edition: E. G. Turner, *The Oxyrhynchus Papyri* 38 (1971) 3–15, with a photograph (pl. II); a preliminary discussion of these and the St. Petersburg fragments is given by Turner, *GRBS* 10 (1969) 307–24.

Testimonia I to VII provide further information about the play that seems worth recording.

Pictorial Evidence

A mosaic of (probably) the late fourth century A.D. from the 'House of Menander' at Mytilene in Lesbos. The mosaic is inscribed ΦΑΣΜΑΤΟΣ ΜΕ(ΡΟΣ) Β (*Phasma*, Act II), but since the three characters portrayed are not identified by name (cf. the *Misoumenos* mosaic in the same house, discussed in vol. II of this edition, pp. 250–51), and the text of the scene which inspired the picture has not been preserved, it is difficult to identify two of the characters or to explain with full confidence the dramatic situation. On the left a girl either emerges from, or stands at, a double door that is wide open; she wears a yellow gown with vertical red stripes, looks to her right, and has her right arm raised. In the middle a grey-haired man, dressed in a basically white gown, takes a step towards the girl, with his right arm raised and a stick clutched in his left. To his right stands a third figure, with very dark hair and a red, white and blue cloak on top of a white ankle-length tunic; the right hand is extended, apparently in a gesture to restrain the man in the centre. The hair colour here suggests youth or middle age, but it is not absolutely clear whether the artist was representing a young man or (more probably) a woman, and this uncertainty increases the difficulty of interpreting the scene. Donatus' summary of the *Phasma*'s plot (testimonium VI) makes it plausible to identify the girl on the left as the illegitimate daughter of the now married woman living next door. The other two figures seem most likely to be the woman's husband, threatening or attacking the girl in a now lost second-act scene after he had learnt of her existence, and the wife herself seeking to restrain him. Such an identification of the figures and situation has one major advantage over others that have been advanced:[1] it makes it possible to interpret this mosaic as a representation of action staged in the play, just like the other mosaics in the Mytilene house. Standard edition of the mosaic: S. Charitonidis, L. Kahil, R. Ginouvès, *Les Mosaïques de la Maison du Ménandre à Mytilène* (*Antike Kunst*, Beiheft 6, Berne 1970), 60–62 and plates 8 (colour) and 24 (black and white). See also T. B. L. Webster, *Monuments Illustrating New Comedy* (3rd edition, revised by J. R. Green and A. Seeberg, London 1995),

[1] See also below.

II p. 471 (6DM 2.11); and L. Berczelly, *BICS* 35 (1988) 119–27.

Donatus (see test. VI) and the extant fragment of the play's divine prologue (vv. 9–25) tell us a great deal about the antecedents of the action in *Phasma*, and Donatus adds something about its dramatic resolution, but our knowledge about what actually happens in the plot is limited, haphazard and often problematic. Even the relationships of the major characters are not entirely clear; the following family trees comply with all the available information, but cannot be considered certain.

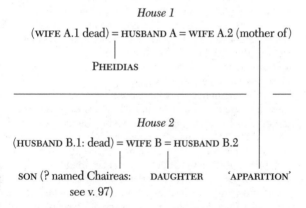

House 1

(WIFE A.1 dead) = HUSBAND A = WIFE A.2 (mother of)

PHEIDIAS

House 2

(HUSBAND B.1: dead) = WIFE B = HUSBAND B.2

SON (? named Chaireas: DAUGHTER   'APPARITION'
see v. 97)

Wife A.2 bore an illegitimate daughter, probably long before she married husband A, whose son Pheidias, now grown up, was issue from an earlier marriage. The illegitimate daughter, now grown up, was reared by and lives with wife B, a friend presumably of wife A.2 or wife A.2's parents. Husband A and wife A.2 now live next door to wife B, who also has a son and daughter, probably by different husbands and now grown up. When *Phasma* begins arrangements seem to have been made for Pheidias to marry wife B's daughter; it is likely that the day of the dramatic action is the planned wedding day.

There is, however, a snag. Wife A.2 had manufactured a device to meet her daughter, without her husband and stepson knowing; they are as yet unaware of her relationship to that daughter. Wife A.2 had made a hole in the party wall between the two houses and turned the area into a shrine, where she was able to meet her daughter under cover of engaging in religious observances. Some time before the action of the play begins Pheidias had caught sight of the daughter at the shrine, believed her to be an apparition, and in his terror had fallen prey to psychosomatic melancholia and insomnia.

By the end of the play Pheidias is in love with the imagined apparition and marries her. How this came about is largely a mystery, although the surviving fragments of text and the Mytilene mosaic provide a few small pieces to insert into what was a large and complicated jigsaw.

(a) If vv. 1–27 in the St Petersburg parchment come before vv. 32–56, it seems likely that the play opened with a scene involving Pheidias and a house slave, in which they discussed Pheidias' sight of the imagined apparition, his resultant illness, and his need nevertheless to go through with his planned wedding to the daughter of husband B.2 and wife B, probably arranged for that very day. When Pheidias discovered (presumably early in the staged action) that what he had seen was a real girl, he fell in love with her, and this at one stroke both cured his indisposition and made him decide to withdraw from his planned wedding to the other girl.

(b) In the second act Pheidias' father must also have discovered some of the truth about his wife's illegitimate daughter, and made threatening gestures at least against her, if my reading of the Mytilene mosaic is correct; this is most likely to have come after Pheidias' discovery that the apparition was a real young lady.

(c) A badly mutilated section of the Oxyrhynchus papyrus (vv. 57–78) contains two references to the wedding being on again (vv. 59, 61), and if a cook is involved in this scene, as seems likely, he may have been hired for the wedding.

(d) A block to Pheidias' planned marriage to the daughter of husband B.2 and wife B appears to be provided by a passage in the Oxyrhynchus fragment (vv. 86–92) where one character (presumably the son of husband B.1 and wife B) hears about the possibility of a man (presumably Pheidias) passionately kissing a girl (presumably the 'apparition') and says that this would dishearten his stepsister, the planned bride.

(e) Another fragment of this papyrus (vv. 193–208 in this edition) apparently has a husband and wife discussing night events during a festival at Brauron[2] on Attica's east coast, when a poor girl wandered off. Although this fragment is severely mutilated, its extant details here point most plausibly to a discussion between husband B.2 and wife B about the rape of wife A.2 long ago. Could the per-

[2] See note on vv. 197-98.

petrator of the rape have been husband A before he married either of his wives?[3]

(f) In a tiny but badly mutilated scrap of this papyrus the name Chaireas has been identified with some plausibility (v. 97); was this the name of the son of husband B.1 and wife B?

In this edition the line numbering differs considerably from that of Sandbach in his Oxford text, who places vv. 32–56 before vv. 1–31 (along with several earlier editors), and then omits three badly mutilated scraps (here vv. 93–98, 99–103, 104–107), the first of which belongs to the papyrus column directly following vv. 75–92. These omissions have made it necessary in this edition to renumber Sandbach's vv. 93–107 as vv. 193–207. Where my numbering differs from that of Sandbach, Sandbach's is added in brackets.

Menander's *Phasma* seems to have become a popular play. Attic inscriptions confirm productions of it in the 250's B.C. (test. I) and 167 B.C. (test. II); it was adapted for the Roman stage by Luscius Lanuvinus (test. V); Fronto mentioned it in a tediously clever epigram (test. IV); and it was included among the Menander titles listed in a shorthand manual of the 3rd or 4th century A.D. (test. III).

No hypothesis, didascalic notice or cast list survives for this play. The date of its first production is therefore unknown.[4]

[3] See further my comments below on test. VI.

[4] More detailed discussions of matters discussed in this introduction, as well as of textual questions in the *Phasma*, will be found in *ZPE* 123 (1998) 35-48.

In addition to the St Petersburg parchment and *P.Oxy.* 2825, three other scraps of papyrus have been (at least tentatively) attributed to Menander's *Phasma*.

(i) T. B. L. Webster (*JHS* 93, 1973, 197 n.6) suggested that *P.Oxy.* 862, a tiny scrap of papyrus from the third century A.D. containing the ends of 19 trimeters (first edition: B. P. Grenfell and A. S. Hunt, *The Oxyrhynchus Papyri* 6, 1908, 171–72), might belong to *Phasma* because in it "a slave tells Pheidias of the birth of a child." The presence of a character named Pheidias is an unreliable clue, however; young men with this name appeared in *Heros* (cast list) and *Kolax* (v. B19), and if the reference in vv. 8–9 of this papyrus is to the birth of a child, it seems more likely to be something happening in the dramatic present, not more than fifteen years ago, as in *Phasma*. *P.Oxy.* 862 is more appropriately included in Kassel–Austin's *fragmenta adespota* (1022).

(ii) With some hesitation Webster (*An Introduction to Menander*, Manchester 1974, 201) also attributed *P.Oxy.* 2329, a better preserved scrap of the second or third century A.D. with the remains of 29 trimeters, to Menander's *Phasma*. It contains a dialogue between a young man who is ashamed (v. 7) and his distraught mother (v. 1) about an aborted wedding (v. 14). The subject matter here would suit Pheidias and his stepmother or even Chaireas and his mother—and doubtless also many other comedies now lost, but none of the character names preserved in this fragment (Dromon v. 25, a woman named Kle[15) reappears in *Phasma,* and so this papyrus too is more safely printed in Kassel–Austin's *adespota* (1091).

(iii) E. W. Handley (with A. Hurst, *Relire Ménandre*, Geneva 1990, 138–43; and *The Oxyrhynchus Papyri* 59,

1992, 51–59) was the first to publish *P.Oxy.* 3966, a scrap written in the first century A.D. and containing 15 lines from comedy, which introduce somebody carrying wine or more probably water for a bride's prenuptial bath (vv. 7–10). Handley's tentative suggestion that this passage might belong to *Phasma* is founded on that play's frequent references to a forthcoming wedding (10, 59, 61, 92) and the presence of lyrics in both *Phasma* (test. VII) and this papyrus (v. 12). Unfortunately, the latter's lyrics are in a metre different from those attested in *Phasma*, and weddings form the climax of too many plays of Menander for Handley's suggestion to be altogether convincing. The handwriting on this papyrus is identical with that on an Oxyrhynchus fragment of Menander's *Karchedonios* (2656), and this makes it more likely that the author of *P.Oxy.* 3966 was also Menander, but the evidence is insufficient to identify the play.

Dramatis Personae, so far as they are known:

Pheidias, a young man

Syros, a senior slave or freedman, probably connected with the household of Pheidias' father

An unidentified divinity, who spoke the prologue

Pheidias' father (husband A)

Pheidias' stepmother (wife A.2)

The illegitimate daughter of Pheidias' stepmother, believed by Pheidias at first to be an apparition, and living with the family of house B, next door to the house of Pheidias' father

A cook hired for the wedding of Pheidias to the stepsister of the young man next door

A young man, son of wife B and husband B.1, possibly
    named Chaireas
A slave from this man's household
The young man next door's stepfather (husband B.2)
The young man next door's mother (wife B)

In the lost parts of the play some other characters doubt-
less had speaking roles; these may just possibly have in-
cluded the daughter of husband B.2 and wife B, although,
if she appeared at all, she is most likely to have been a
mute, like one or more assistants accompanying the cook.
A chorus, probably of tipsy revellers, would have per-
formed four entr'actes.

ΦΑΣΜΑ

(We do not know how much of *Phasma*'s opening scene is missing before v. 1 here, but if that scene matched in length the corresponding scene of *Aspis*, we should have lost something like the first 30 or 40 lines of the play.)

ΦΕΙΔΙΑΣ

1 (26   .νατ[..].[.].εισι.[
Sandbach)

1–27, 31a–56 P, indicating changes of speaker (only in mid-line) by means of a blank space and raised point (·).

---

[1] For a fuller discussion of the troublesome problems here, see *ZPE* 123 (1998) 37–38. The interpretation of vv. 1–56 given above faces one possible objection: if the divine prologue begins at v. 40, the bluntness and directness of its first sentence are without parallel in such Menandrean speeches—but no more surprising than, and theatrically just as effective as, the way in which identification of the speaker in *Perikeiromene*'s prologue is delayed until her very final word (v. 148).

374

PHASMA

(SCENE: A street somewhere in Athens. Two houses are
visible to the audience; one belongs to Pheidias' father, the
other to a family with a son, daughter and another girl
brought up along with them.)

(Vv. 1–27 are written on one side, and vv. 32–56 on the
other, of the St Petersburg parchment leaf. Although it is
not certain which side preceded the other in the play, such
evidence as we have[1] makes it more likely that vv. 1–27
come somewhere in the middle, and vv. 32–39 at the end, of
the play's opening scene, in which Pheidias and a house
slave (here provisionally identified as the Syros named in
vv. 60, 71) are on stage together. We have no means of
knowing how they met, or which entrance was used by the
slave; Pheidias may perhaps have entered at the beginning
of the play on his way from the market, carrying bread and
other purchases that he has made there for his wedding
feast, planned in all probability to take place on that very
day. He is betrothed to the daughter of wife B and husband
B.2 next door. Pheidias is now nervous about his forthcom-
ing marriage, because he feels unwell after one or more
sleepless nights. His indisposition was triggered by a re-
cent experience (described perhaps in a graphic narrative)
when he saw what he believed to be an apparition of a
young girl.

375

ΣΤΡΟΣ (?)

πῶς εἰσιν οἱ πυροὶ [κατ' ἀγορὰν ὤνιοι;

ΦΕΙΔΙΑΣ

τί δ' ἐμοὶ μέλει τοῦτ';

ΣΤΡΟΣ

οὐθέν, [ἀλλὰ τῷ λόγῳ
εἰς τὴν ἀλήθειαν καταχρήσα[σθαι πρέπει.
5 (30S) ἂν τίμιοι, δακέτω σ' ὑπὲρ ἐμ[οῦ τοῦτο τοῦ
πένητος. αἴσθου σαυτὸν ὄντα, [Φειδία,
ἄνθρωπον, ἄνθρωπον δὲ καὶ [τὸν ἐνδεῆ,
ἵνα μὴ 'πιθυμῇς τῶν ὑπέρ [σε πραγμάτων.
ὅταν δ' ἀγρυπνεῖν εἴπῃς, τί σο[ὶ τὸ δυσχερές;
10 (35S) τὴν αἰτίαν γνώσῃ. περιπατεῖς κ[ατ' ἀγοράν.
εἰσῆλθες εὐθύς, ἂν κοπιάσῃς τ[ὰ σκέλη.
μαλακῶς ἐλούσω. πάλιν ἀναστ[ὰς περιπατεῖς
πρὸς ἡδονήν. ὕπνος αὐτὸς ὁ βί[ος ἐστί σοι.
τὸ πέρας· κακὸν ἔχεις οὐδέν, ἡ ν[όσος δέ σου
15 (40S) ἔσθ' ἢν διῆλθες—φορτικώτερο[ν δέ τι
ἐπέρχεταί μοι, τρόφιμε, συγγνώ[μην δ' ἔχε—

2 κατ' ἀγορὰν suppl. Gomperz and Wilamowitz, ὤνιοι Cobet.
3 δ' ἐμοὶ Wilamowitz: δεσοι P. τουτο·ουθεν P. Suppl.
Körte (but τῷ λόγῳ already Cobet at the end of 4).
4 Suppl. Arnott. 5 Corr. Wilamowitz: τειμιος P.
ἐμ[οῦ suppl. Cobet, τοῦτο τοῦ Wilamowitz. 6 Suppl. Cobet.
7 Suppl. Sudhaus (τὸν already Gomperz).
8 επιθυμηις P. Suppl. Wilamowitz. 9 Suppl. Arnott.
10 γνώσῃ P. Suppl. Sudhaus. 11 Suppl. Cobet.
12 Suppl. Gomperz. 13 Suppl. Weil.
14 Suppl. Wilamowitz. 15, 16, 17 Suppl. Cobet.

PHASMA

Only a few letters of v. 1 are preserved, and no word that can securely be translated.)

SYROS (?)[2]
How much does wheat [cost in the market]?

PHEIDIAS
                              What   2
Concern is that of mine?

SYROS (?)
                    None—[yet one ought
[To] check [accounts] and verify the facts!
If wheat's expensive, [that] should prick your conscience   5
On my behalf. [I'm] poor. Remember, [Pheidias],
You're human, and [a poor man]'s human, too!
So don't you crave for what's beyond [your reach]!
When you complain of sleeplessness, what's really
Your [problem]? I'll tell you the cause. You stroll   10
[All round the market], come straight home when [legs]
Are weary, bathe in luxury. Then up you get
And [take a] pleasant [stroll. Your] life itself
[Is] sleep! So, finally, there's nothing wrong with you.
This [sickness] you've described is—well, [a] rather   15
   coarse
Expression comes to mind—forgive me, master—

---

[2] It is a plausible (but not verifiable) guess that Pheidias' slave here is the same character as the slave present with Pheidias in the scene at vv. 57 ff., where he is twice (vv. 60, 71) addressed by name as Syros.

τὸ δὴ λεγόμενον, οὐκ ἔχεις ὅπο[ι χέσῃς
ὑπὸ τῶν ἀγαθῶν, εὖ ἴσθι.

ΦΕΙΔΙΑΣ
μὴ ὥ[ρασί γε
ἵκοιο.

ΣΤΡΟΣ (?)
τἀληθῆ λέγω, νὴ τοὺς θε[ούς·
20 (45S) τοῦτ᾽ ἐστὶ τἀρρώστημα.

ΦΕΙΔΙΑΣ
καὶ μή[ν, ὦ Σύρε,
ἀτόπως ἐμαυτοῦ καὶ βαρέως [ἔχω σφόδρα.

ΣΤΡΟΣ (?)
ἀσθενικόν ἐστι τἀνόητο[ν, Φειδία.

ΦΕΙΔΙΑΣ
ε]ἶέν· πάνυ γὰρ ταυτὶ λελό[γισαι κατὰ τρόπον·
τί] μοι παραινεῖς;

ΣΤΡΟΣ (?)
ὅ τι παρ[αινῶ; τοῦτ᾽ ἐγώ.
25 (50S) εἰ μέν τι κακὸν ἀληθὲς εἶχες, Φειδία,

17–18 cited (without Menander's name) by Marcus Aurelius
Antoninus 5.12.4.   25–31 cited from Menander by Clement
of Alexandria, *Stromateis* 7.27; its beginning matches the muti-
lated remains of vv. 25–27 in P.

18 ισθι· P.   μὴ ὥ[ρασι suppl. Jernstedt, γε Körte.
19 ικοιο· P.   Suppl. Kock.

The saying goes, you're so well off you don't
Have anywhere [to shit], I'd have you know!

PHEIDIAS

Be [damned]

To you!

SYROS (?)
I swear I'm telling you the truth—
That's your affliction!

PHEIDIAS
[Syros,] in myself   20
[I] really [feel quite] strange and out of sorts.

SYROS (?)
The root of your complaint is folly, [Pheidias].

PHEIDIAS
Well, since [you]'ve worked this out so [sensibly],
[What]'s your advice?

SYROS (?)
What's [my] advice? [Just this:]
If your complaint had been a real one, Pheidias,   25

---

20 ταρωστημα· P: corr. Cobet.   μή[ν suppl. Cobet, ὦ
Σύρε Arnott.   21 ἔχω suppl. Cobet, σφόδρα Sudhaus.

22 ἀσθενικόν deciphered by Jernstedt.   τἀνόητο[ν suppl.
Cobet, Φειδία Arnott.

23 ε]ἶέν deciphered and suppl. Jernstedt.   ταυτὶ Jernstedt:
ταυτει P.   λελό[γισαι suppl. Arnott, κατὰ τρόπον Sudhaus.

24 τί] μοι first Jernstedt.   παραινεις· P.   παρ[αινῶ
suppl. Cobet, τοῦτ᾽ ἐγώ Arnott (τοῦτ᾽ also Cobet).

25–26 Φειδία,/ ζητεῖν Grotius: φιλιάζειν ms. L of Clem. (la-
cuna here in P of Men.).

ζητεῖν ἀληθὲς φάρμακον τούτου σ' ἔδει.
νῦν δ' οὐκ ἔχεις. κενὸν εὑρὲ καὶ τὸ φάρμακον
πρὸς τὸ κενόν, οἰήθητι δ' ὠφελεῖν τί σε.
περιμαξάτωσάν σ' αἱ γυναῖκες ἐν κύκλῳ
30 (55S) καὶ περιθεωσάτωσαν. ἀπὸ κρουνῶν τριῶν
31 (56S) ὕδατι περίρραν' ἐμβαλὼν ἅλας, φακούς.

(After v. 27 there is a lacuna of around 25 lines in P, the first 4 of which are supplied by Clement's quotation.)

ΣΤΡΟΣ (?)

32 (1S) Δι]ονυσίων

] ἐπιτελεῖν, συλλαμβάνῃς

26 τούτους σε δεῖ L of Clem.: corr. Grotius.
27 εὑρὲ καὶ Weil: εὕρηκα L of Clem. (lacuna in P of Men.).
28–31 Preserved only in Clem.
30 Corr. Meineke: περιθέτωσαν L.
31 περιρράναι L of Clem.
32 Δι]ονυσίων suppl. Jernstedt.
33 -νῃς read by Körte, Hutloff.

---

[3] Such treatments were the traditional remedies of superstitious folk for imaginary ailments and unpleasant experiences such as nightmares and the apparitions that bad dreams might produce. Cf. especially Plutarch's essay on superstition (*Mor.* 165d–166a), and see G. E. R. Lloyd, *Magic, Reason and Experience* (Cambridge 1979) 10–58, and R. C. T. Parker, *Miasma* (Oxford 1983) 207–34. The best study of depression in antiquity is H. Flashar, *Melancholie und Melancholiker in den medizinischen Theorien der Antike* (Berlin 1966).

You would have had to seek real medicine for it.
You're not now really ill, though! Find a quack
Treatment for your sham illness, and believe
It's helping. Let the women in a circle
Massage and fumigate you. Spray yourself   30
With water from three springs. Add salt and lentils[3]   31

*(After v. 31 there is a gap of about 21 lines. When the text
resumes, it is difficult to make coherent sense of some of the
slave's remarks, but he seems to be advising Pheidias to cel-
ebrate his wedding and not to disclose any of his problems
(melancholia, sleeplessness: see especially vv. 9, 57) to the
stepbrother of his future bride, because those problems
might be misinterpreted next door as an excuse for cancel-
ling the wedding.)*

SYROS (?)

(in mid-speech)

of the [Di]onysia[4]   32
] to celebrate, [that (?)] you may grasp

[4] This reference to the Dionysia, the festival at which
(amongst other things) plays were produced, is puzzling. In
Menander's *Synaristosai*, adapted by Plautus in his *Cistellaria*,
the great procession that preceded the dramatic contests pro-
vided an opportunity for the play's young male hero to catch sight
of a girl and fall in love with her (*Synaristosai* fr. 1 Arnott = 337 K-
A = 382 K-T; cf. Plaut. *Cist.* 89ff.), but the fragments of
Menander's *Phasma* include no other reference to the Dionysia.
The rape of Pheidias' stepmother occurred during a very different
festival at Brauron, some 26 kilometres away from Athens (see on
vv. 197–204).

MENANDER

]ν νυμφίον σαυτὸν φρονεῖν

35   τῆ]ς παρθένου τὴν μητέρα
(5S)   ἑτ]έρῳ τοῦθ᾽ ὁμομητρίῳ τινὶ
      ] μὴ παραδῷς, πρὸς τῶν θεῶν,
προφασιν κατ]ὰ σαυτοῦ μηδεμίαν· οὕτω πόει.

ΦΕΙΔΙΑΣ

39   εἶέν· ποῶ γὰρ τ]οῦτο. τί γὰρ ἄν τις πάθοι;

ΘΕΟΣ

40   τὸ δ᾽ οὐχὶ φάσμ᾽] ἔστ᾽, ἀλλὰ παῖς ἀληθινή,
(10S)   ἐν τῴκίᾳ στε]χθεῖσα τῆς γαμουμένης.
      τίκτει γὰρ ἡ] μήτηρ πρὶν ἐλθεῖν ἐνθάδε
      ] ταύτην, δίδωσί τ᾽ ἐκτρέφειν
      ν]ῦν ἐστιν ἐν τῶν γειτόνων
45   λάθρᾳ τρεφομ]ένη καὶ φυλαττομένη κόρη

34 -νειν read by Hutloff.   35 Suppl. Jernstedt.
36 Suppl. Körte.   τουτο P.   38 Suppl. Jernstedt.
39 Change of speaker noted by Kock.   εἶέν· ποῶ γὰρ
suppl. Arnott (ποήσω Körte, τ]οῦτο Jernstedt.
40 Suppl. Kock.   αληθινηι P: corr. Jernstedt.
41 Suppl. Arnott (ἐν οἰκίᾳ already Turner).
42 Suppl. Körte.
44 Suppl. and corr. Jernstedt: γιτονων P.
45 λάθρᾳ suppl. Körte, τρεφομ]ένη Wilamowitz.

---

5 Literally 'brother by the same mother.' This remark seems to
imply that the two young people born legitimately and living next
door to Pheidias had different fathers (B.1 and B.2 in my sched-
ule; see the introduction), with their mother having married
twice.

382

] to consider you're the bridegroom
] the mother of the girl   35
] this to a second man, a stepbrother[5]
] I insist that you provide [him (?)] with
No [grounds] for blaming you. Just act like that!

PHEIDIAS

That'[s how I'll act.] What else can a man do?   39

(Pheidias and his slave now depart, presumably into their own house, and at v. 40 a divinity appears to deliver a prologue from which portions of its first 18 lines are preserved. These give important details about the antecedents of the plot, closely matching what Donatus says in his own summary of the Phasma story (test. VI), but although Donatus' account helps us to supplement some of the lines in the parchment, this passage is extremely mutilated, many points in Menander's text remain obscure, and no information about the precise identity of the prologue divinity survives.)

A GOD OR GODDESS

[But *that*]'s [no apparition], she's a real   40
Girl [who's been hidden (?) in] the bride's[6] own [house].
[The] mother [bore] this girl before she moved
Here [   ], and she gave the baby to
[A nurse] to rear. [That child] now lives next door,
A girl [raised secretly], and guarded [when]   45

[6] Pheidias' prospective bride. The speaker presumably points to the husband B.2's house (see my introduction).

MENANDER

(15S) ἀνὴρ ὅταν ἔλθῃ] δεῦρο· τὸν δ' ἄλλον χρόνον
        ]ν φυλακῆς τ' ἐλάττονος
    χρεία 'στιν, ἣν εἴλη]χεν οἰκίαν τότε
    εἴωθε καταλιπεῖν.] τίν' οὖν φαντάζεται
50   ἡ παῖς τρόπον; τ]ουτὶ γὰρ ἔτι ποθεῖτ' ἴσως
(20S) ἐμοῦ πυθέσθ'. ἔνδ]ον πεπόηκεν ἡ γυνή,
    διελοῦσα τὸν τοῖχον,] διέξοδόν τινα
             ]παντ' ἐπισκοπεῖν
    ἡ γὰρ διέξοδος κε]κάλυπται ταινίαις
55   μή τις πρ]οσελθὼν καταμάθῃ
56 (25S)   ] τις ἔνδον τῆς θεοῦ

(After v. 56, where P comes to an end, there is a gap of
unknown length—possibly several hundred lines—before
we come to that short section of the play preserved in O's
four badly mutilated columns.)

46 Suppl. Kock.   48, 49 Suppl. Sudhaus.   50 ἡ παῖς
suppl. Sudhaus, τρόπον Kock, τ]ουτὶ suppl. and corr. Jernstedt:
]ουτει P.   51 Suppl. Sudhaus.   52 διελοῦσα suppl.
Wilamowitz, τὸν τοῖχον Körte.   54 ἡ γὰρ διέξοδος suppl.
Allinson, κε]κάλυπται Jernstedt.   55 μή τις suppl. Allinson
(after Körte ἵνα μὴ περίεργός τις), πρ]οσελθὼν Jernstedt.

---

7 Husband B.2. We do not precisely know the implications be-
hind '[when the husband] visits there'; if the supplemented words
are correct, we must presume that this husband was often away
from home, presumably either at his farm or abroad on commer-
cial business.

8 The speaker presumably points to the door of house 2.

384

[The husband[7]] visits there. At other times
[When he's away   ] and [there's call]
For fewer safeguards, [usually she']ll then
[Leave her allotted] quarters. So how does [the girl (?)]
Make her appearance? That may be what you   50
Still crave [to know]. In there[8] that mother's [blitzed]
[The party-wall] and made a passage through
[   ] keep total watch.
[The passage] is concealed by strips of fabric
[so no one] who approached would know.   55
In there the goddess[9] [also has] an [altar]   56

(*Here the St Petersburg parchment breaks off, and it is un-
certain what happened after the prologue speaker had
filled in as many details of the plot's background as in
Menander's view the audience would have needed to know.
Pheidias may have taken his slave's advice to seek quack
therapy (vv. 27–31), but then his depression was cured by
his discovery that the apparition was a real girl. When the
Oxyrhynchus fragments of Phasma come into play, we ap-
pear to be at a later stage of the plot, perhaps already in the
third act and thus after the incident portrayed in the
Mytilene mosaic (see the introduction to this play). The
Oxyrhynchus fragments apparently open (vv. 57–74) with
a dialogue mainly between the slave Syros and a cook[10]
who presumably had been hired for Pheidias' wedding to
the daughter of wife B and husband B.2 next door.*
  Vv. 57–72 are too mutilated for connected translation,

---

[9] The mother has concealed the through-passage by making it
look like a shrine to some goddess; see also test. VI.
[10] See *Aspis* 215–16 n. 2.

ΣΤΡΟΣ

57]ν ὑπεμελαγχόλη[σέ τι
ὄν]τα νῦν ὑγιέστερο[ν
] καὶ γαμεῖ πάλιν.
60]εται τἄνδον.

ΜΑΓΕΙΡΟΣ (?)
Σύρε,

]γειν.

ΣΤΡΟΣ
γαμεῖ πάλιν.
]ς ἀδελφήν.

ΧΑΙΡΕΑΣ (?)
οἴχομ[αι.
ὥ]σπερεί σε νῦν ὁρῶ.

ΜΑΓΕΙΡΟΣ (?)
]ο τοῦ κάπνου βλέπω.
65]ριον καθαρὰ μία
] ἀπόλωλε.

ΣΤΡΟΣ
πλησίον

].

57–107 and 193–208 = O, which indicates changes of speaker
by paragraphi and mid-line blank spaces. Supplements and
corrections in these lines whose author is not named were made
by its ed. pr., E. G. Turner, *GRBS* 10 (1969) 307–24 and *The
Oxyrhynchus Papyri* 38 (1971) 3–15.   59, 61 Or γάμει.

60–62 Spaces after τανδον,]γειν, αδελφην in O.

66 Space after απολωλε in O.

but enough phrases and words can be deciphered to pro-
vide us with some indication of what was going on. Syros
here informs the cook about the background to the wed-
ding. Pheidias, he says, was quite depressed *(57), presum-*
ably after seeing the apparition, but now he's healthier
(58), and once more he's getting wed *(59). He mentions*
things inside *(60) his house. The cook then addresses* Syros
(60) by name, after which Syros repeats the information
that once more he's getting wed *(61), perhaps identifying*
the bride as sister *(62: i.e. presumably stepsister of the son*
of wife B and husband B.1).

 At this point it seems likely that a third character, who
may have been eavesdropping unseen in the background,
says I am done for *(62), following this remark up with a*
puzzling as if I see you now *(63); could this be Chaireas,*
the bride's stepbrother,[11] *opposed to this marriage for some*
reason[12] *and now visualising his stepsister?*

 The cook then continues his conversation with Syros.
The preserved scraps of his remarks are particularly dis-
jointed, but they all apparently refer to his professional ac-
tivities: I see . . . of the smoke *(64),* a single clean . . . *(65),*
it's lost *or* perished *(66); Syros replies with an equally*
puzzling nearby *(66). The cook responds with* Tell me, my

---

[11] See also v. 97.

[12] The reason could not have been that he himself loved and
wished to marry his stepsister, for stepchildren who shared the
same mother were not allowed to marry in Athens. See A. R. W.
Harrison, *The Law of Athens: The Family and Property* (Oxford
1968) 22–23.

ΜΑΓΕΙΡΟΣ (?)

βέλτιστ᾽, εἰπέ μοι,

]δετέραν.

ΣΤΡΟΣ

ἀκούετε

].ρα γὰρ μετέρχεται

70   ]ς αὐτόθεν κάλει

]

ΜΑΓΕΙΡΟΣ (?)

ἐ]ξώλης, Συρε,

ἀπόλοιο   ]ιωνε[....] ἐμοὶ

] ἐπισημαίνεσθ᾽ ἐὰν

ἡ σκευασία καθάρειος ᾖ καὶ ποικίλη.

ΧΑΙΡΕΟΤ ΔΟΤΛΟΣ (?)

75   ] παντοδ[απ

]υπερ[

].εκ.ιτ[

] νῦν ὄντων .[

73–74 *Phasma* fr. 1 Körte.

68 οὐ]δετέραν (Turner) or μη]δετέραν (Austin).   Space
after]δετεραν in O.   69]κ,]υ or]χ.

72 Suppl. Austin, Handley.

73]πισημ[...]εσθεαν O: ἐπισημαίνεσθαι ἂν ms. A of
Athenaeus 14.661f (already corrected by Bentley).

74 καθάριος ms. A of Ath.: corr. Cobet.   ποικίλη A of
Ath.:]ηι O of Men.

77 και or κλι O.

good man *(67) and a disconnected* neither *(68). In 68–71
Syros addresses the cook, first with a plural imperative* Lis-
ten *(68), which implies that one or more mute assistants ac-
companied the cook on stage, and later with two other
badly preserved remarks:* for he (? *Pheidias*) is going for [?
the bride] *(69: a reference perhaps to that stage of a wed-
ding ceremony when the bridegroom goes to the bride's
house and takes her from there to their new home),*[13] *and*
call . . . from where you are *(70). This latter remark is a
command which offends the cook, who responds with*
Syros, damn / [and blast you] . . . to me *(71–72), and then
gives his assistant(s) and Syros a final order (with a plural
imperative) which has been completely preserved in an an-
cient quotation:*

Indicate if your	73
Menu's straightforward or elaborate.	74

*At this point apparently Syros, the cook and his assistant(s)
depart presumably into Pheidias' house in order to prepare
the wedding festivities. A different slave now comes onto
the stage, perhaps from the house next door, and engages in
a conversation with Chaireas, who moves forward from
the place in the background where he had eavesdropped on
the previous scene. Of this new slave's opening remarks
(75–78) too little is preserved for connected translation or
comment (but all sorts of 75, over (?) 76, being now 78), but
from v. 79 onwards a less incoherent text is available. Prob-
ably from its start at v. 75, and certainly from v. 79, this
new scene is written in trochaic tetrameters.)*

---

[13] See notes on *Sam.* 75, 159, and 714, and on *Sik.* 405.

ΧΑΙΡΕΑΣ (?)

οἴχο[μ]αι.

ΧΑΙΡΕΟΤ ΔΟΤΛΟΣ (?)
    τὸ παιδίον [

80 αὐτός. οὐκ Ἔμβαρός ἐσ[τιν οὖ]τος· ὑπενόουν [ἐγὼ
    τὸ πα[ρ]αχρῆμ᾿ ὀ[ρ]θῶς· ἔ[πειτ]α παντοδαπὰ λέ[γων
        φίλως
    ο]ὐθὲν [...]ύνθ...

ΧΑΙΡΕΑΣ (?)
        κ[....]ν ἐμφρόνως ημ[
ἐνέτυχεν.

ΧΑΙΡΕΟΤ ΔΟΤΛΟΣ (?)
        τὸ πρᾶγμα [.... ἐ]πινοῆσαί μοι δο[κε]ῖ·
εἶτα πάλ[ι]ν ἐπῆξεν.

80 *Phasma* fr. 2 Körte.

79 Space after οιχο[.]αι and paragraphus in O.
80 Punctuation after αὐτός by Handley.   οὖ]τος suppl.
Handley.
81 λέ[γων φίλως suppl. *exempli gratia* Arnott (λέ[γοντα already Turner).
82 Probably space before κ[in O.
83, 84 Paragraphi in O.
83 Space after ενετυχεν in O.   ]πινοησε O: corr. Handley.

390

PHASMA

CHAIREAS (?)

I am done for!

SLAVE OF CHAIREAS (?)

[   ] the girl—   79

He himself,[14] yes! He's no mastermind.[15] Right from the   80
start I had

My suspicions. I was right. [Then] when he [said] all
sorts of [

Nothing [   ]

CHAIREAS (?)

[   ] sensibly [

He encountered [her (?)].

SLAVE OF CHAIREAS (?)

I think he planned the situation. Then
Once again he jumped on [her]!

---

[14] The "he" throughout this passage seems to be Pheidias, but
why he should be imagined at this point to be behaving in a frenzy
is a matter of speculation. One possibility is that after recovering
from depression and falling in love with the girl whom he had
thought to be an apparition, he faked fits of madness in an attempt
to caress her.

[15] Literally "He's no Embaros." Embaros was a minor hero of
Athenian folklore famed for the practical application of his brain-
power. According to Pausanias (quoted by the *Suda* s.v. Ἔμβαρός
εἰμι (ε 937) and Eustathius' commentary on H. *Il.* 331.25–32),
during a famine Apollo promised the Athenians succour if one of
them would sacrifice his daughter to Artemis. Embaros agreed to
do this provided his family was awarded the hereditary priesthood
of Artemis. He then hid his own daughter and sacrificed a goat
dressed up in her clothes.

ΧΑΙΡΕΑΣ (?)

[ἠήν· ἀναφρό]διτός εἰμί τις.

ΧΑΙΡΕΟΥ ΔΟΥΛΟΣ (?)

85 τῶν διδόντων δ᾽ εἰς τρ[οφήν γ᾽ εἶ, τρό]φιμε,
κατακεκλειμέν[ῳ,

ἂν τὸ κακὸν αὐτῷ παραστ[ῇ. τῆς] κόρης τὴν <ῥῖν᾽
ἴσως>

ἀπέδετ[αι] καμών—

ΧΑΙΡΕΑΣ (?)

Ἀπολλο[ν], μηθαμῶς.

ΧΑΙΡΕΟΥ ΔΟΥΛΟΣ (?)

νὴ τοὺς θεούς—

ἢ τὸ χεῖλος ἅμα φιλῶν.

ΧΑΙΡΕΑΣ (?)

τί;

ΧΑΙΡΕΟΥ ΔΟΥΛΟΣ (?)

καὶ κ[ρά]τιστα ταῦτ᾽ ἴσως

ἔστ᾽· ἐρῶν παύσει γὰρ οὕτως, ἂν ἴδη[ς] αὐτήν τότε.

84 ἠήν suppl. Handley.   85 εἶς Sandbach (εἰς already
Handley): εκ O.   τρ[οφήν suppl. Handley, γ᾽ εἶ, τρό]φιμε
Turner.   κατακεκλειμέν[ῳ Arnott: -κεκλημεν[O.

86 <ῥῖν᾽ ἴσως> omitted in O, added by Handley.

87 απεδετ[.] O, possibly with -ετε written in error for -εται.

Spaces after καμων and μηθαμως in O.

88 χιλος O.   O's τι so interpreted and given to a separate
speaker by Turner, but O has no spaces after and before it.

τουτ apparently O.   89, 90 Paragraphi in O.

CHAIREAS (?)
> [Oh no!] I've got [no] luck in love!

SLAVE OF CHAIREAS (?)

Master, [you are] one of those provisioning a man locked   85
up,[16]

If the madness comes upon him. Otherwise perhaps he'll
bite

Off ⟨the⟩ girl's ⟨ear⟩ in his frenzy—

CHAIREAS

(interrupting)

> God, not that!

SLAVE OF CHAIREAS (?)

> Oh yes, or else

While he does that, kiss her lips!

CHAIREAS
> What!

SLAVE OF CHAIREAS (?)

> This is for the best, maybe—

That's the way you'll cool your ardour if [you] then
[catch sight of] her!

---

[16] Attempts to decipher, interpret and supplement this line
have severely challenged scholarly effort. The text and translation
printed here imply that Pheidias had been locked up in one of his
fits, with Chaireas one of his guards. This makes reasonable sense
in the context, but I doubt if it exactly reproduces what Menander
originally wrote.

---

89 παυσεγαρ apparently O.   ἴδη[ς] deciphered and sup-
plemented by Handley.

ΧΑΙΡΕΑΣ (?)

90 καὶ παρασκώπτεις μ';

ΧΑΙΡΕΟΥ ΔΟΥΛΟΣ (?)
ἐγώ σε; μὰ τὸν Ἀπόλλω, 'γὼ μὲν οὔ.

ΧΑΙΡΕΑΣ (?)

εἰσιὼν πρὸς τὴν ἀδελφὴν πά[ντ' ἀκού]σομαι σαφῶς·
οἴομαι δ' αὐτὴν ἀθυμεῖν [τῷ πο]ουμένῳ γάμῳ.

(Between vv. 92 and 93 there is a gap of 12 lines. The speakers in vv. 93–98 cannot be identified.)

93 τὴν θύραν [
    ἄτοπόν ἐστ[
95 καὶ μάχεσθ[
    διὰ τὸν οὐκ[
    Χαιρέαν εἰπ[
98 [..].ι.αντα[

(Two other tiny scraps of O may belong to this section of the play, but their precise location is unknown.)

Turner's fr. C (ends of lines: from the top of a column)

99   ]...
100   Ἄπολλον, ὦ π]άροικ' ἄναξ

91 No paragraphus in O.
93 Deciphered by Handley.
95 Paragraphus in O.
97 So Austin, but χαῖρ', ἐὰν is also possible.
100 Suppl. Handley.

PHASMA

CHAIREAS

(angrily)
Are you mocking me?

SLAVE OF CHAIREAS (?)
Me mocking you? Upon my oath, I'm not! 90

CHAIREAS
If I go and see my sister, I'll [hear] plainly all there is.
I imagine she's disheartened by [this] knot that's being 92
  tied.

*(After v. 92 there is a short gap in the papyrus, during
which Chaireas presumably departed into his house in or-
der to talk with his stepsister, but whether his slave de-
parted too or remained on stage is unknown. After the gap
the beginnings of a further six lines are preserved; neither
speaker nor part division can be identified, but one possi-
bility out of several is that Chaireas' exit was followed by a
long monologue by his slave. These six lines (vv. 93–98 Ar-
nott) are still in trochaic tetrameters, and yield only dis-
connected phrases: The door (93), Strange it (?) is (94),
And to fight (95), Through the . . . not (96), and Chaireas in
the accusative case (96: or less probably, Greetings, if). If
Chaireas is correctly deciphered at v. 97, it almost cer-
tainly provides us with the name of the young man living
next door to Pheidias.*

  *Two other tiny scraps of the Oxyrhynchus papyrus may
come from this part of the play. Only one of them (Turner's
fr. C) yields any decipherable words: [Apollo], lord who
dwells with us (v. 100 Arnott) and to see (v. 101). V.100
seems to be a salutation to the altar or pillar erected*

395

101   ]ονθ' ὁρᾶν

103   ]αι

Turner's fr. D (ends of lines)

104   ]ληι
105   ]..ω
                    ].ω.
107   ].

(A further column of O appears to derive from a later part of the play. The lines here have been renumbered: see my introduction.)

ΑΝΗΡ Β΄

193   ]ου τίς ἐστι; τίς καταισχ[ύνει ‾‒
(94S)   ]θεν.

ΓΥΝΗ Β΄

οὐκ οἶδ'· οὖσα γὰρ [×‒‾‒
195   παν]νυχίδος οὔσης καὶ χο[ρῶν ×‒‾‒
(96S)   οὐ μ]ανθάνεις γάρ; τὴν οδ[
ἐξ]ελέγξεις. ἡ δ' ἐρεῖ "Βρ[αυρῶνι, τοῖς
Βραυ]ρωνίοις·" σύ, "πηνίκ';" οὐ π[

101].ντοραν O, with the first letter]ο or]ε.
197 ἐξ]ελέγξεις suppl. Austin, Βρ[αυρῶνι suppl. Webster, τοῖς Arnott (Βραυρωνίοις already Handley).
198 Βραυ]ρωνίοις (mentioned but rejected by Turner) is too long for the space, but O's scribe could have misspelled it as e.g. βαυρωνιοις.

to Apollo Agyieus by the door of the speaker's house,[17]
and since in Plautus' Bacchides 172–73 (adapted from
Menander's Dis Exapaton) Chrysalus utters a similar salu-
tation immediately on return from abroad, it is possible
that at Phasma 100 too the speaker has just come back from
a similar journey; in that case could he have been husband
B.2, whose previous absence would have made his wife's
construction of a party-wall altar less difficult?

A further mutilated column of the papyrus preserves
part of what seems to have been a scene later in the play us-
ing iambic trimeters again. The speakers are most plausi-
bly identified as husband B.2 and wife B.)

HUSBAND B.2

[   ] who is he? Who dishonours [193

[   ]

WIFE B

      I don't know, for then I (or she) was [
It was a gala night, with dancing [195
Well, do[n't] you see? The [road (?)
You'll check [   ] She'll say, "At Br[auron, where
   they had
The festival."[18] You'll ask "When was that?" [   ]
   not [[19]

[17] Cf. Menander, *Dysk.* 659 and n. 3, *Mis.* 715–16 Arnott, *Sam.*
309 and 444.

[18] Brauron, about 26 km east of Athens, was the site of a
famous sanctuary of Artemis. Every four years the Brauronia, a
festival involving young girls, was held there. See the scenic
introduction to *Sikyonioi* and note on *Sik.* 355.

[19] Or: "When was that? Not [.·"

μόν]η πλανηθεῖσ' ἡ τάλαι[να –◡–
200   ]

ΑΝΗΡ Β΄

ἐρωτήσεις τὰ προ[
πλ]εῖστον, εἶτα θαυ[μασεῖ
]ον ποῦ ποτ' ὢν λ[

ΓΥΝΗ Β΄

φίλ'] ἄνερ, γνώριμον τ[
].ς γάρ ποτ' ἐν Βραυ[ρῶνι –
205   ]αιδ' ἐνθαδὶ τὰ π[–◡–
(106S)   ].αντι τῶν γεγ[–◡–
        ].τ' απαντησ[–◡–
208   ]..[

200 Space before ερωτησεις in O.
201 θαυ[μασεῖ suppl. Arnott (θαυ[μα- already Turner).

398

PHASMA

The poor girl wandering [on her own (?)
[   ]

HUSBAND B.2
You'll ask about [   ] before (?)   200
[   ] most, then you['ll show] surprise [
[   ] where he was [

WIFE B
]   Dear (?)] husband, [   ] known [
] for once in Brau[ron
] here the [205
] instead of what [took place (?)
] met[20] [207

*(Here end the papyrus fragments definitely belonging to
Phasma. It seems that wife B and husband B.2 are concoct-
ing a plan (like Habrotonon and Onesimos in Epitrepontes
464–556) to question Pheidias' stepmother about the rape
long ago that led to the birth of the apparition. That rape
presumably occurred during the Brauronia festival, and
probably the investigation that is being planned here led to
the identification of the man who committed the rape.
Could it have been husband B.2 before his marriage to wife
B? The answer to this question, as also to virtually all the
questions about what happened later in this play,[21] is un-
known.)*

[20] Or:] all the [.

[21] Except the one fact that Donatus' account (test. VI) tells us:
Pheidias married the apparition.

MENANDER

Seven Testimonia about Φάσμα

I (Menander, testimonium 53 in Kassel–Austin, PCG VI.2)

An inscription from the Athenian agora (I.2972.982) first published by B. D. Meritt, *Hesperia* 7 (1938) 116–18; see also H. J. Mette, *Urkunden dramatischer Aufführungen in Griechenland* (Berlin & New York 1977) IVa.18–24.

18 Mette)   [ἐπὶ Ἀλ]κιβιάδου ἄρχον(τος)

5   [ἀγων]οθέτης Νικοκλῆς·

        [παλ]αιᾷ κωμῳδίᾳ

        [Καλ]λίας ἐνίκα

        [Μισα]νθρώποις Διφί(λου),

        [Διοσκ]ουρίδης δεύ(τερος)

10 (24 M)   [Φάσμα]τι Μενάνδρ(ου)

4–10 [Μισα]νθρώποις suppl. Capps, the rest Meritt.

4 Ἀλκιβιάδης = 1 in (M.) O(sborne and S.) B(yrne, *A Lexicon of Greek Personal Names* 2, Oxford 1994).

5 Νικοκλῆς = 36 O–B.

7 Καλλίας = 369 in J. B. O'Connor, *Chapters in the History of Actors and Acting in Ancient Greece* (Diss. Princeton, Chicago 1908).

8 Μισάνθρωποι Διφίλου = Kassel–Austin, *PCG* V (1986) pp. 48 test. 5 and 84.

9 Διοσκουρίδης = 157c in I. Parenti, *Dioniso* 35/1 (1961) 3–29.

Seven Testimonia about Phasma

I

An Athenian inscription listing old plays produced in the
Theatre of Dionysus at Athens in the mid-third century
B.C.:

> Archonship of [Al]cibiades:
> [Games] president, Nicocles.
>> Productions of old comedies:
>> [Cal]lias won
>> with Diphilus' [*Mis*]*anthropoi*;
>> [Diosc]urides came second
>> with Menander's [*Phasma*].

(It is uncertain whether this fragment of an inscription lists
productions at the Dionysia or the Lenaea. Alcibiades was
archon in one of the years between 259 and 254 B.C.[22] *Al-*
though only the last two letters of the Menander title are
preserved in the inscription (τι), they provide a dative
ending which fits only Phasma of Menander's known plays.

[22] See especially M. J. Osborne, *ZPE* 78 (1989) 211 and 241.

II (Menander, testim. 55 K-A)

IG ii².2323 col. iii, 206–207; see also Mette, IIIb.3, col. 4a, 17–18.

206 (17M)   ἐπὶ Ξενοκλέους παλαι[ᾷ
              Μόνιμος Φάσματι Μεν[άνδρου

III (Menander, testim. 42 K-A)

P. British Museum 2562 (first published by H. J. M. Milne, *Greek Shorthand Manuals*, London 1934, 21–56) is a shorthand manual of the third or fourth century A.D., with a tetrad of four usually linked words chosen to illustrate each symbol. J. Stroux, *Philologus* 90 (1935) 88–89 first noted that tetrads 330–333 and the first word of tetrad 334 were titles of Menandrean plays, as follows:

330 Ἀνεψιοί, Ἐγχειρίδιον, Θησαυρός, Δύσκολος.
331 Ῥαπιζομένη, Ἐπίκληρος, Χρηστή, Δεισιδαίμων.
332 Ναύκληρος, Ἐπιτρέποντες, Μηναγύρτης,
      Κιθαριστής.

II Suppl. Köhler.   Μόνιμος = 347 in O'Connor.
   III The papyrus has the following misspellings: 330 ενχειρι-
διον, θυσαυρος (corr. Milne). 331 ραπιζομενοι (corr. Körte),
δισιδαιμων. 332 επιτρεποντος (corr. Milne).

PHASMA

II

An Athenian inscription listing productions of comedies between 215 and 141 B.C. at the Greater Dionysia:

Archonship of Xenocles: (production of) old (comedies). Monimus won with Men[ander's] *Phasma*.

(*Xenocles was archon in 168–67 B.C. Monimos produced and possibly also acted in the play.*)

III

A shorthand manual from late antiquity tests its pupils with exercises that contain four words at times related to each other in various ways. One of the two series where the theme is Menander titles runs as follows:

Tetrad 330

Anepsioi *(Cousins)*,
Encheiridion *(The Dagger: Loeb volume I)*,
Thesauros *(The Treasure)*,
Dyskolos *(The Peevish Fellow: vol. I)*.

Tetrad 331

Rhapizomenoi *(The Men Slapped in the Face: an error for* Rhapizomene, *The Girl Slapped in the Face)*,
Epikleros *(The Heiress)*,
Chreste *(The Good Woman)*,
Deisidaimon *(The Superstitious Man)*.

Tetrad 332

Naukleros *(The Shipowner)*,
Epitrepontes *(Men at Arbitration: vol. I)*,
Menagyrtes *(The Beggar Priest)*,
Kitharistes *(The Lyre Player: vol. II)*.

333 Ἀφροδίσιος, Νέμεσις, Δημιουργός, Δίδυμαι.
334 Φάσμα.

IV (Menander, testim. 112 K-A)

Fronto in the *Palatine Anthology* 12.233:

τὴν ἀκμὴν Θησαυρὸν ἔχειν, κωμῳδέ, νομίζεις,
   οὐκ εἰδὼς αὐτὴν Φάσματος ὀξυτέρην.
ποιήσει σ’ ὁ χρόνος Μισούμενον, εἶτα Γεωργόν,
   καὶ τότε μαστεύσεις τὴν Περικειρομένην.

333 αφροδιδιον (corr. Milne, Körte), διδυμοι (corr. Stroux).

---

[23] See particularly R. Reitzenstein in *RE* VII (1912) s.v. *Fronto* (12) col. 112; R. Aubreton and others in the Budé edition of book XII of the *Palatine Anthology* (Paris 1994) pp. 62 and 127 n. 5; and D. L. Page, *Further Greek Epigrams* (Cambridge 1981) 115.

PHASMA

Tetrad 333

Aphrodision *(The Temple of Aphrodite, an error for*
   Aphrodisios, *The Womaniser),*
Nemesis *(Nemesis* or *Retribution),*
Demiourgos *(The Confectioner: vol. III pp. 632–35),*
Didymoi *(Twin Boys: an error for* Didymai, *Twin Girls).*

Tetrad 334

Phasma *(The Apparition).*

(See also Sikyonioi, test. I.)

IV

An epigram by Fronto:

Comic actor, you think you've a TREASURE in your
   beauty now.
   You don't see that it's more fleeting than an APPARI-
   TION. Soon
Time will make you first a HATED MAN, then next a
   FARMER, and
   Finally you'll be pursuing that GIRL WITH HER HAIR
   CUT SHORT!

*(There are two epigrams by 'Fronto' in the Palatine An-
thology (also 12.174), but the precise identity of this writer
is unknown. The candidates include (i) M. Cornelius
Fronto of Cirta in Numidia, suffect consul in* A.D. *143; (ii) a
rhetor from Emesa in Phoenicia (Longinus' uncle) living
around* A.D. *200; (iii) some other Fronto otherwise un-
known. Fronto was a common name during the Roman em-
pire.*[23]

MENANDER

V

(a) Terence *Eunuchus* 9

idem Menandri Phasma nunc nuper dedit.

(b) Donatus (1.271 Wessner) commenting on Terence, *Eunuchus* 9.2: IDEM . . . *haec comoedia Luscii Lanuuini.*

VI

Donatus (I.272 Wessner) commenting on Terence, *Eunuchus* 9.3: PHASMA *autem nomen fabulae Menandri est, in qua nouerca superducta adulescenti uirginem, quam ex uitio quondam[1] conceperat, furtim eductam,[2] cum haberet in latebris apud uicinum proximum, hoc modo secum habebat assidue nullo conscio: parietem, qui medius inter domum mariti ac uicini fuerat, ita perfodit, ut*

[1] *uitĭo quodam* V: *uicio quodam* BK: corr. Kassel.
[2] *fortune* or *furtiue eductam* mss.: corr. Stephanus.

---

[24] On Luscius Lanuvinus and his adaptation of the *Phasma* see C. Garton, *Personal Aspects of the Roman Theatre* (Toronto 1972) 41–129.

PHASMA

In this epigram an older man, who is pursuing a hand-some boy at the height of his beauty, warns him that although the boy is now the apple of everyone's eye, one day he will be turned by time into a man pursuing women. In a rather forced conceit the poet compares each stage in this boy's life to a well-known play of Menander's: the Thesauros, Phasma, Misoumenos (vol. II), Georgos (vol. 1) and Perikeiromene (vol. II).)

V

(a) From the prologue to Terence's *Eunuchus*:

Just now he's staged Menander's *Apparition*.

(b) Part of Donatus' comment on this line: HE . . . this comedy by Luscius Lanuvinus.

Luscius Lanuvinus was an older contemporary and rival of Terence. Terence's Eunuchus seems to have been produced in 161 B.C., so Luscius must have staged his adaptation of Menander's Phasma in 163 or 162. Could his decision to adapt this play[24] have been influenced by Monimos' successful production of it in 167?

VI

A further comment by Donatus on Terence, *Eunuchus* 9: THE APPARITION, however, is the title of a play by Menander. In it a young man acquired a stepmother who had formerly been raped, conceived a daughter and brought her up secretly in hiding under her next-door neighbour's roof. She maintained personal contact with her daughter by the following means, without anyone else

407

MENANDER

ipso transitu sacrum locum esse simularet eumque[3]
transitum intenderet sertis ac fronde felici rem diuinam
saepe faciens et uocaret ad se uirginem. quod cum
animaduertisset adulescens, primo aspectu pulchrae
uirginis uelut numinis uisu perculsus exhorruit, unde
fabulae Phasma nomen est; deinde paulatim re cognita
exarsit in amorem puellae ita ut remedium tantae
cupiditatis nisi ex nuptiis non reperiretur. itaque ex
commodo matris ac uirginis et ex uoto amatoris
consensuque patris nuptiarum celebritate finem accipit
fabula.

[3] *cumque* mss.: corr. Wessner.

knowing. The party wall which joined her husband's and her neighbour's houses was knocked through in a way that allowed her to pretend that there was a shrine in front of the through-passage. She spread garlands and festive greenery across this passage, and as she frequently performed there her acts of worship she could call the girl to her. When the young man saw what was going on, he was startled and terrified by his first sight of the beautiful girl, thinking that he had seen a vision of some spirit, and that is why the play was called *The Apparition*. When he eventually realised the true situation, he fell in love with the girl, with the result that no remedy for so great a passion could be found except marriage. Thus the play reached a conclusion which benefited mother and girl, answered the lover's prayers, and received the father's consent—the celebration of a wedding.

MENANDER

VII

Caesius Bassius, *fragmentum de metris* or Atilius Fortu-
natianus, *Ars* (H. Keil, *Grammatici Latini*, VI.1,255), after
citing as a line of verse *Bacche Bromie Bacche Bromie
Bacche Bromie Bacche*: *nam ithyphallicum metrum saepe
recepit hunc tribrachum, ut etiam apud Menandrum in
Phasmati et apud Callimachum in epigrammatibus* (fr. 402
Pfeiffer) *ostendi potest.*

---

25 The idea of a young man raping or seducing a girl, leaving
her pregnant and deserting her, but coming across her once more
many years later and marrying her, was perhaps a common motif
in New-Comedy plots. Parallels in Menander may have included
Kitharistes (see the Loeb edition, II p. 114) and *Synaristosai*
(above).

26 See especially L. Beauchet, *Histoire du droit privé de la
république athénienne* I (Paris 1897) 488–535, D. Ogden, *Greek
Bastardy* (Oxford 1996) 32–212, and cf. A. R. W. Harrison, *The
Law of Athens: The Family and Property* (Oxford 1968) 61–70 and
R. Garland, *The Greek Way of Life* (Ithaca, NY 1990) 89.

27 Athenian law allowed stepbrothers and stepsisters to marry
provided they had different mothers: see A. R. W. Harrison, *The
Law of Athens* (Oxford 1968) 22–23.

28 But see note 2 of the introduction to *Fab.Inc.* 9.

Pheidias by his first marriage and later married Pheidias'
stepmother without knowing that she had been his rape
victim.[25]

*A subsequent marriage of the parents legitimised a child
born earlier to them out of wedlock, and this yielded real
advantages to mother and especially daughter (only legiti-
mate issue could inherit the parents' estate and be legally
married).[26] And a man who thus turned out to be father of
both bride and bridegroom could by Athenian law give his
consent to a marriage of stepchildren who had different
mothers.[27])*

VII

A Roman metrician cites as a line of verse:

"Bacchus Bromius Bacchus Bromius Bacchus Bromius"

and says: the ithyphallic metre often accepted this tribrach
($\smile \smile \smile$), as can be demonstrated also in Menander's
Phasma and Callimachus' *Epigrams*.

*(An ithyphallic verse normally scans $-\smile-\smile-\times$; the metri-
cian here claims that Menander, when using this metre, re-
solved $-\smile$ into $\smile\smile\smile$ in his Phasma. There is no trace of this
metre in what remains of this play or elsewhere in
Menander, although the dramatist occasionally introduces
anapaests (Leukadia 11–16, fr. 2 and test. I) and dactylic
hexameters (Theophoroumene 36–41, 50 ?, 52, 56) into his
plays.[28])*

OTHER PAPYRI

UNIDENTIFIED AND
EXCLUDED PAPYRI

In the last 120 years or so a good number of comic pa-
pyri have been published, and many of those displaying
typical New Comedy features have been attributed to
Menander on grounds that range from very convincing to
highly implausible. The papyri chosen for this section are
of two kinds: those assigned to Menander with some secu-
rity (*Fab.Inc.* 1, 6), and those where the attribution is
based on a personal feeling that their style and imaginative
vitality seem to compare most closely to those qualities
in accredited plays and fragments of Menander (*Fab.Inc.*
2–5, 7–9). Inevitably with the latter group decisions for
both inclusion and rejection will be largely subjective,
being based at times on unquantifiable feelings about
Menander's creative power and idiosyncrasies of expres-
sion, thought and scansion.

(1) Some previously canvassed attributions have been
omitted because their quality appears unworthy of Me-
nander or because their papyri are too mutilated or too
short to yield a modicum of continuous text. The most im-
portant exclusions are:

(i) *P.Louvre* 7172 = *P.Didot* 1 (fr. adesp. 1000 K-A). This
papyrus of c.160 B.C. includes a passage of 44 iambic

414

trimeters in which a young wife affirms her loyalty to an impoverished husband and opposes her father's wish that she divorce him and marry a wealthier husband. The papyrus assigns these lines to Euripides, but New Comedy seems a likelier source. Its first editor (H. Weil, *Un papyrus inédit de la bibliothèque de M. Ambroise Firmin-Didot* (Paris 1879) 1–15 and plate I) called attention to its 'Menandrean tone,' and various scholars have assigned it firmly to Menander, as follows:

(a) R. Y. Tyrrell, *Hermathena* 4 (1883) 96–102, naming no play; cf. A. Körte, *Hermes* 61 (1926) 134–56, 350–51 and his third edition of Menander, p. xxiii.

(b) D. R. Robertson, *CR* 36 (1922) 106–109 and 348–50, suggesting it was Pamphile's speech to Smikrines in the fourth act of *Epitrepontes*, with support from Chr. Jensen, *Rh.Mus.* 76 (1927) 1 and his edition of Menander pp.xxvi–xxvii, M. Platnauer in J. U. Powell (ed.), *New Chapters in the History of Greek Literature* (Oxford 1933) 168, and J. McN. Edmonds, *Fragments of Greek Comedy* IIIB (Leiden 1961) 1040–43, who prints it as part of *Epitrepontes*. Körte's 1926 papers already demolished Robertson's arguments for its identification as Pamphile's speech long before the new Oxyrhynchus and Michigan fragments confirmed their erroneousness.

(c) H. Lucas, *Philologische Wochenschrift* (1938) 1101–104, attributing it to Menander's first *Adelphoi*, the Greek original of Plautus' *Stichus*; cf. Gianna Petrone, *Pan* 3 (1976) 45–52.

Yet as long ago as 1895 Wilamowitz (*Einleitung in die Griechische Tragödie*[2], Berlin, 42 n.82) drew attention to the woeful mediocrity of these 44 verses, and W. Bühler (*Hermes* 91, 1963, 345–51) underlined both the mechani-

415

cal structure of the speaker's arguments and the poverty-stricken flatness of her words, which nowhere show one glint of Menandrean imagination, and he rightly concluded that here we have the work of a third-rate comic poet with pseudo-tragic ambitions. The best text and apparatus is now in Kassel–Austin; for texts with English translations see D. L. Page, *Greek Literary Papyri* I (London 1942) no. 34 and pp. 180–89, and Edmonds, *loc. cit.* in (b) above.

(ii) *P. Strasbourg* 53 (fr. adesp. 1008 K-A). This is dated to the first century A.D. by W. Crönert, *APF* 1 (1901) 515, and to the following century by E. G. Turner in Christina Dedoussi, *Proceedings of the XIV International Congress of Papyrologists* (1975) 73. It contains 29 comic trimeters with the opening letters of each line (5–10 in vv. 8–29, a larger number in vv. 1–7) torn off, and comes from a divine prologue in which the speaker discusses the function of such prologues before giving a brief account of the plot antecedents: a pair of named brothers got married and then, leaving their families behind, they made a trip to Asia Minor which resulted in one brother being imprisoned and then escaping, while the other was subsequently imprisoned for helping his brother's escape. Their absence from home had lasted sixteen years when the papyrus breaks off. First edition: G. Kaibel, *NGG* (1899) 549–55 (with a photograph), attributing the fragment to Menander or an imitator. Later Christina Dedoussi (*op. cit.* 73–77, and *Dodone* 4, 1975, 268–70) argued that if the son of one brother and the daughter of the other were the play's young lovers, their blood relationship could have been reflected in a title Ἀνεψιοί ('Cousins') which is recorded only for Menander. Unfortunately the papyrus yields no hard evidence in support of Dedoussi's theory, and there is one factor that speaks against Menandrean authorship. The narrative part of this papyrus prologue begins by naming the two brothers (Σωσθένης καὶ Δημέας, v. 16), but Menander's extant prologues, both divine (*Aspis*, *Dyskolos*, *Perikeiromene*, *Sikyonioi*) and human (*Samia*), either avoid naming any character or restrict such naming to one main person (Kleostratos, *Asp.* 110; Knemon, *Dysk.* 6). Accordingly Kassel–Austin are justified in printing this prologue judiciously unsupplemented in their adespota; for a text with English translation see Page, *GLP* no. 60 (pp. 272–76) rather than Edmonds IIIA 316–17.

(iii) *P.Hibeh* 6 (fr. adesp. 1014 K-A). A papyrus of the third century B.C., whose main fragment covers four columns of text, with only the second and third of them preserved well enough to yield some 20 complete and 20 half-complete trimeters. Several characters are named: Noumenios (v. 5), Demeas (40) and perhaps Sostratos (? 122). An unnamed man is told to returned a borrowed basket to Noumenios (5–7); he may be identical with the person sent off by Demeas on a probably long journey with a slave (31–34). Demeas has a wife (32, 42) who is ordered to bring a baby outside (42–45). The first editors of the papyrus, B. P. Grenfell and A. S. Hunt (with F. Blass), *The Hibeh Papyri* 1 (1906) 29–35 with a photograph of vv. 1–46 (pl. IV), claim that 'the style . . . suggests Menander or some contemporary dramatist,' but there are neither links with any known fragments of Menander nor any other clues to its author, although one other comic scrap (*P.Oxyrhynchus* 677 = fr. adesp. 1013 K-A) has a character

417

with the rare name Noumenios (v. 7) and so may derive from the same play. The writing in *P.Hibeh* 6 lacks distinction and imagination, as Wilamowitz noted (*SB Berlin* 1916, 84–85 = *Kleine Schriften* I, Berlin 1935, 437; cf. his edition of Menander's *Epitrepontes*, p. 157 n.1), and is better not foisted on Menander. T. B. L. Webster, *Studies in Later Greek Comedy*[2], Manchester 1970, 172–73, detected similarities in the portrayal of relationships between this papyrus and those plays of Plautus based on Greek originals by Diphilus. The best text and apparatus is now in Kassel–Austin; for texts with English translations see Page, *GLP* no. 63 and pp. 286–90, and Edmonds, IIIA pp. 330–37.

(iv) *P.Louvre* 72 recto = *P.Ghoran* 2 (fr. adesp. 1017 K-A). The partially mutilated remains of five columns from a later Greek comedy (109 vv., of which 65 are complete or plausibly supplemented), copied in the 3rd century B.C. They reveal that Nikeratos has received into his house a girl who had fled from her father's house in some distress (? pregnancy after rape or seduction by a young friend of Nikeratos named Phaidimos) during Phaidimos' absence from home, and that Nikeratos' actions were misconstrued by Phaidimos on his return as an attempt to win the girl's affections for himself. The first editor (P. Jouguet, *BCH* 30, 1906, 123–49) assigned these fragments to Menander, with the concurrence of Blass (*ibid.* 146–47), who suggested that they may have belonged to that poet's *Apistos*; Jouguet's attribution has won general but not warm support (e.g. G. Capovilla, *Bulletin de la Societé Archéologique d'Alexandrie* 17, 1919, 205–29, J.-M. Jacques, *BAGB* 4, 1968, 223, D. Del Corno, *Maia* 20,

1970, 347, the Gomme–Sandbach commentary p. 601 on *Sam.* 507). However, serious weaknesses in the writing—a lack of verbal distinction, with an unimaginative repetition of words and phrases—were first noted by Wilamowitz (*Neue Jahrbücher* 1908, 35 = *Kleine Schriften* I, Berlin 1935, 250) and demonstrated at greater length by Körte (*Hermes* 43, 1908, especially 49 and 54–57); these effectively demolish any attribution to Menander and suggest rather authorship by some inferior comic dramatist of Menander's time or the succeeding generation. The best text and apparatus is now in Kassel–Austin; for texts with English translations see Page, *GLP* no. 65 and pp. 296–307, and Edmonds, IIIA pp. 296–307.

(v) *P.Oxyrhynchus* 862 (fr. adesp. 1022 K-A) was attributed to Menander's *Phasma* by Webster, *JHS* 93 (1973) 197 n.6, but on inadequate evidence (see the introduction to *Phasma* in this volume).

(vi) *P.Berlin* 11771 (fr. adesp. 1032 K-A) was tentatively attributed to Menander's *Perinthia* by me in *ZPE* 102 (1994) 69–70 because of a possible link between v. 57 of *P.Berlin* 11771 and Men. *Perinthia* 13; but see now volume II of the Loeb Menander pp. 477–78, where reasons opposing this ascription are given.

(vii) *P.Cairo* 65445 contains two fragments of comedy (frr. adesp. 1072, 1073 K-A) originally written in a schoolbook and first edited by O. Guéraud and P. Jouguet, *Un livre d'écolier du IIIe siècle avant J.-C.* (Cairo 1938) 27–33 and plates VI, VII; the second fragment was re-edited by K. Gaiser in *Menanders 'Hydria': Eine hellenistische Komödie und ihr Weg ins lateinische Mittelalter* (*Abhand-*

419

*lung der Heidelberger Akademie, Philosophisch–histor-
ische Klasse* 1977/1) 208–10 with a clearer photograph
(p. 86). These two fragments are accompanied by an ab-
breviated version of Strato fr. 1 K-A. The exercise thus
brings together three speeches by cooks in later Greek
comedy. In the first (1072 K-A) the cook complains that he
has completed his initial preparations but cannot now find
his hirer, who has been talking to somebody called Simon.[1]
The second cook (1073 K-A) describes how he has man-
aged to steal some of the ingredients provided for a meal.[2]
Cook speeches of this kind are so common a feature of
Greek comedy from just before the middle of the fourth
century onwards, with a wide range of authors repeatedly
reusing the same motifs and clichés, that it is impossible to
say who composed frs. 1072 and 1073, but their presence
in this schoolbook alongside a speech written by a relative
nonentity such as Strato should be a warning against any

[1] Webster, *An Introduction to Menander* (Manchester 1974)
168 n. 50, was inclined to assign this papyrus, along with
P.Oxyrhynchus 11 (fr. adesp. 1007 K-A) and *P.Vienna* 29811
(fr.adesp. 1081 K-A), to Menander's *Paidion*, but his argument
was based mainly on the alleged presence of characters named Si-
mon in all three papyrus fragments (but not in any of the book
fragments of Menander's *Paidion*). A Simon is attested for *P.Oxy.*
11 (margin, v.43), but hardly for *P.Vienna* 29811 (margin, v.17 has
the abbreviation]σιο, which suggests rather a name ending in
-σιος).

[2] M. Treu, *Philologus* 102 (1958) 236 assigned this speech to
the same play as fr. adesp. 1093 K-A (see (ix) below), with the ap-
proval of Gaiser, *ZPE* 47 (1982) 31, but D. Bain, *Actors and Audi-
ence* (Oxford 1977) 223–26 argues effectively against this sugges-
tion.

assumption that links them necessarily with one of the leading dramatists of New Comedy. Accurate texts and apparatuses are provided by Kassel–Austin; for texts with English translations see Page, *GLP* nos. 59(a) and (b) and pp. 270–73, and Edmonds, IIIA pp. 366–69.

(viii) *P.Oxyrhynchus* 2329 (fr. adesp. 1091 K-A) was also attributed to Menander's *Phasma* by Webster, *An Introduction to Menander* 201, but on inadequate evidence (see the introduction to *Phasma* in this volume).

(ix) *P.Heidelberg* G 406, *P.Hibeh* 5 and *P.Rylands* 16ᵃ are different parts of one papyrus from el-Hibeh dating from the mid-third century B.C., and *P.Lit.London* 90 a different papyrus from the Fayyûm written in the same century; between them they contain just under 400 lines (most of them severely mutilated) of a New Comedy play. The most reliable text is now printed as fr. adesp. 1093 K-A (*PCG* VIII pp. 388–405); its line numbering is adopted here. Clear photographs with facing diplomatic transcriptions are provided by K. Gaiser, *Menanders 'Hydria'* (Heidelberg 1977) pp. 50–83. The extensive damage to the text makes any identification of poet, plot and play very insecure. Named characters include a slave Daos (vv. 79, 84), an old master Demeas (193, 198, 295, 326), a cook Libys (188, 206), Strobilos (probably a parasite:[3] 86, 146, 355, 356) and perhaps a Nikophemos (251). An unnamed young man (84–85) is also involved in the plot; he may be the person in love with a girl (3) who may or may not be (a) the girl (κόρη) of vv. 64 and 105 and (b) the daughter described as trembling with fear (243–44). Only two short

---

[3] See Gaiser, 176–79.

passages give connected sense: some metatheatrical re-
marks by a cook about the thieving behaviour of second-
rate cooks in comedy (155–65: here see D. Bain, *Actors
and Audience*, Oxford 1977, 223–26); and a scene in which
Strobilos seems to sprint onto the stage trying to escape
from somebody or something, then praises the land in
which he finds himself, and comments on the smell (? of
the cook's preparations for a wedding feast: 348–58).

F. Blass (in B. P. Grenfell and A. S. Hunt, *The Hibeh
Papyri* 1, 1906, 25) identified the author of this play as
Philemon on the sole grounds that the four letters κροισ[
(v. 363) only elsewhere began a line in Philemon fr. 159
K-A. J.-M. Jacques in his edition of Menander's *Dyskolos*
(Paris 1963, pp. 55–56 n.3) tentatively assigned these
papyri to Menander's *Thesauros*. C. Austin (*Comicorum
Graecorum in Papyris Reperta*, Berlin & New York 1973,
p. 252) and A. Aloni (*Acme* 27, 1974, 57–64) assigned the
finds to Menander's *Hydria* because the character name
Libys occurs elsewhere only in that play (fr. 359 K-A). The
evidence for the first two identifications is flimsy, but on
the basis of the third one the late Konrad Gaiser re-edited
the papyri, sought out evidence from other papyri, book
fragments of comedy, Plautus and other Latin plays up to
the twelfth century A.D., and produced a massive study
(cited in (vii) above) of minute detail, extensive scholar-
ship and fertile imagination in support of the *Hydria*
identification. The only verbal links that he could add to
the shared name Libys, however, were insufficient to bol-
ster his case strongly (fr. adesp. 1093 K-A v. 5]αρ......
and v. 17]κω.[allegedly matching book frs. 361 K-A
παρουσίαν and fr. 357.1 K-A κακῶν from Menander's
Hydria). And even the absence of the name Libys from

preserved comedies and papyrus fragments elsewhere may be accidental. Cooks named Libys are likely to have been of African origin and black, freedmen basically and slaves.[4] Black cooks cannot have been rare in ancient comedy, since Pollux 4.149–50 includes in his list of masks one that is black and named 'Tettix,' and Athenaeus 14.659a identifies 'Tettix' as a cook. The mask worn by the unnamed cook on the Mytilene mosaic of Menander's *Samia* (see the introduction to *Samia* in this volume) shows him as black. Consequently Gaiser's case must at best be considered unproven (cf. especially J. Blänsdorf, *GGA* 232, 1980, 42–66; R. Hunter, *CR* 29, 1979, 209–11).

Careful and repeated reading of the papyrus fragments of this play suggests to me a general lack of imaginative ideas and wording, and a style that has no distinction even in the better preserved sections, and those who still canvass support for the Austin–Aloni–Gaiser identification must be surprised that in nearly 400 lines of mutilated text no secure tie can be identified with any of the six attested book fragments of Menander's *Hydria* or with any book fragment cited without title. The fact that the play was considered to be worth copying in two different papyri suggests that it was the work of an established comic dramatist, but probably not one of the first order. No full English translation exists, but portions appear in Page, *GLP* no.64 pp. 290–97.

(x) *P.Oxyrhynchus* 1149 (fr. adesp. 4093 K-A), a scrap of the late second or third century A.D. containing the re-

---

[4] There is, however, no evidence that Menander ever introduced a slave cook into his plays. See here my commentary on Alexis (Cambridge 1996) pp.392–93 (on fr. 134 K-A).

mains of 15 comic trimeters with an act break between vv. 5 and 6. Its first editor, E. W. Handley (*The Oxyrhynchus Papyri* 61, 1995, 1–6 with a photograph, plate V) suggested that its source could have been Menander's *Dis Exapaton*. At the beginning of the new act in this fragment two young men appear to be discussing a situation in which one of them is reproached for previous misdemeanours (v. 7) but told to act by handing over some money (10, 15), while the other protests that he couldn't live without the girl (14–15). There are, however, no verbal links with anything known from *Dis Exapaton* or from Plautus' adaptation of this play in his *Bacchides*, and the situation as interpreted seems conventional for New Comedy (cf. e.g. Plautus' *Curculio*, *Epidicus*, *Trinummus*), while it includes one detail that appears to rule out *Dis Exapaton*: the beloved girl is τῆς παρ[θένου] ('the maiden' v. 14) and not a courtesan. Kassel–Austin are accordingly right to include it in their adespota.

(2) Other comic papyri have been excluded from this edition for one basic reason. There seems to be little point in printing a selection of severely mutilated texts which have been attributed to Menander with varying degrees of confidence but contain no single line of unimpaired text: e.g. *P.Oxyrhynchus* 11 (fr. adesp. 1007 K-A), 1239 (Menander fr. 903 K-A), 3969–72 (frr. adesp. 1142–45 K-A) and (with 678) 4302 (fr. adesp. 1152), and *P.Harris* 172 (Menander fr. 908 K-A).

(3) Nor does it seem advisable, given limitations of space, to reprint the book fragments of Menander cited in, and known continuously from, antiquity, even though a

few of these (e.g. Menander fr. 602 K-A) have in modern times had their texts revised and even imperfectly supplemented by papyri. These book fragments, with English translations, are available in F. G. Allinson's Loeb edition of Menander (1921) pp. 307–461 and 474–535, and Edmonds III B (Leiden 1961) pp. 546–77, 586–649, 652–55, 664–709, 712–49, 752–63 and 770–901. However, one papyrus first published in 1966 contains scraps of an ancient anthology which include one probable and two certain fragments of Menander, all three previously unknown. These are printed at the end of this volume.

FABULA INCERTA 1

INTRODUCTION

Manuscript

C = *P.Cairensis* 43227, part of a papyrus codex from Aphroditopolis written in the fifth century A.D. The codex originally contained *Epitrepontes*, *Heros*, *Perikeiromene*, *Samia* and two or more other plays by Menander. One of these was the *Fab.Inc.* 1, from which five mutilated scraps survive. Four of these have been carefully assembled to form most of one papyrus leaf (vv. 2–32 on one side, 33–64 on the other). The fifth scrap (fragment ι) is probably part of the same leaf, but has not been securely placed; it is printed here immediately after v. 64. In his *Fragments d'un manuscrit de Ménandre* (Cairo 1907) pp. 176–80 G. Lefebvre published three of these scraps, mistakenly attributing them to the *Samia*. The same editor's *Papyrus de Ménandre* (Cairo 1911) pp. 44–45 follows Körte in attributing these scraps to an unidentified play, and by now incorporating the fourth scrap into its text it deserves to be considered the first edition proper; it includes photographs (plates D and E, printed before plate I, show the four placed scraps; plate XLVIII has the unplaced fifth scrap). New photographs of C were published in *The Cairo*

Codex of Menander (P.Cair. J.43227) (Institute of Classical Studies, London 1978); *Fab.Inc.* 1 appears on plates XLVII and XLVIII, with the unplaced scrap included in a position questionably assigned to it by S. Sudhaus.

The leaf preserved in C identifies four characters: Moschion (10, 27, 47, 56), his father Laches (19, 22, 26, 30), Kleainetos (28) and Chaireas (31, 51, 52, 59, 60; probably *ι* recto 5; right margin of 36). Moschion, during his father's long absence from home, raped a girl whose father or guardian was Kleainetos, apparently a member of the Areopagus. It seems likely that Moschion was then forced by Kleainetos to marry the girl without receiving a dowry or gaining his own father's consent.[1] Moschion was afraid that on his return Laches would withhold his agreement, and Chaireas, presumably a young friend of Moschion, agreed to take part in a scheme designed to force Laches' consent in this matter.

The papyrus leaf opens after Laches' return, and the scheme is now in progress. Chaireas is conversing with Laches, and tells a largely false story that the girl now married to Moschion had originally been promised to Chaireas, but that Moschion, after trying unsuccessfully to induce Chaireas to give her up, had debauched her. Some badly

---

[1] It used to be believed that in Attica a father's consent was required before his son could be married, but such evidence as we have (Lysias fr. 24 Thalheim; Dem. 40.4) implies rather that in most cases "the father could urge, but not command" a son's obedience in such a matter (A. R. W. Harrison, *The Law of Athens: Family and Property*, Oxford 1968, 18 and n.5; cf. D. M. MacDowell, *The Law in Classical Athens*, London 1978, 86).

mutilated verses at the beginning of the leaf (fr. ι recto) seem to imply allegations by Chaireas that Moschion had been seen (v. 6) committing the offence and then imprisoned (9); neighbours were involved (v. 8). The law of Athens allowed a woman's father or guardian to apprehend or even kill a man apprehended in such circumstances.[2] Laches is naturally horrified by this news, but clearly he hopes that by consenting to Moschion's marriage he will dispel any dangers still threatening, and he offers his own daughter in marriage to Chaireas, in place of the bride that Chaireas claimed to have lost.

Kleainetos now appears on stage, and shortly afterwards Chaireas departs to inform Moschion of the scheme's success. Kleainetos, who in all probability was ignorant of most of the details in Chaireas' stratagem, now explains the true situation to Laches, who is annoyed at

[2] The way in which a crime of this sort was normally punished in Menander's Athens is not absolutely clear. Dracon's law (as cited by Demosthenes 23.53) allowed the girl's father or guardian to kill the malefactor, but a permitted alternative resolution seems to have been for the rapist to marry the girl without a dowry provided the rapist's father consented to this. Unfortunately "we know next to nothing about the way in which rape at Athens was legally regulated" (S. C. Todd, *The Shape of Athenian Law*, Oxford 1993, 276–77). The question has acquired a large bibliography in recent years, although Menander's *Fab.Inc.* 1 has not always been cited in evidence; see A. R. W. Harrison, *The Law of Athens: Family and Property* (Oxford 1968) 13–14, 19 and n.3, 32–37; D. M. MacDowell, *The Law in Classical Athens* (London 1978) 124–26; E. M. Harris, *CQ* 40 (1990) 370–75; D. Cohen, *G&R* 38 (1991) 171–88; P. G. McC. Brown, *CQ* 41 (1991) 533–34 and *CQ* 43 (1993) 196–200.

having been duped but nevertheless steels himself to accept Moschion's marriage and to confirm the offer he has just made to Chaireas.

This account of the lively and imaginative lines preserved in C largely agrees with modern scholarship, but several points need to be stressed here. First, we have no means of knowing how much of the story that Chaireas recounts so graphically at the beginning of C's page is pure fabrication. Moschion's maltreatment of the girl might in truth have been observed, condemning him to an imprisonment by Kleainetos from which release was possible only after Moschion had agreed to marry the girl. It is not impossible, however, that the details about one or more eye-witnesses and Moschion's imprisonment had been invented purely to increase Laches' horror, and that Moschion had previously fallen in love with the girl, debauched her and then gladly offered to marry her without any previous physical restraint on Kleainetos' part.

And who was behind the story that Chaireas embroidered? If Menander was following dramatic convention here, it would not have been Moschion or Chaireas, but a slave probably attached to Laches' or Kleainetos' household.

It is a striking fact that plurals are always used by Kleainetos (28, 46, 48), Chaireas (18) and Laches (51) when reference is made particularly to the person or persons who authorised the girl's betrothal and marriage to Moschion. It seems most likely that Kleainetos himself used these plurals either as an individualising feature of his characterisation (cf. also the plural at v. 49), or with the implication that although he was head of his family, important decisions affecting the family were taken jointly by his wife and himself. We cannot be certain, however, whether Kleainetos was married (? to a dominant wife) and the girl's father, or whether he had become the girl's guardian only after her own father had died.

Finally, was Chaireas' embroidered account of Moschion's past his only function in Menander's plot? We do not know, but it is conceivable that Chaireas had never wished to marry Kleainetos' girl, but was in reality enamoured of Laches' daughter. In that event the stratagem would have been engineered to suit his own wishes as well as those of Moschion.

Four other papyri (*P.Oxy.* 429, *PSI* 1176, *P.Oxy.* 2533 and 4409) have at different times been attributed to *Fab.Inc.* 1. For none of these papyri is the evidence in favour of the assignment either totally convincing or demonstrably incorrect. However, since a correct attachment of any one of them to this play would necessarily affect interpretation not only of the dramatic situations hinted at or clearly present in C, but also of some of the questions and problems discussed in the preceding paragraphs, I have decided to print the texts of all four papyri directly after the two pages from the Cairensis, and there to discuss briefly the arguments for their assignment to *Fab.Inc.* 1 and their potential contributions to our knowledge of its plot.

None of the lines preserved in C's leaf matches any ancient quotation from a named play by Menander, and nothing in its extant words or action points to any specific title. Even so, several attempts have been made to identify the comedy's name, of which only one has attracted mod-

est support, even though based on inadequate founda-
tions. In his second edition of the then known papyri of
Menander (Berlin 1914, p. 95), completed shortly before
he died in the first World War, Sudhaus suggested *Konei-
azomenai*, solely because the character name Chaireas was
shared with that play; it is, however, shared with too many
other comedies by Menander: *Aspis*, *Dyskolos* and per-
haps also *Phasma* (see v. 97).[3]

Dramatis Personae, so far as known:

Laches, an old man, father of Moschion and a nubile
  daughter
Chaireas, a young friend of Moschion, wishing to marry
  Laches' daughter
Kleainetos, an old man, apparently a member of the
  Areopagus[4]
Moschion, married to Kleainetos' daughter

The rest of the cast is unknown, but probably included a
slave who devised the scheme carried out by Chaireas.
There was presumably also a chorus to perform the
entr'actes.

[3] More detailed discussions of matters dealt with in this intro-
duction, along with textual questions and the problems affecting
attribution of other papyri to this play, are to be found in *ZPE* 123
(1998) 49–58.
[4] See on v. 11.

431

FABULA INCERTA 1

(The major papyrus fragment probably comes from one of the last two acts of the play. Who speaks what in vv. 2–9 is uncertain.)

2   [.].[
    ἐπ[
    ἐχ[
5   ἔκσωσ[ον
    μάρτυρα[
    ἐπ᾽ ἄλλα σ[
    γείτοσιν ἕτοιμ[
    τὸν ἐγκεκλει[μένον

     Fragment ι (recto) of C (printed here after v. 64) contains the final letters of 6 lines that have not yet been securely placed but could have come somewhere between the top of this page (before v. 2) and v. 11.   In vv. 2–11 assignments to the speakers (Chaireas, Laches) are uncertain; here C's paragraphi are given.

    4 Paragraphus uncertain.
    5 Suppl. Körte.
    6 μάρτυρα[ς (suppl. Sudhaus) or μάρτυρα [.
    7 Deciphered by Lefebvre.
    9 Suppl. Lefebvre.

UNIDENTIFIED PLAY 1

(SCENE: *a street in an unknown part of Attica, backed by the houses of Laches and Kleainetos. Laches and Chaireas are on stage together. Laches has returned home after a long absence, in which his son Moschion has married Kleainetos' daughter without securing Laches' consent. In order to counter the possibility that Laches would react furiously to this marriage, Chaireas is engaged in a scheme that attempts to exonerate Moschion from blame by portraying Moschion as a victim of force majeure. It is not clear how much of Chaireas' story here is true, and how much is fiction. Only a few letters at the beginning of the first 11 lines are preserved, and identification of who says what in vv. 2–9 is not always clear. But Laches appears to cry* Rescue [him] *in v. 5, to which Chaireas may have responded with references to a* witness *or* witness[es] *v. 6,* for other [things(?)] *v. 7,* ready for *or* with neighbours *v. 8 and* the man imprison[ed] *v. 9. Was Chaireas here telling a story—either true or false—about events during Laches' absence when neighbours of Kleainetos had witnessed Moschion's rape of Kleainetos' daughter, leading to Moschion's subsequent imprisonment by Kleainetos until Moschion agreed to marry the daughter? At v. 10 Laches probably expressed amazement at Moschion's plight, which may have been increased if Chaireas went on to*

433

MENANDER

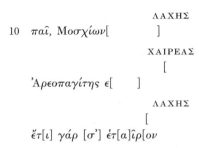

ΛΑΧΗΣ

10 παῖ, Μοσχίων[   ]

ΧΑΙΡΕΑΣ
[

Ἀρεοπαγίτης ε[   ]

ΛΑΧΗΣ
[

ἔτ[ι] γάρ [σ'] ἐτ[α]ῖρ[ον

ΧΑΙΡΕΑΣ

ἀδικεῖ μ' ἐκεῖνος, οὐδὲ[ν] ἐξ ἐμοῦ π[αθών.
ἦρα μὲν ἀεὶ τῆς κόρης κ[αὶ] πολλά μοι
15 πράγματα παρεῖχεν· ὡ[ς δ'] ἐπέραινεν οὐδὲ ἓν
αὐτῷ παραδοῦναι τὸν [γάμο]ν πείθων, ἰδού,
ἐξειργάσατο—

11 Cf. Alciphron 3.36.2 τὸν σκυθρωπὸν Κλεαίνετον, ὃς τὰ
νῦν δὴ ταῦτα πρωτεύει τοῦ συνεδρίου καὶ εἰς αὐτὸν ὁ Ἄρειος
πάγος ἀποβλέπουσιν.

10 Or παῖ·.   Μοσχίων [, or Μοσχίων[α, -ων[ος, -ων[ι?
12 Deciphered and supplied by Jensen, Sudhaus.
13–15 Suppl. von Arnim.   16 Suppl. Körte.

1 The Council of the Areopagus, whose membership was
confined to the city's past archons, had in Menander's time been
given powers to inflict summary punishment on malefactors, and
so Kleainetos' membership of this body would have made him
an especially dangerous enemy after Moschion had raped
Kleainetos' daughter, since the girl's father was then legally enti-

434

mention that Kleainetos was a member of the Areopagus.
In v. 12 Laches seems to have made a comment on the
friendship between Moschion and Chaireas.)

LACHES
Good heavens! Moschion [   ]

CHAIREAS
[   ]   10

[He's (?)] in the Areopagus[1] [

LACHES
For [you], his friend[2] still [

CHAIREAS
I've not done anything to justify
His[3] wronging me. He always loved the girl,[4]
And caused me lots of trouble. When he failed   15
To bring me round and let him [marry] her,
See what he did![5]

tled to execute her attacker if caught in the act; see especially W. S.
Ferguson, *Hellenistic Athens* (London 1911) 24, 99, and the works
cited in note 2 on my introduction to this play. The epistologra-
pher Alciphron may have been influenced by this passage of
Fab.Inc. 1 when he mentioned (3.36.2) "the sullen Kleainetos,
who holds first place in the Council today and is looked up to by
the Areopagus."

2 Laches means "[you] (= Chaireas), Moschion's friend still."

3 "His" and "he" refer to Moschion.

4 Kleainetos' daughter.

5 He shies off from saying openly that Moschion raped
Kleainetos' daughter.

435

ΛΑΧΗΣ

τί οὖν; ἀναίνει τὴν ἐμὴν
ἔχειν θυγατέρα;

ΧΑΙΡΕΑΣ

τοῖς δὲ δοῦσι τίνα λόγον
ἐρῶ, Λάχης;

ΛΑΧΗΣ

γενοῦ γάρ, ἱκετεύω [σ'] ἐγώ—

ΧΑΙΡΕΑΣ

20   οἴμοι, τί ποήσω;

ΚΛΕΑΙΝΕΤΟΣ

τίς ὁ βοῶν ἐστίν ποτε
πρὸς ταῖς θύραις;

ΧΑΙΡΕΑΣ

εὐκαιρότ[α‹τά› γ]ε, νὴ Δία,
νῦν οὗτ]ος ἥ[κει πρό]ς με. τί ποήσω, Λάχης;

ΛΑΧΗΣ

πείθωμεν αὐτόν.

17 Punctuation after τί οὖν by Kuiper.
19 γενοῦ—ἐγώ assigned to Chaireas by Sandbach (para-
graphus below v. 19, probably dicolon after ἐγω in C); end of the
line deciphered and supplied by Jensen.
21 Suppl. and corr. Körte.
22 Suppl. Körte (πρὸς] ἐμε Jensen).

FABULA INCERTA 1

LACHES
Well then, do you refuse

To have my girl?

CHAIREAS
Laches, what am I to say

To my prospective in-laws[6]?

LACHES
Please, just be—[7]

CHAIREAS
(raising his voice and so interrupting Laches)
Oh, what am I to do?

(At this point Kleainetos enters, probably from his house.)

KLEAINETOS
Whoever's bawling at   20

My door?

CHAIREAS
[He's come to see] me [now, and just]
In time, too! Laches, what am I to do?

LACHES
Let's try persuading him!

---

[6] Chaireas falsely pretends that Kleainetos' family had origi-
nally betrothed their daughter to him.

[7] Abrasion makes the text here difficult to read and any transla-
tion uncertain. Laches may have intended to say something like
"Be helpful."

MENANDER

ΧΑΙΡΕΑΣ

ὦ βίας ἐρρωμένης.
πείθω παραδοῦναι τὴν ἐμὴν ἀδικούμενος
25 [α]ὐτός;

ΛΑΧΗΣ

ὑπόμεινον δι᾽ ἐμέ.

ΧΑΙΡΕΑΣ

νὴ τὸν Ἥλιον,
α]ἰσχύνομαι, Λάχης, σε.

ΛΑΧΗΣ

ταῦτα σπ[ε]ύδομεν.

ΧΑΙΡΕΑΣ

ἄ]κουε δή μου. Μοσχίων τὴν παρθένον
ἐλ]ὼν ἔχει, Κλεαίνετ᾽.

ΚΛΕΑΙΝΕΤΟΣ

ἠδικήμεθα.

ΧΑΙΡΕΑΣ

μηθὲν βοήσῃς. γνησίων ἐπὶ σπορᾷ

29–30 γνησίων—παίδων cited by scholion on Euripides,
Andromache 4, without author's name.

25–28 Line openings suppl. Lefebvre.
25–26 νὴ—σε assigned to Chaireas by Körte, Jensen.
26 σπ[ε]ύδομεν deciphered and supplemented by Sandbach,
Koenen.   28 ἐλ]ὼν suppl. Lefebvre. ˙ ἠδικήμεθα assigned
to Kleainetos by Jensen (C has no dicolon either before or seem-
ingly after κλεαινετ᾽).

438

CHAIREAS
                    Yes, rape's effective![8]
Must I ask him to give away my girl,
When I'm the injured party?

LACHES
                    Do that, just for me.   25

CHAIREAS
Laches, I must give way to you.

LACHES
                              It's what we wish.

CHAIREAS
Listen to me. Kleainetos, the girl was [seized]
By Moschion, he's got her.

KLEAINETOS
(*crying out in pretended[9] despair*)
                              We've been wronged.

CHAIREAS
Don't shout. He aims to sire legitimate

---

[8] Chaireas now pretends that Moschion's rape of Kleainetos'
daughter forced her family to reject his own claims to the girl and
instead to support those of Moschion.

[9] If Kleainetos had forced Moschion to marry his daughter af-
ter the rape, he is unlikely at this stage to have complained that he
himself was being ill-treated. Presumably here he is going along
with Chaireas' scheme, without necessarily knowing all its details.

30 παίδων. ὁ πατὴρ αὐτοῦ [παρ]ὼν Λάχης ὁδὶ
    τοῦτ᾽ ἐπιβεβαιοῖ. φὴς σ[ύ];

                    ΛΑΧΗΣ
                [φημ]ί, Χαιρέα.
                      (?)
32 ..] γάρ τι βουλ[.......].[

(After v. 32, which closes one page of C, there is a lacuna
probably of between 2 and 5 lines at the top of the next
page.)

33   ]ε..

35   ἄνθρω]πος ἦν
                        ] ἐμοὶ
                    κα]λῶς ἔχει·
                    κα]τὰ τρόπον
                    ] γάρ μοι διαφέρει

30 Suppl. and deciphered by Jensen.   31 σ[ύ suppl.
Jensen, φημ]ί Sudhaus.   Fragment ι ('verso') of C (printed
here after v. 64) contains the opening letters of 6 lines that have
not yet been securely placed but could have come somewhere be-
tween the top of this page (before v. 33) and v. 43.

33–43 Assignments to the speakers here (Chaireas,
Kleainetos, Laches) are uncertain, but the end of v. 36 is spoken
by Chaireas, and C's dicola are noted.   34 Nothing remains
from a line which must have occupied less space in C.

35 Suppl. Sudhaus.   36 C has χαιρ´ in the right margin to
indicate the speaker.

37, 38 Suppl. Körte.

440

Children.[10] His father's here—Laches, and he   30
Confirms this—don't you now?

LACHES

> [Yes,] Chaireas.

KLEAINETOS *or* CHAIREAS

[I don't] want at all [

*(Between vv. 32 and 33 there is a short gap in the papyrus,
and then only the ends of vv. 34–43 are preserved. At v. 33
the same three characters are still on the stage, but between
vv. 37 and 41 Chaireas made his departure, probably to
pass on to Moschion the news that Laches has accepted his
son's marriage. It often remains difficult to identify the
speakers or make coherent sense of the odd phrases that
can be translated: v. 35 was a man (?) or man (?) was; 36 to
(?) me; 37 it's fine or no, thank you, said by Chaireas and
followed by a change of speaker; 38 all right; 39 you see, to
me it matters; 40 the happenings, followed by a change of
speaker; 41 you're most considerate, probably said by
Kleainetos to Laches (cf. v. 48); 42 a remark beginning And
I don't see you . . . either; 43 displeased. The speakers here
seem to have been mulling over Moschion's present posi-
tion, with Laches' calm acceptance of it surprising
Kleainetos and possibly Chaireas too. From vv. 44 to 47 the
papyrus text is only slightly defective, and from vv. 48 to 64
virtually undamaged. When in vv. 44–45 Laches celebrates
the fact that Moschion's worries seem now to have been*

---

[10] By quoting here part of the normal Athenian betrothal for-
mula (see vol. I, note on *Dysk.* 842–43), Chaireas implies that
Moschion is now legally married to Kleainetos' daughter.

40

τ]ὰ γεγονότα·
]. πρᾶός γ᾽ εἶ σφόδρα
]εν· οὐδὲ γάρ σ᾽ ὁρ[ῶ
] ἀγανακτ[.........]ν

ΛΑΧΗΣ

...].. ἐ[κ τηλι]κούτων νῦν φόβων
45 τὸν υἱὸν ἐκ[λυσά]μενος.

ΚΛΕΑΙΝΕΤΟΣ
                    ἀλλὰ μὴν πάλαι
ἡμῖν ἔδοξ[ε τοῦ]τ᾽. ἔχει τὴν παρθένον
ὁ Μοσχίων. [ἔλα]β᾽ ἐθελοντής, οὐ βίᾳ.
ᾠόμεθα χα[λε]πανεῖν σε τοῦτο πυθόμενον.
ἀστεῖος ἀποβέβηκας· εὐτυχήκαμεν·
50 περὶ τοῦ βοῶμεν;

ΛΑΧΗΣ
                    πῶς λέγεις;

ΚΛΕΑΙΝΕΤΟΣ
                    ὥσπερ λέγω.

ΛΑΧΗΣ
οὐ Χαιρέᾳ τὸ πρῶτον ἐξεδώκατε
τὴν παῖδα;

40 Suppl. Lefebvre.   42 Deciphered and suppl. Sudhaus,
Jensen.   44 Suppl. Wilamowitz.
45 Suppl. Meister.   πάλαι deciphered by Jensen.
46 Suppl. Körte (ἐδοξ[ε ταῦτ᾽ von Arnim).
47 Suppl. and deciphered by Jensen.
48 Suppl. von Arnim, Crönert.

nullified, Kleainetos surprises Laches with the news that
Moschion's difficulties were resolved long ago, presumably
when the young man married Kleainetos' daughter.)

LACHES
    ] dis[pell]ing my son's fears,   44
Which were so anguished now.

KLEAINETOS
         We settled [that],   45
Though, long ago. Your Moschion has got
The girl. [He took] her willingly, not by
Duress.[11] We thought you'd be upset when you
Found out. You've taken it so well. We're lucky!
So why should we complain?

LACHES
        How do you mean?

KLEAINETOS
           It's as I say!   50

LACHES
But didn't you first offer Chaireas
Your girl?

---

[11] It is not clear whether Kleainetos here means that (after
raping her) Moschion married the former's daughter willingly and
without duress, or whether Kleainetos is actually denying the
truth of an allegation by Chaireas (cf. v. 23) that Moschion had
raped the girl.

443

MENANDER

ΚΛΕΑΙΝΕΤΟΣ

μὰ Δία.

ΛΑΧΗΣ

τί σὺ λέγεις; οὐ Χαιρέᾳ;
ἀλλὰ τίν[ι];

ΚΛΕΑΙΝΕΤΟΣ

[π]άνυ γελοῖον. οὐκ ἀκήκοας;
τῷ σῷ νεανίσκῳ.

ΛΑΧΗΣ

τί λέ[γει]ς;

ΚΛΕΑΙΝΕΤΟΣ

νὴ τ[ο]ὺς θεού[ς,
55   καὶ παιδίον γὰρ γέγονεν ἐκ τούτου.

ΛΑΧΗΣ

[τ]ί φ[ῇς;
ἐκ Μοσχίωνος; ὦ πολυτίμητοι [θ]εο[ί,
ἐρρωμένου πράγματος.

ΚΛΕΑΙΝΕΤΟΣ

Ἄπολλον, ν[οῦν ἔχεις;
πρωί γε σ᾽, ὡς ἔοικ᾽, ἐπήνεσ᾽.

ΛΑΧΗΣ

οὐδ[ὲ ἓν
ὁ Χαιρέας ἄρ᾽ ἠδίκηται;

52, 54 C has no paragraphus under these lines.
53 τίν[ι] suppl. Körte, [π]άνυ Lefebvre.

444

FABULA INCERTA 1

KLEAINETOS
Certainly not!

LACHES
                  What's that you say?
Not Chaireas? Who then?

KLEAINETOS
                 That's quite a joke—
You heard me, surely?[12] Your own son!

LACHES
                      What's that
You say?

KLEAINETOS
It's true, and now he's got a baby boy.   55

LACHES
(now flying into a passion)
What's that? Do you mean Moschion? Good god,
That's awful!

KLEAINETOS
          Heavens, [can't you show some sense?]
It looks as if I praised you all too soon!

LACHES
Then Chaireas has not been wronged [at all]?

---

[12] Kleainetos refers to what he said at vv. 46–47.

---

54 τισυλε[C: συ deleted by Jensen, Sudhaus.   λέ[γει]ς
suppl. Körte, τ[ο]ὺς θεού[ς Lefebvre.
   55, 56 Suppl. Lefebvre.   57 Suppl. Sudhaus.
   58 επηνησ᾽ουδ[C: corr. and suppl. Körte.

MENANDER

ΚΛΕΑΙΝΕΤΟΣ

φίλτατος—

60 τί γὰρ ἠδίκηται;—Χαιρέας.

ΛΑΧΗΣ

οὐθέν; τί οὖ[ν
ἐβόα πορευθ[εὶς] δεῦρ’;

ΚΛΕΑΙΝΕΤΟΣ

ἴσως ἐβούλετο—

ΛΑΧΗΣ

ἐβούλετ’; ἐ[π’ ἐμ]ὲ ταῦτα συνετάξασθ’ ἄρα.
ὦ Γῆ.

ΚΛΕΑΙΝΕΤΟΣ

τί πο[ιεῖς;]

ΛΑΧΗΣ

οὐθέν, ἀλλ’ ὅμως ἔα
64 δὶς ἢ τρ[ὶς ἀνακ]ραγεῖν με, πρὸς τῆς Ἑστία[ς].

59–60 φίλτατος—Χαιρέας assigned to Kleainetos with this
punctuation by Sandbach (C has no dicolon either before or after
φίλτατος).

60, 61, 62 Suppl. Lefebvre.

63 C has no paragraphus under the line.

63, 64 Suppl. Körte.

446

KLEAINETOS

How could

He have been—dear, dear Chaireas!

LACHES

Not wronged at all?   60

Why did he come here shouting then?

KLEAINETOS

Perhaps he wished—

LACHES

He wished? So you've all plotted here against [me]![13]

(Here Laches pauses, and then cries out at the top of his voice.)

O world,—

KLEAINETOS

What [are you] doing?

LACHES

Nothing—still, in god's

Name, let me have just two or three [loud] screams!   64

(Here the papyrus breaks off. The play may be in its closing stages, but we do not whether Menander had any new surprises up his sleeve.)

[13] At this point Laches feels that he has been tricked by both Chaireas and Kleainetos.

The unplaced fragment (ι) of C*

(recto side: line ends)

1a
$$]τε$$
$$]..ν\ ἔδει$$
$$]ξας\ ολ.ς$$
$$μ]εγ'\ ἀθλιο[$$
5a
$$]λλα\ Χαι[ρε$$
6a
$$]ουκ[$$

(verso side: line beginnings)

1b ἄ]παντ' ακ[
    ἐκεῖνος [
    ἀναδέξομ[
    φί[λ]ῳ δικαι[
5b ἄπ[αντ]α μελ[
6b π[...] τουτ.[

Four Papyri Tentatively Attributed to
Fabula Incerta 1

(i) P.Oxyrhynchus 429
(fr. adesp. 1010 Kassel–Austin)

A small scrap, written in the 3rd century A.D.; first published (without a photograph) by B. P. Grenfell and A. S. Hunt, *The Oxyrhynchus Papyri* 3 (London 1903) 73–74.

(?)

ἐγὼ δ[ὲ] τ[
καὶ τη.[

(The unplaced fragment ι of C probably came from the same leaf as vv. 2–64. On one side of ι we have six line endings (1a–6a) which could originally have fitted somewhere before v. 11; they provide the following words and phrases: 1b had to, 1c all, 1d very wretched, 1e but, Chai[reas] (?). If 1e is correctly placed before v. 11 and its letters correctly interpreted, the translated words would have been spoken by Laches, the only other character known to have been on stage at the time. On the other side of ι we have six line beginnings (1b–6b) which could have come somewhere between vv. 32 and 43; they yield the following words and phrases: 1b all, 2b he or that, 3b will receive, 4b right for a friend, 5b all (?), 6b this.)

Four Papyri Tentatively Attributed to Unidentified Play 1

(i) P.Oxyrhynchus 429

This scrap preserves the beginnings of 14 verses. An unidentified character speaks from v. 1 to the first part of v. 9; the remainder of what survives is spoken by the father or guardian of a bride, possibly the Laches of Fab.Inc. 1, towards the close of that play. Only individual words and phrases can be identified in each line, as follows: from the unidentified speaker, 1 and I, 2 and the (?), 3 no man or no, 4 to rape or to seizure, 5 Laches, 6 I don't know, 7 as neigh-

---

* See the introduction to this play.
4a, 5a Suppl. Sudhaus.
1b Suppl. Zucker, Gomme.
4b, 5b Suppl. Sudhaus.
P.Oxy. 1 Suppl. Schröder.

οὐθεὶς ὑ[
εἰς ἁρπα[γ
5   Λάχης εν[
οὐκ οἶδα δ.[
ὡς γείτονες συνέδ[ραμον
ἐμοὶ δ’ ἐπεδ[
___ἵνα τὰς θύρας [

ΛΑΧΗΣ (?)

[δίδωμι γνησίων

10   παιδῶν ἐπ’ ἀρό[τῳ
ἐφ’ ἧπερ ὁ πατὴ[ρ
τὰ φίλτατ’, ὦ παῖ, χ[
ἀ]λλουτο[....]ιο[
14   προτερο[

7 ·γιτονες O: corr. Grenfell and Hunt.   Suppl. Sudhaus.
9 δίδωμι suppl. Schröder, γνησίων Grenfell and Hunt.
10 Suppl. Grenfell and Hunt.
13 ἄ]λλου το[(Kassel–Austin) or ἀ]λλ’ (Grenfell and Hunt)
οὐ το[(Schröder) or οὗτο[ς (Sudhaus).

14 See n.1 on Men. *Dysk.* 842–43 (vol. I p. 325).
15 A Laches appears in Menander's *Heros, Kitharistes, Perinthia* and (on the evidence of the Mytilene mosaic) *Plokion*, Crobylus' *Pseudhypobolimaios* and Philemon's *Ephebos.* Cf. also several fragments from unidentified plays: Men. frs. 795.1 and 430 K-A, fr. adesp. 1045 K-A. On *PSI* 1176 and *P.Oxy.* 4409 see below.

bours [ran] (?) together, *8* and to me, *9* in order to . . . the doors; *from Laches, 9–10* [I betroth] . . . to harvest [lawful] children,[14] *11* on condition her *or* your father, *12* my child, the dearest, *14* former *or* former[ly].

The successive mention of a rape *or* seizure *(4), Laches (5) and* neighbours *doing something* together *(7), directly before the introduction of the standard formula of betrothal (10–11), seems clearly to match both a known character and incidents mentioned (vv. 8, 23) in Fab.Inc. 1, and in a letter to Körte Wilamowitz tentatively suggested that P.Oxy. 429 might derive from that play. Körte countered the suggestion (i) by drawing attention to the frequency with which Laches is used as a character name for old men in later Greek comedy,[15] and (ii) by alleging that any combination in one and the same scene of the details about Moschion's arrest (in Chaireas' embroidered story) with (presumably) Chaireas' betrothal to Laches' daughter would be dramatically implausible.*

P.Oxyrhynchus 2533 (see iii below) has also been attributed to the same play as Fab.Inc. 1, but a common assignment of both P.Oxy. 429 and 2533 to the same source would be difficult to sustain, in view of the betrothal formula at v. 10 of P.Oxy. 429. If P.Oxy. 429 belongs to Fab.Inc. 1, that betrothal formula cannot apply to Moschion and Kleainetos' daughter, since this pair apparently were married before the staged action of Fab.Inc. 1 began. Any attempt to refer it to the betrothal of Chaireas and Laches' daughter, however, must rule out a common origin for P.Oxy. 429 and 2533, since the latter papyrus introduces the same betrothal formula (vv. 3–5) for a named Chaireas, and there is no precedent in later Greek comedy for two uses of this formula at a single betrothal.

(ii) *PSI* 1176 (fr. adesp. 1063 Kassel–Austin)

This papyrus, written probably before 60 A.D., contains
the remains of the top 17–18 lines from three adjoining
columns, the third of which preserves only the line
beginnings. It was first published by G. Vitelli in *SIFC* 7
(1929) 235–42, and later (with a photograph: plate iii) in
Papiri greci e latini 10 (Florence 1932) 146–55.

ΜΟΣΧΙΩΝ (?)

1   σοὶ πε]πιστευκώς.

ΜΕΓΑΣ

βάδιζε, μὴ δεδοικὼς μηδὲ ἕν.

The speakers in *PSI* 1176 (abbreviated below to P) are iden-
tified as α (= 1st actor: before βάδιζε v. 1, wrongly in v. 4 (see be-
low), β (= 2nd actor: before ἐγω v. 24, ηρα[κ]λεις 26, ἐδωκ[38)
and γ (= 3rd actor: before μη v. 26, ω 46); the scribe underlines
these letters, and occasionally (see below on v. 4) adds a further
line above.

Those corrections and supplements whose author is not
named in this apparatus were made by the ed. pr., G. Vitelli.

1 σοὶ suppl. Mette.   δεδυκως P.   1 βάδιζε—23 as-
signed to one speaker by Maas.

---

16 If Moschion now leaves the stage expressing his confidence
in this slave, he must presumably have asked him in the lost pre-
ceding context to help him out of his fix.

FABULA INCERTA 1

(ii) *PSI* 1176

This papyrus contains parts of two scenes. The first is in trochaic tetrameters; a slave (apparently bearing the dramatically unique name Megas, v. 3) bids good-bye to another character (v. 1: probably his young master Moschion), and then launches into a long monologue in which he steels himself to tackle a desperate situation facing Moschion (2-4), which he compares to a storm at sea (5-16 at least). There are similar speeches in Roman comedy by slaves who have been asked by their masters to tackle difficult problems but have not so far hit upon a clever stratagem (e.g. Chrysalus in Plautus' Bacchides 760-69, a play adapted from Menander's Dis Exapaton; Pseudolus in Plautus' Pseudolus 394-414, 561-74). At the end of his monologue the slave notices his old master Laches (21, cf. 24) and another man (22) arriving presumably by one of the side entrances, and he disappears offstage into his house. The metre now changes to iambic trimeters, and Laches' companion rebukes Laches for having ill-treated him by sending him (24-26) on a mission connected with the marriage of a son and daughter (29-30).

MOSCHION

(ending a speech of which only the final words are preserved)

Counting [on you]![16]

(As Moschion now moves off into his house, his slave Megas is left alone on stage.)

MEGAS

Go, and don't be terrified of anything! 1

οὗτοσ]ὶ μὲν ἔνδον ἐστίν. ὥστ᾽ ἔγειρ᾽, ἔγειρε δὴ
νῦν σε]αυτὸν μὴ παρέργως. νῦν ἀνὴρ γενοῦ, Μέγα.
μὴ ᾽γκ]αταλίπῃς Μοσχίωνα. βούλομαι, νὴ τοὺς
θεούς,

5 βούλομ᾽,] ἀλλ᾽ ἀπροσδοκήτως εἰς κλύδωνα
πραγμάτων
ἐμπε]σὼν ἠγωνίακα καὶ πάλαι ταράττομαι
μή πο]θ᾽ ἡ τύχη λάβῃ μου τὴν ἐναντίαν κρίσιν.
δειλὸ]ς εἶ, νὴ τὴν Ἀθηνᾶν, δειλὸς εἶ. βλέπω. σύ γε
τὸν π]όνον φεύγων προσάπτεις τῇ τύχῃ τὴν αἰτίαν.

10 τοῖς π]λέουσιν—οὐ θεωρεῖς;—πολλάκις τὰ δυσχερῆ
ἀντίκει]ται πάντα· χειμών, πνεῦμ᾽, ὕδωρ, τρικυμία,
ἀστραπ]αί, χάλαζα, βρονταί, ναυτίαι, σύναγ[μα],
νύξ.
ἀλλ᾽ ὅμω]ς ἕκαστος αὐτῶν προσμένει τὴν ἐλπίδα
καὶ τὸ μέ]λλον οὐκ ἀπέγνω. τῶν κάλων τις ἥψατο

2 Suppl. and corr. Körte (suggesting hesitantly that P may
have had ουτοσ]ει).   δηι P.

3 Suppl. several.   Μέγα identified as a name by Maas,
Wilamowitz.

4 Corr. Maas: μοσχιων $\bar{α}$ βουλομαι P.

5 Suppl. Maas.

7 τυχηι P.

8 συμε corrected to συγε P.

9 Suppl. several.

10 δυσχερηι P.

12 σύναγ[μα] suppl. Morel.

13 Suppl. Maas.

14 απεγνων: P.

454

[He']s indoors. So rouse yourself, yes rouse [your]self to
    action [now],
Give his plight your full attention. Now, Megas, just be a
    man!
Do[n't] run out on Moschion! I swear I want to help the
    boy,
[Yes, I want to], but I've [fall]en into stormy waters,[17]   5
    quite
Unexpectedly, and I'm anxious, ill at ease for many a day,
[Fearing] that my luck may gain an adverse verdict from
    the court.
You are [yellow-bellied], yes indeed, you're yellow, I can
    see!
Seeking to avoid [this] mess, you fix the blame on your
    bad luck!
Don't you realise? All kinds of trouble often [face our]   10
    men
In their ships—storms, savage gales and heavy rain,
    gigantic waves,
[Lightning flash]es, hail and thunder, queasiness,
    collisions[18] (?) too,
Darkness. Every one of them [still] watches for a ray of
    hope,
Not despairing of [his] future. One man grabs the ropes,
    with his

[17] We do not know what these stormy waters were, but they
are most likely to have resulted from some previous attempt by
the slave to help a young master in difficulties.

[18] The Greek word which has been supplemented here is a
ἅπαξ λεγόμενον of uncertain meaning.

MENANDER

15 θοἰστιόν] τ᾿ ἐσκέψαθ᾿· ἕτερος τοῖς Σαμόθραξιν
   εὔχετα[ι
   τῷ κυβερνή]τῃ βοη[θεῖν]· τοὺς πόδας προσέλκεται
   ἄλλος .....].. νετ[....]. υτον.[.......] τ[
        ]. ν[.] φ[.........] αν[.......] α[
19   ]. [

(There is a lacuna of several lines between vv. 19 and 20, in
which Megas continues his monologue.)

20 ....] εις ἅπασιν εὐγενῶς προθυμ[ία]ν
   .... ἀλλ᾿] ὁρῶ γὰρ τουτονὶ τὸν δεσπότη[ν
   καὶ τὸ]ν [.....]νον μετ᾿ αὐτοῦ. θᾶττον εἴσειμ᾿ ἐνθάδε,
23 παρα]φ[ανήσο]μαί τε τούτοις καιρὸν εὐφυῆ λαβών.

(The metre now changes from trochaic tetrameters to
iambic trimeters.)

(?)
24 ἐγὼ μὲν ὕβρισμαι, Λάχης, ὡς οὐδὲ εἷς

15 Suppl. Vitelli (ἱστιόν Eitrem).   τοισομωθραξιν appar-
ently P: corr. several.
16 τῷ κυβερνή]τῃ suppl. Wilamowitz, βοη[θεῖν] Norsa.
17 ἄλλος suppl. Wilamowitz.
21 Suppl. Vitelli (see SFIC 7, 1929, 241).
22 Suppl. several.   εισιμ P.
23 Suppl. Körte (κατα]φ[ανήσο]μαί Vitelli).
24 λαλης P with a diagonal / scribbled beneath λη.

456

Eyes fixed on [the sail]; another begs the gods of   15
  Samothrace[19]
[To bring] succour to [the helmsman; someone else]
  hauls in the sheets

(Lines 17–19 are too mutilated for identification of any in-
dividual word, and after 19 there is a short gap in the papy-
rus. When the papyrus resumes at v. 20, Megas is now ap-
proaching the end of his trochaic-tetrameter monologue.)

[   ] nobly [   ] goodwill to all (?)   20
[but] I see my master here,
[And there's[20]   ] beside him. I shall go in here at
  once,
And I'll choose a more convenient time to [show myself]
  to them.

(Megas exits into his master's stage house, while Laches
and his unidentified companion enter together by one of
the side entrances. The metre now changes to iambic
trimeters.)

LACHES' COMPANION

I've been abused far worse than anyone

---

[19] The 'great gods of Samothrace' were identified with the
Cabeiri, whose cult was widespread in the 4th and 3rd centuries
B.C. It was believed that initiation into their mysteries would pro-
tect one from shipwreck. See further my commentary (Cam-
bridge 1996) on Alexis fr. 183.5 K-A. (pp. 546–47).

[20] Laches was presumably Moschion's father, entering here
with another character whose identity is hidden in the gap.

25 ἄνθρωπος ἕτερος πώποθ᾽, ὕβρικας δέ με
σὺ δεῦρο πέμψας.

ΛΑΧΗΣ
μὴ λέγ᾽ οὕτως.

(?)
Ἡρά[κ]λεις·
ἐγὼ δὲ πῶς σχοίην ἂν ἑτέρως; πολλάκ[ι]ς
ἔλεγον ἐκεῖ σοι "ποῖ με πέμπεις;"

ΛΑΧΗΣ
καὶ μάλα.

(?)
"υἱῷ φέροντα περὶ γάμου, καὶ θυγατέρα
30 δώσοντ᾽;" ἐὰν δὲ μὴ προσέχῃ μοι, πῶς ἐγὼ
ἀναγκάσω σοῦ μὴ παρόντος λαμβάνειν;
.]...δε[.]σει πραγμάτων κατήκοος
].[μέ]μψεθ᾽ ἡ μήτηρ ⟨∪ –⟩
]επείσθη μοι λέ[γειν
35].ν

ΛΑΧΗΣ
ηδ[..]ενπ[
]ννηι[

(There is a lacuna between vv. 36 and 37 roughly equal in
length to that between vv. 19 and 20.)

26 P has a paragraphus under the line.
31 παροντως and λαμβανεις P.

Else ever, Laches! You've abused me by   25
Sending me here!

LACHES
Don't talk like that!

LACHES' COMPANION
                      Good god,
How else could I behave? I often asked
You there, "Where are you sending me,—

LACHES
                    Quite so.

LACHES' COMPANION
—Discussing marriage with a son first, then prepared
To give a girl away?" If he won't listen,   30
How can I force him in your absence to
Accept [   ] listening to events
    ] the mother will blame (?) [
    ] was induced to [say] to me[21]   34

(Verses 35 and 36 of the papyrus are too tattered and torn for coherent translation. After v. 36 there is a short gap in the papyrus. Only the line beginnings of vv. 37–54 in the next column of text are preserved, yielding some disconnected words and phrases, as follows: 37 for not spoken by

[21] Laches' companion had apparently been sent by Laches from another place to one of the stage houses (probably Laches' own), where he was to tell a son residing there 'about a marriage' and to arrange for the betrothal of a daughter of that house. The son seems to have been reluctant, and the mother opposed (v. 33). See below for the alleged connection of this passage to *Fab. Inc.* 1.

37 οὐ γὰ[ρ

(?)

ἔδω[κ
ἰμάτι[
40 οἴκει κ[
τὴν οχ[
τουτ.[
αλλοσμ[
εἶχεν τ[
45 ἕτερος τ[

ΛΑΧΗΣ

ὦ πραγμ[
τοσοῦτο[
ἔασον.

(?)

[
Λάχης δ[
50 σχολὴν κ[
νῦν ἥδιο[ν
ταραττομ[
ἧς ἦν πρ[
54 .[

37 Suppl. Edmonds.
39 ἰμάτι[ον or ἰμάτι(α).
48 P has a paragraphus under the line.
51 Suppl. Edmonds.

460

Laches; 38 gave, 39 cloak *or* cloaks *or* clothes, 40 lives (?),
41 the, 42 this, 43 other, 44 had, 45 other, *all spoken appar-
ently by Laches' companion;* 46 What a . . . affair, 47 so
great, 48 allow *or* let *as a command, all spoken by Laches;*
49 Laches, 50 leisure, 51 more pleasant now, 52 [I] am *or*
[we] are disturbed, 53 of which was, *all spoken by Laches'
companion. Here the papyrus breaks off.)*

In his preliminary publication of PSI 1176 Vitelli hesi-
tantly suggested that it might derive from Fab.Inc. 1, rely-
ing on the presence of a Moschion and a Laches in both the
Cairo and the Italian papyri, and noting that it was "not
impossible" to fit them both into the same plot. Vitelli's sug-
gestion has been opposed for metrical, linguistic and dra-
matic reasons, but the accretion of many new comic papyri
since the 1930s has made some of the earlier arguments un-
tenable and a brief new discussion advisable.

(a) The appearance of Laches and Moschion together in
both papyri is a striking fact, even though this pairing is
known also to occur in Menander's Kitharistes and (ac-
cording to the Mytilene mosaic) Plokion.

(b) The presence in PSI 1176 of a slave who finds the
problems facing his master Moschion hard to resolve fa-
vours (rather than, as Körte thought, impedes) the attribu-
tion of this papyrus to Fab.Inc. 1. Long before our present
bonanza of Menandrean papyri, Roman adaptations of
Greek comedy (e.g. Plautus' Miles Gloriosus and Persa,
Terence's Andria) already made it clear that, even when
free men were involved in carrying a scheme through, it
was normally a slave or a parasite who devised it. The
Bodmer fragments of Menander's Aspis now confirm that
Plautus and Terence here in all probability followed an es-

461

tablished Greek convention. Thus it seems likely that the stratagem of Chaireas in *Fab.Inc. 1* was originally the brainchild of a slave—perhaps the despairing plotter of *PSI 1176*.

(c) The major structural difficulty standing in the way of assigning *PSI 1176* to *Fab.Inc. 1* remains the identity of the man who rebukes Laches (vv. 24–26, 27ff.) and the nature of the mission on which he had been sent by Laches to discuss marriage with a son and to give a girl away in marriage (29–30). The Laches of *Fab.Inc. 1* had a son married without his consent while he was away from home, and a daughter apparently promised originally to someone other than Chaireas, and this at first sight seems compatible with a mission (earlier in the play than the Cairensis page) on which some character had been despatched by Laches to deal with the affairs of his two children. But the known portion of *Fab.Inc. 1*'s plot contains no reference to such a mission.

(d) *Despite some earlier criticism, there are no metrical anomalies in the verses of PSI 1176 to counter its attribution to Menander, and very little in its style and language that raises serious doubts. A few phrases have been singled out as aberrant for an Athenian writer of Menander's period (e.g. [μή πο]θ' ἡ τύχη λάβῃ μου τὴν ἐναντίαν κρίσιν v. 7, καιρὸν εὐφυῆ λαβών 23, υἱῷ φέροντα περὶ γάμου 28, and πραγμάτων κατήκοος 32). Admittedly none of these expressions has yet been attested for Menander, but exact or closely related parallels for all of them can be cited from writers of early Koine Greek.*[22]

However, none of the points discussed above can be considered conclusive. There is as yet no sure way of establishing (a) whether or not PSI 1176 should be attributed to Menander, or (b) if Menandrean, whether or not it belongs to Fab.Inc. 1. The odds are probably rather less than even for a positive answer to (a), and a great deal less than even for a positive answer to (b). PSI 1176 must be judged the weakest of the four candidates for assignment to Fab.Inc. 1.

[22] For a detailed discussion of the alleged metrical, linguistic and stylistic anomalies see my paper in ZPE 123 (1998) 54–57.

MENANDER

(iii) *P.Oxyrhynchus* 2533
(fr. adesp. 1098 Kassel–Austin)

A small scrap of papyrus written in the 2nd century A.D.
and containing the middle portions of 15 lines. It was first
published by J. W. B. Barns (with the help of Sir H. Lloyd-
Jones), *The Oxyrhynchus Papyri* 31 (London 1966) 9–11,
with a photograph (plate ii).

ΧΑΙΡΕΑΣ

1   οὐκ ἔσ]τι, μὰ τὸν Ἥφαιστον, ἀλλ᾽ οὐκ ἔ[στι μοι
ἀφεκ]τέον δήπουθεν ἧς ἐρῶ πάλα[ι.
ἄλλως ἔ]δεισα.

ΛΑΧΗΣ (?)

σοὶ μὲν αὕτη, Χαιρέα·
ὥστ᾽ ἐγγ]υῶ ταύτην, ἐμαυτοῦ θυγατέρα,
5   ......]ων π[αίδων ἐπ᾽ ἀρότῳ γνησίων.
τὴν πρ]οῖκα δ᾽ αὐτὸς οἶσθα.

ΧΑΙΡΕΑΣ

νυνὶ μὲν [δύο
τάλαν]τ᾽ ἐπι[δ]ίδως.

1 Suppl. and corr. Lloyd-Jones: αλουκ O.
2 ἀφεκ]τέον suppl. Handley, πάλα[ι Barns.
3 Suppl. Lloyd-Jones.
4 ὥστ᾽ suppl. Arnott, ἐγγ]υῶ Barns.
6 τὴν πρ]οῖκα suppl. Lloyd-Jones, δύο Barns.   Change of
speaker after οἶσθα suggested by Barns.
7, 10, 13 Suppl. Barns.

464

FABULA INCERTA 1

(iii) *P. Oxyrhynchus* 2533

This brief scrap contains fragments of 17 lines from a scene presumably very near the end of the play, in which a father betroths his daughter to a young man apparently named Chaireas.

CHAIREAS (?)

I swear that it can['t] be! You know [I] can't
Ever [desert] the girl I've loved so long!
My fears were [groundless (?)].

LACHES (?)

Chaireas, she's yours.
So (?)] I [betroth] this girl to you, my daughter,
] to harvest lawful children.[23]   5
[The dowry] you yourself know.

CHAIREAS

Yes, you're now
Offering [two talents].   7

(From here onwards only a few words and phrases can be deciphered: v. 7 The remainder, v. 9 now's the time, 10 Moschion, 11 your two [talents] (?), 12 the wedding hymn,[24] 13 happening.)

Two features of this badly mutilated scrap led its first editor to attribute it tentatively to a closing scene of Fab.Inc. 1. One was the presence of the names Chaireas (addressed at v. 3) and Moschion (a certain supplement at v. 10); although it seems a safe guess that characters with these

---

[23] See note 1 on *Dyskolos* 843.
[24] See note on *Samia* 127.

MENANDER

ΛΑΧΗΣ (?)

τὴν δὲ λοιπ[
]σμε..ξας μηχ[
] νῦν ὁ καιρὸς [
10   Μ]οσχίων μ.[
].τα δύο σοι τ[άλαντα
] τὸν Ὑμέναι[ον
γεγο]νότος· ου[
].ιτας[.]..[
15   ].[

(iv) P.Oxyrhynchus 4409

Four papyrus fragments from the third century A.D.,
perhaps all deriving from one tall column of text. Fr. 1
yields the remains of 21 trimeters (vv. 1–11 with the
second halves of the lines lost, 12–21 nearly complete); frs.
2 and 3, if correctly put together, contain the endings of 17
trimeters. They were first published by E. W. Handley,
The Oxyrhynchus Papyri 64 (1997) 50–59, with a
photograph (plate iv).

Fragment 1

(?)

πατή[ρ .....]μηθ[..].
θυγάτ[ηρ, ἀδε]λφός, α..[
τοῦτ’ ἐκβιάσεται .[...]γ...[

P.Oxy. 2533 v. 11 Suppl. Georgescu.

*names were present together in other plays of Menander
and New Comedy, this pairing has not as yet been found in
any other surviving play or fragment. Secondly, two other
details—a character's confession that he had been in love
with a girl for a long time (v. 2), and a father's use of the for-
mula betrothing his daughter apparently to that character
(3–5)—agree with what we know about the plot of Fab.Inc.
1. The attribution is admittedly speculative, but if it is
correct, the speakers on stage are unlikely to have been
Kleainetos and Moschion, as Barns suggested, since
Moschion seems already to have been legally married to
Kleainetos' daughter, but rather Laches and Chaireas. In
that case Laches would be fulfilling at the end of the play a
promise that he initially made at Fab.Inc. 1 vv. 17–19. On
the difficulty of assigning both P.Oxy. 429 and 2533 to the
same play, however, see the discussion of P.Oxy. 429 above.*

(iv) P. Oxyrhynchus 4409

*This papyrus is made up of four fragments. Fragment 1
comes from a dialogue between a Laches (v. 12) and an
unidentified young man who apparently wants to marry
Laches' daughter but is told that arrangements have been
made for her to marry somebody else. The first 3 lines are
severely mutilated; the young man appears to be speaking,
but all that can be deciphered is a series of disconnected
phrases opening each line: 1 Father, 2 A daught[er,
bro[ther, 3 He (?) will force it. The next 8 lines are less*

P.Oxy. 4409, fr. 1 Those corrections and supplements whose
author is not named in this apparatus were made by the ed.pr.,
E. W. Handley.

δίκαι'· ἃ μὴ †σύμφερε μηδὲ [συντίθει
5 εἰς ταὐτόν· ἀμφοτέρου[.].[.].[

ΛΑΧΗΣ

[ο]ὕτως ἔχεις· οὐ μὴ κολάζε[ιν σπουδάσῃ
ἐκεῖνος ἐξελθών σε.

(?)

ταῦτ.[

ΛΑΧΗΣ

εἴσω βαδίσας αὐτῷ [δί]ελθε σω[φρόνως
τὴν ἀτοπίαν τούτου.

(?)

[π]επόη[κα ταῦτ'.

ΛΑΧΗΣ

[ἴσως

10 ἔσχηκεν ἐξελθών τι.[
προσγέγονεν αὐτῷ ταῦτα τ[.].[

(?)

ἀλλ' ἀξιοῖς, Λάχης, με κηδεστὴν ἔχ[ειν
ἀφελόμενός με τὴν σεαυτοῦ θυγ[ατέρα;

ΛΑΧΗΣ

ἐγὼ γὰρ ἀξιῶ τι νῦν ἢ φθέγγομαι;

Paragraphi are found under the beginning of vv. 5, 7, 9, 11, 13, 14, 17 and 19.
9 [π]επόη[κα ταῦτ' suppl. Arnott, ἴσως Handley.

severely damaged, followed by another 10 virtually com-
plete.

YOUNG MAN 4

Right. Don't collect (?) these or [put them[25] together   5
All in one place. Both [

LACHES

That's how you're placed. He['ll] not [be eager to
Come out and punish you.

YOUNG MAN
That [

LACHES

Go in, talk soberly (?) to him about
The other's strange behaviour.

YOUNG MAN
That [I've] done [

LACHES 10

When he comes out, he's got some (?) [
This too has happened [

YOUNG MAN

But, Laches, do you think that I can be
An in-law now that you've deprived me of
Your daughter?

LACHES
Do I think or say a single word

Now?

[25] With the loss of the preceding context, what 'these' and
'them' are is a mystery. The following 'both' however, implies that
there were two of them.

(?)

15 καὶ τίνι ποτ᾽ ὄψει πρὸς σεαυτὸν ὁ χ[αλεπὸς
ψυχῇ με προσιόντ᾽; ἢ προσειπεῖ[ν σ᾽ ὑπομενῶ
προπηλακισθείς, χἀτέρου τα[ύ]την [ὁρῶν;

ΛΑΧΗΣ

ἤδη γὰρ ἠγγύηκα, κ[ο]ὐκ ἔνεστι [νῦν
ἄλλως γενέσθαι, καὶ ποῶ γάμους ἐ[γω.

(?)

20 ὦ Ζεῦ, γένοιθ᾽ ὃ δεῖ γενέσθαι, καὶ θεῶ[ν
ε]ὔνους παρών τις συλλάβοι. ψοφε[ῖ δέ τις

Fragments 2 and 3

| 1]τω.[| 2]τ᾽η[| 3].ειν[| 4].μ.[|

| 5].ιτρ[.]π.[| 6]οτουτ[| 7]ειδετις: | 8].σεστ᾽αρ.[|

| 9].νθεων | 10].θυμια[| 11]ορει | 12]. |

| 13]ταῦτά τις: or -τα τίς: | 14].ι: | 15]ς |

| 16].ον | 17]αλη | | |

Fragment 4

| 1].[| 2]..[.].[| 3]καιν.[|

Fr. 1 v. 21 ψοπε[corrected to ψοφε[O.

---

26 An indication that somebody is emerging from one of the stage houses. Cf. e.g. *Dysk.* 586, *Misoumenos* 972–73 and note b on *Mis.* 684.

YOUNG MAN

You are [hard]. What feelings will you have   15
When you see me approach? I've been insulted, I
[See] her belonging to another. How'[ll I bear]
Addressing [you]?

LACHES

I've just betrothed her, that
Can't [now] be changed. My present job's the wedding.

YOUNG MAN

O Zeus—let what must happen happen! May   20
A kind god come and help! [But someone]'s rattling[26]

Fragments 2 and 3 have been put together and give the final letters of 17 further lines, perhaps in the same column of text, but only one or two words can be deciphered: v. 7 but if someone or someone (or who) saw, 13 someone (or who) . . . this. Nothing of any value can be deciphered from fragment 4.

Fragment 1 comes from a dialogue between a Laches (v. 12) and an unnamed young man who rebukes Laches for depriving him of his daughter, now apparently betrothed to somebody else; Laches is already arranging the wedding (vv. 12–19). In the earlier and more mutilated portion of the fragment Laches seems to have asked this young man to discuss with a third man (the 'him' of v. 8) a fourth man's 'strange behaviour' (v. 9).

Laches is a common name in later Greek comedy, as I have noted above (n. 15 on the introduction to P.Oxy. 429), but Handley draws attention to the neat way that the recognisable subject-matter of the dialogue in fr. 1 matches

*known elements in the plot of Fab.Inc. 1. If this papyrus
derives from that play, the person rebuking Laches would
be Chaireas, at a much earlier stage in the plot when
Chaireas' wish to marry Laches' daughter was being im-
peded by Laches' betrothal of her to somebody else; the
third man would then be Kleainetos (with a house on
stage), and 'the other's strange behaviour' would presum-
ably refer to Moschion and the whole episode leading up to
his marriage to Kleainetos' daughter without Laches' con-
sent. Assignment of this papyrus to Fab.Inc. 1 would help
to fill in gaps in our knowledge of the latter's plot by reveal-
ing that a previous arrangement by Laches lay behind his
rejection of Chaireas as a suitor for his daughter. Even so,
it must be admitted that the apparent links between P.Oxy.
4409 and Fab.Inc. 1 could be adventitious, with the two
papyri deriving from separate plays.*

FABULA INCERTA 2

INTRODUCTION

Manuscript

D = a papyrus originally styled *P.Didot*, but now cata-
logued as *P.Louvre* 7172. It was written by three different
scribes at the Memphis Serapeum in or around 160 B.C.
The papyrus contains this speech from an ancient comedy
(*P.Didot* 2), together with a much longer speech (*P.Didot*
1) attributed incorrectly by its scribe to Euripides and by
some modern scholars to Menander (see above on
Unidentified and Excluded Papyri), as well as other ex-
tracts from Aeschylus (fr. 99 Radt), Euripides (*Medea* 5–
12) and two poems by the Hellenistic epigrammatist
Posidippus (11, 12 Gow–Page). First edition: H. Weil, *Un
papyrus inédit de la bibliothèque de M. Ambroise Firmin-
Didot* (Paris 1879) 25–28. There have been several further
editions; that by K. Gaiser, *Gymnasium* 75 (1968) 193–219
includes an excellent photograph (pl. xxiv). The speech is
fr. com. adesp. 1001 in Kassel–Austin, *PCG* VIII.

This speech was written down, probably from memory,
by a Macedonian boy in his mid-teens called Apollonius,
the younger brother of one Ptolemy, a recluse from the

temple of Sarapis at Memphis.[1] Although the boy's hand-writing, spelling and—at times—memory leave much to be desired, a reasonably accurate text can be teased out of his scrawl. Apollonius, however, fails to name either the dramatist or the play that he is quoting. The style and content of the speech point to its source in a comedy written in the fourth or third century B.C. Its male speaker, almost certainly in an entrance monologue and possibly even at the very beginning[2] of the play, enthusiastically tells the audience about a recent conversion which has turned him into a born-again thinker. His obvious excitement has led some scholars to assume that he must be young, and likely in the course of the play to have had experiences that challenged his confidence in his personal transformation. These are plausible but totally unverifiable speculations.

Many and varied have been the attempts to name the speech's author. Blass and Kock alleged similarities in Philemon and Theognestus respectively;[3] Bergk assigned it to the *Asotodidaskalos*, a play in my view incorrectly attributed to Alexis, and Edmonds named Posidippus' *Anablepon* without compelling reason.[4] Herzog[5] argued for Menander's *Hypobolimaios*, identifying a young rustic

[1] On Ptolemy and Apollonius see now Dorothy J. Thompson, *Memphis under the Ptolemies* (Princeton 1988) 212–65.

[2] Cf. D. Bain, *Actors and Audience* (Oxford 1977) 186 n. 3, with a useful bibliography.

[3] *RhMus* 35 (1880) 89 and 277.

[4] *RhMus* 35 (1880) 257 (cf. my commentary on Alexis, Cambridge 1996, 819–30) and Edmonds' *Fragments of Attic Comedy* IIIA, 228–30.

[5] *Philologus* 89 (1934) 195–96.

character in that play as the enthusiastic speaker of D. Although Herzog's suggestion has won some support,[6] the only evidence in its favour is a partial resemblance between the ideas expressed in D and those of fr. 373 K-A from Menander's *Hypobolimaios,* and scholars today tend to reject D's ascription to *Hypobolimaios* while still accepting Menander as its most likely author. Certainly the quality of imagination and expression in the lines of D seems higher than that achieved in the remains of any of his comic rivals.

[6] E.g. A. Barigazzi, *Athenaeum* 33 (1955) 271–77; G. Zuntz, PBA 42 (1956) 239–40; M. van der Valk, *Ant.Class.* 37 (1968) 477.

FABULA INCERTA 2

ἐρημία μέν ἐστι, κοὐκ ἀκούσεται
οὐδεὶς παρών μου τῶν λόγων ὧν ἂν λέγω.
ἐγὼ τὸν ἄλλον, ἄνδρες, ἐτεθνήκειν βίον
ἅπανθ' ὃν ἔζων· τοῦτό μοι πιστεύετε.
5 πᾶν ταὐτὸ τὸ καλόν, τἀγαθόν, τὸ σεμνὸν ⟨ἦν⟩,
τὸ κακόν. τοιοῦτον ἦν τί μου πάλαι σκότος
περὶ τὴν διάνοιαν, ὡς ἔοικε, κείμενον,
ὃ πάντ' ἔκρυπτε ταῦτα κἠφάνιζέ μοι.
νῦν δ' ἐνθάδ' ἐλθών, ὥσπερ εἰς Ἀσκληπιοῦ
10 ἐγκατακλιθεὶς σωθείς τε, τὸν λοιπὸν χρόνον

Those corrections and supplements whose author is not
named were made by the ed.pr., H. Weil. 1 ερημεια D orig-
inally, with ε crossed out. εστεινκαιουκ D.

2 ουδισπαρωμου D. 3 τεθνηκει D. βίον Bücheler:
παλαι D. 4 απαντα ωνεζη D. πιστεύετε Bücheler:
πιστευσεται D. 5 ταὐτὸ Bücheler: τηκτο apparently D.
τοαγαθον D. ἦν added by Bücheler, Kock.

6 Paragraphus under the line in D, presumably intended to
mark the beginning of a new theme; it would have been better
placed under v. 8. 7 κιμενον D. 8 παντεεκρυπτα and
καιφαινησε D: κἠφάνιζ' ἐμοί Weil (-ιζέ μοι Blass, Kock).

9 ωπερ D. 10 ενκατακλιθισωσνισθε D: ἐγκατακλιθεὶς
Weil, σωθείς τε Bücheler.

UNIDENTIFIED PLAY 2

(Entrance speech of a man, probably young, in a play whose scene, to judge from the references in v. 15, must have been Athens.)

I'm all alone, and nobody is here
To hang on any words of mine that may
Be dropped. Sirs,[1] I was dead all through the life
I've lived till now. You must believe this claim.
To me all beauty, virtue, piety   5
Were all alike—vice, too! Such was the dark
Cloud blanketing my mind, or so it seems.
It shrouded and blacked out all this for me.
But here[2] I've come now, like a patient on his bed
In hospital[3] when he's been cured! I'm born again   10

---

[1] Here and at v. 14 the speaker addresses the audience directly; cf. D. Bain, *Actors and Audience* (Oxford 1977) 185–89.

[2] By 'here' the speaker means the centre of town, but whether he has arrived there from abroad or just from the countryside surrounding the city is unknown.

[3] Literally, 'put to bed in Asclepius' shrine'. Sick people were often taken to a local shrine of Asclepius, where overnight they expected to have a dream in which Asclepius prescribed treatment; medical therapy normally followed. See F. Graf in *OCD*[3] s.vv. *Asclepius* and *Incubation*.

MENANDER

ἀναβεβίωκα. περιπατῶ, λαλῶ, φρονῶ.
τὸν τηλικοῦτον καὶ τοιοῦτον ἥλιον
νῦν τοῦτον εὗρον, ἄνδρες· ἐν τῇ τήμερον
ὑμᾶς ὁρῶ νῦν αἰθρίᾳ, τὸν ἀέρα,
15 τὴν ἀκρόπολιν, τὸ θέατρον.

11 περιπατων D: περιπατῶ several.
12 Corr. Blass: τηντηλικουντον D.
13 τοντονευρμα D: τοῦτον Blass, εὗρον Herzog (εὑρών Blass). τήμερον Bücheler, Kock: σημερον D.
14 Corr. Herzog: ορωτονθριαι D with ννν written as correction above ονθρ. ἀέρα Kock: αρα D.
15 τονθατρον D. Underneath this speech Apollonius writes ἀρίστων φιλόσοφος μαθήματα, perhaps added as an appropriate if misspelled (? and misquoted) tag (e.g. ἄριστον φιλοσόφοις μαθήματα Gaiser).

478

To live my future life. I walk[4] and talk
And think. This great and glorious sun I've now
Discovered. In today's clear light I can
See you now, gentlemen, I see blue sky,
And the Acropolis, the theatre.[5]   15

[4] The speaker has apparently been converted by some philosopher or teacher. On the habit of philosophers and their pupils walking up and down during their lessons cf. my commentary (Cambridge 1996) on Alexis fr.151.1–3.

[5] These references to the Acropolis and the theatre in close conjunction must indicate that the dramatic scene was Athens, where the upper seats of the audience in the Theatre of Dionysus were on the southern slopes of the Acropolis.

FABULA INCERTA 3

INTRODUCTION

Manuscript

O = *P.Oxyrhynchus* 10, a mutilated scrap from the second or third century A.D. containing 20 iambic trimeters, the last nine less severely damaged. First edition: B. P. Grenfell and A. S. Hunt (with the assistance of F. Blass), *The Oxyrhynchus Papyri* 1 (1898) 21–22; it was republished by M. Gronewald, *ZPE* 84 (1990) 1–3 with a photograph (pl. I), and is now fr. com. adesp. 1006 in Kassel–Austin, *PCG* VIII.

The best preserved chunk of this papyrus (vv. 7–20) comes from a speech by a slave, saying that he expects punishment after (?) an intrigue designed to promote his young master's love affair has failed, and that he intends to avoid involvement in any future intrigue of this kind. Whether this decision is firm and permanent or reversed later by pleas or threats from his young master is unknown. The papyrus was included by F. H. Sandbach in his Oxford Text of Menander among his fragments by unidentified authors (pp. 336–37), but the lively imagination which it reveals strongly favours its attribution to Menander.

FABULA INCERTA 3

1   ετ[
    χαρ[
    ἐχρ[
    και[
5   δει[
    μετα[
    μὴ και[. . . . . . ἐντ]αῦθ'.

ΔΟΥΛΟΣ

ὅμως δ' α[

   τῶν π[λημμελου]μένων γὰρ ἡμε[ῖς αἴτιοι
   ὑπὸ τ[οῦ τροφίμου, κὸ]ν μειράκιον ἔνθε[ρμον ὂν
10 ἐρῶν [τ'. ἐκεῖνός] μ' εἰς τὸ βάραθρον ἐμβ[αλεῖ,
   πρόφασ[ιν λαβὼν] μικράν. τὸ μὲν τού[τῳ τάδε

Those corrections and supplements whose author is not named were made by the first editors, B. P. Grenfell and A. S. Hunt.

7 ανθ: O.   ἀ[μελητέον Schröder.

8 αἴτιοι suppl. Gronewald, the rest Blass.

9 τ[οῦ suppl. Schröder, τροφίμου Gronewald, the rest Blass.

10 τ' suppl. Gronewald, the rest Sudhaus (ἐμβ[αλ already edd. pr., ἐμβ[αλεῖν Blass).   11 λαβὼν suppl. either Schröder or Sudhaus, τού[τῳ Blass, τάδε Gronewald.

UNIDENTIFIED PLAY 3

(Of the first six lines in this papyrus only the initial two to four letters survive, yielding virtually nothing that can be safely translated: perhaps and *v. 4,* must *5, with* or *after 6. Verse 7 begins with someone saying* Not . . . here *or* there too *(?), to which a slave appears to respond with the following speech. It is uncertain whether he is now alone on stage or addressing one or more other characters.)*

SLAVE

Still, [it must be overlooked! (?)]   7
We're held [responsible] for our [young master's
[Misdeeds], and not the boy, [who's] fired up [and]
In love [as well! He]'ll[1] not [need] much excuse   10
To cook my goose![2] Explain [it] to his father?

---

[1] Presumably the slave's young master.

[2] Literally 'throw me in the pit'. That pit was a cleft of rock in Athens probably on the west side of the Hill of the Nymphs, into which certain types of criminal were thrown for execution. The expression became an imprecatory formula which occurs frequently in comedy. See my commentary on Alexis (Cambridge 1996) p. 467 (on fr. 159.1 Kassel–Austin).

φράσαι γάρ;—ἄπαγε· κρον[ι]κόν, ἀρχαίου τρ[όπου.
ἵνα χ[ρ]ηστὸν εἴπῃ τις; χολή. φιλοδέσπ[οτον;
ἔμετο[ς. τ]ὸ πλουτεῖν ἡδύ, τἄλλα δ᾽ ἐστὶ [— φῦ.
15 ἐκ μὲν ταπεινῶν καὶ παραδόξων η[
     ὑπ]ερβολή τις. ἀλλ᾽ ἐλεύθερόν με δεῖ
     πρ]ῶτον γενέσθαι, καὶ τυχόν, νὴ τ[ὸν Δία,
     τὸ] νῦν με τῶν ἐνταῦθ᾽ ἀμελῆσαι πρα[γμάτων
     ἀρχὴ γένοιτ᾽ ἄν. πεύσεται γὰρ αὐτίκα
20 ἐλθὼν ὁ τρόφιμος πρῶτον, ἡ παῖς π[ῶς ἔχει

12 γάρ; so punctuated by Arnott.
13 So punctuated by Sudhaus.   φιλοδέσπ[οτον suppl.
Lloyd-Jones (-δέσπ[οτος edd.pr.).
14 ἔμετο[ς suppl. Sudhaus, φῦ tentatively Arnott.
15 ἡ[δονῆς edd.pr.
17 Or τ[οὺς θεούς Schröder.
20 Suppl. Austin.

FABULA INCERTA 3

No—that's outdated now, old [hat]! Me win
A name for virtue? Makes me fume! Or loyalty
To master? Makes me puke! Wealth's nice, but all
The rest is—[yuck]! The best [of pleasure] comes   15
From humble, unexpected things. But first
I must secure my freedom, and perhaps
Abandoning these [intrigues] here today
Would be a start. When he arrives, young master
Will hear at once first [how] the girl[3] [is placed (?)] . . .   20

[3] Presumably the young master's girlfriend, who may now perhaps either be pregnant by him or have borne his child.

FABULA INCERTA 4

INTRODUCTION

Manuscript

F = *P.Freiburg* 12, a school exercise written in the second or first century B.C. It includes a collection of literary extracts—these eight trimeters assigned provisionally to Menander and written here as if they were prose, four lines from an unidentified epic poem (J. U. Powell, *Collectanea Alexandrina*, Oxford 1925, p. 281), two lines from the *Certamen Homeri et Hesiodi* (lines 213–214 Allen = p. 41.24–25 Wilamowitz), and Homer, *Iliad* 5.385–91. First edition: W. Aly, *Sitzungsberichte der Heidelberger Akademie der Wissenschaften, Philosophisch-historische Klasse* (1914/2) 7–22 (7–9, 11–14 on the comic extract) and plate I.a+b. The extract is fr. com. adesp. 1027 in Kassel–Austin, *PCG* VIII.

This short passage, a speech[1] made by a loyal slave to a young master worried in all probability by the difficulties of a love affair, was ascribed to New Comedy (possibly Philemon) by its first editor, but Wilamowitz' suggestion[2]

---

[1] So first A. Körte in K. Fuhr's review of Aly, *BPW* (1915) 809.

[2] In *Menander, Das Schiedsgericht* (Berlin 1925) 107 n. 1.

that here we have the opening speech of a play by Menander seems rather more plausible. Wilamowitz drew attention to the very similar speech at the beginning of Plautus' *Pseudolus* addressed by the slave to the lovelorn Calidorus.[3] The attribution to Menander is based partly on the imaginative quality of the writing, but it is reinforced by the fact that Lucian, a notorious plagiariser of other writers' openings,[4] purloins three of its first four lines at the start of his *Juppiter tragoedus* without naming his source; Lucian would have been less likely to do this, and a schoolboy in Ptolemaic Egypt to make his copy, from the work of an inferior New Comedy dramatist.

[3] See also E. Fraenkel, *Kleine Beiträge zur klassischen Philologie*, I (Rome 1964) 489, and D. Bain, *Actors and Audience* (Oxford 1977) 157 n. 3.

[4] See G. Anderson, *BICS* 23 (1976) 59–68.

FABULA INCERTA 4

ΟΙΚΕΤΗΣ

ὦ Ζεῦ, τί σύννους κατὰ μόνας σαυτῷ λαλεῖς,
δοκεῖς τε παρέχειν ἔμφασιν λυπουμένου;
ἐμοὶ προσανάθου· λαβέ με σύμβουλον πόνων·
μὴ καταφρονήσῃς οἰκέτου συμβουλίας.
5 πολλάκις ὁ δοῦλος τοὺς τρόπους χρηστοὺς ἔχων
τῶν δεσποτῶν ἐγένετο σωφρονέστερος.
εἰ δ᾽ ἡ τύχη τὸ σῶμα κατεδουλώσατο,
8 ὅ γε νοῦς ὑπάρχει τοῖς τρόποις ἐλεύθερος.

1, 3 and 4 plagiarised (with some adaptation and no source
named) by Lucian, *Juppiter tragoedus* 1; 1 σὺ δὲ δὴ τί σύννους
quoted (with no source named) by Cicero, *Att.* 13.42.1; 7–8 =
Comparatio Menandri et Philistionis (hereafter *CMP*) II.131–32
Jäkel.

Those corrections and supplements whose author is not
named were made by the ed.pr., W. Aly.

1]ονας—λαλεις F: ὦ Ζεῦ Arnott, and τί σύννους κατὰ
μόνας Fuhr, both from Lucian.   σεαυτω F.

2 τε Wilamowitz: τι F.   λυπουμένου Körte (in Fuhr, *BPW*
1915, 809): λυπουμενωι or -ενω F.

488

UNIDENTIFIED PLAY 4

(At the opening of the play a slave and his young master enter, apparently in mid-conversation.)

SLAVE

God! Why gripe to yourself, alone and ill
At ease? The impression that you give, it seems,
Is one of anguish. Talk to *me*, and take
Me as your trouble-shooter! Don't despise
A servant's counsel. With integrity   5
Slaves can prove wiser than their masters.
If destiny's enslaved their bodies, still
The mind that serves their characters is free.   8

---

3 πόνων om. F, added by Fuhr from Lucian.

4 συμβουλίας Wilamowitz: συμβουλιαν F, φλυαρίας Lucian.

7 ειδη F: ἡ δὲ ms. Q of *CMP*.

8 ογενους F: τὸ γένος *CMP*.   τοιστροποισελευθερος F: τῇ φύσει *CMP*.

FABULA INCERTA 5

INTRODUCTION

Manuscript

H = *P.Hamburg* 656 (= fr. 951 in the second edition, Leipzig 1959, of the Körte–Thierfelder edition of Menander, II pp. 272–78), a papyrus of unknown Egyptian provenance written in the first half of the third century B.C., and thus one of the oldest Greek dramatic papyri known. It contains the remains of 42 trimeters (21 severely, 9 moderately and 12 only slightly mutilated). First edition: B. Snell (with the assistance of A. Thierfelder), *Griechische Papyri der Hamburger Staats- und Universitäts-Bibliothek* (Hamburg 1954) 20–27 with a photograph (pl. 2). It is now fr. com. adesp. 1089 in Kassel–Austin, *PCG* VIII.

This papyrus introduces the reader to four named characters: a young man Moschion (cf. elsewhere in Menander certainly *Kith.*, *Pk.*, *Sam.*, *Sik.*, *Fab.Inc.* 1[1]), his slave Par-

---

[1] The name appears also in several other unattributed or less certainly attributed papyri: *PSI* 1176.4 and *P.Oxy.* 2533.10 (possibly from *Fab.Inc.* 1 and printed in this volume along with it), *P.Antinoopolis* 55 (printed here as *Fab.Inc.* 7), *P.Oxy.* 3218.5 and 10, 3431.42 and 3432.6 (= frr. com. adesp. 1125, 1129 and 1130 K-A respectively).

menon (slave of a Moschion also in *Sam.*; elsewhere in Menander also *Theophoroumene*, *Hypobolimaios* and probably *Plokion* (frs. 373 and 300 K-A), a young woman whose name Dorkion may imply that she was a *hetaira* (cf. Asclepiades' epigram in *Anth.Pal.* 12.161 = 20 Gow–Page, and my commentary on Alexis, Cambridge 1996, p. 177 n. 2),[2] and a female slave named Doris (in Menander also *Encheiridion*, *Pk.* and *Kolax* B.18)[3] who appears to have been played by a mute in the portion of text preserved on this papyrus. Doris' mistress, who is not named in the surviving fragment, also takes part in the dialogue.

In this fragment actions occur which in all probability were of crucial importance for the plot. The unnamed woman, whose status is uncertain—wealthy bawd, retired or still practising *hetaira* are perhaps likelier possibilities than respectable free wife or widow—enters, accompanied by Doris; she offers as a loan or gift to Moschion some valuable clothes and jewelry which Moschion can then pawn for ten minas (vv. 5, 13). That sum is to be paid to the *hetaira* Dorkion, whose connection with the unnamed woman is unknown; Dorkion presumably is intended to use it either as a final payment to secure her freedom or as recompense to a client with whom she formerly had a con-

---

[2] Its Latinised form Dorcium is the name of the slave Geta's partner in Terence's *Heauton Timorumenos* 252, adapted from Menander's homonym, and of a girl of uncertain status in fr. XVI of Turpilius' *Leucadia*, adapted from Menander's *Leukadia* (see the Loeb Menander II pp. 223-24).

[3] Doris appears additionally in two unattributed comic papyri, *P.Oxy.* 2658.25, 44 and 3971.4 (= frr. com. adesp. 1103 and 1144 K-A respectively).

tract that she now wishes to repudiate.[4] Eventually the unnamed woman and Doris go off into Dorkion's house followed by Moschion, leaving Parmenon alone on stage to deliver a long monologue whose content is now uncertain because of severe mutilation.

It can be presumed that Moschion is in love with Dorkion and desires her undivided affection, but the legal and social intentions of this pair are unclear. If Dorkion is a native of Moschion's city and either is free or can be freed, Moschion may intend to marry her; if she comes from elsewhere or wishes to retain her independent status as a *hetaira*, Moschion may desire to have her as a lifelong partner or a fixed-term mistress. Moschion's father may favour or oppose his son's wishes. The action in the papyrus fragment seems to come from a later stage in the play when the knots are being unravelled, but we are in no position to guess what came before this action or what followed it; it is not even certain that Moschion's love affair had a happy ending. It has been suspected that the jewelry or clothes brought out by the unnamed woman and Doris may have contained a token or tokens which led to Dorkion's recognition as that woman's or some friend's daughter; in that event the mother would presumably have been raped, borne an illegitimate daughter and exposed her with the tokens. Yet such speculations are unverifiable and may be

[4] The figure of 10 minas is important here. It is not high enough to secure an attractive young female slave her freedom, at any rate within the confines of ancient comedy (20 minas are required in Plaut. *Pseud.* 51, 30 minas in *Rud.* 45, 40 minas in *Epid.* 52 and *Curc.* 343; in the last passage 10 minas is the figure given for the slave's clothes and jewelry alone.

misleading; it is perhaps more important to note that gifts of clothes and jewelry were normally added to a free girl's dowry by the bridegroom's family,[5] while similar presents were made to concubines and *hetairai* by their lovers.[6]

Several attempts have been made to identify the play from which this papyrus derives. Its first editor (p. 24) suggested Menander's Κεκρύφαλος (*The Hair Net*), since a variant wording of the proverb ἀπὸ μηχανῆς θεὸς ἐπεφάνης ('You've turned up like a god upon a crane') appears in v. 12 of the papyrus and is attested by a scholiast on Plato (*Clitopho* 407a.2, p. 187 Greene) for both *Kekryphalos* and *Theophoroumene* (fr. 5: Loeb II, pp. 74–77), while the badly mutilated last line of the papyrus (v. 42 παρὰ το[or τη[) could be the opening of fr. 208 K-A from that play. Snell's suggestion has its attractions and supporters, but the wording of the proverb in v. 12 of the papyrus does not correspond exactly to that given by the scholiast, while the matching of only two nondescript words at the beginning of v. 42 is not enough to add weight to the argument.

No more convincing are two later suggestions. L. A. Post (*AJP* 77, 1962, 215) tentatively mentioned Menan-

---

[5] In fourth-century Athens such gifts to the precise value of 10 minas are attested in Dem. 41.27 and (with the addition of furniture and cups) 27.10. Although these gifts were morally regarded as belonging to the wife, it is uncertain whether she could legally dispose of them without her husband's permission. See A. R. W. Harrison, *The Law of Athens*, I (Oxford 1968) 112–14.

[6] Cf. e.g. Men. *Misoumenos* 39–40 Arnott = A39–40 Sandbach, *Samia* 381–82, Plautus *Curculio* 488, *Miles Gloriosus* 980–83.

der's *Heauton Timoroumenos* because the situation in the papyrus is similar to that invented by Syrus at the end of Act III of Terence's adaptation of Menander's play, while the figure of 1000 drachmas given there (vv. 601, 606) for the girl's purchase matches that mentioned in the papyrus. True: but Syrus is here devising a confidence trick, and there is no suggestion of any such trick in the papyrus fragment. Konrad Gaiser (*Menanders 'Hydria': Abhandlung Heidelberg, Philosophisch-historische Klasse*, 1977/1, 454–61) proposed Menander's *Leukadia*, because a girl named Dorcium (the Latin version of Δορκίον) appears in Turpilius' adaptation of that play (fr. XVI), while four known Menandrean and Turpilian characters (Dorcium, a mature woman (sc. the priestess), a young man in love and his slave) can be made to tie in with personnel in the papyrus. The matches, however, are too flimsy either to support or to oppose Gaiser's suggestion.

Even so, there is nothing in the metre or diction of the Hamburg lines that is unmenandrean, while the writing has a liveliness, wit[7] and imagination not unworthy of that dramatist, even if the staging of the exits in vv. 15–21 seems rather pedestrian.[8] Although a papyrus in Egypt at this early date could have contained work by other late fourth-century or early third-century dramatists, it seems to me more likely than not that this Hamburg fragment derives from Menander.

---

[7] Cf. vv. 12–14, with their amusing contrast between divine and human capabilities.

[8] Cf. the Gomme–Sandbach *Commentary*, p. 738.

FABULA INCERTA 5

(SCENE: unknown, perhaps Athens. A street probably, backed by two houses. In one Dorkion apparently lives, with Moschion having some right of access. The other house may—or may not—be where Moschion lives.)

ΠΑΡΜΕΝΩΝ

]υνα[.].α Μοσχίων, ἰδού.

(ΜΟΣΧΙΩΝ?)

[?]

ΓΥΝΗ

[?]ταῦθ' ἱμάτια καὶ χρυσία

]νων ἔχω· νῦν Δορκίῳ

Those corrections and supplements whose author is not named were made by the ed.pr., B. Snell.

1 Either]υν, ἀ[λ]λά, (Snell) or γ]υνα[ῖ]κα (Paoli).   At line end a dicolon, followed by XNX (most probably a coded abbreviation announcing the unnamed woman's entry at this point and/or identifying her. There is, however, no exact parallel in extant dramatic papyri, and the code remains uncracked).

2 Either ταῦθ' or ἐν]ταῦθ'.

UNIDENTIFIED PLAY 5

*(The first eight lines of this papyrus fragment are mutilated
and impossible to supplement with any confidence, but it
opens apparently with young Moschion and his slave
Parmenon in conversation.)*

PARMENON
] Moschion, [the] woman (?)—look!   1

*(Parmenon's remark appears to have been inspired by the
entry of an unnamed woman, probably by one of the side
entrances. She is accompanied by Doris, her female slave,
carrying a quantity of clothes and jewelry.[1])*

MOSCHION
(moving into the background)
[   ]

WOMAN
(addressing Moschion and Parmenon jointly)
        These [are (?)] clothes and jewelry;
[All, Parme]non (?), belong to me. [They are (?)] for
    Dorkion

---

[1] On these clothes and jewelry see the introduction to this
fragment.

MENANDER

τ]αῦτα θέντες ἐνέχυρα
5   ] δύνησθε δραχμὰς χιλίας
     ]

ΠΑΡΜΕΝΩΝ
Ἡράκλεις.

ΓΥΝΗ
                    ἀποδώσετε,
ὅταν τύχῃ] τε, ταῦτά μοι, καλῶς τ᾿ ἔχῃ.
ἐὰν δὲ τοῦτο] μὴ δύνῃ, συμβάλλομαι
εἰς τὴν ἐκεί]νης ταῦτ᾿ ἐγὼ σωτηρίαν.

ΠΑΡΜΕΝΩΝ
10 νὴ τὸν] Δία τὸν Σωτῆρα, γενναία τε [κ]αὶ
γλυκεῖ]α—τί γὰρ ἂν ἄλλο τις λέγειν ἔχοι;—
ἀπὸ μη]χανῆς τις τῶν θεῶν σοι, Παρμένων,
μνᾶς δ]έκα δέδωκεν, ὥσπερ ἐν τραγῳδίᾳ.
ἀνθρώ]πινον τὸ λοιπὸν ἤδη γίνεται.

4 [λαβὼν ἔνεγκε] suppl. Sandbach.
6 Ἡράκλεις given to Parmenon by Gaiser: dicolon after it
in H.
7 Suppl. Gronewald.
8, 9 Suppl. Thierfelder (εἰς τὴν Snell).
10 νὴ τὸν] suppl. Thierfelder apparently, τε [κ]αὶ deciph. and
suppl. Arnott (γε [κ]αὶ already Gronewald).
11 Suppl. Arnott.
14 Suppl. Thierfelder.

Now [   ] pawning them,
[To raise] a thousand drachmas, possibly.   5
[   ].

PARMENON

My god!

WOMAN

You'll let me have
Them back [one of these days], if all goes well.
[But if] you can't [do that], they're my donation
[Towards] achieving [her] security.[2]

PARMENON

By] Zeus our Saviour, O you noble and   10
[Sweet (?)] lady—for what else could any man
Say? Parmenon, a god [upon] a crane,
Just like in tragedy,[3] has given you
Ten [minas]![4] Now the rest can be performed
[By humans]!

---

[2] It is uncertain whether the 1000 drachmas likely to be received from pawning the clothes and jewelry were to be used by Dorkion as a final payment of the sum owed to gain her freedom (if she was a slave) or to withdraw from a contract tying her (if she was a practising hetaira) to a lover other than Moschion. See the introduction.

[3] See *Theophoroumene* fr. 5 (the Loeb Menander II, pp. 74–77). The appearance here of this reference to tragedy's 'god upon a crane' has led to the tentative assignment of this Hamburg papyrus to Menander's *Kekryphalos:* see the introduction.

[4] Ten minas = 1000 drachmas. Cf. note 2 above.

MENANDER

ΓΥΝΗ

15 εἴσω β]αδίζω δεῦρο πρὸς τὴν Δορκίον·
    αὐτὴ π]ρὸς αὐτὴν συνεθέμην γὰρ ἀρτίως.

ΠΑΡΜΕΝΩΝ

καὶ ταῦ]τα μετὰ σαυτῆς γε πάντ᾽ εἴσω φέρε.

ΓΥΝΗ

καὶ μὴν] ἀγαθῇ τύχῃ γ᾽· ἀκολούθει, Δωρί, μοι.

ΜΟΣΧΙΩΝ

ἀλλ᾽ αὐτ]ὸς αὐτὴν βούλομ᾽ εἰσελθὼν ἰδεῖν,
20 ὦ Παρμ]ένων.

ΠΑΡΜΕΝΩΝ

    εἴσελθε καὶ θαρρεῖν λέγε
αὐτῇ, παραμύθησαί τε.

ΜΟΣΧΙΩΝ

    τοῦτο β[ού]λομα[ι.

15, 16 εἴσω and αὐτὴ suppl. Thierfelder.
16 συνεθεμηγγαρ H.
17 καὶ suppl. Thierfelder.
18 Suppl. Arnott.   Punctuation after γ᾽ by Gomme.
19 αυτημβουλομ H.
20, 21 Dicola after]ενων and τε.
21 β[ού]λομα[ι deciph. and suppl. Fleischer.

500

WOMAN

(addressing Parmenon, and pointing to Dorkion's house)
I'll now visit Dorkion   15
In there. I came to terms with her just now.[5]

PARMENON

[And] take all that you've brought inside with you!

WOMAN

Yes, [and] good luck! Now, Doris, follow me.

*(The woman goes off into Dorkion's house. Doris follows
her inside, carrying the clothes and jewelry. After their
departure Moschion steps forward.)*

MOSCHION

[And] I should like to go inside and see
Her, [Parm]enon.

PARMENON

Go in and tell [her] to   20
Cheer up, be nice to her.

MOSCHION

That's my intention.   21

*(Moschion now follows the other two women into Dork-
ion's house, leaving Parmenon alone on the stage, where
apparently he delivers a monologue of at least 21 lines. Un-
fortunately only the opening words of each line have been*

---

[5] A reference presumably to some action earlier in the play.

MENANDER

ΠΑΡΜΕΝΩΝ

22 εἰέν· τί .[
    κατὰ λό[γον
    ἀργύρι[ον
25 τῶν αλ[
    δι᾽ ὃ γὰρ .[
    οὐκ ἔστ[
    πρόφασι[
    καὶ πισ[τ
30 ὁ λέγων [
    φίλοι δε[
    εὖ πρασ[
33 οἱ πατέ[ρες

34 τὰ τῆς π[
35 οὐκ ἔστ[
    καὐτὸς [
    τί οὖν α[
    οἴμοι· δ[
    ἦ φα.[
40 ἀποδρα[
    πα[.]ακ[
42 παρατ.[*

22 τιμ[or τιν[H.
26 γαρπ[or γαρν[H.
39 φαμ[or φαν[H.
42 τη[or το[H.

* On the tentative linkage of these letters with the beginning of Menander fr. 208 K-A from the *Kekryphalos* see the introduction to this play.

502

preserved: 22 Well then, what, 23 Reasonably, 24 Money, 25 Of the [remainder (?)], 26 For why (?), 27 Is not, 28 Excuse, 29 And faithful, 30 The man who says, 31 Friends, 32 Do[ing] *or* Far[ing] well (?), 33 The fathers, 34 The . . . of the, 35 Is not, 36 And I myself *or* You yourself *or* He himself, 37 So what *or* why, 38 Oh dear, 39 By which (?), 40 [I'll (?)] run off, 42 From *or* With the. *These pitiful remains seem to indicate that Parmenon may have been reflecting on the futures of Dorkion (v.24) and Moschion and their families (33), as well as on his own (38, 40) if things go wrong.)*

FABULA INCERTA 6

INTRODUCTION

Manuscript(s)

Ant.15 = *P.Antinoopolis* 15, a mutilated and abraded page from a codex of the fourth century A.D. One side originally contained the author's name, play title, cast list and the opening lines of the play, the other side apparently a continuation of the opening scene; an unknown number of lines has been torn off the lower part of the page. First edition: C. H. Roberts (with help from several Oxford colleagues), *The Antinoopolis Papyri* I (London 1950) 30–35 with a photograph (pl. I) of the opening side. It was republished by J. W. B. Barns and H. Lloyd-Jones, *JHS* 84 (1964) 21–31 (= Sir Hugh Lloyd-Jones, *Collected Papers: Greek Comedy, Hellenistic Literature, Greek Religion, and Miscellanea,* Oxford 1990, 94–114) with ultra-violet photographs of both sides (*JHS* pl. I), and is now numbered fr. adesp. 1084 in Kassel–Austin, *PCG* VII.

Three other papyri have been attributed to the same play as Ant.15. Two of them are:

(i) *P.Berlin* 13982 (alternatively styled *P.Schubart* 23), hereafter designated B.1. It comes from a codex of the third century A.D., written in a hand similar to, but not identical with, that of Ant.15; one side contains the ends of 18 lines, the other the beginnings of 18 lines. Its attribution to the same play as Ant.15 rests partly on the similarity of the handwriting, but more on an address to a character named Kantharos in v. 1 of B.1; this name appears in the cast list of Ant.15, but nowhere else in what remains of Menander or New Comedy. Additionally, a female servant occurs in Ant.15's cast list while a nurse is mentioned in B.1 (vv. 13, 15). The argument linking Ant.15 and B.1 to the same play is neither compelling nor implausible. First edition: W. Schubart, *Griechische literarische Papyri = Berichte der Sächsischen Akademie der Wissenschaften zu Leipzig, Philologisch-historische Klasse*, 97/5 (1950) 50–53. It too was republished by Barns and Lloyd-Jones, *JHS* 84 (1964) 31–33 (= Lloyd-Jones, *Collected Papers*, 110–13), with an improved text based on a photograph (printed in *JHS* as pl. II); when the first edition was published, Schubart had no access to either papyrus or photograph. It is now numbered fr. adesp. 1085 in Kassel–Austin, *PCG* VIII.

(ii) *P.Berlin* 21184, hereafter designated B.2. This scrap of papyrus from Hermopolis, written in the third or fourth century A.D., contains on one side the beginnings of 9 lines, on the other the ends of 7. It was tentatively assigned to the play from which Ant.15 and B.1 allegedly derive because of H. Maehler's claim that the handwriting of B.2 is 'somewhat similar' to that of Ant.15 and B.1. Nothing in the content of B.2 links it to either Ant.15 or B.1, and it is difficult to assess the strength of Maehler's claim without publication of a photograph of B.2. First edition: C. Austin (with the help of H. Maehler), *Comicorum graecorum*

fragmenta in papyris reperta (Berlin 1973) no. 368 p. 368.
It is now numbered fr. adesp. 1122 in Kassel–Austin, *PCG*
VIII.

Both of these papyri are published here. The third,
P.Antinoopolis 16, is not; dated to the late third or early
fourth century A.D. and containing the beginnings of 14
and the ends of 13 iambic trimeters, it was first published
by Roberts, *The Antinoopolis Papyri* I 35–36 and repub-
lished by Barns and Lloyd-Jones, *JHS* 84 (1964) 33–34
(= Lloyd-Jones, *Collected Papers*, 113–14). W. Morel
(*Philologus* 107, 1963, 151) noted that the scrap had a line
starting with κανθαρ[(2), assumed that this was the name
Kanthar[os], and concluded that this fragment too be-
longed, along with Ant.15 and B.1, to one and the same
play. However, we do not know whether κανθαρ[in
P.Antinoopolis 16 is part of a proper name or simply means
'wine-cup,' but we can be certain that this scrap does not
come from a New Comedy play; its mixture of (para)tragic
language (vv. 8, 9, 16, 19), divine and satyric names (vv. 3,
5, 6), and comic rhythms and scansion (vv. 17, 20, 23) indi-
cates that its origin is most probably a satyr play, or a myth
travesty in all probability dating thirty years or more be-
fore the period of Menander.

In the heading to the play preserved in Ant.15 the
scribe wrote its title and the name of the author, but both
are now badly abraded; only]ε.[..].ρο. [   ]..ς can be read
with any confidence. The author's name is more likely to
have been Μενάνδρου (Menander's) than that of any other
comedian—the readable traces seem consistent with this,
although not enough ink remains for a totally positive

identification—and there is nothing in the style and language of Ant.15's text that conflicts with, but much that suggests, Menandrean authorship. Too little of the play's title, however, is preserved on the papyrus for any confident supplementation. All that can be made out in the photograph published by Barns and Lloyd-Jones is the top of a final sigma; in front of that, with the papyrus itself before him, Barns tentatively deciphered το, but there is no sign in the photograph of a tau's crossbar, and this absence decreases the plausibility of C. Austin's suggestion[1] that the intended title was Ἄπιστος (An Untrustworthy Person), the one preserved Menandrean title ending in -τος; there is no reference to anyone untrustworthy in Ant.15's text, scanty though that is, and in any case Menander's *Apistos* seems more likely to have been the Greek original of Plautus' *Aulularia*. Two other attempts to identify Ant.15's title have been made: Θησαυρός (Treasure)[2] and Δακτύλιος (The Ring).[3] The latter seems more promising; the opening scenes of Menander's plays at times have the play's title, or words associated with it, unobtrusively inserted into the text (*Aspis* 16, *Dyskolos* 7, *Samia* 21, cf. *Misoumenos* 43 Arnott = A43 Sandbach, *Sikyonioi* 13).[4] In Ant.15's opening scene we find ὁ δακτύλιος mentioned at v. 27.

[1] *CR* 17 (1967) 134.

[2] A. Seeberg, *Classica et Mediaevalia* 31 (1970) 221–22.

[3] T. B. L. Webster, *Classica et Mediaevalia, Dissertatio IX, Francisco Blatt dedicata* (1973) 138–39. See also Anna Bandini, *Ann. Fac. Lett. Siena* 5 (1984) 158–59.

[4] Cf. W. G. Arnott, *Drama* 2 (1993) 29.

This play's opening engages its audience with features both striking and puzzling. A young man emerges from one of the stage houses, probably followed by a female servant carrying a sizable container and trying in vain to attract his attention. He turns away to face the audience, informing them that it is night, and that he has now been married for more than four months, during which time he has been faithful to his wife and they have come to love each other. He married at his father's bidding, but presumably at the time of the wedding the young man was not in love with the bride.

Eventually the servant induces the young man to open the container, which has inside it recognition tokens that include half a moth-eaten old cloak. Presumably these objects had been placed there by a girl who had been violated before marriage by a drunken male and snatched the cloak from him at the time of the rape. The girl had as a result become pregnant and caused her offspring at birth to be exposed along with the tokens. Two important details here have been shrewdly appraised by A. Seeberg.[5] If the cloak was old and moth-eaten,[6] the rape could not have been recent or involved the opening scene's young husband or his wife; it was most probably committed a generation ago by a

[5] *Classica et Mediaevalia* 31 (1970) 218–19.

[6] Seeberg notes also that papyrus B.1 appears to mention a sword (v. 9) that cannot be drawn from its sheath (21–22) because of rust (20) apparently; if B.1 does derive from the same play as Ant.15, the rusty sword may be a further memento of that rape long ago. Combination of sheathed sword and cloak would imply that the raper had at the time been either a soldier or perhaps an ephebe serving in the cavalry.

now elderly man on a woman old enough to be the young man's mother. In fact one possible interpretation of vv. 19–22 would make the young man's mother the victim. Secondly, only half a cloak is present in the container. Might the pregnancy perhaps have produced twins, with the babies exposed separately, each with half of the cloak?

The young man on stage, however, has more immediate problems on his mind that make him postpone further investigation of the items in the container. These problems clearly concern his marriage, but the lines preserved in Ant.15 do not identify what these problems were. Menander here, like Aristophanes often long before him, has chosen to open his play with a striking and puzzling mime that he does not immediately explain. He would have unravelled all the mysteries later in the play, but experience has taught us that Menander's solutions are usually more ingenious and effective than modern scholarship has been able to conjure up. It is accordingly more sensible here to admire the puzzle than to attempt its resolution.

Along with the play's title and author, Ant.15 originally contained a list of the play's ten characters, almost certainly presented in the order of their first appearance. Unfortunately no trace of the first two now survives, hardly any of the third, and only part of the fifth. This means that we do not know the name of the young man who enters at the beginning of the play, while it remains uncertain whether the slave who follows him onto the stage is the unnamed θεράπαινα (female servant) postponed to the end of the list because she was not given a proper name, or was listed separately as the second entry. Both are possible; in the margin of the text at v. 16 the slave speaking there seems to be identified in the margin as].ρ, which can be supplemented either as θ]ερ⟨άπαινα⟩ or as Σ]ύρ⟨α⟩. Syra would be an appropriate name for an elderly female slave; we may compare Menander *Misoumenos* 555 Arnott, Philemon fr. 117 K-A, Plautus *Mercator* and *Truculentus*.[7]

[7] Further discussion of matters dealt with in this introduction, along with some textual questions in *P.Ant.* 15, are to be found in *ZPE* 125 (1999) 61–64.

FABULA INCERTA 6

Ant.15

a $ξα$

b   .]ε.[..].ρο.   Λύσιππος
c   ]..ϲ   Κάνθαρος
d   ]..[Γοργίας
e   Κρατῖνος   Φιλῖνος
f   ].α   ...   θεράπαινα
g

In the apparatus those corrections and supplements whose
author is not named were made by the ed.pr., C. H. Roberts.

Line b M]εν[άν]δρου Roberts.

c The missing name in the left-hand column was perhaps
Σύρα: see below on v. 16.

e Κρατῖνος deciphered by Barns.

f B]ία suppl. Webster.

On this portion of the heading see the introduction to this
play.

See also the introduction.

512

UNIDENTIFIED PLAY 6

Papyrus Ant.15

(*SCENE: Unknown, but probably a street somewhere in Attica, with two houses belonging to characters in the play.*)

(*Papyrus Ant.15 numbers its first page as 61, gives the author's name and play title (? [M]en[ander]'s [   ]s:[1]), and lists the characters, probably in the order of their first entrances. Only six of them can now be read clearly:*

Kratinos (*an elderly man in Terence's Phormio 348ff., of uncertain age in Plautus' Asinaria 866, Ter. Adelphoe 581*)
Lysippos (*unknown elsewhere as a comic character*)
Kantharos (*elsewhere only in B.1, see below: the name suggests a drunkard and would suit best a soldier or a parasite*)
Gorgias (*a young farmer in Men. Georgos and Dyskolos, young shepherd in Heros 25–27*)
Philinos (*elderly man in Men. Pk. 1076, of uncertain age in Apollodorus fr. 7, Strato fr. 1.13 and fr. adesp. 821.2 K-A*)
Female Slave[2]

A prologue divinity, who would have entered after one or

513

ΝΕΑΝΙΑΣ

δεινότ[ερ]ά τις πέπονθε τῶν ἐν τῇ πόλει
ἐμοῦ; μ[ὰ] τὴν Δήμητρα καὶ τὸν Οὐρανόν.
πεμπτ[ὸ]ν γεγάμηκα μῆνα, πεισθεὶς τῷ πατρί.
ἀφ' ἧς γ[εγά]μηκα νυκτός—ὦ δέσποινα Νύξ,

5 σὲ μά[ρτυρ' ὀ]ρθὴν ἐπάγομ' οὗ λέγω λόγου—
μί[αν οὐ γε]γένημαι νύκτ' ἀπόκοιτ[ο]ς πώποτ[ε
ἀπὸ τῆ[ς γυναι]κός, ὅσιον ἦν ἔχειν ‹μ'› ἔδε[ι·
οὔποτ[ε πονηρ]ὸς γέγονα, κοὐκ ...[
μετὰ τοὺς γάμους [

10 δίκαιον ἤρων· καὶ οτ..[...].[..]εται..[
αὐτῆς ἐλευθέρῳ γὰρ ἤθει καὶ βίῳ
δεθεὶς ἀπλάστῳ τὴν φ[ι]λοῦσαν ἠγάπ[ων.
τί προσφέρεις μοι δει[κ]νύουσα καθ' ἓν [
ἅπαντ', [ἐπεὶ τὴν κ]αρδίαν ἀλγῶ γ' ὁρ[ῶν;

15 τιθε.[   ].... οὗ καὶ νῦν [

1 τις Morel (correcting Roberts' τίς).   2 μ[.]τον Ant.15
with correcting η written above the o.   3 πεισθεισπατρι
Ant.15 with omitted τωι written above πατ.   5 ὀ]ρθὴν suppl.
Pfeiffer.   7 Corr. Arnott: ὅσον or ὅτον or ὅγον Ant.15 with
one or two letters written above the second letter.

8 πονηρ]ὸς suppl. Arnott *exempli gratia*.   γέγονα or
γέγονε Ant.15.   8–10 E.g. κοὐκ ἔρω[τ' ἐγὼ] / μετὰ τοὺς
γάμους [ἀνόσιον ἐνθάδ', ἀλλ' ἀεὶ] / δίκαιον ἤρων suppl. Ar-
nott.   13 δι[.]νουσα Ant.15.   14 [ἐπεὶ] suppl. Lloyd-
Jones.   15 οὖν Ant.15 with ν deleted.

more opening scenes, may also be listed, perhaps [Vio-
lence]. *The names of the two characters who appeared at
the beginning of the play have not been preserved in the
cast list.*)

(*The papyrus contains the play's opening lines. It is night.
A young man enters from one of the stage houses, followed
by a female slave (perhaps named Syra) carrying a lamp
and a container. She tries, at first in vain, to engage his at-
tention. He instead turns to face and address the audience.*)

YOUNG MAN

Has anyone been treated in this town
[More] terribly than me? I swear there's none!
Four months now I've been married, at my father's
Wish. Lady Night, I call on you to bear
True [witness] of my claim—I've never once   5
Slept elsewhere since my wedding night, away
From my own [wife], whom I was bound in honour
To cherish. Never have I [failed her], since
My wedding [I've] not [misbehaved here, she]
[Was always my] true love, and [10
For, charmed by her frank disposition and
Her artless ways, [I] liked her, and she me.

(*At this point the female slave succeeds in gaining the
young man's attention. She places the container in front of
him, and shows him a ring and some small objects that she
is holding.*)

Why must you bring and show me one by one [
All these, [when my] heart's sore and grieves to see
Them? Put [   ], which even now [15

515

MENANDER

ΣΤΡΑ (?)

ἵν᾽ ᾖ [   ] πρὶν [
αλ.[
18 .[

(Between vv. 18 and 19 there is a lacuna of probably
between 12 and 17 lines.)

ξ[β]

NEANIAΣ

19 [ἐμ]ῆς γυναι[κὸς

ΣΤΡΑ (?)

[

20 [τῆς μ]ητρὸς .[   ]ιδε τῇ γυ[ναικί σου
    ἔδωκε· καὶ δι[   ]βεβλητ[
    ὁ δακτύλιος [....] ἐκείνης· ου.[

NEANIAΣ

ἄνοιξον, εἴ τι καὶ φυλάττει χρήσιμο[ν
ἵν᾽ ἴδωμεν.

ΣΤΡΑ (?)

    αἴ.

16].ρ in left margin of Ant.15 to identify new speaker:
Σ]ύρ‹α› suppl. Arnott, θ]ερ‹άπαινα› Barns and Lloyd-Jones
(see the introduction to this play). Possibly a paragraphus under
this line in Ant.15.   Above v. 19 ξ[β] suppl. Lloyd-Jones.
19 [ἐμ]ῆς suppl. Mette.
20 γυ[ναικί suppl. Lloyd-Jones, σου Mette.
22, 24, 26 Paragraphi under these lines in Ant.15.

516

FABULA INCERTA 6

SLAVE
In order that it (?) may [   ] before [

*(Nothing intelligible can be read in vv.17–18, and after
that there is a shortish gap in which the slave woman must
have succeeding in persuading the man to look at the ob-
jects she is holding and to examine the container. When the
text resumes at the top of the next page in the papyrus
(numbered 62 by the scribe at its head), one of those ob-
jects, a ring, is being discussed, although the text at first is
too mutilated for secure interpretation.)*

YOUNG MAN
(in mid speech)
Of [my] own wife.

SLAVE
[19
Of [your] own mother [   ], but if (?) she gave them to   20
[Your wife], and [   ] the ring
Belonged to her (?) [   ] thrown—don't [you see? (?)]

YOUNG MAN
Just open it, in case it's got inside
Something that helps, let's see!

SLAVE
*(opening the container and taking out a tattered piece of
clothing)*

Oh!

---

23 φυλάττει (with omitted ε written above the second τ) deci-
phered by Rea.

ΝΕΑΝΙΑΣ

τί ἐστι;

ΣΤΡΑ (?)

χλαμύδο[ς] ἥμισυ
25 διεσπαραγμένης παλαιᾶς, ὑπὸ [σέ]ων
σχεδόν τι καταβεβρωμ[έν]ης.

ΝΕΑΝΙΑΣ

ἄ[λ]λ᾽ οὐδὲ ἔν;

ΣΤΡΑ (?)

καὶ περιδέραια καὶ περισκελὶς [μ]ία.

ΝΕΑΝΙΑΣ

ἐμοὶ προσένεγκε, τὸν λύχνον τε φ[αῖν᾽] ἅμα.
29 οὐκ εἶδες ἐπιγεγραμμέν᾽ α[ὐτοῦ ζῷ]δια;
ὠή,
30 ἄνοιγ᾽ ἄνωθεν.

ΣΤΡΑ (?)

γρά[μματ᾽ ἐστίν, ὦ] τάλαν,
τ]άδε, γράμματ᾽ εἶδον.

ΝΕΑΝΙΑΣ

τί [ποτε ταῦτα] βούλεται;
...........] ἔνεστ᾽ ἐν αὐτῷ παιδίου

24 ἥμισυ deciphered by Lloyd-Jones, ημισης by Barns.
25 διασπαραγμενης Ant.15.
26 ἄ[λ]λ᾽ suppl. Woodward.
27 Paragraphus under this line in Ant.15.   [μ]ία suppl.
Barns.

FABULA INCERTA 6

YOUNG MAN

What is that?

SLAVE

Half of a torn old cloak, that's eaten up   25
By [moths], almost completely.

YOUNG MAN

Nothing else?

SLAVE

Some necklaces too, and a single anklet.

YOUNG MAN

Bring them to me, and [shine] the lamp as well.
Didn't you see [there toy animals] inscribed?
Oh! Open it on top!

SLAVE

(obeying the orders

Dear me, these are   30
Letters, I saw them—letters.

YOUNG MAN

(examining further the contents)

What can [they] mean?
[   ] Inside there are a baby's

---

28 προσενεγκελυχνον Ant.15 with the omitted τον written
above κελ.   φ[αῖν]' suppl. Lloyd-Jones.   ἅμα deciphered
by Barns.   29 ιδες Ant.15.   α[ὑτοῦ ζῴ]δια suppl. Lloyd-
Jones.   30 Paragraphus under the line and dicolon after
ανωθεν in Ant.15.   [ἐστίν, ὦ] suppl. Mette.

31 [τ]άδε suppl. and deciphered by Barns.   Dicolon after
ειδον in Ant.15.   ποτε suppl. Roberts, ταῦτα Mette.

519

γ]νωρί[σμαθ', ἡ] μήτηρ δ' ἐτήρει ταῦτα. θὲς
πάλιν ὡς ἔκειτο, σημανοῦμαι δ' αὖτ' ἐγώ.
35 ο]ὐ νῦν ἐπιτηδείως ἔχει, μὰ τὸν Δία,
ζ]ητεῖν ἄφαντ'. οὐχ ἡμέτερον. τὴν ἐμποδὼν
τα]ραχὴν ἱκανῶς θεῖμεν ποτ'. ἂν ἐντός ποτε
γέ]νωμ' ἐμαυτοῦ κ[   ].ξω πάλιν
...]ητεσ.[ο]ὐδὲ ἕν
40   ]σῇ[
41   ]..[

Two Papyri Possibly Deriving from
the Same Play as Ant.15

(1) B.1

recto

            ]μ....., Κάνθαρε·
            ].δ'[...]ικ.μα·
            ]..κ ἔχω δέ πῶς;
            ]..[..].αν λάβῃς
5   ].[.].. καταλιπὼν
            ].. γὰρ τῷ λαβεῖν
        ] θορυβούμενος:
        ] χρόνον
            ].θὲν τοῦτο ξίφος
10   ]πεῖν δέ σε
            ].ῆσιν· κατέλιπον·
            ].θ' ἄρρενα
            ]δον τὴν τρόφον

FABULA INCERTA 6

Keepsake[s, its] mother kept them. Put them back,
Just as they were. I'll seal them up again.
I say it's not appropriate now to try   35
To dig up secrets—not our job. The turmoil
That faces us will be enough, let's hope!
If I keep calm [   ] I'll [open it (?)] again
                                    ] nothing
                    ] your [40

Papyrus B.1

*(This papyrus, conjecturally assigned to the same play as
Ant.15, contains on one side the ends of 18 lines, on the
other the beginnings of 18 more, but it is uncertain (i)
which side came first in the play, and (ii) how many lines
(but probably between 15 and 35) intervened between the
two sides. On the side containing line endings (the recto)
the following words and phrases can be made out: 1 an ad-
dress to Kantharos, 3 but I don't know (?) how (or where),
4 if (?) you take, 5 some male having left, 6 in or by taking,
7 some man being disturbed (followed by a change of
speaker), 8 time, 9 this a sword, 10 but you to say (?), 11 I or
they left behind, 12 male, 13 the nurse inside (?), 14 a male*

---

33 Suppl. Maas.   36 αφανθ.αιμετερον Ant.15 with ..χ
written above αι.   37 θεῖμεν ποτ' deciphered by Barns.

38 Suppl. Maas.   3 B.1 adds που in the right margin as a
correction of or alternative reading to πῶς.

4 λαβης B.1 with ε written above the η.

5].ν or].ν B.1.   6 Above the α of λαβειν B.2 has either an
acute accent or λ.   10 καταλι]πεῖν suppl. Snell (cf. vv.5, 11).

12 θἄρρενα B.1.   13 ? ἔν]δον.

521

] ἠδικηκότα
15   ]ης τρόφου·
τα]ράττομαι:
] Δία
18   ] παιδίων

verso

ΘΕΡΑΠΩΝ or ΘΕΡΑΠΑΙΝΑ (first speaker)

19 ὃ μὲν ἐδεδοίκεις τι[
20 ἀπὸ τοῦ γὰρ ἰοῦ: το.[
$\overline{\text{ἕλκυσον· ἵν᾽ εἰδῇ[}}$
$\overline{\text{οὐχ ἕλκετ᾽ ὄντως [}}$
$\overline{\text{νεόπλουτος.: ω.[}}$
$\overline{\text{αὐτὴ πόθεν λαβ[οῦσα}}$
25 $\overline{\text{σὸν δ᾽ ἐστὶ τοῦτο .[}}$
$\overline{\text{εἰ τοῦ πριαμέ[νου}}$
$\overline{\text{κεκτημέν.[}}$
$\overline{\text{ἄνω ῥέουσι.: κα[}}$
ὁ τοὐμὸν εὑ[ρὼν

17 Or]δια.   19 θεραπ· added in B.1's left margin to indicate speaker.   μενδεδοικεις B.1 with omitted ε added above νδ.   21 ινιδη[B.1 with omitted ε added above νι.   εἰδῇ[ς suppl. Schubart.   24 Or αὕτη.   λαβ[οῦσα suppl. Kassel–Austin.   26 Suppl. Schubart.

29 Words so divided by Austin, εὑ[ρὼν suppl. Webster.

3 See especially D. L. Page's commentary on Euripides' *Medea* 410 and C. Collard's on *Supplices* 520b–521.

having wronged, *15* nurse, *16* I'm being [harassed (?)], *followed by a change of speaker, 17* Zeus (?), *18* children.

   Kantharos and one or two other characters take part in this scene. If Kantharos is here identical with the Kantharos of Ant.15, one possibility is that he was involved in a recognition scene which required the presence of a nurse and confirmed the identity of a male with the help of a sword. The mention of children in v.18 might perhaps be significant if in this play twins and not a single child had been abandoned at birth. See also the comments on the other side of B.1 which directly follow.)

   (The other side of papyrus B.1 (the verso) has only the line-beginnings of some quickfire dialogue with many changes of speaker; there are paragraphoi under vv.20, 21, 22, 23, 24, 25, 26, 27, 30, 31, 32, 33, 34 and 35, and dicola in 20, 23 and 28. In the left margin of B.1 the speaker of vv.19–20 is identified as a slave, but the abbreviation used does not reveal whether that slave was male or female; if female, this could have been either the θεράπαινα or the Syra of Ant.15. The following words and phrases can be made out: 19 What you had feared, *20* From rust, you see! *followed by a change of speaker, who begins with* This (?). *21* Pull it, *followed by a change of speaker, who says* So you may know. *22* It really can't be pulled, *23* With newfound wealth, *followed by a change of speaker, 24* From where has she got, *25* But this is yours, *26* If the (male) buyer, *27* Having acquired, *28 a speech ending* They flow uphill *(a proverb indicating that something has disturbed or is likely to disturb a normal course of events),*[3] *29* The man

30   τἀλλότριον. ὡς .[
    <u>φυλάττομεν ..[</u>
    <u>φυλάττετε γν[</u>
    <u>ὁ τὸν φανέντ[</u>
    <u>ἡμῶν τις .[</u>
35   <u>.έξω. τὸ ποῖ[ον</u>
    τοῦθ' οἰδ[

(2) B.2

recto

.].ασερ[
.]αι τὰς θύρ[ας
.].ι πρότερ[ον
ὡραιοτέραν [
5   κόψω δὲ κ.[
  <u>τίς τὴν θύ[ραν</u>
  <u>πρῶτον [</u>
  <u>ἄρχων α[</u>
9   ...[

32 γν[B.1 with αι written above and blotted out.
35 .έξω.τ B.1 with ι added above ω.τ.   ποῖ[ον suppl. Schubart.
8 Or δ[.   10 Or οχ[.   11 Suppl. Austin.

who's found my, *30* What's owned by someone else, as, *31*
We're guarding, *32 a plural* You're guarding, *33* He who
... the ... that's *or* who's appeared, *34* Who *or* one of us, *35*
What kind of, *36* This.

*These fragments of a lively but puzzling dialogue appear
to tie up with remarks on the other side of the papyrus leaf;
it seems that a vain attempt is being made to draw a sword
out of a scabbard to which it has been fused by rust. If this
was a sword that a young girl (cf. the she in v.24) seized
from a soldier or cavalryman who was violating her, there
is a plausible link with Ant.15. Such a military figure had
then become wealthy after serving as a mercenary abroad
(cf. v. 23), and been named Kantharos because, like other
soldiers in later comedy, he was fond of wine. The raper's
sudden discovery that he was the father of either one or
two grown up children would certainly have upset (v.28)
the normal tenor of his life.)*

Papyrus B.2

*(It is uncertain whether this scrap is rightly assigned to the
same play as Ant.15, but it makes little difference either
way; B.2 yields virtually no new text of any consequence.
On one side (the recto) we have the beginnings of nine
lines, in which an unidentified character, perhaps after en-
tering with a monologue, knocks on one of the stage house
doors, and either someone comes out of the house or a char-
acter already on stage intervenes. There are paragraphi
under vv.6 and 7. The following words and phrases can be
made out: 2 the doors (i.e. presumably the two leaves of a
double door), 3 First, 4 More blooming (probably with ref-*

verso

10
]..αλ[
] γὰρ καλῶ[ς
].τησητε.[
]ψηφίζετε
]λας·

15
].εις·
]ιων·

erence to a girl), 5 But I'll knock. *The other character responds with* Who [is knocking at] the door 6, *and the first speaker responds with* First 7. *Line 8 begins either with a puzzling* Beginning *or* Ruling, *or with a character's name: e.g.* Archon[ides].

On the other side (the verso) are the ends of seven further lines, giving very little that is translatable: 11 excellently, you see, *and* 13 you *(plural)* count up *or* decide by vote.

FABULA INCERTA 7

INTRODUCTION

Manuscript

Ant.55 = *P.Antinoopolis* 55, fragments from a parchment codex written in the fourth century A.D. First edition: J. W. B. Barns (with help from other scholars), *The Antinoopolis Papyri* 2 (London 1960) 8–29, with photographs (plates I and II). These fragments are republished as fr. adesp. 1096 in Kassel–Austin, *PCG* VII, pp. 246–51.

Nine fragments (a–i) survive, eight of them with text on both sides of the page. The largest of these (a) preserves enough text to show that each page contained two columns of text, although we do not know the original height of a page (and thus also the number of lines in a column) because neither fr. a nor any other retains both top and bottom margins. The script, however, is both exquisite and small, and we should accordingly allow for original columns between 30 and 50 lines.[1] There is no sure way of deciding the dramatic order either of the fragments themselves or of recto and verso in each individual fragment, although in the case of fragment a it seems possible to guess that verso precedes recto. The text published here follows

[1] E. G. Turner, *GRBS* 10 (1969) 311.

MENANDER

Mette,[2] Austin[3] and Kassel–Austin in giving a continuous
line numbering, although vv. 1–32 reverse the previously
printed order of the two sides of fr. a, and here the Kassel–
Austin numbering is added in brackets.

Although these fragments do not contain any ties with
previously known quotations from Menander, their lan-
guage, style, metrics and imaginative quality combine to
indicate a common source in one of his plays. So far, how-
ever, its title remains a mystery. The first editor of the
parchment opted for Menander's *Misogynes*, and Thomas
Williams[4] for the *Proenkalon*, but there are no identifiable
links with either play, no solid arguments to support the
attributions, and one counter at least to the former sugges-
tion: the absence of any misogynistic character or expres-
sions in the Ant.55 fragments.

A third suggestion may perhaps be tentatively ad-
vanced: Menander's *Thrasyleon*. Admittedly there are
again no links with known quotations from this play (frs.
181–85 K-A), but two small details may point in its direc-
tion. A speaker in one of the Ant.55 fragments has his
name abbreviated to θρασ΄ in the left margin of v. 55, and
this is most plausibly filled out to Thras(on), Thras(onides)
or Thras(yleon). Menander is not known to have given
the same name to soldiers in different plays. Thrasonides

[2] The appendix to his second edition of Men. *Dysk.* (Göttingen
1961) 60–64.

[3] *Comicorum graecorum fragmenta in papyris reperta* (Berlin
& New York 1973) no. 242 pp. 246–51. Cf. also the second edition
of Sandbach's Oxford text of Menander (1990) pp. 354–55.

[4] *RhM* 105 (1962) 223–25.

was used for the title figure in Menander's *Misoumenos*, while Thrason may have been the soldier's name in his *Eunouchos*, unless Terence changed it when adapting that play for his *Eunuchus*. This makes Thrasyleon the most plausible supplement in *P.Ant*.55, with the play named after him. Secondly, in one of the essays written to oppose Epicureanism, Plutarch (*Mor.* 1095d) referred to Θρασωνίδας τινὰς καὶ Θρασυλέοντας ὀλολυγμοὺς καὶ κροτοθορύβους ποιοῦντας ('characters like Thrasonides and Thrasyleon, with their howls and noisy applause'). Although Plutarch does not mention Menander's name here as the author who invented these celebrated characters, and although the words κροτοθορύβους ('noisy applause') and ὀλολυγμούς ('howls') seem to have been introduced into this passage primarily for their Epicurean resonances (cf. 1117a later in Plutarch's essay, and Epicurus fr. 143 Usener), it is worth noting that in a very mutilated fr. (b) of Ant.55 (v. 47) some unidentified characters ὀλο]λύζουσιν, 'howl.' Could the howlers there have been associates of Thrasyleon, and Plutarch have recalled that passage too at *Mor.* 1095d?

Three characters are named in the Ant.55 fragments. Thras(yleon) in the margin at v. 55 has already been discussed. The others are the slave Dromon (vv. 29 Arnott = 13 K-A, 38, 95, and left-hand margin of 16 Ar = 32 K-A) and a young man Moschion (66).

Of the fragments two (a, b) in particular yield information that seems vital to the plot. On the verso side of fr. a (vv. 1–16 Ar = 17–32 K-A) two characters discover a document on an altar where the fire is still burning. The document either contains, or (less probably) is accompanied by, a πρόκλησις: that is, a legal challenge that often played a part in Athenian private lawsuits. The πρόκλησις had several functions; it could require one's opponent to carry out an obligation or observe its execution by the challenger, to submit his slaves for interrogation or agree to the interrogation of the challenger's slaves, or finally to swear his own or accept the challenger's oath endorsing a statement.[5] The discovery of this πρόκλησις reduces one of the two speakers to distraction (v. 10 Ar = 26 K-A).

The second column of the recto side begins with two speakers, one of whom is identified as the slave Dromon (v. 29 Ar = 13 K-A). The other person first tells Dromon to deal with the problem (v. 28 Ar = 12 K-A) and then disappears from the stage, leaving Dromon alone to consider his future action and the situation of his infatuated young master (v. 32 Ar = 16 K-A). If the two sides of fr. a are read in this order,[6] the likelihood is that Dromon and his young

[5] See especially A. R. W. Harrison, *The Law of Athens* II (Oxford 1971) 135–36, 150–53, D. M. MacDowell, *The Law in Classical Athens* (London 1978) 242–47, C. Carey and R. A. Reid, *Demosthenes: Selected Private Speeches* (Cambridge 1985), commentary on 54.27, and M. Gagarin in *Symposium 1995: Akten der Gesellschaft für griechische und hellenistische Rechtsgeschichte* 11 (1997) 125–34.

[6] So first T. B. L. Webster, *An Introduction to Menander* (Manchester 1974) 196–98, and *Studies in Later Greek Comedy* (2nd edition, Manchester 1974) 207. There is also a subsidiary argument for this sequence: it makes better dramatic sense to assume a long discussion between Dromon and his young master after the unsettling discovery of the πρόκλησις, followed by Dromon's self-addressed (v. 29 Ar = 13 K-A) monologue after his young master's departure.

master were the speakers on both sides of this parchment page, that the discovery of the πρόκλησις severely disturbed the young master, and that Dromon needed to think of some scheme to help him out of his difficulty.

There is a gap, however, of just under three columns of text between vv. 1–11 Ar = 17–27 K-A and vv. 22–32 Ar = 6–16 K-A, probably amounting to between 80 and 140 lines, in which the nature of this particular πρόκλησις would doubtless have been clearly explained.

Fragment b may perhaps provide some ambiguous clues here. On its verso side the soldier whose name begins with Thras- is involved in a discussion which refers to a daughter (v. 56) who seems to have 'borne a child to' an unidentified male (58); 'the adulterer' is mentioned (59) and a young man called Moschion (66). It is possible that the daughter in question was the soldier's partner but had had intercourse on at least one occasion also with this Moschion, which may have been the name of Dromon's young master. In that case a legal dispute between Moschion and the soldier might have arisen, with a πρόκλησις in which an oath had been either sworn by the girl or demanded from Moschion or the soldier about the paternity of the baby. Such a scenario would have paralleled the antecedents of a real-life lawsuit in mid-fourth-century Athens, when Boeotus was claiming to be the legitimate son of Mantias and Plangon, and Mantias then tried to bribe Plangon into refusing to swear in a πρόκλησις that Boeotus was her son.[7]

---

[7] See Demosthenes 39.1–5, dated probably to 348 B.C., and the introduction to the Carey–Reid commentary (*Demosthenes: Selected Private Speeches,* pp. 160–67).

We do not know whether the recto side of fr. b came
before or after its verso side, but in it Dromon and an-
other character seem to be discussing the tablet left on the
altar (vv. 44–45, 48). The identity of this other character is
uncertain; it is perhaps unlikely to have been Dromon's
young master, although he seems to be just as surprised by
the situation as the young man (v. 45).

The other fragments complement or embroider the in-
formation supplied by frs. a and b. The recto side of fr. c
describes a woman (? a *hetaira* or her bawd, a midwife or
nanny to the baby of v. 58) supplying over-watered wine to
one or more other people. Its verso side has a character
(most probably the father or a friend of the young lover)
telling Dromon that he knows all about the scheme that
the slave was working out in fr. a. The recto side of frag-
ment d accuses a slave (presumably Dromon) of having
been ordered by an infatuated master to devise a scheme
for him; the speaker here is likely to have been the young
man's father or friend. On the verso side of this fragment
Dromon is named (v. 95), while a loyal man and a rogue are
mentioned in quick succession (92, 94). The recto side of
fr. e repeats a phrase in v. 30 Ar = 14 K-A, while its verso
mentions young men 'who'll soon be here ($\H{\eta}\xi ov\sigma$') . . .
with force' (vv. 114–15); these are likely to be either a cho-
rus of tipsy young men whose arrival to perform the first
entr'acte is conventionally announced at the end of the
first act, or alternatively a band of the young man's or the
soldier's associates bent on abducting a beloved girl.

The fragments thus reveal a few incidents from what
may have been a complex plot, whose ramifications can no
longer be unravelled. Pivotal details, such as the legal pro-
cess employed (? lawsuit, arbitration), the status of the girl

who bore the baby, and the present object of the young man's affections (? the aforementioned girl, or someone else: cf. v. 32 Ar = 16 K-A), remain uncertain. It is advantageous to remember that Menander's plot constructions tend to be more imaginative and surprising than those imposed upon him by the guesses of scholars.

FABULA INCERTA 7

fr. a (verso)

column i

1 Ar στεφαν[
(=17 KA) [...]ʼ..[
       πε..[   ]...[
       κερδ..[

                    ΜΟΣΧΙΩΝ (?)
                        ]αν. ὦ δέσπ[ο]τα
5 Ar Ἄπολλον· ἐ[πʼ ἀγαθῇ] τύχῃ· τί τοῦτο, παῖ;
(=21 KA)

Supplements whose author is not identified in this apparatus
were made by the ed.pr., J. W. B. Barns.

3 πεν.[or πεπ.[Ant.55.

Under v. 5 Ant.55 may have a paragraphus.   ἐ[πʼ ἀγαθῇ]
suppl. Handley.

UNIDENTIFIED PLAY 7

(SCENE: uncertain, but possibly a street in Athens, with two houses backing onto it. One would probably have belonged to Moschion and his family, the other to one of the other major characters such as the soldier or the family of the girl mentioned in vv. 56-57. An altar is also visible, perhaps attached to a shrine separating the houses.)

Fragment a (verso: *vv. 1-16 Ar*)

(This page contains the remains of the last 11 lines of one column of text, and minuscule traces of the last 5 lines of the column to its right. Only the opening letters of the first 4 lines of the first column are preserved, yielding Garland 1 *and* Gain 4, *before a fuller text from the end of v. 4 to v. 11 allows continuous translation. Two characters appear to be on stage, plausibly identified as the slave Dromon and his master, who may be called Moschion. It is likely that on entrance both have caught sight of a fire burning on an altar just after a sacrifice; hence perhaps the presence of v. 1's discarded (?) garland, since sacrificers were garlanded.)*

MOSCHION (?)
(noticing something else on the altar, besides the garland)

O Lord   4
Apollo! [Bless my] soul! Hello! What's this?   5

537

MENANDER

ΔΡΟΜΩΝ

πρόκλ[η]σιν [ἐ]πὶ τὸν βωμὸν ἐκτέθηκέ τις.
καινόν γε πῦρ πάρεστιν.

ΜΟΣΧΙΩΝ (?)

ἐπίμεινον βραχύ.

τ]ουτ[ὶ δὲ δὴ] τί ποτ᾽ ἐστί; πρῶτον βούλομαι
ἰδε[ῖν. τί ἐσ]τι τοῦτο;

ΔΡΟΜΩΝ

γραμματείδιον.

ΜΟΣΧΙΩΝ (?)

10 Ar   θεο[ί] με νοῦ κενοῦσιν.

(=26 KA)

ΔΡΟΜΩΝ

οὐθὲν δ[ια]φέρει.

ΜΟΣΧΙΩΝ (?)

11 Ar   ἐγώ] σε κρίνω τῶν φ[ί]λων εὐνο[ύστατ]ον.

(=27 KA)

6 ἐκτέθεικε Ant.55: corr. Austin.   τις with full stop Williams: alternatively τις or τίς with question mark.

8 δὲ δὴ suppl. Lloyd-Jones.   Under v. 9 Ant.55 has a paragraphus, and a dicolon before but not after γραμματειδιον; in left margin it has δρομ(ων) to indicate speaker.

---

[1] This translates the Greek term πρόκλησις; see the introduction to this play.   [2] Literally, a wooden tablet, either coated with wax and written on with a stylus, or whitened and written on in ink, here presumably containing the text of the πρόκλησις. See F. G. Kenyon, *Books and Readers in Ancient Greece and Rome* (2nd edition, Oxford 1951) 42-43 and 92.

DROMON

(*going up to the altar and picking up a document laid there*)

Somebody's left a legal challenge[1] on
The altar. There's a new fire, too!

MOSCHION (?)

(*joining Dromon at the altar*)

                                        Just wait
A bit! Whatever's that? I'd like [to] see
It first. [What *is*] it?

DROMON

                    It's a document.[2]

MOSCHION (?)

(*taking and reading the document*)

                            The gods
Are driving me insane.

DROMON

(*reading the document himself*)

                    It's nothing.

MOSCHION (?)

                            I   10
Consider you the kind[est] of my friends.

(*At this point, with Moschion flattering Dromon before
presumably asking for his help in the new situation that the
legal challenge has created, the column of text ends, and
virtually nothing is preserved from the second column on
this page.*)

column ii

12 Ar (28 KA) .[, 13 Ar [, 14 Ar .[, 15 Ar __[, 16 Ar (32 KA) ω[.

fr. a (recto)
column i

17 Ar (1 KA)   ]ους

                                               ].ν

                                               ]

20 Ar (4 KA)   ]

21 Ar (5 KA)   ]η...ο

column ii

22 Ar (6 KA)   ] νεωτέρων

                                   ]..[

        ]..[   ]..ο.[

25 Ar   ....]ε τοιοῦτ᾽ ε..[   ].[.]. ἐμοὶ

(=9 KA) ο]ὕτως ἔσομ᾽ ὑμῖν σ..[   ]ο.[.]ν ἐγὼ

        ἄχρηστον.

NEANIAΣ

ἀλλ᾽ εἰ ταῦτα [σ]αυτ[ῷ] συμφέρειν
ἡγεῖ, πέραινε. τί γὰρ ἂν ἀντιλέγοιμί σοι;

21]ησατο Snell.   22–27 Division between the two speak-
ers is unknown, except that vv. 26–27 ἄχρηστον were spoken by
Dromon.   22 τῶν] Mette.   23]ρθ[?   24]φιο.[?
25 Or ἐμοῦ Ant.55.   27 Change of speaker after
ἄχρηστον suggested by Barns: Ant.55 has paragraphus under the
line, but places its one dicolon after συμφέρειν.

FABULA INCERTA 7

fragment a (recto: *vv.* 17-32 Ar)

(After v. 11 there is a gap probably of between 80 and 140 lines before we reach the next well-preserved section of text containing the bottom 11 lines of the second column on the other side of fr. a. Before that we have a few letters from the ends of three lines in column i (vv. 17, 18, 21) yielding no complete word. It seems likely that Dromon and his master continued their conversation throughout the gap, discussing the document on the altar and wondering how to deal with it. Dromon doubtless would have been pressed by his master to formulate a plan, and at the point when continuous translation is possible Dromon seems to have agreed. Before Dromon speaks in v. 26, however, there are traces of a few letters from the preceding four lines, giving young (men ?) 22 *and* such a thing . . . me 25.*

DROMON

That way I'll be [   ] no use   26
To you.

MOSCHION (?)
But if you think this benefits
You, do it! Why should I oppose you there?

(Here Moschion, apparently reassured by what Dromon has said, makes his exit, leaving Dromon the only character on stage.)

ΔΡΟΜΩΝ

εἶἑν· μόνος δὴ γενόμενος νυ[νί, Δ]ρόμων,

30 Ar   λογισμὸν ὧν μέλλεις διοικε[ῖν πραγ]μάτων
(=14 KA)   σαυτῷ [δ]ός, ἐν ὀλίγοις δὲ καὶ μὴ διὰ μ[α]κρῶν.
32 Ar   τρόφ[ιμο]ς ἐρῶν, ἧς δήποτ᾽ οὐθὲν διαφ[έρει
(=16 KA)

fr. b (recto)

33   ]ν[.]ιδα[
                          ]..εινα.[
35   ]..[.
                     ]ταλλ᾽ οὐδενὶ
                ἤ]δη μ᾽ ἐξάγων.:
             ].....[σ]οι, Δρόμων
             ]ες ἤδη κατ᾽ ἀγορὰν
40   ] ἔρωτι δ᾽ ὡς ἐγὼ
         , ν]ὴ τὸν Ἥλιον
         ταῦτ]α μὲν [χ]αίρειν ἔα
         ἐσ]τὶ μοχθηρὸν δρ[..].
      ]. γραμματείδιόν τινος
45   ] τὸν βωμόν.: ὦ δεινοῦ λόγου.:
         πρό]σειμι δὲ

29 Deciphered (with Turner's support) and suppl. Williams.
37 Suppl. Austin.   38 σ.[or ε.[.
42 ταῦτ]α suppl. Lloyd-Jones.   μιν Ant.55 with a correct-
ing ε above the ι.   At line end ἔα or ἐᾶ[ν.
43 ἐσ]τὶ suppl. Austin.   At line end Δρ[όμω]ν is tempting,
but would overrun the available space.

DROMON

Well then, Dromon, you're now alone.[3] Apply
Your mind to these concerns that you appear   30
To be directing. Briefly, though, no blather!
Master in love—no matter who's the girl!   32

(At this point the fragment ends.)

fragment b (recto: *vv.* 33-52)

*(It is uncertain whether recto or verso comes first in this
fragment, but the references in the recto to the* document
*(44, 48) and the altar (45) suggest that its subject matter
was identical with that in the verso of fr. a (vv. 4-11
Ar = 20-27 K-A). Dromon is addressed in this fragment
too (v. 38), but it appears unlikely that the recto of fr. b
comes from the gap between vv. 11 Ar = 27 K-A) and 27
Ar = 11 K-A. Such a placing would inevitably bring fr. b's
verso also into the same gap, although the verso's introduc-
tion of the soldier into the characters present (v. 55) and its
reference to Moschion as if he were not on stage (v. 66)
would make its plausible integration into the assumed dra-
matic developments at this point very difficult. For this
reason it seems preferable to assume that the recto of fr. b
contains a later discussion about the document on the altar
between Dromon and somebody else—while fr. b's verso
comes from a preceding or following scene involving the
soldier and an unidentified character.*

[3] Monologues of this sort, delivered by a slave left alone to
contemplate a problem and possibilities of its solution, seem to
have been a convention of later comedy: cf. e.g. Plautus, *Epidicus*
81-103, *Pseudolus* 394-414, *Trinummus* 717-28.

ὀλο]λύζουσιν[
γραμ]ματείδιον
      ]ν γε, νὴ Δία.:
50   ].. τὸν χρόνον
      π]ρόσεχε σὺ
52   ]θαν.[

fr. b (verso)

53   ]σα.[
      ]εστ...[
55   ].ε.[
τὴν θ[υ]γατέρ᾽ ἔγ[νω
ἐπὶ τὴν θύραν [
καὶ τέτοκεν αὐ[τ]ῷ [παιδίον
..]χης. : σὺ μοιχὸν [
60 ἑ]ορακέναι τῶν πα[
ἑ]λαφρωτε[..]υσοκ[
υ]περμετρῆσαι. : τ.[
ἐρ[ῶν πε]παῦσθαι τῆς [
ἐὰν τὸ λαβεῖν τὸν κα[ιρὸ]ν ..[
65 π.....ωι πραττο....[
τὸν Μοσχίων᾽ ε[

47 ὀλολύζουσι ν[ῦν Lloyd-Jones.

55 θρασ´ in left margin of Ant.55 naming the speaker
(Θρασυλέων, Θράσων or Θρασωνίδης ?).

56 Suppl. Handley.   58 παιδίον suppl. Lloyd-Jones.

59 τύχης suppl. Lloyd-Jones.

60 πα[ρθένων suppl. Mette.   63 ἐρ[ῶν suppl. Mette.

Since only the line ends of fr. b's recto are preserved, continuous translation is impossible, and assignment to the presumed two speakers, Dromon and someone else, is often uncertain.

Lines 33-35 yield nothing to the translator. We do not know who says the rest *(or* but*) to nobody (or* nothing*) at* 36 *and* now leading *(masculine)* me away *at* 37. 38 to you, Dromon *and* 40 in *or* with love, like me, *however, clearly belong to Moschion. In between,* 39 now in the market *could come from either speaker, as could everything after v. 40:* 41 yes, by the Sun!, 42 [this] you must forget!, 43 [is] wicked, [, 44 some[one]'s document, 45 the altar, *followed by the other speaker exclaiming* What an awful tale!, 46 but I'll approach *or* I'm [here], 47 they're howling,[4] 48 document, 49 yes, I swear!, 50 the time, 51 you pay attention. *Line 52 yields nothing.)*

fragment b (verso: *vv.* 53-72)

(This side of fr. b, which apparently comes from the scene that preceded or followed that of the verso (q.v.), preserves only the mutilated openings of 20 lines. One of the speakers is identified in the margin of v. 55 as Thras(yleon *?: see the introduction to this play), presumably a soldier, but we do not know who is on stage with him, nor who speaks what. The subject of their conversation is someone's daughter, who has had a baby, and an adulterer (who may be named seven lines later as* Moschion*), but the relation of these statements, if any, to the document on the altar of frs. a and b recto is uncertain, although one possibility is outlined in the introduction to this play.)*

[4] On this remark see the introduction to this play.

πε...ο.ευρ[
πυθόμενος η[
.].εαση.....[
70 ἐν τῷ βίῳ .[
    ἑόρακα τὴ[ν
72 οὕ]τως

          fr. c (recto)
73   ].ρθ[...].ν[
            ]ε τῷ δ' ὑδαρεῖ [ποτῷ
75   ]..[   ]νπερ ἀρτίως τρο[φ]ὸ[ς
    ]κεράσασ' ἔ[δω]κεν ἡ συνετὴ πιεῖν
77]ισαυτα[....]ουτο κακοήθως γενη[

          fr. c (verso)
78   ]ε..[..]νε[
    πρ]όφασιν δ' εὑρ[
80 ..]ρουμεν διακεκ[
    α..τα τούτων δ' εἰφα.[...].ζωσ[
82 .. διὰ μακρὰν πρόφασ[ιν ..]εστ.ν.[

    72 Suppl. Arnott.
    73 Or].ρε[Ant.55.
    75 Suppl. Mette.
    82 Either]εστον.[or]εστιν.[Ant.55.

546

Lines 53, 55, 67 and 69 yield nothing that can be securely translated, but 54 gives is, *56* The daughter, *57* Towards the door, *58* She's borne him [a baby] *(but the father's identity is not revealed in the preserved fragments), 59-60 a speech beginning* You [claim ?] to have observed / A seducer of the [girls ?], *61* More nimble *or* More fickle, *62* To go too far, *63* To have stopped yearn[ing] for the [girl ?], *64* If seizing the opportunity, *65* act[ing ?], *66* Moschion, *68* Discovering *(masculine), 70* In life, *71* I've seen the, *and 72* Thus (?).

fragment c (recto: vv. 73-77)

(A scrap of five mutilated lines, in which a woman is described as serving wine which has had too much water added to it.[5] The woman's identity and her role in the dramatic plot are uncertain, but see the introduction to this play. Line 73 yields nothing translatable, 74 and the watery [drink], *75-76* [wine,] which recently a n[urse (?)] / Had mixed and served for drinking, clever girl!, *77* wickedly become.*)

fragment c (verso: vv. 78-82)

(The other side of fr. c also has bits of five lines, but they yield little intelligible sense. Line 79 has but find[ing (?)] an excuse, *80* we *followed by a verb, 81* of these, *82* through a tedious excuse. *The references to* an excuse *are now inexplicable.)*

[5] Tipplers in ancient Athens, both male and female, normally drank their wine mixed with water, and there were complaints sometimes when too much water was added. Cf. my commentary (Cambridge 1996) on Alexis fr. 228.2 with the works there cited.

fr. d (recto)

83 ἐπέτα]ξέ σοι τάχ' οὖν τιν' εὑρεῖν μ[ηχανὴν
α]ὐτῷ· σὺ δ' ὑπέσχου τοῦτο. διὰ τίν' [αἰτίαν;
85 πρῶ]τον μέν ἐστι κύ[ριος σ]οῦ. δεύ[τερον,
πισ]τός. τρίτον ⟨δ'⟩, ἐρᾷ. .[....]ος· εμη[
πῶς] οὐ δικαίως τοῖς ἐρω[μέν]οις [τε καὶ
σαυτῷ] βοηθεῖς ἄμα; πεπ[
....].. .[..]...ωμηθ[
90   ]προσ[

fr. d (verso)

91   ].ξα.τασω † ἐμοὶ δὲ χρησι[μ
                         ].δων τὸν πιστὸν ἐξ ἀρχῆς εν.[
                         ]ν.ηνε[...].' οὕτω ῥαδίως [
                         ]..ον [γυν]αῖκα τῷ μαστιγίᾳ
95   ].....[..]ω Δρόμων ἡμῖν ..[
                         ]..[......]του κρίνετ' οὐχο.[
                         ]αλλον ......[.]οι[
98   ].ειν[..]..[

86 πισ]τός suppl. several, ⟨δ'⟩ Arnott.
87 πῶς suppl. Austin.
91 χρήσιμο[ν δοκεῖ Mette.
92 τῶν ἐλπ]ίδων Mette.   του corrected to τον Ant.55.
93 νδην or νλην Ant.55.
96 οὐχ ὁ or οὐ χο.[.
97 β.[or ρ.[Ant.55.

548

fragment d (recto: *vv.* 83-90)

(This fragment comes from the top of a page, providing us with six slightly and two severely mutilated trimeters whose speaker (? the father or a friend of the young man) tells Dromon that he knows about the slave's activities staged in fr. a.)

And so he may have [told] you to work out   83
A s[cheme] for him. You said you would. The [reason]?
First, he's your master. Second, he's [reli]able.   85
Third, he's in love [   ] my [   ].
You're [surely] right to help young men in love,
[And] at the same time help [yourself].   88

(From vv. 89 and 90 nothing can be safely translated.)

fragment d (verso: *vv.* 91-98)

(The eight vv. on this side of fr. d are much more mutilated than the recto, and although they provide us with a number of phrases, nowhere do we have a passage of connected sense. Line 91 has but to me [it seems (?)] a help, *92 the* loyal fellow from the start, *93 so easily, 94* woman . . . to *or* with the rogue, *95* Dromon to us, *96* is judged *(?). Situation and speaker(s) are uncertain, and the identities of the loyal fellow, the rogue and the woman unknown.)*

fr. e (recto)

99   ]...[

100   ].[..]....με[.]α.[

        δι]οικεῖν [π]ράγμ[ατα

        ]ησενοσω....[.].[

        ].ι τουτί· λαβὼν [

        ]..μενος γὰρ ἕξεις .[

105   ]εσωσδ..λ' ἐκεῖνον του[

      ].[   ]ας τισυ[..]ε.[

              ]του[

108   ].ειντ[

fr. e (verso)

109   ]...[

110   ]ω[..]α.[...]..[

        ]ο[..]..[.]. πατερ[

        ]..ε : τί ἐστι τουτί; [

        ]τιδ' αὐτίχ' ἤξουσ' ε.[

        ] νεανίσκοι βίᾳ .[

115   ].σονται τὴν εβρ...' εξ[

      ].ν.[..].ντεσ.[

      ].ερ.[

118   ]....[

fr. f (recto)

119   ]. ἐξέλθη πάλιν

120   ]..[   ]ε[

FABULA INCERTA 7

fragment e (recto: *vv*. 99-108)

*(A tiny scrap, with a few words readable in its ten muti-
lated lines: 101 yields* to manage concerns *(cf. v. 30 Ar = 14
K-A), 103* this here. Taking *(masculine), 104* for you'll
have, *105* that [man (?)]*.)*

fragment e (verso: *vv*. 109-18)

*(The other side of fr. e also has bits of ten mutilated lines,
containing only a few decipherable words: v. 111* father,
112 somebody asks What's this?*, 113* they'll soon be here,
114 young men with force. *If it is the* young men *who will
soon be here, these newcomers could either be the chorus,
whose arrival was being announced at the end of the first
act, or a group of the soldier's or young man's associates
bent on abducting a young girl with whom one of the arriv-
ing party was besotted.)*

fragment f (recto: *vv*. 119-20)

*(A minuscule scrap from the top of a page, with the end of
the top line and traces from the next. From v. 119 may
come back out* can be read*.)*

106]ας τις υ[or κ]ᾰστι συ[.
113–14 ἐμ[βεβρεγμένοι τινὲς / ἡμῖν] νεανίσκοι e.g. Mette.

fr. f (verso)

121   .[..] δὲ κἀγὼ προσ.[
122   ].[   ]ν[

fr. g

(recto)   (verso)
123   .[134   ]..
      π[135   ].ς
125   ημα[   ]
      ηιθα[   ]φη
      λαθρ[   ]ξοτε
      αιτ.[   ]
      .φ.[140   ]κος
130   τ.[141   ]ε
      νη[
      .[
133   .[

fr. h

(recto)   (verso)
142   ]δ' ἔχω[149   .[
      ].   150   α[
      ]   τ.[
145   ]α σοι   οπ.[
      ]σως   ἐμοῦ δ[
      ].ν.ν   ο....[
148   ]αμ.[155   .[.

FABULA INCERTA 7

fragment f (verso: *vv.* 121-22)

(The other side of fr. f has and I too *in the middle of v. 121.)*

fragment g (recto: *vv.* 123-33)

(A minuscule scrap with the first one to four letters of 11 lines, with the one word Secretly *identifiable in v. 127. Paragraphi under vv. 129 and 130 indicate that these lines come from a dialogue.)*

fragment g (verso: *vv.* 134-41)

(The other side of fr. g has either the ends or the margins to the right of eight lines. No words can be deciphered.)

fragment h (recto: *vv.* 142-48)

(Another minuscule scrap with the ends, near ends, or margins to the right of seven lines. In v. 142 and I have can be read, *in 145* to you.*)*

fragment h (verso: *vv.* 149-55)

(The other side of fr. h has the opening letters of seven lines, with Of me *legible in v. 153. The presence of paragraphi above and below v. 149 and under vv. 150, 151 and 153 indicates that hereabouts there was lively dialogue.)*

---

121 Traces of a character name in the left margin of Ant.55 suspected by Barns.   127 λάθρ[ᾳ e.g. Mette.

128 τε[or τω[.   Before v. 134 came three trimeters which all ended to the left of this scrap.   135]ος or]ως.

153 The paragraphus under this line in Ant.55 is not certain.

fr. i

(recto)

156   ]…ημ.[

157   ]αττειν[

(verso is blank)

fragment i (recto: *vv.* 156-57)

(Another minuscule scrap with letters from the middle of two lines, but no identifiable words.)

fragment i (verso)

(This side of fr. i is blank, perhaps because its area coincided with an act-break or space at the end of the play.)

FABULA INCERTA 8

INTRODUCTION

Manuscript

The extant passages and fragments come from mummy cartonnage made apparently from one long roll of papyrus, which may have contained the text of just one play, transcribed in the third century B.C.[1] The scribe normally used paragraphi and dicola to indicate changes of speaker, but his practice appears to have been erratic; these signs are often omitted, and occasionally (vv. 5, 50 Arnott = 122 Kassel–Austin, 53 Ar = 125 K-A) dicola are replaced by spaces left between letters. The papyrus roll was eventually separated into at least three parts, first published as follows:

[1] Although there is no physical join linking the fragments of Col.1, Col.2 and Mich., the evidence for their derivation from the same roll—and almost certainly from one play—is convincing. Wherever a full column of text is preserved, with margins to top and bottom, the height is an unvarying 15.5cm, and such columns contain between 18 and 20 lines of text. The writing appears to be by one hand, and the text is set out always in the same way. The reference to a man who is either described as ἡδύς or named Hedys at v. 27 (Col.1) seems to be picked up again in v. 145 (Col.2), and the mention of an Ephesian at v. 27 (Col.1) similarly to be endorsed at v. 168 (Mich.).

(i) Col.1 = *P.Cologne* 203 (vv. 1–39, 58–129 Ar = 1–111 K-A): K. Maresch (with the assistance of many colleagues), *Kölner Papyri* 5 (Cologne 1984) 1–21 with photographs (plates XXVII, XXVIII);

(ii) Col.2 = *P.Cologne* 243 (vv. 40–57, 130–66 Ar = 112–66 K-A): K. Maresch (with the assistance of many colleagues), *Kölner Papyri* 6 (Cologne 1987) 52–60 with a photograph (pl. XIX);

(iii) Mich. = *P.Michigan* 6950 (vv. 167–244 Ar and K-A): R. Nünlist, *ZPE* 99 (1993) 245–78 with photographs (plates III, IV).

Nünlist's paper also republishes Col.1 and Col.2, with a photograph (pl. V) of vv. 58–93 Ar = 40–75 K-A which corrects slightly the placing of a loose scrap at vv. 70–73 Ar = 52–55 K-A. Col.1, Col.2 and Mich. are printed as fr. adesp. 1147 in Kassel–Austin, *PCG* VIII. The text printed here places Col.2's fr. a+b directly after Col.1's fr. B, and this has necessitated renumbering vv. 40–129 Kassel–Austin; for these lines the Kassel–Austin numberings are appended to the Greek text in brackets. It must be recognised, however, that the original placing and sequence of the many tiny scraps are quite uncertain.

Three of Col.1's fragments are substantial, each consisting of a whole column of text, with some mutilation or abrasion. The first two are:

(i) Fr. A, vv. 1–19. At sunrise a young man stands outside the locked door of the girl he loves. On stage with him is in all probability just one other character, whose remarks—at times sardonically dismissive, coarse but not entirely unsympathetic—make it likely that he is an elderly slave who had been the young man's tutor, rather than a free young companion. The locked door seems to indicate that the young man's beloved is either a practising or a trainee *hetaira*, although the possibility that she was an impoverished free girl cannot be ruled out. One remark by the young man is clearly designed to intrigue and puzzle the audience: he is in love with a girl whose face he has never seen (vv. 9–11). The extant fragments of this play do not explain how this could have happened; there are many possibilities—for instance, the passion might have been inspired by a portrait of the girl, a glimpse of her from behind, a dream, or he could even have raped her at a festival in the dark during the previous night.

Four features of this fragment combine to indicate its original position in the play. Puzzles of the sort posed in vv. 9–11 are regularly introduced into opening scenes by comic playwrights as devices to attract an audience's attention. The typical plot of New Comedy covers the events of a single day, beginning early in the morning and ending at dusk.[2] Elsewhere in comedy locked-out lovers appear habitually at the start of plays (e.g. Plautus *Curculio*, *Truculentus*, Terence *Eunuchus*; cf. Menander's *Misoumenos*, where a rejected lover shuts himself out). And finally, much of the material in this fragment seems to be expository. Fr. A of Col.1 must come from the play's initial scene, perhaps with only a few lines lost before v. 1.[3]

[2] See especially my papers in *Drama* 2 (1992) 14–18, 24–25 and *PLLS* 2 (1979) 344–52, and R. Nünlist, *ZPE* 99 (1993) 261.

[3] If the play's opening lines appeared in the column immediately preceding fr. A of Col.1, that would mean a maximum of 20 vv. lost before the opening line preserved in the papyrus. Yet if the scribe added prefatory material (e.g. cast list, hypothesis) to

(ii) Fr. B of Col.1, vv. 20–39. Here the same young man is on stage, talking probably to the same companion, since the latter's ripostes and comments here share the same characteristics as those in fr. A. The conversation once again is expository, supplying extra information about the young man's infatuation. There are further enigmatic remarks leaving it uncertain how much the young man has yet seen of his beloved (vv. 29–31, 34–35). The girl is characterised as a beautiful *hetaira* (34–35), and a man who has come from Ephesus seems to be connected with her (26–27), presumably as a rival, a relative, or an owner and pimp. Although fr. B does not directly follow fr. A but is separated from it by one or more columns, it may come from a later part of the same scene or (perhaps more probably) from a new scene involving the same two characters not too long afterwards.

(iii) A mutilated fragment assembled from two scraps (a and b) of papyrus Col.2 seems to contain two commands ('Sell me!' 45 Ar = 117 K-A, 'Even kill me!' 48 Ar =120 K-A), mentions 'the famine' (46 Ar = 118 K-A) and an 'old man' (47 Ar = 119 K-A), and follows these remarks with an accusation of drunkenness (51–52 Ar = 123–24 K-A). These cannot all be convincingly integrated into what must have been an intriguing context, but only a slave who had misbehaved (? by stealing money from an old man,

his text in this opening column, as his counterparts did in the Cairo papyrus of Menander's *Heros*, the Bodmer codex of the *Dyskolos*, and *P.Antinoopolis* 15 (= *Fab. Inc.* 6) there would then be room for only a very few lines of play text in that opening column.

perhaps his master and the young man's father, in order to further the young man's love for a *hetaira*) would be likely to expect punishment such as sale or even execution.[4] This sequence of phrases immediately precedes an announcement of the arrival of the chorus, with the customary indication of their performance (54–56 Ar = 126–28 K-A, followed by χορ[οῦ]). This must be the end of the first act; it thus comes later in the play than frs. A and B of Col.1, and probably (but not certainly) earlier than fr. C of Col.1.

(iv) The third substantial fragment is fr. C of Col.1, column i, vv. 58–75 Ar = 40–57 K-A. A character who appears to be tipsy (cf. v. 63 Ar = 45 K-A) enters; he is carrying one or more containers of wine to one of the stage houses. After being intercepted by another man already on stage, he goes on to knock and kick the door savagely, but nobody opens it for him in the lines of the fragment that are preserved in this column. Here we seem to have reached a later stage in the plot, but it is impossible to identify with any confidence either the act to which it belongs or the characters involved. Presumably the wine is being carried to a stage house for an intended party; we can speculate

[4] Cf. e.g. A. R. W. Harrison, *The Law of Athens, II: Procedure* (Oxford 1971) 225–26, D. Cohen, *Theft in Athenian Law* (Munich 1983) 48, 72–79, and S. C. Todd, *The Shape of Athenian Law* (Oxford 1993) 117–18, 140–41. Anyone caught in the act of stealing 50 drachmas or more could in Athens be either killed by his victim or arrested, sentenced to death in court and then publicly executed. A similar crime may well have led to the threatened burning of the slave Daos in Menander's *Perinthia* (see the Loeb edition II, p. 481 and note on v. 18).

that the carrier is probably a slave, the partygoers free
young men, and the house the dwelling of the *hetaira*, but
the occasion remains a mystery. The man who intercepts
the carrier has previously "served" the people in the stage
house (vv. 73–74 Ar = 55–56 K-A); this may imply that he
was a cook or a trusted slave—perhaps even the slave of
frs. A and B.

The other fragments are virtually all insignificant
scraps, but one or two of them may supplement slightly the
limited information provided by frs. A, B and C of papyrus
Col.1.

(v) Fr. D column ii of Col.1 contains the remark "I carry
the Thasian wine" (v. 101 Ar = 83 K-A); this is likely to
come from an entrance speech by the wine carrier of
Col.1's fr. C preceding the dialogue in vv. 58–75 Ar = 40–
57 K-A of that fr.

(vi) Fr. a column i of Mich. mentions a man of Ephesus
who is described as fat, stupid or rich (v. 168) and a girl who
is quivering (173); are these the man from Ephesus men-
tioned in fr. B of Col.1 (vv. 25–27) and the girl with whom
the young man of frs. A and B of Col.1 is in love?

One remarkable fact about the text preserved on this
papyrus roll is that none of the characters there is certainly
named, although attempts have been made to supplement
or interpret five ambiguous letter sequences as proper
names: ἡδύς at vv. 25 and perhaps also 145 as the name
(Hedys) of the man from Ephesus, χρυσι[at v. 81 Ar = 63
K-A (cf. χρυ[at v. 216) as a *hetaira* Chrysi[s], and δρομ[at
v. 47 Ar = 119 K-A as a slave Drom[on]. The last of these is
more plausible than the others.

Scholars who have dealt with this papyrus readily acknowledge that nothing in the preserved portions of text ties in with any known quotation from Menander or any other comic poet, but there is a general—if subjective—feeling that the style of the comic trimeters, particularly in its imaginative use of language, brings Menander to mind more than anyone else. But if Menander, what play?

In his publication of the Col.1 fragments Maresch (pp. 2–3) noted that Menander's *Kitharistes* (vv. 93–98) and *Ephesios* introduced the city of Ephesus into their plots, yet the incidents known from the *Kitharistes* fragments appeared to derive from a plot irreconcilably different from that containing the dialogue and events of Col.1.[5] Gaiser (*ZPE* 63, 1986, 15–22) assigned Col.1 to Menander's *Hydria*, and Nünlist (*ZPE* 99, 1993, 271–78) assigned Col.1, Col.2 and Mich. to Menander's *Dis Exapaton*. Gaiser's suggestion, however, is ruled out partly because it assumes that the play's young man was in love not with a girl but with a valuable treasure, partly because it requires the entry of the chorus at the end of the first act to be signalled twice in different passages of text.[6] Nünlist's theory would compel Plautus, when adapting Menander's *Dis Exapaton* for his *Bacchides*, to have altered the original plot more substantially than he is ever known to have done elsewhere.[7]

Menander's *Ephesios*, on the other hand, faces no such

---

[5] Cf. *ZPE* 31 (1978) 26–29 and my Loeb Menander II, pp. 112–15.

[6] Cf. P. G. McC. Brown, *ZPE* 65 (1986) 34–35 and Nünlist 270.

[7] Cf. *ZPE* 123 (1998) 59–60.

objections. The surviving fragments from that play do not clash with the papyrus fragments of Col.1, Col.2 and Mich., while fr. 150 Kassel–Austin (assigned to the *Ephesios* by Harpocration)[8] presents a slave envisaging his being sold in the market. This could possibly come from a monologue by the same slave at or near the beginning of the next act, explaining his remark "Sell me" at v. 45 Ar = 117 K-A of the papyrus (Col.2).

Titles such as *Ephesios* seem normally to involve the presence of the titular ethnic in another town,[9] and this seems to be the case with the Ephesian at vv. 25–27 (Col.1). Gaiser admittedly once argued for Menander's *Ephesios* as the source of Plautus' *Miles Gloriosus*,[10] and if

[8] The relevant part of Harpocration's text (κ 91 Keaney) runs as follows: . . . κύκλοι ἐκαλοῦντο οἱ τόποι ἐν οἷς ἐπωλοῦντό τινες· ὠνομάσθησαν ἀπὸ τοῦ κύκλῳ περιεστάναι τοὺς πωλουμένους. Μένανδρος Ἐφεσίῳ·

ἐγὼ μὲν ἤδη μοι δοκῶ, νὴ τοὺς θεούς,
ἐν τοῖς κύκλοις ἐμαυτὸν ἐκδεδυκότα
ὁρᾶν κύκλῳ τρέχοντα καὶ πωλούμενον.

(1 ἤδη ms. N of Harpocration: οὖν ἤδη QPM, οὖν δὴ K. 2 ἐκδεδυκότα B: ἐνδε- the other mss.)

This translates: 'The places in which people were put up for sale were called "rings". They were given this name because those up for sale stood round in a ring. Menander in the *Ephesios*:

I think I see myself—yes, yes, I do—
Stripped naked in the market rings and there
Cavorting round and being up for sale.'

See also my paper in *ZPE* 125 (1999) 66.

[9] Cf. e.g. my *Alexis, The Fragments: A Commentary* (Cambridge 1996) 120, 128–29, 210.

[10] *Poetica* 1 (1967) 436–61.

that were correct, the differences in plot between the Latin play and the papyrus fragments from Cologne and Michigan would rule out any attribution of the papyrus to Menander's *Ephesios*. Gaiser's argument, however, has won little support.[11]

---

[11] See e.g. the Gomme–Sandbach commentary on Menander (Oxford 1973) pp. 7–8.

FABULA INCERTA 8

Col.1: fr. A

ΝΕΑΝΙΑΣ

]δ[

2 οἴκαδε κα[τα]γ[α]γὼν σ[ῶς], ἐὰν ἑτο[ιμ ◡–
ἔλθῃς ἀπ[αντ]ῶν αὐτός· οὕτω γὰρ κ[αλῶς
φαίνοντα φανὸν πό[θ]εν ἂν ἀγοράσειέ [τις];

ΠΑΙΔΑΓΩΓΟΣ (??)

5 ὑπαδολέσχης ἐστί.

1–166 Those corrections and supplements whose author is not named were made by the ed. pr., K. Maresch.

2 κα[τα]γ[α]γὼν σ[ῶς] suppl. Austin.

3 ἀπ[αντ]ῶν suppl. Kassel, κ[αλῶς Lloyd-Jones and West.

4 [τις] suppl. several.

5 Space after εστι indicating change of speaker in Col.1.

UNIDENTIFIED PLAY 8

(SCENE: A street in a city or village which is not identified in the surviving portions of this play; it is more likely to have been Athens than anywhere else. The street is probably backed by two houses, in one of which a courtesan lives. The fragments preserved in papyrus Col.1 begin shortly after the opening of the play. It is early morning. A young man has entered by one of the side entrances, and he now stands outside the closed door of the courtesan's house. He is now joined by another character, most probably the elderly slave who took the young man to and from school when the latter was a boy.)

Papyrus Col.1 (fragment A)

YOUNG MAN

(in mid-speech)
[Arriv]ing home [safe], if you come yourself   2
[Ready (?) to meet me]. Where could [any man]
Purchase a torch that shines so [brilliantly]?[1]

SLAVE TUTOR (?)

(probably aside)
He's quite an orator!

---

[1] It is now sunrise, and the speaker makes the point that the sun's light is far brighter than that provided by any torch.

MENANDER

ΝΕΑΝΙΑΣ

διαφέρει δέ μ[οι
ὁ κῶμος οὐδέν· πᾶσαν ὥραν γάρ—μέσ[ων
νυκτῶν, ἕωθεν, ἑσπέρας—ἀποκλείομαι.
προσκαρτερῶ δὲ καὶ πορεύομ᾽ ἐπιμ[ελῶς.
ἐρῶ γὰρ ὁ ταλαίπωρος ἀνθρώπων ἐ[γὼ

10 καινότα[τ]α πάντων, [ο]ὐχ ἑορακὼ[ς πώποτε
τὴν ὄψιν [ἧ]ς ἐρῶ, μὰ τοὺς δώδεκα θε[ούς.

ΠΑΙΔΑΓΩΓΟΣ (??)

πῶς οὖν ἐρᾷς, ὦ τρισκακόδαιμον; τ[ίνι τρόπῳ;

ΝΕΑΝΙΑΣ

πολλοῖς ἀπίθανον φαίνετ᾽ εἶναι τ[οῦτ᾽ ἴσως.

ΠΑΙΔΑΓΩΓΟΣ (??)

κ]ινητιᾶν τε καὶ τρυφᾶν λίαν δοκ[εῖς.

6 ωραγγαρ Col.1.
8 Suppl. Austin, Handley.
9 Suppl. Kassel.
10 πώποτε suppl. Kassel.
11 Suppl. Kassel, Merkelbach.
12 Suppl. Merkelbach.
13 This line assigned to the young man's companion by
Maresch (Col.1 has no paragraphus under it).   τ[οῦτ᾽ ἴσως
suppl. Gronewald.
14]εινητιαν and τρυφαλιαν Col.1.

FABULA INCERTA 8

YOUNG MAN
A revel[2] means   5
Nothing to me, for every single minute—
Midnight, sunrise and evening—I'm locked out.[3]
I persevere, though, and on purpose I
Keep coming, for my love is more unusual
Than anyone's. Poor me! By the twelve gods[4]   10
I swear I've never *seen* [my] darling's face!

SLAVE TUTOR (?)
Then how are you in love, poor boy? [What way]?

YOUNG MAN
People may think [this] quite absurd, [perhaps].

SLAVE TUTOR (?)
[You] seem to crave sex and delights too much!

[2] It was the practice of wealthy young males to drink heavily after dinner and then roam the streets together generally misbehaving and creating a nuisance. See especially H. Lamer in *RE* XI (1921) s.v. *Komos* 1286–1304, the Headlam–Knox commentary (Cambridge 1922) on Herodas 2.34–37, and cf. my commentary (Cambridge 1996) on Alexis fr. 112.1.   [3] The lover shut out by his beloved (usually a *hetaira*) and spending the night complaining at her door was a popular theme in ancient literature, and was developed in various ways at the beginning of several comedies (e.g. Menander *Misoumenos*, Plautus *Curculio, Truculentus*, Terence *Eunuchus*). See the Headlam–Knox commentary on Herodas 2, 34–37, F. O. Copley, *Exclusus Amator* (Baltimore 1956, reprinted Chico 1981) 1–42, 144–56, the Nisbet–Hubbard commentary (Oxford 1970) on Horace *Carm.* 1.25 (pp. 290–91, 293–94), and F. Cairns, *Generic Composition in Greek and Roman Poetry* (Edinburgh 1972), index s.v. komos.   [4] The twelve gods of Olympus: see note d on *Kolax* E232 (vol. II).

MENANDER

ΝΕΑΝΙΑΣ

15 φ]ὴς ἄτοπον. ἱκετεύω σε, πυθό[μενον σαφῶς
ἀ]στεῖον ἦθος, ἡδέως σχεῖν· δ.υ[
εἴ]ρηκ[α] τὴν ὄψιν γὰρ εἶναι μήποτε
......]εις ὥστ᾽ ἐκπεπλῆχθαι κ[
19 ....]τῳ κοσμίαν δειν.[

At v. 19 fr. A of Col.1 comes to an end, and there then is a
gap of around 20, 40 or 60 lines before fr. B of Col.1 comes
into play.

Col.1: fr. B

ΠΑΙΔΑΓΩΓΟΣ (??)

20 ἃ δὴ λογίζου. [πα]ραδέδωχ᾽ ὁ τυφ[λὸς Ἔρως
τὸ λαμπαδεῖον τοῦ πόθου γὰρ σοὶ λ[αθών.

ΝΕΑΝΙΑΣ

ὦ λῃστά.

ΠΑΙΔΑΓΩΓΟΣ (??)

σαυτὸν οὐ καθέξεις, ἄθλ[ιε;
ὡς σοὶ κέχρηται, νῦν ἀκμὴν χρῆτα[ι πάλιν.
σὺ γὰρ παρέδωκας σαυτόν, ἐμβρόν[τητε σύ.

15 Suppl. Merkelbach.
16 σχειν.υ Col.1 (ευ or ου) with the omitted δ written above
the ν.   17 εἴ]ρηκ[α] suppl. Austin.
20 [πα]ραδέδωχ᾽ ὁ Maresch:]ραδεδωκεν[Col.1.   τυφ[λὸς
Ἔρως suppl. Austin, West.   21 Suppl. West.
22, 23, 24 Suppl. Kassel.
24 σαυτόν Maresch: αυτον Col.1.

570

YOUNG MAN

You've got this wrong. I beg you, [when you] know [   ]   15
Her charming ways, be nice. [
You see, [I've said (?)] her face is never [
[   ] so as to be amazed [
                    ] well-behaved [19

*(Here there is a gap of one or more columns until the next
fragment of text is preserved. The same two characters may
be involved, but whether they are continuing the same
scene or appearing in a new one is uncertain.)*

Papyrus Col.1 (fragment B)

SLAVE TUTOR (??)
                                    . . . .
Your present thoughts. Blind [Cupid]'s [gone behind]   20
[Your back and] handed you the torch of passion!

YOUNG MAN
(angrily)
You thug![5]

SLAVE TUTOR (??)
          Poor chap, can't you control yourself?
Love's treating you [again] now as it has
Before. You've given in, [you] silly fool!

[5] Literally 'pirate' or 'brigand', but used here and at v. 51 ap-
parently as a general term of vituperation.

NEANIAΣ (?)

25 τί ἂν λέγοις; ἡδύς γ᾿ ἐληλύθειν, φ[ύσει
    ἄνθρωπος ὢν ὑπερηδύς, ὦ πότνι᾿ Ἄ[ρτεμι,
    κληδοῦχ᾿ Ἐφεσία· σὸς πολίτη[s] ε[
    ταῦτ᾿ εἰ πέπ[ον]θα—τί δὲ πέπονθα, πρὸς [θεῶν,
    τὸ δεινόν; ἤρ[ων] οὐκ ἰδὼν τρόπου τιν[ός,
30 καὶ νῦν ἐπαινῶ τοῦτον. ὄψεως τυχεῖ[ν
    ἠβουλόμην ἧς εἶδον, οὐχ ἧς ᾠόμην.
    οὐκ οἶδ᾿ ὅ τι λέγω, πλὴν ἀρέσκει μοι σφόδ[ρα,
    τό τ᾿ ἀγνόημα τοῦτ᾿ ἔχει μοι κατὰ τρόπον.
    ὑπερευπρόσωπός ἐστιν, ἣν ἑόρακ᾿ ἐγώ,
35 ἐν τοῖς λόγοις ἡδεῖ, ἑταίρα τῷ τρόπῳ.
    ἀπόπληκτος εἶναι βούλομαι ταύτην ἔχ[ων
    καὶ συνδιαπλέκων τὸν ἐπίλοιπον τοῦ β[ίου.

ΠΑΙΔΑΓΩΓΟΣ (??)

    οὐδ᾿ ἂν θεῶν σώσειεν οὐδεὶς τουτονί.

25 Change of speaker suggested here by Gaiser (Col.1 has no
paragraphus under it: cf. Maresch, ZPE 63, 1986, 15–16).
Ἡδύς interpreted as a proper name by Ameling, cf. v. 145.
γ᾿ Austin: τις Col.1.   ἐληλυθειμφ[Col.1: φ[ύσει suppl.
Austin.
    26 ποτνια.[(-αλ[or -αα[Col.1): suppl. Sheldon.
    28 πέπ[ον]θα suppl. Lloyd-Jones, [θεῶν Gronewald.
    29 ἤρ[ων] suppl. Kassel.
    35 ηδι Col.1.

YOUNG MAN

What can one say? A man of pleasant [mould]⁶   25
Had come—yes, very pleasant—from your town,
O Lady A[rtemis], Warden of Ephesus⁷ [   ]
If I have suffered—what's so dreadful, though,
In that? [I] loved a girl's demeanour, though
I never saw her. Now I praise it. I desired   30
To win a glimpse of one I saw, not one I thought
I saw. I don't know what to say, except
I'm very pleased—for me this ignorance is fine.
The girl I've seen is most attractive—she
Talks nicely, and acts like a courtesan.⁸   35
I want to be quite mad—possessing her
And spending all the rest of [life] with her.

SLAVE TUTOR (??)

(aside)
No god in heaven could rescue this chap here!

---

⁶ Or, just possibly, 'A man Hedys by name.'

⁷ The young man seems to imply that his new love sprang from the arrival of the man from Ephesus—was he a pimp who controlled his inamorata? Artemis was worshipped at Ephesus as the city's presiding divinity. See especially G. Seiterle, *Antike Welt* 10/3 (1979) 6–16, G. M. Rogers, *The Sacred Identity of Ephesos* (London 1991), and W. Burkert, *Greek Religion* (Oxford 1985) 149–52, 406–408.

⁸ Lines 31–35 are puzzling. The speaker apparently fell in love with the girl without seeing her face (vv. 10–11: see the introduction), but now (vv. 34–35) he has seen her and heard her talking. Did he first see her in the lost scene or scenes between v. 19 and v. 20?

MENANDER

ΝΕΑΝΙΑΣ (?)

39 τί φῄ[ς];

ΠΑΙΔΑΓΩΓΟΣ (??)

σὺ πορνοκοπεῖν προῄρησ᾽, εἰπέ μοι;

At v. 39 fr. B of Col.1 ends, and there is a gap of perhaps several acts between frs. B and C of Col.1. In between almost certainly comes fr. a + b of Col.2.

Col.2: fr. a + b

40 Ar	ειν.[..]..· οιμ[
=112 KA)	τοῦτ᾽ ἀναβαλο[
	εἴσω δ᾽ ἴωμεν π[
	.[
	..[....].[
45 Ar	ἀπόδου μ᾽ ἀκο[.......]ντ[
=117 KA)	τὸν λιμὸν οὐδε.[....].ρ.[
	γέρων ἀνὴρ τ[.....]μη Δρόμ[
	καὶ σὺ καταλ[...]. : εἰ γὰρ εἰδ[

39 Change of speaker after φῄ[ς] indicated by Maresch (but Col.1 has no space for a dicolon in the gap before συ).

40 εἶ, νύ[μφ]ιε Austin.

41 ἀναβαλο[ῦ or -ο[ῦμαι or -ο[ύμεθ᾽ Austin.

42 π[ρὸς Austin.

46 οὐδέπ[οτε Austin.

47 Δρόμ[ωνα Austin, Lloyd-Jones.

48 κατάλ[υσο]ν Austin.   εἰδ[ον Lloyd-Jones, εἶδ[ες Austin.

574

FABULA INCERTA 8

YOUNG MAN

(half hearing the aside)
What's that?

SLAVE TUTOR (??)

(sarcastically)
　　　　　Tell me, have you resolved to pimp?　　　　39

*(Here this fragment of text ends, and there is a gap of un-
known but not inordinate length before a further fragment
yields lines from the end of Act I. This is Papyrus Col.2
(fragment a + b), which has been assembled from the care-
ful juxtaposition of two small scraps which do not physi-
cally join at any one point. It contains the opening portions
of 18 lines, and is chiefly notable for containing a reference
to the arrival of the play's chorus, such as is signalled else-
where in Greek New Comedy always at the end of the first
act.[9]*

*There appear to be two or three characters on the stage
at the beginning of the fragment, one of whom is a slave.
Continuous translation is impossible, but the extant lines
yield the following snatches:* 40 You are (?) *and* Oh dear *or*
I think, *not necessarily spoken by the same character,* 41
Put this off, 42 Let's go inside, 45 Sell me!, 46 The famine,
nor *(it is uncertain whether this refers to a real contempo-
rary famine or one invented here for unknown dramatic
reasons),* 47 An old man *and* Don't, Drom[on], *two
phrases which were not necessarily spoken by the same
character,* 48 And kill (?) me too *(? spoken by the person
who said* Sell me! *at 45) followed by the reply* If only *(or*

---

[9] See also the introduction.

49 Ar   λέγων καθ᾽ ἑκά[στη]ν ἡμέραν [
=121 KA)   ..]νω τυχον.[....]ν μετρ.[

      <u>εὔτακτος ὅτι β[ούλ]ει παροιν[ῶν</u>
      <u>ἐγὼ παροινῶ[....]....ενφ[</u>
      <u>ἡμεῖς. τίς οὐκ [ἂ]ν ἀποπνιγε[ίη</u>
      <u>ἀλλ᾽ οὗτος εἴτ᾽ ἔστ᾽ ἐκ προ[</u>

55 Ar   χορός τις, ὡς ἔοικ[ε
=127 KA)   οὐκ ἐν ἀκροασ[

ΧΟ Ρ [ΟΥ]

49 λεγωγκαθ Col.2.

50, 53 Spaces after]νω and ημεις indicating change of speaker.

50 τυχονε[or -ονθ[Col.2.   ο]ὐ μετρί[ως Maresch.

51 Or εὖ τάκτὸς (Austin).   ὅτι β[ούλ]ει Merkelbach, παροιν[ῶν Austin.

53 ἀποπνιγε[ίη Maresch, then τοῦτ᾽ ἰδών Arnott, τοῦθ᾽ ὁρῶν Gaiser.

54 προ[αστίου ποθὲν Lloyd-Jones, προ[νοίας εἴτε μὴ Austin.

55 ἔοικ[εν, εἴτ᾽ ἀπὸ τῶν ἀγρῶν Lloyd-Jones, ἐνθάδ᾽ ἔρχεται Gaiser.

56 ἀκροάσ[ει τῶνδε συμφέρει μένειν West.

---

10 See the introduction.

For if) I *(or you)* had seen, *49* Saying every day. *From this point on to the end of the scene there seems to have been a series of short exchanges, although it is often uncertain where each remark begins and ends:* 50 perhaps . . . not moderate[ly], *51* Well-mannered since *(?)* . . . [you're] drunk, *followed at 52 by* I'm drunk?, *evidently a riposte from the person so accused,* 53 We, *followed by another character saying* Who wouldn't choke? *Lines 41–53 are too mutilated for a clear understanding of the scenario at this point, and speculation about it is perhaps unwise. One possibility is that in the lost scenes between vv. 39 and 40 the young man wished to win over the hetaira he loved by parties at which much wine was drunk, and money would have been needed to pay for these and for the hetaira's services. The slave who appeared in the opening scenes (perhaps named Drom[on], if that name is correctly supplemented at v. 47) might have sought to help by stealing money from the young man's father (? the old man of v. 47) in order to finance the affair. If he had been caught in the act, as punishment he could well have faced sale or even execution.*[10]

At v. 54 the approach of the chorus, ready to deliver their entr'acte at the end of Act I, is signalled, apparently by the character who said We *in v. 51.)*

But here's a band of revellers, [from some]   54
Place [in the suburbs or beyond], it seems.
[To stay here] within earshot [is]n't [wise].   56

(After the choral performance, this fragment preserves the first two words of Act II (57 The so-called*), and then breaks off. There is then a gap of perhaps several hundred*

⟨ΜΕΡΟΣ Β΄⟩

57 Ar   ὁ καλούμενος [

(=129 KA)

Col.1: fr. C
(column 1)

ΔΟΥΛΟΣ Α

58 Ar   .....]ταλ..δον[....].......αν, ἀλλὰ δεῖ

(=40 KA)   τού]τους ταράττειν, εἰς τ[ὸ] βά[ρ]αθρον.

ΔΟΥΛΟΣ Β

πρὸς θεῶν,

60 Ar   οὐ]χ οὗτός ἐσθ᾽ ἄνθρωπος ὁ φέρων ἐνθάδε

(=42 KA)   τ]ὸ Θάσιον.

ΔΟΥΛΟΣ Α

ἤδη δ᾽, ὡς ἔχω, πρὸς τὴν θύραν

π]ορεύσομ᾽ αὐτῶν.

ΔΟΥΛΟΣ Β

οὐδὲ εἷς ἄλλος μὲν οὖν.

εἰ]ς καιρὸν ἑόρακά σε.

60 οὐ]χ deciphered and suppl. Merkelbach.   εστ Col.1.

---

11 Slave A was presumably bringing the wine for a party, but
both occasion and participants are unknown. The wine of Thasos
was highly praised in antiquity; it was dark red and had a bouquet
suggesting apples. Cf. my commentary on Alexis (Cambridge
1996) fr. 232.4 (pp. 658–59).

lines before the next chunk of continuous and fairly complete text is available. It appears to begin with a tipsy and aggressive slave (here A), who has just entered with a large jar of wine, delivering an entrance monologue. He is on his way to one of the stage houses (the courtesan's ?), and does not at first notice that another character—probably also a slave, just possibly the tutor of the earlier scenes—is already on the stage. Since his identity is uncertain, he is here called Slave B.)

Papyrus Col.1 (fragment C)

SLAVE A
．．．．．．., but I must blast   58
[Them] to perdition.

SLAVE B
               Heavens, is[n't] that
The man—the one who's bringing here that load   60
Of Thasian wine?[11]

SLAVE A
(still not noticing slave B)
            And now, just as I am,
I'll walk up to their door.

SLAVE B
            Yes, it's the man himself!
(addressing slave A)
A timely meeting!

MENANDER

ΔΟΥΛΟΣ Α

σὺ δ᾽ εἶ τίς;

ΔΟΥΛΟΣ Β

φῦ ἰού.

ΔΟΥΛΟΣ Α

ἄ]νθρωπος οὐδ᾽ ἄπε[ι]σιν ἀπὸ τῆς οἰκίας;

ΔΟΥΛΟΣ Β

65 Ar   ἔ]τ᾽ ἐξ ἐκείνου περιπατεῖς σύ;

(=47 KA)

ΔΟΥΛΟΣ Α

φαίνομαι,

ν]αὶ μὰ Δία, ταῖτιον δέ—

ΔΟΥΛΟΣ Β

χρηστῶς δηλαδὴ

ἠρίστικας σεαυτὸν [....].†ηπαυνετο†
μαίνει· κατάξεις] τ[ὴ]ν θύραν τῇ χειρί.

ΔΟΥΛΟΣ Α

ναί,

ὦ λῄ]στ᾽ ἀναιδές.

ΔΟΥΛΟΣ Β

νῦν δὲ τῷ σκέλει πάλιν

70 Ar   κό]ψας—

(=52 KA)

63 τιφυ Col.1: correction made by Maresch, change of
speaker indicated by Handley.
67 Corr. Gronewald: ηριστικασεαυτον Col.1.
70 κό]ψας and ἄπει]σιν suppl. Austin, [δ᾽ οὐκ] Koenen.

580

SLAVE A

(coming up to slave B)
Who are you?

SLAVE B

(now able to smell the other slave's alcoholic breath)
Ugh! Oh!

SLAVE A

(aside)
That fellow—won't he move off from the house?

SLAVE B

Still on your way from him,[12] are you?

SLAVE A

Yes, it appears   65
So, and the reason—

SLAVE B

(as slave A starts knocking vigorously on one of the house doors)
Clearly you have had
A splendid lunch [
[You're mad! You'll smash] the door with your fist!

SLAVE A

(knocking first with his fist and then with his foot)
Yes,
[You] cheeky thug![13]

SLAVE B

Knocking again now, with
Your foot—

---

[12] The surviving fragments of this play do not reveal the identity of 'him.'   [13] See note on v. 22.

MENANDER

ΔΟΥΛΟΣ Α

ὁ [δ' οὐκ ἄπει]σιν;

ΔΟΥΛΟΣ Β

ὦ τεράστιοι
δαίμον[ες· ἄκου]σον, πρὸς θεῶν, βέλτιστ', ἐμοῦ.

ΔΟΥΛΟΣ Α

πάλιν [θέλεις κό]πτειν με;

ΔΟΥΛΟΣ Β

γινώσκεις γ᾽ ἐμὲ
πολὺ μᾶλ[λον ἢ] τοὺς ἔνδον.

ΔΟΥΛΟΣ Α

οὐκ ἐδιακόνεις
ἔνδον σὺ παρὰ τούτοισι;

ΔΟΥΛΟΣ Β

καὶ κόπτων ἐμὲ

75 Ar   ×–ū–]εις, φίλτατ'· ἐπιδεῖται λογου
(col. 2)   τὸ πρᾶγμ[α

The rest of column 2 preserves only the opening letters of
the lines; assignment of speakers is impossible.

71 δαίμον[ες suppl. Nünlist, ἄκου]σον Austin.
72 [θέλεις suppl. Arnott, κό]πτειν Austin.   ]πτειμμε
Col.1.   -εισεμε Col.1 with the omitted γ written above σε.
73 Suppl. Nünlist.

582

SLAVE A

(aside)

Will he [not] go [away]?

SLAVE B

(exasperated)

O gods,   70

We need a miracle! Sir, [hear] me, please!

SLAVE A

[Want] me once more to go on knocking?

SLAVE B

You know me

Far better [than] the people there.

SLAVE A

Didn't you

Once serve the folk in there?

SLAVE B

And boring (?) me

[   ], dear fellow. This affair requires   75

Some talking over. [76

(Lines 58–75 come in one well-preserved column of Col.1's fragment C, but vv. 76–93 yield only the opening four to seven letters in each line of the following column, together with an occasional dicolon and twelve paragraphi. This suggests that the lively conversation of vv. 58–75 continued into the next column, although we have no means of knowing when—or if—slave A's onslaught on the house door won any response from inside. Slave B may have added to his remark in vv. 75–76 a question Do they say that . . . not

77 Ar (59 KA) <u>οὔ φασιν[</u>

<u>οὔ φασι.: ν[</u>

<u>κόπτειν[</u>

80 Ar (62 KA) <u>μᾶλλ[ον</u>

<u>καὶ χρυσι[</u>

<u>μενοῦμ[εν</u>

<u>ὡς ἀνοσι[</u>

<u>ἐπίσχες .[</u>

85 Ar (67 KA) <u>δευρί τισ.[</u>

<u>τ[.]ν εν[</u> 86 Ar (68 KA)

<u>τί φής; οφ[</u>

<u>εὐθὺς ποθ[</u>

<u>καὶ ταῦτ[α</u>

<u>ποῦ δ' ἐστὶ[</u> 90 Ar (72 KA)

<u>κακῶς.: α[</u>

<u>οὐχὶ πα[</u>

<u>π.[.]ω.[</u> 93 Ar (75 KA)

Col.1: other fragments

fr. D

(column 1)   (column 2)

<u>κα.[.........]..[</u> 97 Ar (79 KA)

ερωτικηδει..ν...[

94 Ar   ]ει

(=76 KA)   ]ενους

96 Ar   ].ιν

(=78 KA)

<u>κε[ῖ]ται προσελθὼν ...[</u>

<u>ἔοικέ τις τῶν ἔν[δ]ον [</u> 100 Ar (82 KA)

<u>ἐνθ[ά]δε φέρω τὸ Θάσ[ιον</u>

<u>τ[οὺ]ς δ' ἄνθρακας μετα[</u>

..[.......]....[103 Ar (85 KA)

81 χρυσί[ον Gaiser.   83 Sc. either some part of ἀνόσιος
or ἀνοσίως (Maresch).   84 Or ἐπισχε σ.[.

86 τ[ὴ]ν or τ[ὸ]ν or τ[ῶ]ν.   89 Suppl. Gaiser.

93 πο[θ]ω.[West.   98 ἐρῶ· τί κήδει τὸν πόθ[ον Maresch
(τὸν πόν[ον Gaiser).   99 Suppl. West.

100 Suppl. Austin, West.   101 ἐνθ[ά]δε suppl. Austin,
Θάσ[ιον Gronewald.   102 μετὰ [ταῦτα Austin.

... (77), *eliciting from slave A the reply* That's what they say *78. Thereafter it is hard to decide who says what. Line 79 opens with* To knock, *presumably with reference to the closed door, then 80–93 produce only a few contextless words and phrases:* 80 More, *81 the response* And gold *(or, less plausibly,* And Chrysi[s], *with the assumption that this was the name of a hetaira in the play), 82 the response* We'll stay *(slave A in front of the house door, or slave B?), 83 the response* How wicked[ly?], *84 a responding command* Stop *(could this have been voiced by somebody eventually opening the door?), 85* Here someone, *87 as a response* What do you say?, *88* Straightway, *89* And this, *90 (in response to v. 89)* Where is, *91 the response* Badly, *92 the response* Not).

Papyrus Col.1: other fragments

Fragment D. *A small scrap, with a few untranslatable letters from the ends of three consecutive lines in one column (94–96), and more substantial fragments of the openings of six consecutive lines in the next column (97–102). The position of this scrap and frs. E, F and G of Col.1 is totally obscure. Fragment D yields the following snippets: 98* I am in love. What do you care? *(spoken by the young man of frs. A and B?), 99* He's come here and is lying down *(a reference to the man from Ephesus?), 100* One of those inside is likely, *101* I'm bringing here the Thasian wine *(spoken presumably by slave A of fr. C), 102* The charcoal. *If this scrap comes shortly after fr. C of papyrus Col.1, it might imply that the young man of fr. A had eventually been allowed inside the hetaira's house, and was now planning a wine party there for the hetaira and himself. In that event the*

fr. E

		fr. F	
104 Ar	] .αι χρόνον	]..[	122 Ar (104 KA)
105 Ar (87 KA)	]λ.πε.	]και[	
	π]άρελθε, παῖ	]σασκ[	
	]ει δοκεῖ	]μαλ[	125 Ar
	]πνίγομαι	]..[	126 Ar (108 KA)
	]ητις τῷ τρόπῳ	fr. G	
110 Ar (92 KA)	]α λιτῆς κακῶν	].νωμ[	127 Ar (109 KA)
	]κακὸν εἴσομαι	].ειον[	
	]πιθε.ν...ον	]..[	129 Ar (111 KA)
	]ενος		
	]ποτοι		
115 Ar (97 KA)	]ταχὺ		
	]..		
	]τικῶς ἔχει		
	]ων ἐστὶ γὰρ		
	ἐ]ν τῇ πόλει		
120 Ar (102 KA)	]παύομαι		
121 Ar (103 KA)	] δ' ἀπέρχομαι		

Col.2: other fragments

fr. c

130   ῥ]ᾷστα τη[...]..πω[
     ]τιν ὃ λέγω......[
     μ]εμαθήκατ[
     ]μ' ὑφαρπ[α
134   ]ασαυτη[

FABULA INCERTA 8

wine carrier slave A would doubtless be a slave in the young man's household.

Fragment E. *A small scrap with 18 line ends (104–121), yielding little that can be translated: 104 time, 106 come in, my boy (could this have been addressed to slave A of fr. C when he finally gained admittance?), 107 seems, 108 I choke, 109 in the manner, 110 a simple . . . of evils or of troubles, 111 I'll know . . . bad, 114 carousals (?), 115 quick, 117 is + unknown adjective, 118 for he or she or it is, 119 in the city, 120 I'm stopping, 121 I'm off.*

Fragments F and G. *Two miniscule scraps. F has a few letters from five lines (122–126), perhaps yielding* and *in v. 123; G has a few letters from three lines (127–29), yielding nothing that can be translated.*

Papyrus Col.2: other fragments

Fragment c. *A tiny scrap, unplaced like the others in this section. Letters from the middle of several lines are preserved in this and the following five scraps (d–h), and in*

---

105 κόλ[λοπες Maresch.   106 Deciphered and supplemented by Maresch, Gronewald:]αρελε Col.1 with missing θ written above the λ.   108 Deciph. Gronewald.

114 Deciph. Maresch, Gronewald.   117 ἐρω]τικῶς Maresch.   131 ἔσ]τιν Merkelbach.   132 Suppl. Parsons.

135 διοι[κῆσαι or διοι[κεῖν πράγματα Austin.

138 μὰ] or νὴ] Lloyd-Jones.   140 δ᾽ ἥκον[τα or δ᾽ ἡ κόν[ις Austin.   145]μ᾽ Ἡδὺς ἐγγ[ὺς ἵσταται Austin, cf. v. 25.

587

	fr. d			fr. e
135	].ης καὶ διοι[κ	143	]..[...].[	
	]αι ῥᾳδ[ι.]..[		]πραγματ[	
	]τουταδ[	145	]μηδυσεγ.[	
	]τοὺς θεο[ύς		]..πυγοτ[	
	]ουτ’ ἐστ[ι		]...ιβουλε[	
140	]δηκον[		]...ἀγαθὸν [	
	]πωσπ[	149	]....δαμη[	
142	].μητ[			

fr. f

150   ].σει...[
151   π]νιγομεν.[

	fr. g			fr. i
152	].δε.[	159	ἄθ]λιοι	
	λ]αβονη[	160	]ος ἄθλιος	
	]..σινω[			
155	]..[			

	fr. h			fr. j
156	].ειδε[	161	] χρόνον	
	]πλησ[	162	].σεδει	
158	]...[			

146–47 και]λιπυγότ[ατος Maresch, whence τῆς και]λιπυ-
γοτ[άτης κόρης / πληγεὶς ἔρωτ]ι βούλε[ται γαμεῖν Austin.

150].σειελ.[or].σεισα.[Col.2.

159–66 Frs. i, j and k seem to fit in at the ends of some of the
lines in frs. a + b (40–57 Ar = 112–29 K–A), so that vv. 165–66 =
43–44 Ar = 115–16 K–A.

159 Suppl. Kassel.

*none of them (nor in fragments i–k) can any of the speakers
be identified. In fr. c we have bits of five lines (130–34). No
character or characters can be identified. The following
words and phrases can be translated:* 130 *most easily,* 131
[it]*'s what I say,* 132 *you've learnt (with a plural you),* 133
filch from me.

Fragment d. *A tiny scrap, with bits of eight lines (135–42).
These lines yield the following words:* 135 *and . . . manage,*
136 *easy,* 138 *the gods (? part of an oath),* 139 *nor or nei-
ther is,* 140 *coming (?).*

Fragment e. *A tiny scrap, with bits of seven lines (143–49).
The following words emerge:* 144 *business,* 145 *pleasant
(or just possibly the name* Hedys: *see above, note on v. 25),*
146 [with fairest] *buttocks (?), possibly describing the
young man's beloved),* 147 *wishes (?),* 148 *good.*

Fragment f. *A minuscule scrap, with bits of two lines (150–
51) only.* 151 *seems to give* choking.

Fragment g. *A minuscule scrap, with bits of four lines
(152–55).* 153 *may give* took.

Fragment h. *A minuscule scrap, with bits of three lines
(156–68) yielding nothing securely translatable.*

Fragment i. *A minuscule scrap, containing the ends of two
lines (here 159–60).* 159 *gives* wretched *in the masculine
plural,* 160 *wretched in the masculine singular.*

Fragment j. *A minuscule scrap, also containing the ends of
two lines (161–62).* 161 *yields* time, 162 *perhaps* you must
or you had to.

fr. k

(column 1)   163   ]   (column 2)   165   <u>.....[</u>
             164   ]..ου   166   <u>..[.]...[</u>

Mich.: fr. a (column 1)

167   ]ην οὗτός ἐστιν .υ.[
              ]..δ᾽ [᾽Ε]φέσιος παχὺς
              ἀ]λλὰ τὴν θύραν ψοφε[ῖ
170   ].εχε βεβουλεῦσθαι δ᾽ ὅμ[ως
              τ]αῦτα νῦν ἁγὼ λέγω
              ]ται, μὰ τοὺς δώδεκα θεούς,
              ]. ἥτις ἐπτοημέ[ν]η
              ].χικο..υ..οσ[..]...
175   ]..ε.πε...[
              ].............ω
177   ]του

167–244 Those corrections and supplements whose author is
not named were made by the ed.pr., R. Nünlist.
167 E.g. εὔλ[ογος or εὐχ[ερής Nünlist.
174 υτειοσ[?
175 περιτ[?

---

[14] The word thus translated has a wide range of meanings, in-
cluding fat, stupid and rich. It is uncertain which one was in-
tended here.   [15] See note d on *Kolax* E232 (vol. II, p. 183).
[16] See v. 81 and the introduction.

Fragment k. *A minuscule scrap, with the ends of two lines and the beginnings of two lines at the same level in the next column. These four lines are numbered 163–66 opposite and in the edition of Kassel–Austin, but 165–66 seem rather to provide the openings of vv. 43–44 Ar = 115–16 KA. Unfortunately no single word can be securely read in any of the four lines.*

Papyrus Mich. (fragment a, column 1)

(Fragments a and b of papyrus Mich. have been skilfully juxtaposed to yield the line ends in one column and begin-nings or middles of lines from the next. In column 1 of frag-ment a (vv. 167–81) an unidentified character seems to be speaking while someone else prepares to enter from one of the stage houses. The opening lines of column a, though mutilated, deserve to be set out as follows:)

]this man's good-[	167
] fat[14] cat (?) from Ephesus	
] but the door's being opened	
] still, though, to have planned	170
] these things that I now say	
] by the twelve gods,[15]	
] a girl who, quivering	173

(The references here to the man from Ephesus and the quivering girl are intriguing but in the absence of context problematic. The Ephesian is probably the man previously mentioned in vv. 25–27, the quivering girl possibly the one loved by the young man of frs. A and B of papyrus Col.1, and the speaker perhaps that young man himself.

MENANDER

Between vv. 177 and 178 there is a gap of 4 lines.

178   ]. λόγῳ
                                           ]εμιᾶς
180   ]διαλέξομαι
181   ] : νὴ τοὺς θε[ού]s

                    Mich.: fr. a (column 2) + fr. b
182   ]μελετῶ δ[
                             ]παρουδοπ[
                             ] οὐθεὶς ..[
185   ]αρβω.....[
                             το]ῦτο καὶ μειρ[άκιον
                             ]. πολυσημα[
                             κα]ὶ λαλεῖς πρὸ[s
                             ].ε....[
190   ..[   ].πολ.λα.[
191   το..[   ]....[

Between vv. 191 and 192 there is a gap of 5 lines.

192   ..[.   ].[.]πρ[
      σ.[   ]..[
      διδοντ[........]....[.....]α[
195   ἄνθρωπος ....ν ὄλεθρος α....[
      πίστευσον, ὦ τᾶν, οὐχ .π..τ..ε[

        183 παρ' οὗ δ' ὁ π[αῖς Nünlist.   184 α.[or λ.[.
        187]σ or]ν.   189 Or].σ.   190]ἀπόλωλα Nünlist.
        192 α.[or λ.[at beginning of line.
        194].σαι[or].θαι[or]αθλι[.   196 .πειτεδε[?

592

FABULA INCERTA 8

*After v. 173 the papyrus is badly torn and abraded.
Lines 174–77 yield no identifiable words, followed by four
unnumbered lines where nothing at all can be read, and
then four lines at the bottom of the column (178–81) con-
taining in 178* speech *or* word, *179 an adjectival* no, *180* I'll
have a talk, *and 181 (as a response perhaps from the person
whose entrance was signalled at 169)* yes, by the gods!)

Papyrus Mich. (fragment a + b, column 2)

*(Column 2 of this fragment (vv. 182–96) yields far less than
column 1. The following words, however, can be made out
in vv. 182–91: 182* I practise (?), *183* from whom the (?),
184 nobody *or adjectival* no, *186* this *or* it, *and a young
man (?), 187* [things] with many meanings, *188* and you're
chattering to, *190* done for. *After v. 191 there are five un-
numbered lines where nothing can be read. Then at the
foot of the column five further lines (192–96) yield a few
words: 194* Giving, *195* The man['s] a pest, *196* Trust me,
sir . . . not.)

Mich.: other fragments

<table>
<tr><td>fr. c</td><td>fr. d</td></tr>
</table>

fr. c

197　δ..[

 οὐκ ἔλεγον α[

ἐμὲ γὰρ πρ[

200　ἤδη περιπα[τ

πασῶν νεν[ομι

φλύαρον ε.[

ὡς μήποτ[

οὐδ᾿ ἐμφερ.[

205　σωθεὶς ἐγ[ὼ

[gap of 7 lines]

206　σὺ δητ[

τὸ πνεῦ[μα

208　ἄφες φε[

fr. d

209　].μον.[

210　]απολωλ[

].τινα

].[

].γρ[

214　]ου

[gap of 2 lines]

215　]δητω[

]ει γε χρυ[

] τὰς θύρ[ας

]ηλο..[

]λαμβα[ν

220　]ν και..[

]τουτω[

]..[

].α[

224　].[

199 Mich. has a trace of a letter in the left margin.

204 Or ουδεμ (for οὐδὲν) φερ[ω Mich.

205–206 The writing in this gap is abraded, but in the left margin level with the fifth missing line].πα[can be read.

208 φέ[ριστε Nünlist.

209]μμ or]ημ, with traces of a correcting letter over the μ.

210 ἀπόλωλ[α or ἀπολώλ[αμεν Nünlist.

216 χρυ[σίον or oblique case of name Χρυ[σίς Nünlist.

Papyrus Mich.: other fragments

Fragment c. *A tiny scrap, unplaced like the others in this section. Fragments c and e contain the opening letters of several lines: fragments d, f and g middle bits of several lines. Fragment c (vv. 197–208) is notable in that under six of its 12 readable lines there are paragraphi, suggesting that here a lively conversation was in progress. The following words can be made out:* 198 I *or* They didn't say, 199 For . . . me, 200 Now . . . walk, 201 Of all . . . have thought (?), 202 Nonsense, 203 Never, 204 *either* Nor resembling *or* . . . carry nothing, 205 Rescued, I. *Seven unnumbered lines follow, where no letters can now be read, apart from an uninterpreted note in the left margin. The three final lines in this fragment give only* You (206), The breath (207) *and* Let go (208).

Fragment d. *A tiny scrap with only a few letters preserved in each of its 16 readable lines (209–24); between vv. 214 and 215 there are two unnumbered lines, where nothing can now be read. Few words, however, can be made out anywhere:* 210 done for, 211 some, 216 gold (?: *or, less probably, the name* Chry[sis][16]), 217 the doors, 219 take, 221 this.

---

[16] See v. 81 and the introduction.

fr. e

225 ἐπιτ[
     ἔγωγ[
     τίς οὗτ[ος
     ἐνεργὸς ε.[
     εὖ γ᾽, ὦ κράτιστ[
230 ἔλθ᾽ †ἐζομεν†[

fr. f

231].υθε[
     ]ωστ[
     ]νην[
     ].αν.[
235]....[
     ]..[
237]το[
     [gap of 2 lines]
238]οκα[
     [gap of 3 lines]
239]ου.[
     ]...[
241].[

fr. g

242]..[
     ]....[
244]τα...[

228 ἐνεργὸς εἶ Nünlist.
234]σαν or]καν.

Fragment e. *A tiny scrap with the opening letters of six lines (225–30). The following words and phrases can be made out:* 225 On, 226 I, 227 Who [is (?)] this, 228 You're busy, 229 *(probably a different speaker)* That's fine, sir, 230 Come . . . sitting (?).

Fragment f. *A tiny scrap with very few letters preserved in its 11 identifiable lines (231–41); between 237 and 238 there is a gap of two and between 238 and 239 a gap of three unnumbered lines. No single word can be confidently deciphered.*

Fragment g. *A minuscule scrap with traces of writing in its three lines (242–44), but barely three letters can be deciphered.*

FABULA INCERTA 9

INTRODUCTION

Manuscript

O = *P.Oxyrhynchus* 3966, a small scrap containing the
remains of 15 verses at the foot of a column. The hand-
writing, dated to the first century A.D., seems to be iden-
tical with that of *P.Oxyrhynchus* 2654 (a fragment of
Menander's *Karchedonios*; see vol. II, pp. 83–98) and
P.Cologne 4 (possibly a further scrap of *Karchedonios*, see
vol. II, pp. 100–103), but *P.Oxy.* 3966 shows no traces of
dicola or paragraphi. First edition: E. W. Handley in
Handley and A. Hurst (edd.), *Relire Ménandre* (Geneva
1990) 138–43, cf. 162–66; it was republished by Handley
in *The Oxyrhynchus Papyri* 59 (1992) 51–59 with a photo-
graph (pl. I).

Lines 6–16 of this fragment present a character (A) of
unidentifiable status and sex commenting on the arrival of
some people bringing spring water to a bride's home for
her prenuptial bath. If this scrap came from the same
roll as *P.Oxy.* 2654, it could also be part of Menander's
Karchedonios, although it contains nothing that indisput-

ably links it with what little is known of that play.[1] If it derives from another play, not necessarily by Menander, its source cannot be guessed, since weddings appear to close a substantial proportion of known New Comedy plays. As Menandrean possibilities Handley (51–54) suggested *Phasma*, Thomas Gelzer (*Relire* 165–66) *Georgos*, and Netta Zagagi (*Relire* 165) *Kres*; to sustain any of these proposals the limited evidence needs to be pressed very hard.[2]

A reference in this passage (v. 13) to the future bride's being asleep at the time when the water was being fetched for the nuptial bath has led two scholars (H.-D. Blume, P. Brown in *Relire* 162) to assume that a night intervened

[1] See also volume II, pp. 84–85. For one possible identification of character A, however, if this scrap does come from the *Karchedonios*, see below.

[2] Handley notes that in P.*Oxy.* 3966 the bride was sleeping indoors in a locked room (v. 13) and that v. 12 can partly be interpreted as sung lyrics, while *Phasma* (v. 14) referred to 'a girl kept secretly shut up indoors' and (test. VII) allegedly contained ithyphallics resolved into tribrachs. Yet although the surviving portion of v. 12 in P.*Oxy.* 3966 can (not must) be scanned as lyric tribrachs, the situations of the two girls in that papyrus and *Phasma* do not seem identical; we have no evidence that the *Phasma* girl was still in seclusion on her wedding day, nor was she described in any of the extant fragments as 'shut up.' Gelzer's theory is based on ingenious but unverifiable speculations about dramatic developments in the missing portions of *Georgos*. Zagagi suspects that vv. 8–10 of P.*Oxy.* 3966 may be introduced to explain a custom that was unfamiliar to one of the play's characters; this requires that character to have come from outside the Greek part of the world, like, e.g., the Carthaginian title figure of Menander's *Karchedonios*.

between this act and the beginning of the play, as happened in Menander's *Hauton Timoroumenos*.[3] The assumption may be correct, but it is equally possible that a young bride-to-be was enjoying a siesta before the wedding ceremonies that same evening.

[3] See also *ZPE* 70 (1987) 22–23, 72 (1988) 26 and the fragmentary plot summary of *Demiourgos* below.

FABULA INCERTA 9

P.Oxyrhynchus 3966

```
1        ]...[
         ]..[.]ιν[
         ]σ.....[
4        ]ης, ἐὰν δέηθ᾽, ἅ[μα.
5             Χ]Ο  Ρ  [ΟΥ
```

Those corrections and supplements whose author is not named were made by the ed. pr., E. W. Handley.

---

1 On prenuptial baths see R. E. Wycherley, *The Athenian Agora, III: Literary and Epigraphical Testimonia* (Princeton 1957) 137–52 (especially testim. 438, 439, 452 and 455), R.

UNIDENTIFIED PLAY 9

P.Oxyrhynchus 3966

(*Lines 1–4, which are so torn and abraded that only* if need
be, to[gether (?)] *at or near the end of v.4 can tentatively be
deciphered, appear to come from the end of one act, and
vv.6–16, which are better preserved, open the following
act. At the beginning of the new act a character emerges in
all probability from one of the stage houses and observes
the approach of at least three people: a hired female singer,
a piper, and a young slave who carries a large vase filled
with water from a local spring (Callirhoe, if the scene is
Athens). This water is destined for the ceremonial bath that
the bride took directly before her wedding.[1] The identity of
the character who observes the approach is unknown and
unguessable, unless this scrap derives from Menander's
Karchedonios; in that case one possibility would be the
Carthaginian title figure, noting in vv. 8–10 his unfamiliar-
ity with one feature of Greek weddings.*)

Ginouvès, *Balaneutikè* (Paris 1962) 265–82, R. Garland, *The
Greek Way of Life* (Ithaca NY 1990) 220, J. H. Oakley and
Rebecca H. Sinos, *The Wedding in Ancient Athens* (Madison
Wisc. 1993) 5–6, 15–16 (with illustrations in figs. 16–19 of an Attic
red-figure vase portraying a group seeking water for such a bath at
the spring), and my note on *Samia* 157–59.

(A)

6   ].τερον νῦν αὐτοσ.[
      ......]μ᾽ ἀληθές· ο[ἰ]νοχο[ῶν τις ἔρχετ᾽ ἢ
    φέρων] τὰ λουτρά· τοῦτο γὰρ [νομίζεται
    τὰ λουτρ]ὰ τοῖς γαμοῦσιν ἀπ[ὸ κ]ρή[ν]ης φέρειν,
10 ᾄδειν πρ]ὸς αὐλόν· καί τι μέντοι—πρὸς θεῶν,
    πάρες] ποτ᾽—ἐπακούσαιμ᾽ ἂν ἡδέως, γύνα[ι.

Η ΜΕΛΩΙΔΟΤΣΑ (B)
ἀφύπ]νισον, ἀφύπνισον, ἀ.[.].[

(A)

αὐτὴ κάθευδεν ἔνδον ἐγκεκλειμ[ένη·
ᾄ]δειν γὰρ ἐμεμίσθωτο πρὸς τουτο[

ΤΔΡΟΦΟΡΟΣ (C)
15 πρὸς ποῖον ὑδροφορεῖν με δεῖ μέλος ποτε;

(A)

16 παιδάριον οἰκότριψ γὰρ εἶναί μοι δοκεῖ.

6]ε,]ο, or]σ (νῦν—αὐτὸ ση[μανεῖ—τόδε tentatively
Handley). 7 τὸ πρᾶγ]μ᾽ suppl. Turner. 10 Suppl. Turner.
11 γύνα[ι suppl. Turner. 12 Suppl. Handley, interpret-
ing this line as lyrical anapaests resolved into proceleusmatics.
After the second αφυπνισον O adds αφυπνισον.[.]. but crosses
φυπνισον out. 13 Deciphered and suppl. Turner.
16 Or δοκεῖ[ς.

---

[2] But not Act II, since the decipherable words in v. 4 show no
links with any of the conventional phrases used to introduce the
chorus at the end of Act I. [3] These remarks suggest that the
arrival of this group proves to the speaker that a previously ar-

ACT III, IV OR V[2]

CHARACTER A
(as the party arrives)
[It's even clear]er now—events [will show]—   6
[The whole thing]'s true.[3] A lad's here [bringing[water
For wine[4] or wedding bath—that [is the custom],
To fetch spring [water] for the bridal pair
And [sing], backed by a piper. I should like   10
To hear some music, please [allow me], ma'am.[5]

SINGER
(?: with the piper accompanying)
  Awake, awake [

CHARACTER A
The bride was sleeping, shut inside her room.
A singer had been hired for this [

BOY CARRYING THE WATER
What is the song that fetching water calls for?   15

CHARACTER A
I think he's[6] just a young lad from the house.

ranged wedding, which for some reason had been cancelled, postponed or impeded (cf. e.g. in Menander Act II of *Aspis*, Acts IV and V of *Samia*), was in progress again.   [4] The lad was carrying a λουτροφόρος, a large vase (see Oakley and Sinos, *The Wedding in Ancient Athens,* p. 6) filled with water that could be used for either a prenuptial bath or for mixing with wine at the wedding dinner.   [5] It is uncertain whether here he addresses the singer, who must then be female, or another person in charge of the group.   [6] Presumably the young slave carrying the water. The translation would need to be changed to 'I think [you're] just' if the papyrus originally had δοκεῖ[ς].

A PAPYRUS WITH NEW
QUOTATIONS FROM
MENANDER

INTRODUCTION

Manuscript

F = a papyrus in Florence (to be given definitive publication eventually in *PSI* vol. XV as no. 1476) written in the second or early third century A.D. Six scraps (A–G) survive from an anonymous anthology of quotations, which are assembled (as in Stobaeus) under a series of headings (περὶ ἀρετῆς / λόγου / πλούτου / τύχης: On Excellence / Speech / Wealth / Chance). They include two certainly and one probably by Menander, all unknown before, from the section 'On Chance.' First edition: V. Bartoletti, *Atti dell'XI Congresso Internazionale di Papirologia* (Milan 1966) 1–14 (without any photograph).

MENANDER

Menander fr. 89 Kassel–Austin

(quotation 4 in the papyrus, scrap B: p. 11 Bartoletti)

Μενάνδρ[ου ἐ]ξ Ἀχαιῶν·

                ἀλλ' ἐγύμνασ' ἡ τύχη

τοῦτον πένητα καὶ ταπεινὸν ἐν πόνοι[ς

ἵν' ἀναφέρῃ τὰ λαμπρὰ μεταβολῆς τυχών.

Those corrections and supplements whose author is not
named in this and the two following apparatuses were made by
the ed.pr., V. Bartoletti.

  Lemma: αχεων F.
  1 εγυμνασεν F.
  2 ταπινον εν πονυ[F.
  3 ιναφερη F.

NEW QUOTATIONS

Menander fr. 89 K-A

By Menander, from *Achaioi* ('Achaeans'),

> But chance trained him
> To poverty and meekness in his troubles,
> So when things changed he might regain his glory.

(Elsewhere this play's title is once listed (Kassel–Austin PCG VI.2, testim. 41.12) as 'Achaeans or Peloponnesians.' This is the only fragment surviving from the play, although a mosaic from Oescus now in Pleven Museum (MNC³ II p. 468, 6DM1: black and white illustration in S. Charitonidis and others, Les mosaïques de la Maison du Ménandre à Mytilène, Berne 1970, pl. 27) depicts a scene from the play. On the left is a door; an old man with his back to it has a stick; he seems to be in conversation with another old man in the badly damaged centre of the picture. Behind and to the right of this second old man stand two youths wearing military cloaks and apparently listening hard to the old men's conversation. Presumably one of the young men would have been a mute. If the alternative title is correctly attached to this play, it seems more likely that its plot involved contemporary Greeks in a conventional New Comedy intrigue than Greeks of myth in a burlesque of the Trojan War.

The papyrus fragment, spoken by an unknown character in an unknown situation possibly towards the end of the play (cf. Dyskolos 961–65), expresses a conventional view of Chance's ability to change a person's situation in one fell swoop; see especially G. Vogt-Spira, Dramaturgie des Zufalls, Zetemata 80, Munich 1992, 51–59, with 58–59 devoted to this fragment.)

Menander fr. 126 K-A

(quotation 5 in the papyrus, scrap B: p. 11 Bartoletti)

ἐξ Ἐπαγγελλομένου·

φρονοῦντός ἐστι ζημίας ὀρθῶς φέρειν·
πλ[ο]υτοῦντος, οὐ φρ[ο]νοῦντος, ἔργον μὴ λέγ[ειν.

1 Cited also (with variants) in the monostichs attributed to
Menander (v. 818 Jäkel)

Lemma: απαν.ελλωμενου F.
1 ἐστι mss. of monostichs: εστιν F.   ζημίας F and mss. KP
of monost.: ζημίαν other mss. of monost.   ορθῶς F: πρᾴως or
καλῶς or (!) γενναίως mss. of monost.   φέρειν mss. of
monost.: φεριν F.
2 οὐ deciphered by Snell.

NEW QUOTATIONS

Menander fr. 126 K-A

From his *Epangellomenos* (? 'The Man Making an Offer'),

A man with sense bears losses honestly;
A rich man without sense should hold his tongue!

*(The title here is of uncertain application. Five fragments
survive from this play (124–28 K-A); v. 1 here is an expres-
sion of conventional wisdom (see K. J. Dover, Greek Popu-
lar Morality in the Time of Plato and Aristotle, Oxford
1974, 167–69, and my paper in Philologus 125, 1981, 219),
but v. 2 more unexpectedly (if I interpret it correctly) re-
quires wealthy dunderheads to keep their misfortunes to
themselves, and makes our ignorance of speaker and situa-
tion all the more regrettable.)*

Menander fr. dubium 67 K-A

(quotation 14 in the papyrus, scrap E: p. 13 Bartoletti)

[ἐξ] Αὐλητρίδων·

ἡ δ᾽ ἀνὰ μέσον θραύουσα ‹–×–∪–›
τύχη λογισμὸν καὶ τὰ προσδοκώμενα
οὐκ ἐκτελοῦσ᾽, ἀλλ᾽ ἕτερα διανοουμένη,
ὀρφανὰ ποεῖ τὰ πάντα

Lemma: the author's name was not mentioned presumably because it was identical with the one named in the previous extract (cf. quotations 4 and 5).

3 διανωουμενη F.   4 ποεῖ Arnott: ποιει F.

---

[1] The ἀρρηφόρος (cf. Pausanias 1.27.3, with J. G. Frazer's commentary, II.344–45) was one of two to four Athenian girls between the ages of seven and eleven chosen to serve Athena Polias for a whole year. They lived on the Acropolis and helped to weave the robe offered to the goddess at the Panathenaea. At the end of their service they were given covered baskets, which they carried on their heads as they descended from the Acropolis by an underground passage to a precinct on its north side, where they left their baskets and then returned to the Acropolis carrying some other ritual objects, also concealed. See especially L. Deubner, *Attische Feste* (Berlin 1932) 9–17; H. W. Parke, *Festivals of the Athenians* (London 1977) 141–43; W. Burkert, *Homo Necans* (English translation by P. Bing, Berkeley 1983) 150–54; and E. Simon, *Festivals of Attica* (Madison Wisc. 1983) 39–46.

NEW QUOTATIONS

Menander (?), fr. 67 K-A

[From] *Auletrides* ('Girl Pipers')

And in between Chance <   >
Destroys all logic and runs counter to
Our expectations, planning other outcomes.
Chance makes all efforts futile . . .

(*The writer here omits to give the author's name presumably because it was the same as that of the previous fragment in the papyrus, now lost. It is most likely to have been Menander, who composed a play with the alternative titles of Arrhephoros ('The Girl Carrying the Goddess's Symbols'[1]) and Auletris ('Girl Piper') or Auletrides (-ers), from which ten fragments have been preserved (64–73 K-A). However, an Auletrides is attested also for Phoenicides (Kassel–Austin, PCG VII, pp. 388–89), and an Auletris for both Antiphanes (II, pp. 336–37) and Diodorus (V, p. 26), and so the author's identification cannot be considered certain, although the imaginative vigour of the language is typical of Menander.*

These lines, spoken by an unknown character in an unknown plight, express the conventional view that the actions of Chance are illogical and unexpected; see especially Vogt-Spira, Dramaturgie des Zufalls, 37–42, although he does not discuss this fragment.)

THREE PAPYRI
WITH PLOT SUMMARIES
OF MENANDER'S PLAYS

Manuscripts

O.i = *P.Oxyrhynchus* 1235, three columns (one severely, the other two at times mutilated) from a papyrus of the first half of the second century A.D. It deals mainly with Menander's *Hiereia* and *Imbrioi*. First edition: A.S. Hunt, *The Oxyrhynchus Papyri* 10 (London 1914) 81–88. Plate no. 44 in E. G. Turner, *Greek Manuscripts of the Ancient World*[2], *BICS Supplement* 46 (1987) pp. 80–81 is a clear photograph of all the manuscript apart from frs. iii and i.3–4, which have been omitted, lost or cut off. Its text is reprinted in Kassel–Austin, *PCG* VI.2 pp. 135, 137–39 and 140.

O.ii = *P.Oxyrhynchus* 2534, a small scrap of papyrus written in the first century A.D. It contains mutilated fragments from a section dealing with Menander's second *Adelphoi* and his *Hauton Timoroumenos*. First edition: R. A. Coles and J. W. B. Barns, *Classical Quarterly* 15 (1965) 55–57; cf. Barns, *The Oxyrhynchus Papyri* 31 (1966) 12–13. Its text is reprinted in Kassel–Austin, *PCG* VI.2 pp. 47 and 82 (fr. 76).

615

MENANDER

P = *PIFAO* inv. 337, a small scrap of papyrus belonging to
the Institut Français d'Archéologie Orientale de Caire,
written in the second century A.D. It contains mutilated
fragments from a section dealing with Menander's
Demiourgos and *Dis Exapaton* (cf. Loeb Menander I,150–
53). First edition: B. Boyaval, *ZPE* 6 (1970) 5–7 with a
photograph (pl. IIa). The fragments dealing with the
Demiourgos are reprinted in Kassel–Austin, *PCG* VI.2
p. 98.

The *Suda* (o 254, cf. σ 213) identifies a certain Sellius
(or Sillius), who also went by the name of 'Homer', as a
grammarian who wrote a work with the title Περιοχαὶ τῶν
Μενάνδρου δραμάτων (*Summaries of Menander's Plays*),
and it is possible[1] that papyrus O.i at least comes from that
work. In that case Sellius would have been active some
time between the third century B.C. and the end of the first
century A.D. This and the other papyri appear to structure
their material in the same way. The plays of Menander are
listed roughly in alphabetic order. The section on each play
begins with its title, the play's opening line, and informa-
tion about its original production and its numerical posi-
tion in Menander's works. Then comes a concise prose
summary of the plot which identifies characters as (e.g.)
young or old, slave or priestess but does not name them.
Finally there is a brief evaluation of the main characters
and the play's quality. Papyrus summaries of Euripidean

[1] See A. Körte, *Berliner Philologische Wochenschrift* (1918)
787–89.

616

tragedies and satyr plays[2] apparently share the same format, and it seems clear that both format and practice were pioneered by early Alexandrian scholarship; the works cited in Callimachus' *Pinakes*, for example, were presented in alphabetical order and had their first line cited directly after the title.[3]

[2] They are most conveniently assembled in C. Austin, *Nova Fragmenta Euripidea in Papyris Reperta* (Berlin 1968) 88–103; see also J. Diggle, *Tragicorum Graecorum Fragmenta Selecta* (Oxford 1998) 80–81, 120, 128–29, 135, 150, 161, 164.

[3] See R. Pfeiffer, *History of Classical Scholarship* I (Oxford 1968) 129–31, 192–96.

P.Oxyrhynchus 1235 (O.i)

(a) End of the summary of (probably) Θυρωρός
(lines 1–13)

]α 1,]λεν 2,]ρος 3,]μει 4,]σ 5,] 6,]τον or]γον 7,]ιχα 8,
]ελι 9,]σω 10,]εται 11,]ινο 12,] 13.

(b) Summary of Ἱέρεια (lines 14–102)

[Ἱέρεια, ἧς ἀρχή·] 14, διέφθ]ορε (?) 15,]αα 16,]ειν 17,
]να 18,]ι 19,] 20, [ἡ δ᾽ ὑπόθεσις·] 21,]ε 22,]κυ 23,]αι 24,
]διε 25,]ηι 26,]α 27,]εισ 28,]ο 29,]ε 30,].. 31.

Those corrections and supplements whose author is not
named were made by the ed.pr., A. S. Hunt.   1–13 Assigned
to Θυρωρός by Körte.   15 Suppl. Schmidt.

P.Oxyrhynchus 1235 (O.i)

(a) End of the section on (?) *Thyroros* (The Doorman)

(Only a few final letters are preserved of the first column of text in this papyrus. Its first 13 lines come from the end of the summary of the play that preceded Hiereia in this author's alphabetical sequence. That play is likely to have been the Thyroros, if that sequence included all the titles known to us. Unfortunately, none of those 13 lines yields a single translatable word.)

(b) Section on *Hiereia* (The Priestess)

(This section presumably began in the standard way with the play title [HIEREIA] *(line 14), the play's first line, the date of its first production and its numerical place in the playwright's work, followed by a heading* The Plot *(line 21) and the beginning of the author's synopsis, but only the final letters of the first 18 lines of this section have been preserved, giving no intelligible word except for a possible* has deflowered *as part of the play's opening verse. The next 11*

MENANDER

From lines 32 to 76 of O.i the text can be presented continuously; a vertical bar identifies the line ends hereafter in all such passages of the papyrus:

.........]ιτ[......]λυσα(32) |........]ετ.[.....]ν καὶ | ...
..]ον· ἡ δ' ἱέρ[εια πο]λὺ μὲν |.....]ησεν τὸν σ[....]εουν
(35) |....] κατώρυξεν ο[....]σηι....]νῆλθον οἱ πα[ῖδε]ς·
ὁ | δὲ τὸ πρ]ότερον γε[νό]μενος | ....]ας ἀνὴρ
ν.[..]ας παι........] ἐπισκεπτ[ομ]ένης (40) |........]δος

35 τὸν σ[ιδη]ροῦν suppl. Körte.

---

[1] That neighbour's name may have been Rhode, if she was the person addressed (by her husband) in the one major book fragment (186 K-A) surviving from the play. That fragment is printed in the Addendum at the end of this section.

[2] The great mother goddess Cybele was believed both to induce and to cure madness; her epithets included 'Healer' ('Ιατρός Diogenes Athen. trag. fr. 1.5; 'Ιατρείνη *IG* ii² 4714, 4759, 4760; cf. Pindar, *Pyth.* 3.77–79, Diodorus Siculus 3.58). See especially A. Barigazzi, *Prometheus* 6 (1980) 100–102, G. Sfameni Gasparro, *Soteriology and Mystic Aspects in the Cult of Cybele and Attis* (Leiden 1985) 86–88, and R. Parker, *Athenian Religion* (Oxford 1996) 159–60, 188–94.

[3] First by K. F. W. Schmidt, *GGA* 178 (1916) 398, opposed by A. Körte, *Hermes* 75 (1940) 109–10, but supported by W. E. J. Kuiper, *Mnemosyne* 8 (1940) 289–90.

lines yield words and phrases but no connected sense: sep-
arated (?) *32,* and (?) *33,* and the priestess very much *34,*
the iron (?) *35,* he *(or* she) buried in the ground *36,* the
boys came, and the man who was formerly (?) *37–39,* she
considering *40.*

These disconnected phrases do not permit any secure re-
construction of our summariser's version of the plot ante-
cedents and early stage action of the *Hiereia,* but the in-
formation provided by the virtually complete text that
follows in lines *43–75* and the more easily supplemented
passage in *84–92* enable us to infer or guess that the title
figure was raped as a young girl a generation ago and bore
a son who was brought up by a female neighbour.[1] Later
on, either before or after she began to serve the goddess
Cybele as priestess and healer,[2] the title figure married a
man different from her raper, had a daughter by him but
was widowed some time before the stage action of the play
began. The female neighbour, who may have been single or
married when she began to foster the priestess's child, ei-
ther was already or later became the mother of a son and
daughter of her own. When the staged action of *Hiereia* be-
gins, all these children have grown up and the man who
committed the rape has been suffering probably from a
psychosomatic illness and visited the priestess as a patient
hoping for a cure, without realising that she was the victim
of his past rape. Few, however, of the disconnected phrases
in lines *32–42* can be matched with details in the above sce-
nario, although the boys at *37* are likely to refer to the
foster and natal sons of the priestess's neighbour. Two
phrases, however, are puzzling. Who buried *what,* and for
what reason, in *36?* It has been suggested[3] that the priest-
ess was burying tokens which could later be used to iden-

621

MENANDER

πα[....]σας | ......].[.]σ.[.......]α|...... ἀν]ασφή-
λας ζητεῖν | [ἐπε]χείρησεν τὸν ἀγαπητόν. | οἰκέτης δὲ
πεισθεὶς ἠνέχθη (45) | πρὸς τὴν ἱέρειαν ὡς θεοφο|
ρούμενος, θεραπείας ἵνα ἀ|ξιώθῃ λάθρᾳ· τὴν δ' ἀλή-
θει|αν πεπεισμένος ἐξίχνευ|σεν. ὁ δὲ τῆς ὑποβεβλη-
μέ(50) |νης τὸν υἱὸν αὐτ[ῆ]ς γνήσιος | μειρακίσκος τὴν
τῆς ἱερείας θυγατέρα γῆμαι προαιρού|μενος εἰσέπεμ-
ψε τὴν μη|τέρα διαλεξομένην πρὸς (55) | τὴν ἱέ[ρ]ειαν
περὶ αὐτοῦ. λα|λουσῶν δὲ τῶν γυναικῶν, | ὑποψίαν
λαβὼν καὶ μάλισ|θ' ὑπὸ τοῦ θεράποντος δι|δαχθεὶς
προσώπῳ διαλ(60) |λάττειν τὸν νεώτερον τῶν | γειτό-
νων υὸν ὡς ἑαυτοῦ | προσφωνεῖ.

γνοὺς δ' ἐκεῖ|νος αὐτοῦ τὸ διαμάρτη|μα τὸν
ἀδελφὸν προδια(65)|σείει, λέγων μεμανηκέ|ναι τὸν
πρεσβύτην καὶ πάν|τας τοὺς νέους υἱοὺς ἀπο|φαίνειν
αὐτοῦ. διὸ καὶ με|τὰ ταῦτα τὴν ἀλήθειαν ἐ(70)
|ξετάσαντος τοῦ γέροντος | καὶ τὸν πρεσβύ[τερον]
προσ|φωνοῦντος υὸ[ν ὡ]ς μαινό|μενον ἐκεῖ[νος
ἀπο]πέμπει. ἅμα δ' ὁ τ[.......]ς (75) | ὑπὸ τοῦ
θερά[ποντος ....] (76).

49 εξειχνευται O.i.
60–61 Corr. Wilamowitz: διαλλαττων O.i.
61 των O.i.
62 γιτονων O.i.   After εαυτου O.i adds > as a line-filler.
63 Paragraphus under the line in O.i, marking an alleged new
section in the summary.
66–67 Corr. Wilamowitz: μεμενηκεναι O.i.
72–73 προσφωνουντας corrected to -τος O.i.

tify her son's origins, but why should these have been bur-
ied and not passed on to the foster mother? The second
puzzle concerns the identity of the man . . . formerly *in lines*
37–39. Was it the man who had previously raped her, or
the man who previously became her husband?)

Fortunately the writer's concise but flat prose is well
preserved in lines 43–75:

. . . (43) Having recovered his health, he (*sc. the old man
who had raped the title figure long ago*) tried to look for his
beloved son. (45) A male house slave was won over and
brought to the priestess, pretending demoniac possession,
in order to be accorded treatment without anybody else
knowing. Having been won over he tracked down the
truth. (50) The young man who was the true son of the
woman who had passed off the priestess's child as her son
desired to marry the priestess's daughter and sent his (55)
mother in to talk to the priestess about him. While the
women were chatting he (*sc.* the old man) became suspi-
cious and, (60) being informed by his slave that his neigh-
bours' younger son had different features, he greets him as
his own son. The latter realises the other's mistake (65) and
throws his brother first into confusion by claiming that the
old man is out of his mind, identifying every young man as
his own son. And so (70) when afterwards the old man
works out the truth and greets the old[er] brother as his
son, the latter sends him [packing] as a lunatic. (75) At the
same time the . . .

From lines 77 to 83 the papyrus is severely mutilated:

77 πο.[+ gap about 18 letters, 78 τατ[......]ωτ[+ 8, 79 μη[.......]ερω[+ 8, 80–81 ανι[.......] γαμ[+ 6 ἐ]|παγ[γειλά]μενος α[+ 7, 82 απα[.....]περιδ[+ 8, 83 κον[.....]ων δεῖ [+ 7.

In lines 84–102 O.i's text is better preserved:

ελθ[......] ὁ μὲν π[ρεσβύτης] (84) | τὸν υἱὸν ἀπ]ολαβὼ[ν γαμεῖ] (85) | τὴν [ἱ]έ[ρειαν, ὁ δὲ υἱὸς αὐτοῦ] | λαμβάν[ει τὴν θυγατέρα τῶν] | θρεψάν[των, ὁ δὲ νεώτερος] | καὶ γνήσ[ιος τῶν γειτόνων] | υἱὸς λαμ[βάν]ει τὴν [τῆς ἱερεί](90)|ας ἣν ἠγάπησεν, κα[ὶ ποιοῦν]|ται γάμοι τῶν τριῶν [......]. | Ἔρως προὐξένησε ε.δ[.....]| τῶν διδόντων ον δ[.....].

τὰ [μ]ὲν [οὖν] τῆς ὑποθ[έσεώς] (95) | ἐσ[τι ταῦτα.] τὸ δὲ δ[ρᾶμα τῶν] | ἀ[ρίστων. ἔχ]ει δὲ πρ[εσβύτην] | εὐ[......]ν νεανί[σκους] | φι[......]υς οἰκέτη[....]|λο[.. .....]ν καὶ παν[....](100) |ε.[... ἐ]πὶ πᾶσιν καὶ τ[.. ..]|τ.[.] παραφώνησ[ι]ν πρ[.....].

77 που[or ποψ[or πον[O.i.
80–81 Suppl. Barigazzi (ἐπαγγελλόμενος already Körte).
87–89 Suppl. Wilamowitz.   93 ει or συ, then δ[or β[O.i.
94 Paragraphus under the line in O.i at the end of the summary proper.   95–96 Suppl. Wilamowitz.
97 πρ[εσβύτην suppl. Körte, the rest Wilamowitz.
98 Suppl. Sandbach.
102 Paragraphus under the line in O.i marking the end of the section on *Hiereia*.

(What followed next is uncertain, since lines 75 to 84 are badly mutilated, giving once again only a few unrelated phrases: by the servant 76, young [man] in love . . . [order]ing . . . [to] marry *(?)* 79–81, [neck]lace 82, must *or* needs *(?)* 83, come 84; *here there would be no way of deciding which young lover ordered which person to get married, even if the mangled text of 79–81 were correctly so interpreted after supplementations that remain doubtful. Lines 85–92, however, where the gaps in the Greek text are easier to fill, inform the reader of the play's happy ending:)*

(84) The o[ld man (85) re]covers his [son and marries] the priestess, his son takes [the daughter of the] foster parents, [the neighbours' younger] and true (90) son takes the daughter [of the priest]ess whom he loved, and [together] a triple marriage [takes place]. The god of love manipulated . . . those who give . . .

(95) [So these] are the details of the plot. The play is one of the b[est. It has] a well-[.....] o[ld man], young [men] who are fond of [.....], a (?) house slave who is (100).....and every.....in all.....(102) a diction (?) that is [appropriate (?)].

(Thus after ending his summary of the plot the writer assesses the quality of the play, its characters and possibly also its diction, if that is a correct translation of an otherwise unknown word.)

MENANDER

(c) Beginning of the summary of Ἴμβριοι
(lines 103–22/23)

Ἴμβριοι, ὧν ἀρχή· (103)|

δι᾽ ὅσου χρόνου σέ, Δημέα| βέλτιστ᾽, ἐγώ . . .
(= fr. 190 K-A)

ταύτην [ἔγρα](105)|ψεν ἐπὶ Νικοκλέο[υς, ...]|την καὶ
ἑβδομηκοστ[ὴν, καὶ] | ἔδωκεν εἰς ἐργασίαν [εἰς τὰ] |
Διονύσια, οὐκ ἐγένετο δ[ὲ διὰ | Λαχάρην τὸν τυρανν.[+
3–5 letters](110)]|τα ὑπεκρίνετο Κάλ[λιπ]ος Ἀθηναῖος.
|

ἡ δ᾽ ὑπόθεσις |

δύο πένητες ἀλλήλω[ν φί]|λοι, κοινὸν ποιησάμεν[οι
τὸν] (115) | βίον, Ἴμβρον ᾤκησαν κ[αὶ] | διδύμας

104 δημε O.i, with the omitted α added above the ε and a final
horizontal stroke added after the ε apparently as (part of ?) a line-
filler.   106 νεικοκλει[O.i.
106–107 [πρώ]την or τρί]την or ἔκ]την or ἐνά]την O.i.
109 Suppl. Wilamowitz.   110–11 τυραννε[ύσαν]τα·
(Luppe) or τυραννε[ύον]τα· (Gronewald) or τυραννὸ[ν· ἔπει]τα
(Wilamowitz).
111 ὑπεκρεινετο O.i.

---

[4] An island (now Imroz) between Lemnos and the coast of Eu-
ropean Turkey. In Menander's time it still had a close association
with Athens. See especially E. Oberhummer in *Beiträge zur Alte
Geschichte und Geographie: Festschrift für Heinrich Kiepert*
(Berlin 1898), 275–304 and C. Fredrich in *RE* (1914) s.v. *Imbros*,
1105–07.   [5] Literally, 'since I [saw (?)] you.' Demeas was
probably the name of one of the two Imbrian friends.

(c) Beginning of the section on *Imbrioi*
(The Men of Imbros[4])

(103) *IMBRIOI*, which begins with:

How long it's been since we two, noble Demeas[5]

This play he (106) wrote when Nicocles was archon
(302/01 B.C.)—it was his seventy-[.....][6]—and he handed
it in for production [at the] Dionysia, but it was not per-
formed then [because of] (110) Lachares' seizure of
power.[7] Callippus of Athens [subsequently (?)] took the
lead in its performance.[8]

The Plot

Two poor mutual friends (115) dwelled in Imbros, shar-
ing their lives there, and they married twin sisters. Sharing

---

[6] Mutilation at the end of this line makes it uncertain whether
71st, 73rd, 76th or 79th was written here.

[7] Production was presumably intended at the Dionysia in the
spring of 301 B.C., but Lachares' seizure of power at that time may
well have prevented either the festival from being held or at least
any dramatic productions at the festival. The author's statement
here effectively settles a long dispute about the date when the
Athenian general Lachares seized power to become tyrant for a
short time before he was ousted by Demetrius Poliorcetes. See es-
pecially M. J. Osborne, *Naturalization in Athens* 2 (Brussels 1982)
144–53, and Christian Habicht, *Athens from Alexander to Antony*
(Cambridge Mass. 1997) 82–87.

[8] Several members of an Athenian family of actors bore this
name at the end of the fourth and in the first half of the third cen-
tury B.C. See especially P. Ghiron-Bistagne, *Recherches sur les
acteurs dans la Grèce antique* (Paris 1976) p. 335, and I. E.
Stefanis, Διονυσιακοὶ Τεχνῖται (Heraklion 1988) p. 247.

ἀδελφὰς ἔγη[μαν], | κοινοποιησάμενοι π[ᾶσαν] | ἅμα
τὴν ὕπαρξιν. φ[ιλο]πόνως δὲ καὶ κατὰ γῆν [καὶ] (120) |
κατὰ θάλατταν ἐργαζ[ομε]|[νοι] (122) ...

(d) Three unplaced fragments of
P.Oxyrhynchus 1235 (O.i)

	(i)	(ii)	(iii)
1	]την δε[	]θεισ[	].[
	]κακαι ο[	]νειν[	]πουτ[
	].υπετε[	]την[	
4	]ο[		

P.Oxyrhynchus 2534 (O.ii)

(a) End of the summary of (probably) Ἀδελφοί β′
(lines 1–5)

μ]ητέρα χηρὰ[ν + c.10 letters]|..]ῳ τὸ χρυσ[ίον + c.5
λα]|βὼν ταῦτ[α + c.12]|πρόσοδον ε[+ c.11]| τὸ δὲ

118 Suppl. Wilamowitz.

O.ii: Those corrections and supplements whose author is not
named were made by the edd.prr., R. A. Coles and J. W. B. Barns.
The gaps in each line are of uncertain length, perhaps as many as
c.12–13 letters on each occasion.

2 χρυσ[ίον] suppl. Lloyd-Jones.

---

9 So first T. B. L. Webster, *Classica et Mediaevalia, Diss. IX: F.
Blatt septuagenario dedicata* (1973) 132.

[all] their property too, and work[ing] industriously on the land and (121) at sea . . .

(*At this point the main papyrus text breaks off. There are also three minuscule scraps—(frs. i, ii and iii opposite)— whose position in the text is unknown; none of them yields a certainly translatable word, and fr. iii may even not belong to this papyrus.*)

P.Oxyrhynchus 2534 (O.ii)

(*This papyrus was written some years before P.Oxyrhynchus 1235 (O.i), but its structure and arrangement have a great deal in common; each section begins with the title and the play's first line, there follows probably a brief reference to its date of composition, then comes the plot summary and finally a brief evaluation. Even the physical appearance of the manuscript, with its lines of 19–23 letters, seems similar. Yet the preserved scrap of O.ii lacks any description of the characters or reference to a dramatic production at one of the Attic festivals, and so it would be unwise automatically to assume that it comes from the same work as O.i.*)

(a) End of the section on the second play, probably titled
    Adelphoi (The Brothers)

(*Just a few words are preserved from the end of the plot summary, dealing presumably with the dénouement:* widowed mother 1, the money 2, taking these (2–3), income (4). *These words can be slotted neatly into the final scene of Terence's Adelphoe,[9] a play modelled on Menander's 2nd Adelphoi. In that scene Micio agreed to marry Sostrata,*

629

δρᾶμα [(5). A partially or wholly blank line followed.

(b) Beginning of the summary of Αὐτὸν
τιμωρούμενος (lines 7–18)

β′ Αὐτὸν [τιμωρούμενος, (7)], [οὗ αρχή·]] βραχ[
]] τε γέγον[ε   ](10)]αι. ἐποιήθ[η   ]]ταύτης ζη[

7 β′ presumably = the number 2, implying that this summary
was the second in a list arranged in (roughly) alphabetical order.

widowed mother *of Aeschinus' inamorata (930–45), gave a farm to Hegio (949–56), and then offered income to Syrus after Demea had promised to provide money to buy freedom for Syrus' wife (977, 979–85). Thus Terence would have preserved more of Menander's ending than some scholars have thought. After these references to the dénouement the writer then begins a very brief evaluation of the comedy's dramatic quality with (5) The play, but unfortunately the rest of this line, containing his verdict, is torn off.)*

(b) Beginning of the section on *Hauton Timoroumenos*
(The Self-Tormentor)

(line 7) No. 2: *HAUTON [TIMOROUMENOS,*
which begins with:]
Brief and [   ] has been [
(11) It was composed [. . . . .

So opens the section on this play, where comprehension—if not supplementation—of the papyrus' meagre fragments is once again helped by Terence, who modelled his Heauton (or Hauton) Timorumenos on this play. When the author of this work identifies Menander's play as No. 2, we have to assume that this was where it came in his sequence; that involves us in assuming that either he was summarising only a selection of Menander's plays or that his adherence to alphabetical order went no further than the initial letter; the second Adelphoi now comes no. 2, and Hauton Timoroumenos no. 12, in an alphabetical list of Menander's plays.

The first line of Terence's play, after its extra-dramatic prologue, runs 'quamquam haec inter nos nuper notitia

631

|σις καὶ τὰ κα.[|περὶ πρεσβύ[του |νου-
θετῶν τ[   ](15) |μετ' ἐρωμέν[ης | αὐτὸν οὐτ.[
| .αθ ... [   ]|ιτην.[(19).

PIFAO inv. 337 (P)

(a) Ending of the summary of Δημιουργός
(lines 1–6)

[εἰς] | ἅπαν εἰσιὼν ἐλευθέρως .[+ c.11 letters](1)
|[.]ωτος διακονῶν ἑτοίμ[ως πρὸς τὰ πρά]|γματα χωρὶς
θ[ε]ραποντ[... τὸ δρᾶμα ἔχει]| καὶ πρεσβύτας
χρηστοὺς [καὶ ἑταίραν θρα]|σεῖαν μέν, οὐ πονηρὰν
δ[έ. καὶ περιέχει] (5) | [τ]οῦτο δυεῖν ἡμερῶν χρόν[ον.
(6)

14, 16 Suppl. Lloyd-Jones.

P: Those corrections and supplements whose author is not
named were made by the ed.pr., B. Boyaval.   Before 1 [εἰς]
suppl. Koenen.   ιστων P.   ο[or σ[or ω[.
  2 ἑτοίμ[ως suppl. Koenen, πρὸς τὰ Turner.
  3 Either θεράποντ[ος (ed.pr.) or θεραπόντ[ων (Turner).
τὸ δρᾶμα suppl. Koenen, ἔχει Turner.
  4 καὶ suppl. Koenen, the rest Turner.
  5–6 Suppl. Handley ([τ]οῦτο ed. pr.).
  6 Paragraphus under the line in P marking the end of the sec-
tion on *Demiourgos*.

---

10 On the dating of this play (306–301 B.C.) see St. Schröder,
ZPE 113 (1996) 42–48.
  11 Cf. H. Lloyd-Jones, *CQ* 15 (1965) 57.

admodumst' (v. 53: Though our acquaintance here is pretty short*), and this may well have been a close translation of Menander's opening words.*

Thereafter the words it was composed *(11) were followed presumably by an indication of date*[10] *or the play's chronological position in Menander's works; here, however, only* of this *(corrected from* third*), followed perhaps by* [is] sought, *can be read.*

The plot summary may have begun in the lost part of line 13. Only a few words now survive: about an old man *(14), a man* rebuking *(15),* with a beloved [girl] *(16),* him nor *(17). These must come from an account of the play's opening scene or scenes, which Terence may have faithfully adapted; his first scene presents one* old man (Chremes) *rebuking* another *old man (Menedemus) for working too hard (53–96); Menedemus explains that he is now punishing himself for* rebuking *his son Clinia (103–12) when the son* fell desperately in love *with* a girl *from Corinth (98–100).*[11]

PIFAO inv. 337 (P)

(This tiny scrap comes from a work that seems to have been structured in the same way as P.Oxyrhynchus 2534.)

(a) End of the section on *Demiourgos*
(The Confectioner)

. . . (1) entering (?) [into] everything like a free man [and . . . .] willingly responding to events as a slave would, without the presence of any slave[s (?). The play introduces] both excellent old men [and a courtesan who is] audacious but not wicked. [And] (6) this play's action [covers] a period of two days.

MENANDER

(b) Beginning of the section on Δὶς ἐξαπατῶν

Δὶς ἐξαπατῶν, ο[ὖ ἀρχή· (7)

πρὸς τῶν θεῶν, μειράκιο[ν (8)

Addendum

(1) Menander, fragment 188 K-A = 210 K-T
(Ἱέρεια)

[Justin], *De Monarchia* 5.2 (p.95.8–15 Marcovich, Berlin 1990): ὁ αὐτὸς Μένανδρος ἐν Ἱερείᾳ, citing the whole fragment; and Clement of Alexandria, *Protrepticus* 75.4 (p.57.22 Stählin): πάλιν δὲ ὁ αὐτὸς κωμῳδιοποιὸς (after citing Menander fr. 156 K-A) ἐν Ἱερείᾳ τῷ δράματι χαλεπαίνων πρὸς τὴν συνήθειαν διελέγχειν πειρᾶται

---

12 *Aegyptus* 49 (1969) 82–84.
13 Cf. *ZPE* 72 (1988) 26.
14 Texts and translations of Menander fr. 110 K-A and Turpilius, *Demiurgus* fr. IV are printed below in the addendum to this section.
15 See volume I, pp. 150–53.
16 See note 1 above.

634

(*A. Borgogno*[12] *demonstrated that this untitled scrap closes the section on Menander's Demiourgos, the play that comes two places before Dis Exapaton in the alphabetical list of his plays, by noting that (i) responding* . . . *as a slave* (διακονῶν, *line 3 of the hypothesis) picks up a comment in fragment 110.1–2 K-A quoted from that play:* You've come forward, just like a slave (διακονικῶς); *(ii) the reference to the action in this play unusually covering* a period of two days *(line 6) neatly explains a comment in v. 3 of that same fragment,* We've been up all night; *while (iii) Turner's supplement of* courtesan (ἑταίραν) *in line 4 of the hypothesis is confirmed for Menander's play by the presence of such a character in Turpilius' Demiurgus (fr. IV), which was adapted from Menander's Demiourgos.*[13]

Here at the end of this section the author calls attention to one of the play's male characters who acted like a slave without being one; was he perhaps a parasite?[14])

(b) Beginning of the section on *Dis Exapaton*[15]

Dis Exapaton, which [begins thus:]

In heaven's name, young man [

Addendum

(1) A fragment cited from Menander's *Hiereia* in antiquity[16]

An essay *On Monarchy* falsely attributed to Justin cites the whole fragment with the heading 'the same Menander in *Hiereia*', and Clement introduces his quotation of v. 2 (from 'If a man') to v. 6 with 'And again the same comic poet (sc. Menander) in his play *Hiereia*, angered by the

τὸν ἄθεον τῆς πλάνης τῦφον, ἐπιφθεγγόμενος
ἐμφρόνως, citing v. 2 (from εἰ γὰρ) to v. 6 (as far as
ἀνθρώποισιν (sic)):

οὐδεὶς δι᾽ ἀνθρώπου θεὸς σῴζει, γύναι,
ἑτέρου τὸν ἕτερον· εἰ γὰρ ἕλκει τὸν θεὸν
τοῖς κυμβάλοις ἄνθρωπος εἰς ὃ βούλεται,
ὁ τοῦτο ποιῶν ἐστι μείζων τοῦ θεοῦ.
5 ἀλλ᾽ ἔστι τόλμης καὶ βίας ταῦτ᾽ ὄργανα
εὑρημέν᾽ ἀνθρώποις ἀναιδέσιν, Ῥόδη,
7 εἰς καταγέλωτα τῷ βίῳ πεπλασμένα . . .

(2) Menander, fragment 110 K-A = 100 K-T
(Δημιουργός)

Athenaeus 4.172a and c: τοὺς δὲ τὰ πέμματα προσέτι τε
τοὺς ποιοῦντας τοὺς πλακοῦντας οἱ πρότερον δημι-
ουργοὺς ἐκάλουν . . . (172c) ὅτι δὲ ἐκεχώριστο τὰ τῆς
ὑπουργίας, πεμμάτων μὲν προνοουσῶν τῶν δημιουρ-
γῶν, ὀψαρτυτικῆς δὲ τῶν μαγείρων, . . . διεσάφηνεν
. . . Μένανδρος Δημιουργῷ (Δημιουργῷ ms. A: title
omitted by Epitome mss.)·

frag. 188, line 1 οὐδεὶς Clement: οὐθεὶς Justin.
2 τὸν Clement: τινὰ Justin.
5 βίας conj. Bentley: βίου mss. of Clement, Justin.
6 ἀνθρώποις Justin: ἀνθρώποισιν Clement.

17 Cymbals were particularly associated with the worship
of Cybele (e.g. Men. *Theoph.* 51, Diogenes Ath. trag. fr. 1.4);

custom (sc. of divine healing), attempts to expose the un-
godly senselessness of this delusion, speaking with intelli-
gence':

Dear wife, no god will use one man to save
Another. If a man by clashing cymbals[17]
Can lure the god to do just what *he* wants,
The one achieving this is mightier than
The god! But these are tools of reckless folly   5
And violence, devised by shameless men, Rhode,
And forged to make a mockery of life . . .

*(Rhode was presumably the name of the neighbour who
had fostered the priestess's child, and these words were
presumably addressed to her by a husband who disap-
proved of attempts by the priestess to heal sick visitors at
the shrine of Cybele. It is impossible to gauge at what point
in the play this speech was made, but it would have greater
relevance at the time when the old man who had raped that
priestess long ago was receiving treatment at the shrine.)*

(2) A fragment cited from Menander's *Demiourgos*
in antiquity

Athenaeus: Earlier writers called those who made pastries
and also flat cakes 'confectioners' . . . That their (sc. cater-
ers') duties had been categorised, with the 'confectioners'
taking care of cakes, and the 'cooks' of meat and fish, . . .
was clearly demonstrated by Menander . . . in his
Demiourgos:

see especially M. J. Vermaseren, *Cybele and Attis* (London 1977)
108–10.

ΜΑΓΕΙΡΟΣ (?)

τί τοῦτο, παῖ; διακονικῶς γάρ, νὴ Δία,
προελήλυθας.

ΔΗΜΙΟΥΡΓΟΣ (?)

ναί· πλάττομεν γὰρ πλάσματα
τὴν νύκτα τ᾽ ἠγρυπνήκαμεν. καὶ νῦν ἔτι
4   ἀποίητα πάμπολλ᾽ ἐστὶν ἡμῖν.

(3) Turpilius, fr. IV (Ribbeck, Rychlewska)
of his *Demiurgus*

Nonius, 438.18 *'Quaesti' uel 'quaestuis' dictum pro
quaestus* . . . *(29) Turpilius Demiurgo:*

mulier meretrix, quae me quaesti causa cognouit sui

Men. fr. 110, line 1 νὴ Δία A: omitted by Epitome mss.
3 τ᾽ A: omitted by Epitome mss.

COOK (?)

Oho, what's this? I swear that you've come forward,
Just like a slave.

CONFECTIONER

Yes—we're creating cakes,
And we've been up all night. There's still a lot
For us to cope with, even now!

*(This fragment, and Athenaeus' introductory remarks to it,
implies that the 'confectioner craftsman' of Menander's
title was a maker of cakes.)*

(3) A fragment of Turpilius' *Demiurgus*

Nonius: *quaesti* or *quaestuis* (irregular genitive singular
forms of *quaestus*, 'gain') is used in place of *quaestus* (the
regular genitive singular form) . . . Turpilius in the
Demiurgus:

She's a courtesan, who's let me have her just for her own
    gain![18]

---

[18] The relevance of these two fragments to the interpretation
of lines 1–6 of PIFAO inv. 337 (P) is discussed above.